Redefining
Urban and Suburban
America

JAMES A. JOHNSON METRO SERIES

**JAMES A. JOHNSON
METRO SERIES**

The Metropolitan Policy Program at the Brookings Institution is integrating research and practical experience into a policy agenda for cities and metropolitan areas. By bringing fresh analyses and policy ideas to the public debate, the program hopes to inform key decisionmakers and civic leaders in ways that will spur meaningful change in our nation's communities.

   As part of this effort, the James A. Johnson Metro Series aims to introduce new perspectives and policy thinking on current issues and attempt to lay the foundation for longer-term policy reforms. The series examines traditional urban issues, such as neighborhood assets and central city competitiveness, as well as larger metropolitan concerns, such as regional growth, development, and employment patterns. The James A. Johnson Metro Series consists of concise studies and collections of essays designed to appeal to a broad audience. While these studies are formally reviewed, some will not be verified like other research publications. As with all publications, the judgments, conclusions, and recommendations presented in the studies are solely those of the authors and should not be attributed to the trustees, officers, or other staff members of the Institution.

Redefining Urban and Suburban America

EVIDENCE FROM CENSUS 2000

VOLUME TWO

Alan Berube, Bruce Katz, and Robert E. Lang
Editors

BROOKINGS INSTITUTION PRESS
Washington, D.C.

Library of Congress Cataloging-in-Publication data
Redefining urban and suburban America : evidence from Census 2000 /
Bruce Katz and Robert E. Lang, eds.
    p.   cm.
Includes bibliographical references and index.
  ISBN-13: 978-0-8157-4896-0 (cloth . alk. paper)
  ISBN-10: 0-8157-4896-5
  ISBN-13: 978-0-8157-4897-7 (pbk. : alk. paper)
  ISBN-10: 0-8157-4897-3
1. Metropolitan areas—United States. 2. Suburbs—United States. 3. City and town life—United States. 4. United States—Population. 5. Sociology, Urban—United States. I. Katz, Bruce. II. Lang, Robert, 1959–
HT334.U5 R43 2003
307.76′4′0973—dc21   2002151690

9 8 7 6 5 4 3 2 1

The paper used in this publication meets minimum requirements of the American National Standard for Information Sciences—Permanence of Paper for Printed Library Materials: ANSI Z39.48-1992.

Typeset in Minion and Univers Condensed

Composition by Circle Graphics
Columbia, Maryland

Printed by R. R. Donnelley
Harrisonburg, Virginia

Contents

Foreword

Urban areas will claim nearly all of the world's population growth during the next thirty years, according to the United Nations. It is no surprise, then, that the fortunes of cities and metropolitan areas figure prominently among the concerns of leaders across the globe. Public- and private-sector officials from Philadelphia to London to Beijing are grappling with the universal challenges of population growth or decline, poverty, housing, traffic, and their effects on metropolitan dwellers and urban form.

The rising importance of these issues led Brookings in 2004 to establish the Metropolitan Policy Program as the institution's fourth major program, our first new program since 1948. Under the direction of Bruce Katz, the Metro program enjoys a reputation as a unique model for research, analysis, and public education on the issues confronting metropolitan areas. That reputation is built in part on the program's Living Cities Census Series, a three-year effort to distill major findings from Census 2000 for a wide audience of public- and private-sector leaders across the United States.

Brookings's interest in this area follows naturally from the essential role the census plays in our nationhood. Conducted every ten years since 1790, the census links each generation of Americans across the whole of our history. It yields the population counts on which our representative democracy depends, provides an essential evidence base for implementing a host of federal policies, and effectively tells us "who we are" as a society.

The Metro program's work in this area acknowledges that the influence of the census extends far beyond Washington. Urban and suburban leaders recognize the unique capacity of the census to describe the state of places that define our day-to-day lives: metropolitan areas, big cities, small towns, even neighborhoods and streets. That information helps local corporate, political, and civic officials to understand their customers, their voters, and their communities. Increasingly, mayors and other local elected leaders are using census results to establish baselines and set targets for future performance. They are also identifying peer cities and suburbs, in order to exchange ideas and aspirations with counterparts who face similar opportunities and challenges.

Census research by the Metro program and its network of scholars, and by the Fannie Mae Foundation, has provided a critical framework for those efforts. This second volume of *Redefining Urban and Suburban America* unites the two organizations once again and collects several of their best census analyses to portray the disparate demographic trends affecting cities and metropolitan areas in the 1990s.

The first volume in this series focused on population growth and decline, and dramatic changes occurring in the racial and ethnic makeup of cities and suburbs. The current volume focuses on an even richer set of subjects from Census 2000—migration and immigration; income and poverty; and housing and homeownership. The findings in this volume demonstrate the continued ascendance of the Sunbelt, whose cities and suburbs are growing magnets for both domestic migrants and immigrants. They portray stunning improvements in the conditions of the nation's poorest neighborhoods, alongside growing numbers of lower-income households in cities. And the chapters highlight significant progress on homeownership, amid a troubling countercurrent of families increasingly burdened by housing costs.

This book and this series represent a continuing partnership among Living Cities (formerly the National Community Development Initiative), the Fannie Mae Foundation, and the Brookings Institution's Metropolitan Policy Program. The collection further cements the 1990s as a time of profound change in metropolitan America, foreshadows important developments in the current decade, and urges new thinking about the role of our nation's cities and suburbs in an emerging global urban age.

STROBE TALBOTT
President

Washington, D.C.
February 2005

Redefining
Urban and Suburban
America

Introduction

ALAN BERUBE, BRUCE KATZ,
AND ROBERT E. LANG

To many, the 1990s probably seem like an innocent bygone era, with twenty-four-year-old dot-com millionaires, governments awash in surplus cash, the discovery of the *grande latte*, and the nation (mostly) at peace. Beyond these historical hallmarks, however, the 1990s brought unparalleled economic and demographic change to the United States, the effects of which will be felt for many decades to come. The nation added more people—32 million—over the decade than in any other ten-year period in its history, fueled by a new wave of immigration to its shores.[1] Between April 1990, when the nation teetered on the verge of an economic recession, and April 2000, when unemployment hit a postwar low of 4 percent, the nation experienced its strongest economic expansion on record. That expansion lifted homeownership to new highs, with lower-income and minority families making especially large gains in the latter half of the decade.

The United States does not require a full census of its inhabitants, of course, to chart these overall trends. Income, employment, and housing trends are followed closely on a monthly or quarterly basis through large federal surveys. Population estimates and projections are updated annually. Moreover, a lot can happen during ten years, and the decennial census provides a simple point-in-time depiction of the nation at the beginning and end of that interval.

---

1. Indeed, the latest population projections from the Census Bureau show the nation gaining only 27 million people between 2000 and 2010, well short of the increase in the 1990s.

Yet the decennial census stands alone in the breadth, and depth, of its inquiry. In a country of 3.5 million square miles and nearly 300 million people, national trends tell only a small part of the stories experienced by individuals and communities. Most monthly and annual surveys conducted by federal agencies at best provide information down to the state level. Only the census provides detailed demographic and economic information for all metropolitan areas, cities, towns, and neighborhoods—the geographies that define our day-to-day lives. Moreover, the decennial census provides an important benchmark of our nation's progress during that decade. The trajectories of income and employment trends may shift from year to year, but longer-term changes in the geography of immigration, poverty, and homeownership have likely continued their course.

Using results from Census 2000, volume 1 of *Redefining Urban and Suburban America* showed that population growth and racial or ethnic change in the 1990s varied greatly among metropolitan areas, cities, and suburbs. Not all places shared in the significant population growth occurring at the national level. And while nearly all areas of the nation grew more racially diverse over the decade, changes occurred much more rapidly in some areas than others.

Census 2000 also offers crucial insights into social and economic changes that took place across and within U.S. regions in the 1990s. This second volume of *Redefining Urban and Suburban America* brings several of the most compelling of these changes into sharper focus:

—The number of high-poverty neighborhoods declined dramatically in most U.S. metro areas, even as the overall metropolitan poverty rate remained unchanged.

—After several decades of migration to the North and West, African Americans returned to the South in record numbers.

—Homeownership rose across the nation, but large urban counties, and small towns witnessing new immigration, saw significant increases in household overcrowding.

THE CENSUS "LONG FORM"

These and other findings explored in this volume derive largely from analysis of the census "long form." The previous volume featured chapters based on the decennial census "short form"—seven survey questions mailed to all households in the United States asking how many people live at the address, their age, gender, race, Hispanic origin, relationship to one another, and whether or not they own their home.

One in six U.S. households, however, received a much longer survey, with more than fifty questions covering a wide range of subjects: migration, education, work, income, commuting, disability, housing—even whether the household has indoor plumbing. The Census Bureau statistically weights these sample data so that the reported results reflect the characteristics of all households. And because the sample is so large, the bureau is able to report long form data that correspond to areas as small as neighborhoods. With such a rich mine of information for small geographic areas, the long form is one of the research community's most used data sources.

In a nation that values highly the privacy of individuals, however, such a wide-ranging survey distributed to roughly 17 million households can generate its share of controversy. In 2000, as households began to receive the forms in the mail, some members of Congress reported receiving hundreds of angry calls from constituents protesting questions they perceived to be too intrusive. In response, some members—including then Senate majority leader Trent Lott—urged people to answer "basic" census questions but to leave blank questions they felt invaded their privacy (despite the fact that federal law prescribes a penalty of $100 for failing to answer any question on a decennial census—a penalty rarely, if ever, enforced).[2] In the end, the percentage of households who mailed back their Census 2000 forms was 9.5 percentage points lower for long form recipients than short form recipients (versus 4.5 percentage points in 1990).

Yet the long form is not merely an academic exercise conducted by the Census Bureau. Every question ties back to a data need expressed in federal law or program implementation. For instance, questions on household income are required under federal law for rural housing programs, the Community Reinvestment Act, and the Head Start program, among several others. Data collected from migration questions allow the Department of Labor to implement provisions of federal immigration law. Information on indoor plumbing is required to set subsidy levels under the Housing Voucher Choice program. In the end, answers to census long form questions inform the distribution of a significant portion of the $200 billion in federal, state, local, and tribal funds allocated annually.[3] And as with all of its data collection, the Census Bureau vigorously safeguards the privacy of individual respondents to its surveys.

Neither are these social and economic inquiries all that new to the census. Article I of the U.S. Constitution requires an "enumeration" to be per-

2. D'Vera Cohn, "Census Too Nosy? Don't Answer Invasive Questions, GOP Suggests," *Washington Post*, March 30, 2000, p. A1.
3. U.S. Census Bureau (2002).

formed every ten years in order to apportion seats in the House of Representatives among the states—a purpose the census still serves today. But as early as 1810 Congress, responding to difficulties it faced importing manufactured goods during the Napoleonic Wars, commissioned a "census of manufactures" alongside the population census to find out what Americans produced. In 1820 Congress collected information on the size of the nation's growing foreign-born population and the industries in which Americans worked. Between 1830 and 1850, the census added questions concerning the disabled population, educational attainment and literacy, migration, poverty, and wage levels.[4] While the exact nature of these questions has changed over time, the Census 2000 long form collected information on all of these subject areas.

And yet, Census 2000 could mark the last appearance of the long form as we know it. The Census Bureau has developed the American Community Survey (ACS) to improve the quality and timeliness of data traditionally provided by the long form. The ACS is a continuous version of the long form, collecting very similar data through a series of monthly household surveys. By providing annual long form data at all levels of geography, the survey could greatly enhance the utility of census data for metropolitan areas, cities, suburbs, and neighborhoods. If the ACS is fully implemented on schedule in 2009, Census 2010 will not conduct a long form survey. However, the ACS is subject to an annual appropriations process in Congress, and budget pressures continually threaten to derail its full implementation in time for the next decennial census.[5]

As of today, though, the census long form remains the federal government's premier instrument for collecting social science data. The range of data available for very small levels of geography helps researchers analyze the spatial nature of many important questions. Sociologists, for instance, use long form data to study the movements of people into the United States from abroad, and across counties and regions within the United States. Economists are able to examine income and poverty dynamics for metropolitan areas, which approximate local labor markets. And long form data enable political scientists to model the relationship between small-area voting behavior and the socioeconomic characteristics (household type,

---

4. Anderson (1988).
5. Sabety, Reamer, and Clark (2004). For fiscal year 2005, the Census Bureau did receive its full budget request, enough to continue toward full implementation of the ACS. However, the Government Accountability Office has found that to provide small geographic area data consistent with what would be available from the 2010 long form, additional funding will be needed to increase the ACS sample size. Government Accountability Office (2004).

income, education) of the voters who live there. No other survey covers such an exhaustive set of subject areas for as large a number of places as the decennial census.

THIS VOLUME

The contributors to this volume all make use of the geographic specificity of long form census data to adopt a metropolitan frame for their analyses. The first three chapters recognize that metropolitan areas function as migration gateways for individuals entering the United States from abroad, and for those relocating domestically. Household movements reveal the relative economic strength of regions, but also speak to the influence of social ties and the physical manner in which different metropolitan areas are developing.

The second group of chapters examines the divergent economic fortunes of U.S. metropolitan areas and their constituent cities, suburbs, and neighborhoods. These patterns reflect supra-regional employment and productivity trends, as well as population dynamics that affect wealthy and impoverished communities alike.

The third section sheds light on emerging issues in state and regional housing markets, recognizing that policies to promote homeownership and serve the homeless have implicit spatial implications at the neighborhood, city, and metropolitan levels.

These analyses add texture to the short form population and racial/ethnic trends analyzed in volume 1 of *Redefining Urban and Suburban America*. The chapters in this volume "get behind" those trends to examine how migration contributed to population growth and decline across different areas of the country, how economic trends related to those changes, and how these demographic and economic dynamics reverberated in the housing market. As with the first volume, most authors focus their attention on the country's largest metropolitan areas, and the cities, suburbs, and neighborhoods therein.

MIGRATION RESHAPES DESTINATION REGIONS

America is a mobile society. Between 1995 and 2000, 46 percent of U.S. residents changed address. This far exceeds residential mobility in Europe, and even that in relatively mobile nations like Canada and Australia, where about 42 percent of households moved in the late 1990s.[6] Moreover, the United States

---

6. Long (1991); Statistics Canada (2002); Australian Bureau of Statistics (2002).

remains an immigrant-rich nation, with about 11 percent of its residents born abroad. The first three chapters of this volume show that destinations for domestic migrants and immigrants—and the places from which they came—have undergone significant transition in recent decades. These migration patterns helped to drive overall population gains and losses in different regions of the country. And the varying locational preferences expressed by different groups of migrants help explain the changing racial and ethnic makeup of cities and suburbs nationwide.

Important features separate the movements of immigrants and domestic migrants, who often have different reasons for moving and thus choose different destinations across—and within—regions. In chapter 1, William Frey identifies distinct metropolitan destinations for these two groups. He shows that in the 1990s immigrants headed mostly for large coastal metropolitan areas, like New York, Los Angeles, and San Francisco, sustaining population growth by offsetting the out-migration of existing residents. Meanwhile, domestic migrants headed in large numbers for Sun Belt locales, contributing to significant population growth throughout that region. Within metropolitan areas that attracted both types of migrants, Frey finds that the two groups selected distinct county destinations—immigrants tended to settle closer to the urban core, while domestic migrants more often chose outlying suburban areas. These parallel migration trends pinpoint the demographic forces responsible in part for the "dualistic" economies that have materialized in large, multiethnic urban areas like Los Angeles, where workers increasingly cluster at the low and high ends of the skills spectrum. They also reveal the importance of domestic migrants in fueling the rapid, low-density metropolitan growth occurring throughout the South and in fast-growing suburbs and "exurbs" nationwide.

Beneath these distinct international and domestic migration trends lies a subtle, more recent shift in where immigrants are heading. In chapter 2, Audrey Singer charts the historical metropolitan destinations of immigrants, highlighting how the last two decades have seen an upsurge in immigration reminiscent of the turn of the twentieth century. She shows that while international migrants still populate historical centers of immigration like New York, Chicago, and Boston in large numbers, they are also heading for a new set of "emerging gateways" in the South, such as Atlanta, Dallas, and Washington, D.C. Not only are more immigrants moving to a new set of metro areas, they are also increasingly heading to suburbs, a decided shift from past preferences for cities. The recentness of immigration to these metropolitan areas means that many of their suburban communities are for the first time grappling with how to provide public services like schools, health care, and safety to new populations.

Immigrants were not the only group who shifted their destinations in the late twentieth century. In chapter 3 William Frey turns his attention to a group of domestic migrants whose movements turned a long-term trend fully on its head in the 1990s. For the better part of the last century, blacks moved from the South to cities throughout the North in what was termed the "Great Migration." But Frey shows that between 1995 and 2000, blacks returned on net to the South from every other region in the country. Metropolitan areas such as Atlanta, Charlotte, and Memphis led the way, attracting blacks from northern and western metro areas, including New York, Chicago, Los Angeles, and San Francisco. And in further contrast to the historical pattern, which saw less-skilled black workers move northward largely for manufacturing jobs, the most highly educated African Americans are now moving southward, contributing to a "brain gain" throughout the region. Frey cites a number of factors that may account for this "New Great Migration," including blacks' long-standing cultural and family ties to the South, a much improved racial climate in the region, and the economic boom the South enjoyed during the late 1990s. Whatever its drivers, this shifting locus of growth in the black middle class carries major social and economic implications not only for the South, but also for the places blacks are increasingly leaving behind.

POVERTY AND INCOME TRENDS REVEAL VARIABLE METROPOLITAN ECONOMIC FORTUNES

The decennial census, by its very nature, is a "snapshot" of the nation at one moment in time. As an economic portrait of the United States, the census captures places at somewhat different positions in their own economic cycles, yet it nonetheless offers a regular point at which to assess how larger trends have affected smaller locales. The chapters in this second section point to shifting poverty levels across regions between 1990 and 2000, with the South and Midwest performing better than West and Northeast; and shifting poverty within regions, as inner cities witnessed dramatic declines in the spatial concentration of poor households. While these trends may reflect changes specific to the 1990s, longer-term movements are apparent as well: the growing suburbanization of poverty nationwide, exemplified by the Los Angeles region; and a loss of higher-income households in most large cities. The economic downturn of the past five years has likely altered some of the trends witnessed in the last decade, but the longer-term shifts highlighted in this section no doubt persist.

In chapter 4, Alan Berube and William Frey begin by surveying the location of poverty across and within metropolitan areas. They find that central cities still exhibit an overall poverty rate double that of their suburbs, although the gap did narrow slightly in the 1990s. At the same time, rapid suburban growth, in combination with increasing suburban population diversity, meant that by 2000 in the nation's largest metropolitan areas the numbers of poor individuals living in cities and in suburbs were nearly identical. But even as the overall metropolitan poverty rate remained unchanged at 12.5 percent, Berube and Frey show that U.S. regions diverged dramatically on this measure. Poverty rates rose in northeastern and western cities and suburbs, while they declined in southern and midwestern areas. These trends related not only to regional differences in economic growth in the late 1990s, but also to differing regional impacts of the economic recession of the early 1990s. Berube and Frey's analysis raises a number of questions about the demographic, economic, and policy forces driving changes in poverty, and whether the nation can hope to achieve widespread reductions in poverty during the present decade, given its inauspicious start.

It is well known not only that the level of poverty affects outcomes for places and people, but also that the spatial organization of poverty—especially severe concentrations—may impose significant costs on families, neighborhoods, and society as a whole. So it is remarkable that amid the decade's "mixed blessings" on overall metropolitan poverty identified by Berube and Frey, Paul Jargowsky finds in chapter 5 that the 1990s produced a stunning decline in a seemingly intractable social problem—long-term growth in the concentration of poor households in inner-city neighborhoods.

Jargowsky demonstrates that after doubling in the 1970s and 1980s, the share of poor individuals living in high-poverty neighborhoods (where the poverty rate exceeds 40 percent) declined by nearly one-quarter in the 1990s—most dramatically in inner cities in the Midwest and South, like Detroit, Chicago, and San Antonio. He finds especially striking declines in concentrated poverty for African Americans and children. Jargowsky also notes some warning signs, including an increase in concentrated poverty in the West (owing to an increase in predominantly Hispanic high-poverty neighborhoods) and rising poverty rates in many inner suburban neighborhoods. His analysis suggests several factors that may account for these changing patterns of neighborhood poverty, including metropolitan economic performance, federal policy changes to promote work and residential mobility among the poor, and broader patterns of residential decentralization that increasingly affect the nation's older suburbs.

Shannon McConville and Paul Ong effectively take Jargowsky's research "to ground" in chapter 6 with their analysis of the Los Angeles region, one of the few areas that actually experienced an *increase* in concentrated poverty during the 1990s. Between 1990 and 2000, the proportion of poor individuals in the five-county Los Angeles region who lived in neighborhoods of high poverty rose from 7 percent to 12 percent. The authors show how that rise represented an acceleration of longer-term trends toward increased concentration of poverty in the area, especially in the suburbs, where most of the region's poor live today. McConville and Ong examine in particular how significant international migration to the region may have contributed to rising concentrated poverty, and they find a complicated and changing relationship between the two phenomena over time. They conclude that these worrying trends signal a need for a broader approach across the region to promote economic opportunity, and emphasize the role for education in catalyzing upward economic mobility for the children of the region's immigrants. Their findings should hold lessons for the growing number of metropolitan areas now receiving immigrant workers in record numbers as Los Angeles did in the 1970s and 1980s.

Of course, poverty is only one important barometer of the economic health of a region. In chapter 7 Alan Berube and Thacher Tiffany look at the distribution of household incomes in urban areas as an indicator of cities' fiscal capacity and social health. Focusing on the nation's 100 largest cities, they find a significant overall decline between the 1980 and 2000 censuses in the proportion of city households with high incomes. They note, however, that the household income profiles of large cities vary widely, and identify six predominant types of distributions. While some growing cities, like Columbus and Nashville, boast a healthy middle-class profile and a balance of low- and high-income households, most lack the nation's full spectrum of incomes. Many, like New Orleans and Buffalo, contain highly disproportionate shares of low-income households. A handful, like Atlanta and Washington, D.C., have a relatively small middle class. Berube and Tiffany argue that the varying "shape of the curve" among big cities suggests the need to look beyond poverty to fully understand urban income dynamics, and that individual cities need to pursue very different strategies to achieve greater income diversity, secure their fiscal health, and promote economic mobility.

GROWING HOUSING ISSUES ACCOMPANY HOMEOWNERSHIP BOOM

Housing attracts a great deal of attention in the census. The Census Bureau's two principal releases of Census 2000 data to the public (Summary File 1 and Summary File 3) contained a total of 385 tables on housing topics alone.

Researchers have many compelling reasons to be interested in the state of housing. Housing provides shelter, a basic necessity. For most homeowners, housing is the largest asset they hold—and increasingly, many use that asset to finance their consumption of other important goods, such as education, health care, or improvements to the home itself. In macroeconomic terms, strong house price growth in the late 1990s continued into the current decade, helping boost consumption during the recent recession and otherwise sluggish recovery. For policymakers in Washington, increased homeownership is one of the few goals on which Democrats and Republicans agree. And housing—or a lack thereof—dictates one's access to opportunity in terms of schools, jobs, amenities, and a safe neighborhood. The contributors to this section examine both the upside and the downside of the homeownership boom in the 1990s, and two housing issues that affect some groups and places disproportionately: sheltered homelessness and overcrowding.

In chapter 8 Dowell Myers and Gary Painter present the first of two analyses of homeownership trends in the 1990s. They highlight widespread increases in homeownership for young households over the decade, most notably gains made by African Americans. These increases helped make up for declines in homeownership among young age groups in many states during the 1980s. Myers and Painter note, however, that this particular trend was not uniform across the country. Metropolitan areas with large populations of young black or Latino households showed greater advances in homeownership among those groups than did other places. For instance, New York, Washington, and Atlanta all boasted large increases in black homeownership, while Latinos made more significant gains in California and Texas metro areas.

These increases may have come at a price, however: the increasing number of homeowners severely burdened by housing costs—those paying half or more of their income on housing. In chapter 9, Patrick Simmons finds that the number of homeowners facing severe affordability problems shot up by more than half over the 1990s. Just as with growing homeownership, the affordability problem was widespread. The proportion of homeowners with severe affordability burdens increased in forty-seven out of fifty states, and forty-three out of the nation's fifty largest cities. Simmons demonstrates that those burdens fell heavily on urban minorities, especially blacks, who were more than twice as likely to have severe affordability problems as homeowners generally. He warns that efforts to expand homeownership in the 1990s could leave many new homeowners in the red over the longer term, particularly given the economic downturn that occurred after Census 2000. Simmons argues that supplemental efforts are surely needed to sustain the benefits of these gains, and to put cost-burdened homeowners on more solid long-term financial footing.

The ups and downs of homeownership affect a large proportion of the U.S. population, and the economy as a whole. In chapter 10 Barrett Lee and Chad Farrell remind us, however, that a large number of homeless Americans face a much more dire situation. Lee and Farrell use a special tabulation of census data to examine the types of metropolitan neighborhoods that house the sheltered homeless. They find that even in neighborhoods with significant sheltered populations (at least 100 persons), the homeless constitute a visible but rarely dominant group—about 10 percent of population on average. In line with historical patterns, central cities still contain the vast majority of these neighborhoods, despite the suburbanization of larger shelters in some Sunbelt metro areas, like Atlanta and Fort Lauderdale. Neighborhoods with large shelters exhibit high levels of disadvantage generally—suggesting that current siting decisions are driven largely by neighborhood acceptance of, or resistance to, these facilities. The degree to which shelters remain in and around inner city neighborhoods will, the authors argue, depend on the willingness of localities to invoke "fair share" principles to spread human service facilities more widely, and efforts to build more permanent assisted housing for homeless families.

Patrick Simmons returns in chapter 11 to round out the volume's housing analyses by examining an area of growing concern in cities, suburbs, and rural areas alike: overcrowding. After decreasing for most of the postwar period, overcrowded households began to multiply in the 1980s, and increased even more rapidly during the 1990s. The incidence of the problem is highly variable, however, being much more prevalent in western and southwestern states, like Texas, California, and Arizona. Simmons identifies seven types of counties that experience high rates of overcrowding, running the gamut from large, multiethnic urban counties to American Indian/Alaska Native land, to small suburbs and towns attracting new waves of Latino agricultural workers. The analysis highlights a vexing issue for local governments: the need to balance competing factors of health and safety, housing affordability, labor demand, and cultural preferences. Nor is the problem likely to abate in coming years, given continued international and domestic migration to the suburbs, and the resulting mismatch between affordable housing needs and available housing stock.

SUMMARY

Although the United States is now in a somewhat less favorable economic situation than it was five years ago, the contributors to this volume paint a compelling portrait of a nation, its cities, suburbs, and neighborhoods undergoing significant change. The policy issues highlighted by each chapter spring not from the fleeting conditions of the places they describe on April 1, 2000, but from the long-term trends affecting all types of communities and the need to view them from a metropolitan angle. As always, leaders in the public, private, and nonprofit sectors can benefit from understanding the demographic and economic contexts in which their decisions take shape. For leaders at the state and national levels, these chapters reinforce the facts that not all metro areas are alike, and that differing local settings should influence the contours and implementation of policy. In short, this volume provides a clear and useful assessment of the dynamics that underlie the challenges urban decisionmakers will face in the next decade and beyond.

REFERENCES

Anderson, Margo J. 1988. *The American Census.* Yale University Press.

Australian Bureau of Statistics. 2002. "Australians on the Move." *Australian Demographic Statistics,* December.

Government Accountability Office. 2004. "American Community Survey: Key Unresolved Issues." GAO-05-82.

Long, Larry. 1991. "Residential Mobility Differences among Developed Countries." *International Regional Science Review* 14 (2): 133–147.

Sabety, Pari, Andy Reamer, and Lindsay Clark. 2004. "Understanding Our Communities: Funding the American Community Survey." Brookings.

Statistics Canada. 2002. "Canadians on the Move: Highlight Tables, 2001 Census." Ottawa.

U.S. Census Bureau. 2002. "Census 2000 Basics." Washington.

1

Metropolitan Magnets for International and Domestic Migrants

WILLIAM H. FREY

Hundreds of thousands of people move to the United States each year seeking a better life. Millions of Americans move to new locations within the United States each year for the same reason. The respective destinations of these two groups—immigrants and domestic migrants—shape the physical landscape, public service needs, business patterns, and political culture of our nation's metropolitan areas. For those reasons international and domestic migration trends in the late 1990s, and how they shaped metropolitan growth dynamics, are some of the most eagerly anticipated findings from U.S. Census 2000.

In recent decades immigrants and domestic migrants headed for different parts of the United States. Following the 1990 census studies showed that during the 1980s some large metropolitan areas had grown mostly as the result of immigration. A different set of metropolitan areas had grown primarily due to migration of individuals and families from other parts of the United States. In light of these divergent growth patterns it was posited that the demographic profiles for these "immigrant magnets" and "domestic migrant magnets" would, over time, become different.[1] For example, the former metropolitan areas, with strong immigrant-driven growth and young, culturally diverse populations, might follow global economic and demographic

The author is grateful to senior project programmer Cathy Sun and other support staff at the University of Michigan Population Studies Center, to John Haaga for comments, and to Alan Berube for review and editorial assistance.
1. Frey (1996); Frey and Liaw (1998).

trends. The latter areas, by contrast, could become more "suburban-like" with less diverse, more middle-aged populations. With immigration rising to even higher levels in the 1990s, migration data from Census 2000 provide an opportunity to reassess these growth patterns.[2]

This chapter examines how immigration and domestic migration contributed to population change and residential composition in the nation's largest metropolitan areas in the late 1990s. It first identifies the metropolitan areas that experienced the greatest influx of immigrants, and compares them to the metropolitan areas that exhibited the strongest growth—and largest declines—in domestic migrants from 1995 to 2000. Second, the study examines the racial/ethnic and educational characteristics of individuals who left the metropolitan areas that exported the most residents to other parts of the United States during that time. Third, it examines the contributions that domestic migrants made to the rapid growth in metropolitan areas in the "New Sunbelt" states in the South and West. Fourth, it distinguishes between growth sources within metropolitan areas, as immigrants drive population growth in core urban counties, and domestic migrants fuel growth in outlying counties. The chapter concludes with a brief discussion of the possible implications of these trends for the metropolitan United States in the coming decade.

METHODOLOGY

This study evaluates migration trends within the nation's eighty-one largest metropolitan areas—those in which Census 2000 recorded populations of at least 500,000.

Metropolitan Area Definitions

The metropolitan types analyzed include Consolidated Metropolitan Statistical Areas (CMSAs), Metropolitan Statistical Areas (MSAs), and New England County Metropolitan Areas (NECMAs) in the New England states, as defined by the U.S. Office of Management and Budget (OMB) in 1999 and in effect for Census 2000.[3] These eighty-one areas represent 65 percent of the U.S. population, and include sixty MSAs, eighteen CMSAs, and three NECMAs.

---

2. Martin and Midgley (2003).

3. This survey uses data from metropolitan areas defined by OMB as of June 30, 1999, and in effect for Census 2000. The OMB announced new metropolitan area definitions in June 2003. Schachter, Franklin, and Perry (2003).

This study differs from other Brookings census analyses in its use of CMSAs rather than their component parts, Primary Metropolitan Statistical Areas (PMSAs). CMSAs are metropolitan areas of 1 million or more people divided into two or more PMSAs. For example there are four PMSAs within the Los Angeles–Riverside–Orange County CMSA: the Los Angeles–Long Beach PMSA (consisting of Los Angeles County); the Orange County PMSA (Orange County); the Riverside–San Bernardino PMSA (Riverside and San Bernardino counties); and the Ventura PMSA (Ventura County). This study uses CMSAs rather than PMSAs to reflect how migration patterns affect broad metropolitan regions, and to ensure that estimates of domestic migration capture geographically significant changes in residence, rather than moves between two jurisdictions within the same region.

Migration Data

The migration data analyzed in this study draw from the decennial census question, "Where did this person live five years ago?" Using the answers to this question, the study analyzes migration trends over the 1995–2000 period from Census 2000, and for the 1985–90, 1975–80, and 1965–70 periods from the last three decennial censuses.

This chapter reports findings on two basic migration concepts: migration from abroad and net domestic migration. Migration from abroad is defined as in-migration to a given metropolitan area or county among persons who resided outside the United States at the beginning of the five-year period, including in Puerto Rico or another U.S. possession. Although the terms "migration from abroad" and "immigration" are used interchangeably in this chapter for ease of exposition, not all in-migrants from abroad are foreign-born. National figures show that 25 percent of 1995–2000 in-migrants from abroad were U.S.-born, and 75 percent were foreign-born.

Net domestic migration for a metropolitan area or county is defined as the difference between the number of in-migrants to that area from elsewhere in the United States, minus the number of out-migrants from that area to other parts of the United States, during the five-year period. The bulk of domestic migrants (89 percent in 1995–2000) are U.S.-born. Secondary migration (domestic migration among the foreign-born) is, however, increasingly common. Indeed, states like Nevada, Georgia, Arizona, and Colorado received large numbers of foreign-born residents from other parts of the nation during the late 1990s.[4] The percentage of domestic migrants in these fast-growing states who are U.S.-born is therefore lower than the national average.

4. Perry and Schachter (2003).

The migration from abroad and net domestic migration concepts can also be distinguished from one another in that the former describes a flow of people in one direction (into an area from outside the United States), whereas the latter captures the combined effect of two population flows (into an area from elsewhere in the United States, and out of an area to elsewhere in the United States). As such, migration from abroad statistics here do not take into account people who leave a particular area for a destination outside the United States—chiefly because they are not recorded in the U.S. census. Compared to migration from abroad, however, emigration from the United States to foreign countries is small. Total annual emigration of the foreign-born is estimated at 220,000 a year, whereas the United States received an average of 1.5 million immigrants a year in the late 1990s.[5]

The migration data used in these analyses draw primarily from the full "long form" sample of responses from the decennial censuses of 1970 to 2000. The data are based on an approximate 16 percent sample of all respondents in these censuses, and are statistically weighted to represent 100 percent of the population. This study's analyses of metropolitan migration among racial/ethnic subpopulations, and by educational attainment, are based on tabulations of 1995–2000 migration data from Census 2000 1-Percent Public Use Microdata Sample (PUMS) files.[6]

FINDINGS

Results from Census 2000 confirm that trends in immigration and domestic migration diverged significantly in the late 1990s.

The Largest Metropolitan Areas Attract International Migrants and Lose Domestic Migrants

During 1995–2000 four of the nation's five largest metropolitan areas—New York, Los Angeles, San Francisco, and Chicago—led all others in the number of immigrants they attracted. At the same time, however, they led all other metropolitan areas in the number of domestic migrants they lost to other parts of the United States (top and bottom panels, table 1-1). New York and Los Angeles had especially large gains and losses in both respects. The

5. Perry and Schachter (2003); Martin and Midgley (2003).
6. U.S. Census Bureau (2003). Throughout the chapter, the term "white" refers to non-Hispanic individuals who identified "white" as their sole race. "Black" refers to individuals who identified African American as their race regardless of ethnicity. "Hispanic" individuals are those who identified Hispanic or Latino ethnicity regardless of race.

T A B L E   1 - 1 .   Migration Magnets: Migration from Abroad and Net Domestic Migration, Large Metropolitan Areas, 1995–2000

Number of migrants

Metropolitan area	Migration from abroad	Net domestic migration
Magnets for migrants from abroad[a]		
New York-Northern NJ-Long Island, NY-NJ-CT-PA CMSA	983,659	−874,028
Los Angeles-Riverside-Orange County, CA CMSA	699,573	−549,951
San Francisco-Oakland-San Jose, CA CMSA	373,869	−206,670
Chicago-Gary-Kenosha, IL-IN-WI CMSA	323,019	−318,649
Washington-Baltimore, DC-MD-VA-WV CMSA	300,266	−58,849
Miami-Fort Lauderdale, FL CMSA	299,905	−93,774
Dallas-Fort Worth, TX CMSA	231,494	148,644
Houston-Galveston-Brazoria, TX CMSA	214,268	−14,377
Boston-Worcester-Lawrence, MA-NH-ME-CT CMSA	196,042	−44,581
Atlanta, GA MSA	162,972	233,303
Magnets for domestic migrants[b]		
Phoenix-Mesa, AZ MSA	135,017	245,159
Atlanta, GA MSA	162,972	233,303
Las Vegas, NV-AZ MSA	62,255	225,266
Dallas-Fort Worth, TX CMSA	231,494	148,644
Austin-San Marcos, TX MSA	51,795	104,340
Tampa-St. Petersburg-Clearwater, FL MSA	67,664	103,375
Orlando, FL MSA	78,939	101,226
Denver-Boulder-Greeley, CO CMSA	93,970	93,586
Charlotte-Gastonia-Rock Hill, NC-SC MSA	41,485	93,505
Raleigh-Durham-Chapel Hill, NC MSA	47,710	91,272
Greatest domestic migration losses[c]		
New York-Northern NJ-Long Island, NY-NJ-CT-PA CMSA	983,659	−874,028
Los Angeles-Riverside-Orange County, CA CMSA	699,573	−549,951
Chicago-Gary-Kenosha, IL-IN-WI CMSA	323,019	−318,649
San Francisco-Oakland-San Jose, CA CMSA	373,869	−206,670
Detroit-Ann Arbor-Flint, MI CMSA	108,975	−123,009
Miami-Fort Lauderdale, FL CMSA	299,905	−93,774
Philadelphia-Wilmington-Atlantic City, PA-NJ-DE-MD CMSA	127,921	−83,539
Honolulu, HI MSA	38,619	−69,866
Cleveland-Akron, OH CMSA	36,257	−65,914
Washington-Baltimore, DC-MD-VA-WV CMSA	300,266	−58,849

Source: Author's calculations from U.S. Census Bureau data.

a. Metro areas with largest migration from abroad, 1995–2000.

b. Metro areas with largest net domestic migration and where net domestic migration exceeds migration from abroad.

c. Metro areas with largest net domestic migration loss.

New York metropolitan region, which extends from southern Connecticut through central New Jersey, gained almost a million immigrants, but at the same time lost 874,000 residents to other parts of the United States. The five-county Los Angeles region gained nearly 700,000 immigrants, but lost 550,000 domestic migrants.

That the nation's largest metropolitan areas appear on both lists is perhaps not surprising, given their sheer size. Yet the rates at which these mega-regions gained immigrants and lost domestic migrants are striking. In 2000, roughly 5 percent of the population of these four metropolitan areas had arrived from abroad within the last five years.[7] At the same time they exported a combined 4 percent of their residents to other parts of the United States (figure 1-1). Both of these rates exceeded the averages across all metropolitan areas that experienced net domestic out-migration during the 1990s (see table 1A-2 in the appendix).

The loss of domestic migrants was not limited to these four immigrant magnets. The top six immigrant-gaining metropolitan areas each exported people to other domestic destinations in the late 1990s. However, losses in the Washington, D.C., and Miami metropolitan regions were smaller than in the other four. Consequently, the two metropolitan areas each experienced a net gain of at least 200,000 migrants (immigration plus domestic migration) in the late 1990s—more than in the New York, Los Angeles, Chicago, or San Francisco areas.

The nation's top metropolitan area domestic migrant "donors" have not always included the immigrant magnets. In the late 1960s four of the six metropolitan areas posting the largest net domestic migration losses were located in the economically declining "Rustbelt" (Pittsburgh, Cleveland, Detroit, and Buffalo) (see table 1A-1). None of these metropolitan areas was among the leaders in immigration. By the late 1990s, however, the degree of overlap between the top immigrant magnet metropolitan areas and domestic out-migration areas was significant, with five of six appearing on both lists. Of the aggregate net domestic out-migration experienced by the thirty-eight large metropolitan areas that experienced losses from 1995 to 2000, the nation's six largest immigrant magnet metropolitan areas accounted for 68 percent (versus 54 percent of population generally—table 1A-2).

Not every large "exporter" of domestic migrants in the late 1990s attracted immigrants. Although the four largest immigrant magnets top the list of metropolitan areas with the greatest net domestic migration losses (bottom panel, table 1-1), other economically stagnating metropolitan areas also appear in the top ten, including Detroit, Philadelphia, Honolulu, and Cleveland. None of these areas received anywhere near the number of immigrants that the "big six" did from 1995 to 2000.

This pattern of large immigrant gains and significant domestic migration losses is not a new one for some areas. Census data from 1970 onward indicate that for several decades, New York and Chicago—two long-standing immigrant ports of entry—have gained immigrants even as they have lost significant numbers of residents to other parts of the nation (table 1A-1.) The

---

7. These growth rates are calculated as a percentage of metropolitan population in 2000 age five and over.

FIGURE 1-1. **Migration Flows, Selected Immigrant Magnet Metropolitan Areas**

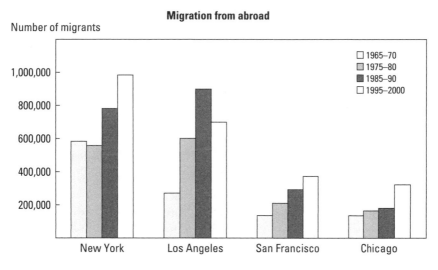

Migration from abroad

Number of migrants

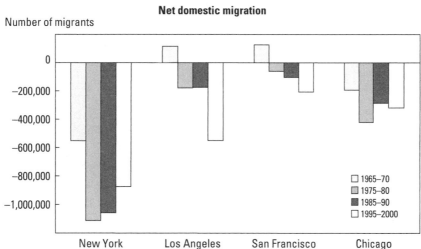

Net domestic migration

Number of migrants

Source: Author's calculations from U.S. Census Bureau data.

domestic migration losses that New York sustained from 1995 to 2000, in fact, were not as severe as those it experienced in the late 1970s or late 1980s.

Net domestic out-migration accelerated, however, in the Los Angeles and San Francisco regions in the 1990s. San Francisco's net loss of residents to other parts of the United States in the late 1990s was double that of the late 1980s, and

Los Angeles tripled its earlier losses. Although this trend was pronounced in these two regions, it reflects a broad domestic out-migration across California.[8] California did experience sharp economic shocks during the past decade, but most of that downturn and associated net out-migration occurred in the early 1990s.[9] The next section analyzes the demographic characteristics of that coastal out-migration as a first step toward assessing its causes.

Migrants Leaving Immigrant Metropolitan Areas in 1990s More Diverse than Their Predecessors

Past evidence of strong domestic out-migration from the largest immigration magnets engendered much discussion. A similar but less striking pattern identified subsequent to the 1990 census fueled speculation regarding a "linkage" between immigration and subsequent domestic out-migration from these areas.[10] The long-term domestic out-migration from immigrant magnets in the Northeast and West can be viewed as a product of general movement to the Sunbelt, driven in part by the broader regional economic restructuring occurring during this period. Yet the new pattern prevailing in regions such as Los Angeles and San Francisco suggested that in addition to the "pull" of favorable economic circumstances in other regions of the country, rising immigration to these areas might also help explain their domestic migration losses.

One perspective viewed the domestic patterns as a nationwide version of the "white flight" phenomenon that characterized local city-to-suburb movements in the 1950s and 1960s.[11] This explanation alluded to the almost "suburbanlike" out-migration from these increasingly urbanized metropolitan areas and the rising costs of their public services and housing, rather than an underlying motivation of racial or ethnic prejudice. Census data from the late 1980s indicated that families with children and middle-income families were more likely than other groups to leave California for surrounding states, and that whites constituted a plurality of these movers.

A related hypothesis, advanced by economists, suggested that lower-skilled workers in these metropolitan areas were displaced from jobs, and their wages reduced, by new immigrant workers who tend to disproportionately occupy the lower-skilled segment of the labor market. Because of this labor market competition some posited that longer-term residents left the immigrant mag-

8. Genaro Armas, "Californians Leaving Faster than Other Americans Arrive," *Chicago Tribune,* August 6, 2003, p. 12.
9. Kotkin (1997); California Department of Finance (2003).
10. Frey and Liaw (1998).
11. Frey (1994a, 1994b).

net areas for employment opportunities elsewhere.[12] Evidence consistent with this explanation included a unique and fairly consistent pattern of higher domestic out-migration from major immigrant gateways among less-educated adults between 1985 and 1990.[13] Other research did not find evidence, however, of a link between immigration and out-migration of native-born workers.[14]

This section begins to update these inquiries by analyzing the demographic characteristics of domestic out-migrants from the immigrant magnet metropolitan areas. As noted above this chapter employs 1-Percent Public Use Microdata Sample (PUMS) files from Census 2000 to identify out-migrants from the New York, Los Angeles, Chicago, and San Francisco regions, and to examine their dominant racial/ethnic characteristics. It also considers the educational attainment of domestic out-migrants as a proxy for their labor market skills.[15]

Most notably the new 1995–2000 data show that domestic net out-migration from California metropolitan areas, especially Los Angeles, was no longer dominated by whites (figure 1-2). Indeed, the racial and ethnic profile of net out-migration from each area was similar to that area's overall population characteristics. In the Los Angeles metropolitan area, whites made up a minority, and Hispanics a bare majority (51 percent), of net out-migration. This contrasted sharply with the makeup of the 1985–1990 net out-migrant pool, which was 78 percent white.[16] In fact whites were slightly under-represented in 1995–2000 net out-migration (35 percent) compared to their proportion of the metropolitan area population in 1995 (41 percent).

The profile of out-migrants in San Francisco changed as well. Whites still made up a majority of that area's net domestic out-migration, but 35 percent of out-migrants were racial and ethnic minorities, up from 23 percent in the late 1980s. Blacks constituted a substantial share (14 percent) of the metropolitan area's net population loss to other parts of the country.[17]

12. Borjas (1999).
13. Borjas (1999).
14. Kritz and Gurak (2001); Wright, Ellis, and Reibel (1997).
15. The PUMS data used in this section, including in figures 1-1 and 1-2, permit detailed analyses for close approximations of the actual boundaries of these metropolitan areas, which are constructed using areas called "Migration Super-Pumas." These approximations increase the populations of the New York and Los Angeles CMSAs by 3.9 percent and 0.8 percent, respectively. The approximations reduce the populations of the Chicago and San Francisco CMSAs by 5.1 percent and 3.7 percent, respectively.
16. Frey (1994a).
17. The higher share of blacks among out-migrants in San Francisco derives in part from the fact that the area actually experienced net domestic in-migration of Asians, thus increasing other racial/ethnic groups' shares of total net domestic out-migration.

FIGURE 1-2. White Share of Net Domestic Out-Migration, 1985–1990 and 1995–2000, and White Share of Population, 1995, Selected Immigrant Magnet Metropolitan Areas

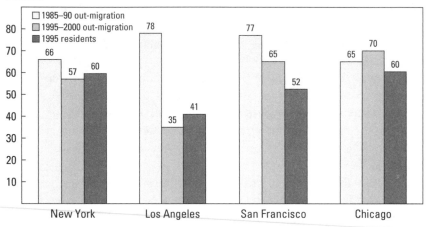

Source: Author's calculations from U.S. Census Bureau data.

Although the changing profile of out-migrants from Los Angeles and San Francisco reflects in part these areas' changing overall racial/ethnic makeup, the large shift suggests that the migration pattern in the late 1990s was significantly different than that of previous decades. In fact the trend in these large metropolitan areas contributed substantially to California's domestic migration loss in the late 1990s, during which nonwhites represented three-fifths of the state's domestic out-migrants.[18]

The move toward a more diverse set of domestic out-migrants was not confined to California metropolitan areas. Consistent with their overall racial/ethnic profiles, out-migrants from the New York and Chicago metropolitan areas in the late 1990s were more likely to be white than people leaving the Los Angeles and San Francisco areas (figure 1-2). In the New York region whites made up a smaller share of out-migrants from 1995 to 2000 (57 percent) than they did from 1985 to 1990 (66 percent), which was roughly equivalent to their proportion of the metropolitan area population. Whites did make up a slightly larger share of out-migrants from Chicago in the late 1990s than in the late 1980s, but so too did Hispanics (not shown). Overall, the increased diversity of domestic out-migrants from the four

18. Tilove (2003).

immigrant magnet metropolitan areas counters the "white flight" characterization that prevailed in previous decades.

The profiles of domestic out-migrants in the other large immigrant magnet metropolitan areas, Washington, D.C., and Miami, were different. As noted above each experienced lower levels of out-migration than the other four areas. Miami mirrored the other metropolitan areas in sustaining domestic migration losses of whites, Hispanics, blacks, and Asians. The Washington, D.C., region, however, showed substantial out-migration only among whites in the late 1990s. Minorities, led by Hispanics and blacks, actually registered domestic migration gains over the five-year period.

The combination of high diversity among international migrants, smaller overall out-flows, and somewhat smaller minority population shares among out-migrants created more racially diverse populations in the immigrant magnet metropolitan areas by 2000. More specifically, all six metropolitan areas gained Hispanics and Asians due to the two migration flows.

Although the racial and ethnic profile of domestic out-migrants from these metropolitan areas signals a change from previous decades, migration trends by educational attainment accentuate patterns identified in the 1990 census.[19] Figure 1-3 shows the percentage gain or loss in population by educational attainment that resulted from domestic migration and migration from abroad in the four immigrant magnet metropolitan areas. The highest rates of domestic out-migration occurred among adults who have not obtained a college degree. In each metropolitan area, net domestic out-migration reduced the population of adults who have not obtained a college degree by 4–5 percent. By contrast, out-migration served to reduce the pool of college graduates in New York and Chicago by smaller amounts, and college graduates actually migrated *into* the Los Angeles and San Francisco metropolitan areas from elsewhere in the United States. This pattern of less-educated out-migrants, and more-educated in-migrants, held for most racial and ethnic groups.

The out-migration of less-educated workers differs from long-established migration patterns between labor markets. That migration typically draws on the "best and the brightest"—that is, the educated and professional workers who respond to changes in a nationwide labor market.[20] The educational profile of domestic migrants observed in Los Angeles and San Francisco, and to a lesser extent in the other immigrant magnet metropolitan areas, may be attributable to those areas' unique economic and demographic dynamics. The high costs of residing in these urbanized metropolitan regions, reflected

19. Tilove (2003).
20. Long (1988).

FIGURE 1-3. **Migration Rates by Educational Attainment, Selected Immigrant Magnet Metropolitan Areas, 1995–2000**[a]

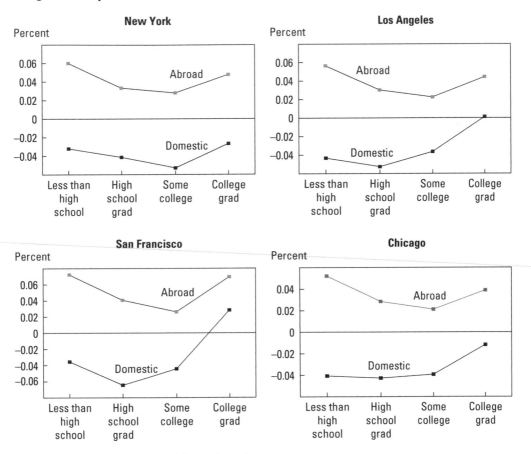

Source: Author's calculations from U.S. Census Bureau data.
a. Rate = (net subgroup domestic migration 1995–2000) / (2000 subgroup population)

in the prices of housing, public services, and commuting, may exert their greatest impacts on residents at the middle and lower ends of the socio-economic ladder, and induce these individuals to move to lower-cost areas of the United States.

The rates for migration from abroad in the four largest immigrant magnets, shown in figure 1-3, show that immigration served to increase their numbers of both low- and high-skilled residents in the late 1990s. Immigrants without a high school education made the largest impact on their destination metropolitan areas, raising the number of residents with that level of attainment 5–7 percent. Yet immigrants with college degrees were not far behind, increasing the ranks of that education group 4–5 percent (even higher in San Francisco).

The pattern of in-migration from abroad of less-educated groups, combined with continued domestic out-migration of similar groups, suggests that competition at the lower-skill end of the labor market may have contributed to domestic out-migration in the late 1990s. Further research is needed to determine whether these patterns are directly linked, or whether other factors played a more important role. The racial and ethnic profile of out-migrants indicates that regardless of the factors, both native-born and foreign-born workers contributed to the "flight" from these metropolitan areas. It is notable, however, that both Los Angeles and San Francisco experienced significant in-migration of college graduates from elsewhere in the United States and from abroad. It may be that these labor markets were able to absorb higher-skilled domestic migrants and immigrants, or that both of these more-educated groups were better able to afford the higher cost of living in these coastal regions.

Domestic Migrants Are Moving to the Southeast and West

Having established that large numbers of people left the nation's most populous metropolitan areas during the late 1990s, this survey now turns to an analysis of where these migrants and others headed over the five-year period.

The metropolitan areas that gained the most domestic migrants in the late 1990s—the "domestic migrant magnets"—are a different set than those that gained the most immigrants (table 1-1, middle panel). Led by Phoenix, Atlanta, and Las Vegas, these metropolitan areas are located in either the traditional Sunbelt states of Texas and Florida, or the band of "New Sunbelt" states that stretch across the Southeast and non-California West.[21] Some of these metropolitan areas, such as Atlanta, Austin, Denver, and Raleigh-Durham, benefited from the 1990s growth in new economy, high-tech sectors. Others, such as Phoenix and Tampa-St. Petersburg, are attracting particular segments of the population, such as retirees. Seven of these top ten metropolitan areas netted more than 100,000 residents from domestic migration over the five-year period. All are characterized by a lower-density style of urban and suburban development than most of the immigrant magnet metropolitan areas.

In contrast to the immigrant magnet metropolitan areas, which have included the same six metropolitan areas over the past four decades, the top

21. Frey (2002a).

domestic migrant magnet metropolitan areas have varied considerably from decade to decade (table 1A-1). For example, in 1965–70, none of the top three domestic magnets from the late 1990s (Phoenix, Atlanta, Las Vegas) were among the top six metropolitan areas for domestic migration gains. Phoenix emerged in the third spot in the late 1970s, and Atlanta and Las Vegas advanced into the top six in the late 1980s. The Miami region further highlights this variability: in the late 1960s it ranked second in domestic migration growth, but it now occupies one of the top positions among the nation's largest losers of domestic migrants.

Why are the immigrant magnets so stable over time, whereas the domestic migrant magnets change from decade to decade? In general the former areas continue to attract new immigrants to the United States who depend on established racial and ethnic enclaves and family connections to provide them with social and economic support. This relates in no small part to our nation's immigration laws, which give strong emphasis to family reunification in the preference system.[22] In contrast, domestic migrants are decidedly more "footloose" in their migration patterns and more responsive to geographic shifts in employment location and amenities. For example, Houston ranked first among major metropolitan areas in domestic migration gains (215,000) during the late 1970s. As the "oil bust" hit in the following decade, however, Houston experienced the nation's fifth-largest domestic outmigration (−142,000) from 1985 to 1990.

Recent domestic migration to these traditional and New Sunbelt destinations has contributed to rapid growth in their overall populations. In several of these metropolitan areas, net domestic migration between 1995 and 2000 boosted population by at least 5 percent overall (table 1-2). In Las Vegas in-migration from other parts of the nation alone contributed nearly 16 percent to the area's population in 2000, far more than in the other domestic migrant magnets.

Some metropolitan areas are increasingly attracting both immigrants and domestic migrants. Dallas fits into this category, as it registered significant gains in each migrant population during the late 1990s. In fact, the top domestic migrant magnets—Phoenix, Atlanta, and Las Vegas—drew substantial numbers of immigrants during this time. As figure 1-4 shows this is a relatively new phenomenon in these metropolitan areas, each of which witnessed comparatively little immigration in previous decades. Other places that previously attracted smaller numbers of immigrants, such as Orlando,

---

22. Martin and Midgely (2003).

TABLE 1-2. **Large Metropolitan Areas with Highest Domestic Migration Growth Rates, 1995–2000**[a]

Percent

		Growth rate	
Rank	Metropolitan area	Net domestic migration	Migration from abroad
1	Las Vegas, NV-AZ MSA	15.54	4.30
2	Sarasota-Bradenton, FL MSA	9.14	2.53
3	Austin-San Marcos, TX MSA	9.01	4.47
4	Raleigh-Durham-Chapel Hill, NC MSA	8.25	4.31
5	Phoenix-Mesa, AZ MSA	8.17	4.50
6	Charlotte-Gastonia-Rock Hill, NC-SC MSA	6.71	2.98
7	Orlando, FL MSA	6.58	5.13
8	Atlanta, GA MSA	6.13	4.28
9	West Palm Beach-Boca Raton, FL MSA	5.70	4.37
10	Tampa-St. Petersburg-Clearwater, FL MSA	4.57	2.99
11	Columbia, SC MSA	4.38	2.06
12	Tucson, AZ MSA	4.05	3.12
13	Greenville-Spartanburg-Anderson, SC MSA	3.98	1.69
14	Nashville, TN MSA	3.98	2.20
15	Denver-Boulder-Greeley, CO CMSA	3.90	3.92

Source: Author's calculations from U.S. Census Bureau data.
a. Rate = (net domestic migration 1995–2000) / (2000 population, ages 5 and over) × 100.

Charlotte, and Raleigh-Durham, are now attracting many more, contributing to growth in their minority populations, particularly Hispanics.[23]

Although domestic migration to these areas still outpaces international migration, recent immigrants contributed 4–5 percent to overall metropolitan area population in most of the fastest-growing metropolitan areas in the late 1990s (table 1-2). It is likely that new immigrants, as well as foreign-born individuals who moved to these areas from elsewhere in the United States, were attracted by the lower-skill service, construction, and retail jobs that rapid domestic in-migration created in the late 1990s.[24]

Immigrants Settle in Inner Core; Domestic Migrants in Outer Suburbs

This section examines where immigrants and domestic migrants tended to move within metropolitan areas, as well as the places within those areas from which domestic migrants moved.

Overall about half of the nation's 3,141 counties experienced net out-migration over the 1990s. Yet only 95 of these counties had declines of at

23. Suro and Singer (2002); Frey (2002a).
24. Frey (2002b).

FIGURE 1-4. **Migration Flows, Selected Domestic Migrant Magnet Metropolitan Areas**

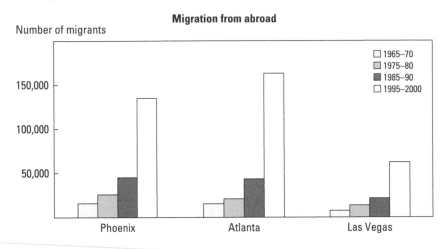

Migration from abroad

Number of migrants

□ 1965–70
▨ 1975–80
■ 1985–90
□ 1995–2000

Phoenix   Atlanta   Las Vegas

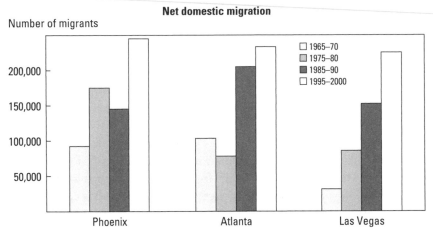

Net domestic migration

Number of migrants

□ 1965–70
▨ 1975–80
■ 1985–90
□ 1995–2000

Phoenix   Atlanta   Las Vegas

least 10,000 people, and they are heavily represented by the kinds of areas shown in table 1-3. It is immediately clear that the most urbanized counties in large metropolitan areas—those containing the central cities—sustained the greatest domestic migration losses in the late 1990s. Nine of these counties lost more than 100,000 net domestic migrants over this period, including the core counties of the Los Angeles, Chicago, New York, and Miami metropolitan areas. For the most part these counties lie within high-immigration coastal metropolitan areas (including Chicago), or within stagnating Midwest/ Rustbelt areas such as St. Louis, Cleveland, and Cincinnati. Some inner-

T A B L E 1 - 3 . Counties with Largest Net Domestic Migration Losses, Large Metropolitan Areas, 1995–2000

Number of migrants

Rank	County and state	Inside metropolitan area	Net domestic migration	Migration from abroad
1	Los Angeles, CA	Los Angeles-Riverside-Orange County, CA CMSA	–567,271	466,605
2	Cook, IL	Chicago-Gary-Kenosha, IL-IN-WI CMSA	–377,902	230,922
3	Kings, NY	New York-Northern NJ-Long Island, NY-NJ-CT-PA CMSA	–233,555	160,306
4	Queens, NY	New York-Northern NJ-Long Island, NY-NJ-CT-PA CMSA	–168,505	169,784
5	Miami-Dade, FL	Miami-Fort Lauderdale, FL CMSA	–159,714	206,689
6	Wayne, MI	Detroit-Ann Arbor-Flint, MI CMSA	–115,437	42,730
7	Harris, TX	Houston-Galveston-Brazoria, TX CMSA	–114,892	181,509
8	St. Louis city, MO	St. Louis, MO-IL MSA	–105,224	11,944
9	Santa Clara, CA	San Francisco-Oakland-San Jose, CA CMSA	–105,088	124,793
10	Philadelphia, PA	Philadelphia-Wilmington-Atlantic City, PA-NJ-DE-MD CMSA	–94,158	46,177
11	Baltimore city, MD	Washington-Baltimore, DC-MD-VA-WV CMSA	–92,223	12,656
12	Dallas, TX	Dallas-Fort Worth, TX CMSA	–89,724	137,081
13	Bronx, NY	New York-Northern NJ-Long Island, NY-NJ-CT-PA CMSA	–87,430	76,736
14	Nassau, NY	New York-Northern NJ-Long Island, NY-NJ-CT-PA CMSA	–72,284	26,840
15	Honolulu, HI	Honolulu, HI MSA	–69,866	38,619
16	Cuyahoga, OH	Cleveland-Akron, OH CMSA	–68,198	23,096
17	Orange, CA	Los Angeles-Riverside-Orange County, CA CMSA	–59,686	128,204
18	San Francisco, CA	San Francisco-Oakland-San Jose, CA CMSA	–58,197	49,743
19	New York, NY	New York-Northern NJ-Long Island, NY-NJ-CT-PA CMSA	–57,249	104,054
20	Hamilton, OH	Cincinnati-Hamilton, OH-KY-IN CMSA	–50,750	12,567

Source: Author's calculations from U.S. Census Bureau data.

suburban counties make the list as well, including Nassau County in the New York region and Orange County in the Los Angeles area. The District of Columbia and the inner-suburban county of Fairfax, Virginia, in the Washington, D.C., region, although not among the top twenty, had net losses of roughly 40,000 domestic migrants in the late 1990s.

In light of these large domestic migration losses in core and inner counties of metropolitan areas, migration from abroad is an increasingly important source of their population gains. Miami-Dade County's gain of 206,000 immigrants in the late 1990s more than compensated for its net loss of 160,000 domestic migrants. Similar migration-driven gains characterize Harris and Dallas counties in Texas and Manhattan in New York.

Many Midwest and Rustbelt metropolitan areas, on the other hand, offer a contrast to the immigration "cushion" that sustained population gains in larger metropolitan areas. For example, the city of St. Louis lost 105,000 domestic migrants over the 1995–2000 period, but received fewer than 12,000 immigrants. Wayne County, containing the city of Detroit, gained over 40,000 immigrants—not enough to make up for its loss of 115,000 domestic migrants. Immigrants contributed little population to core counties in the Baltimore, Cleveland, and Cincinnati regions, and to other smaller urban counties experiencing out-migration (for example, Buffalo, Milwaukee, New Orleans, and Pittsburgh). Thus it is not surprising that many mayors of struggling cities in the Northeast and Midwest are looking to immigrants as a source of potential demographic gains.[25]

In some metropolitan areas immigrants do not head primarily for the core urban counties. In the Washington-Baltimore area, for example, the core counties of Baltimore City and the District of Columbia lost more domestic out-migrants than they gained immigrants in the late 1990s. The inner-suburban county of Fairfax, Virginia, however, gained roughly twice as many immigrants as it lost domestic migrants during that time. This owes in part to Washington's unique settlement pattern, where immigrants have for some time chosen suburban over city residences.[26]

Although inner counties of major metropolitan areas increasingly depended on migration from abroad to fuel population growth in the late 1990s, the opposite occurred on the periphery of these areas. Suburban counties, often those at the exurban edges of their metropolitan areas, dominate the list of counties with the highest rates of growth from domestic migration (table 1-4). At the same time most experienced little migration from abroad.

---

25. Robert L. Smith, "Can Immigrants Save the Region: The Right Kind Can Not Only Boost Population, But Also Create Jobs," *Cleveland Plain Dealer,* July 13, 2003, p. A1.
26. Singer (2003).

T A B L E 1 - 4 . Counties with Highest Domestic Migration Growth Rates, Large Metropolitan Areas, 1995–2000[a]

Rank	County and state	Inside metropolitan area	Growth rate	
			Net domestic migration	Migration from abroad
1	Douglas, CO	Denver-Boulder-Greeley, CO CMSA	33.3	2.4
2	Forsyth, GA	Atlanta, GA MSA	30.5	2.5
3	Henry, GA	Atlanta, GA MSA	23.3	1.2
4	Paulding, GA	Atlanta, GA MSA	22.0	0.8
5	Delaware, OH	Columbus, OH MSA	21.4	0.7
6	Loudoun, VA	Washington-Baltimore, DC-MD-VA-WV CMSA	21.4	4.2
7	Williamson, TX	Austin-San Marcos, TX MSA	20.8	2.0
8	Nye, NV	Las Vegas, NV-AZ MSA	19.9	1.2
9	Collin, TX	Dallas-Fort Worth, TX CMSA	18.9	4.5
10	DeSoto, MS	Memphis, TN-AR-MS MSA	17.1	1.0
11	Hays, TX	Austin-San Marcos, TX MSA	17.0	1.6
12	Pinal, AZ	Phoenix-Mesa, AZ MSA	16.9	2.3
13	Cherokee, GA	Atlanta, GA MSA	16.3	2.4
14	Williamson, TN	Nashville, TN MSA	16.2	1.5
15	Union, NC	Charlotte-Gastonia-Rock Hill, NC-SC MSA	16.1	2.5
16	Clark, NV	Las Vegas, NV-AZ MSA	16.0	4.7
17	Denton, TX	Dallas-Fort Worth, TX CMSA	15.7	3.1
18	Pike, PA	New York-Northern NJ-Long Island, NY-NJ-CT-PA CMSA	15.6	0.4
19	Barrow, GA	Atlanta, GA MSA	15.2	1.1
20	Shelby, AL	Birmingham, AL MSA	15.1	1.2

Source: Author's calculations from U.S. Census Bureau data.
a. Rate = (1995–2000 migration component) / (2000 population, ages 5 and over) × 100.

Not surprisingly, the list includes counties within domestic magnet metropolitan areas such as Atlanta, Phoenix, Las Vegas, Austin, Dallas, and Charlotte. For instance, domestic migration contributed 30 percent to the population of Forsyth County, Georgia, on the periphery of the Atlanta metropolitan area, between 1995 and 2000 alone, whereas migration from abroad contributed only 2.5 percent to Forsyth's population. This decidedly smaller immigration contribution to population characterized other fast-growing counties in the Atlanta region and in other large metropolitan areas.

The disparity between growing suburban and exurban counties, where domestic migration dominates, and inner counties depend on migration from abroad to forestall population decline, is not limited to the domestic migrant magnet metropolitan areas. It is also evident in some of the nation's largest regions, including New York and Washington, D.C. In the New York region, twenty-two of twenty-nine counties registered net losses of domestic migrants between 1995 and 2000. Yet Pike County, Pennsylvania, on the periphery of the region, had one of the highest growth rates from domestic migration in the country. Similarly Loudoun County, Virginia, located within the Washington, D.C., metropolitan area, remains one of the fastest-growing suburban counties in the country due largely to rapid domestic in-migration.

This general pattern is pervasive nationally. Of the nation's 3,141 counties, just 239 grew from domestic migration at rates higher than 10 percent in 1995–2000. Of these only five counties grew at a rate of more than 5 percent due to migration from abroad; and 183 did not register even 2 percent growth from immigration. In general domestic migrants are increasingly choosing residences in the periphery of metropolitan America, whereas immigrants continue to fuel growth in urban and inner-suburban jurisdictions.

CONCLUSION

This study finds that the nation's metropolitan areas can be distinguished by the degree to which they attracted, or lost, international and domestic migrants over the late 1990s. During that five-year period the nation's largest metropolitan areas acquired the most immigrants, but lost the most domestic migrants to other parts of the country. Los Angeles and San Francisco in particular lost more domestic migrants than in decades past, fueling overall domestic migrant losses for the state. The recent trend establishes these two West Coast immigrant ports of entry as "redistributors" of population to fast-growing metropolitan areas in the interior United States, a role that New York and Chicago played in earlier decades.

Moreover, the domestic out-migrants from these "immigrant magnets" are more diverse than residents who left in previous decades. Many out-migrants from these regions are Hispanics, blacks, and Asians, so that "white flight" no longer characterizes the nature of that out-migration. At the same time, these areas are losing population disproportionately among residents without college degrees, who may have difficulty affording the high cost of living in these metropolitan areas, and may see greater economic opportunity in the Sunbelt states. Nevertheless, these dynamic "world city" regions continue to attract highly skilled immigrants and, in some cases, from inside the United States. The challenge for these regions over the next decade will be to grow physically and economically in ways that make them more attractive to moderate-income and middle-income families of all races and ethnicities.

The metropolitan areas that gained the most in-migrants from other parts of the United States in the late 1990s are located throughout the Southeast and non-California West. The movement of new residents into these metropolitan areas followed—and fueled—the growth of new industries and expanding urban and suburban developments in metropolitan areas such as Phoenix, Atlanta, and Las Vegas. These domestic magnets also attracted new immigrant populations, perhaps in response to the lower-skilled labor demands created by rapid new growth.[27] The integration of immigrants into these heretofore largely white or (in the case of the South) white and black metropolitan areas will be the subject of much research and policy focus.[28] Moreover, it remains to be seen whether the low-density physical development patterns that characterize most of their cities and suburbs can sustain rapid population and job growth, as well as demands for affordable housing and other public services, over the longer term.

Within metropolitan areas, immigrants have invigorated city and neighborhood populations in core urban counties in large metropolitan areas like New York, San Francisco, Washington, D.C., and Boston, offsetting their losses of domestic migrants to the suburbs and other parts of the country. At the same time core counties in the Midwest and Rustbelt are sustaining some of the nation's greatest domestic out-migration losses but attracting few immigrants. Some local officials have concluded that attracting immigrants could help rekindle economic and residential life in declining urban neighborhoods, and are beginning to market their cities nationally and internationally in hopes of reversing population declines and increasing ethnic

---

27. Frey (2002b).
28. Singer (2004).

diversity.[29] In addition, population gains in fast-growing peripheral counties accrue almost entirely from domestic migration, with little migration from abroad. These divergent patterns suggest that the demographic profiles and associated public service needs, tax bases, and political orientations of inner and outer jurisdictions in the nation's major metropolitan areas may diverge. Such distinctions appear not only in domestic migrant magnets, such as Atlanta and Denver, but also in immigrant magnet metros such as New York and Washington, D.C.

Future research will undoubtedly go deeper in describing the demographic and socioeconomic profiles of international and domestic migrants in metropolitan areas. This chapter, however, confirms that new immigrants and ongoing domestic migration continue to affect metropolitan America in sharply different ways.

29. Genaro Armas, "Old Cities Make the Pitch for Residents," *Chicago Tribune,* April 27, 2003, p. B1.

TABLE 1A-1. Top Migration Metropolitan Areas, Selected Periods, 1965–2000[a]

Number of migrants

1965–70		1975–80		1985–90		1995–2000	
Greatest migration from abroad							
New York	583,388	Los Angeles	601,613	Los Angeles	899,007	New York	983,659
Los Angeles	271,029	New York	558,051	New York	781,474	Los Angeles	699,573
Washington-Baltimore	136,827	San Francisco	210,566	San Francisco	293,306	San Francisco	373,869
San Francisco	136,191	Chicago	165,482	Washington-Baltimore	228,278	Chicago	323,019
Chicago	135,636	Washington-Baltimore	153,961	Miami	210,609	Washington-Baltimore	300,266
Miami	123,244	Miami	131,153	Chicago	180,875	Miami	299,905
Greatest net domestic migration gains							
Dallas	191,329	Houston	215,343	Atlanta	205,010	Phoenix	245,159
Miami	185,965	Tampa-St. Petersburg	185,182	Seattle	183,820	Atlanta	233,303
Seattle	177,609	Phoenix	175,075	Tampa-St. Petersburg	159,112	Las Vegas	225,266
Tampa-St. Petersburg	146,770	Dallas	164,951	Orlando	154,520	Dallas	148,644
Houston	145,156	Seattle	154,412	Las Vegas	152,197	Austin	104,340
San Diego	135,838	San Diego	114,734	Phoenix	145,226	Tampa-St. Petersburg	103,375
Greatest net domestic migration losses							
New York	−552,020	New York	−1,112,404	New York	−1,058,078	New York	−874,028
Chicago	−192,876	Chicago	−420,926	Chicago	−285,204	Los Angeles	−549,951
Pittsburgh	−82,706	Detroit	−236,920	Los Angeles	−174,673	Chicago	−318,649
Cleveland	−48,835	Los Angeles	−179,032	Detroit	−161,042	San Francisco	−206,670
Detroit	−39,743	Cleveland	−166,263	Houston	−142,562	Detroit	−123,009
Buffalo	−39,265	Philadelphia	−153,481	San Francisco	−103,498	Miami	−93,774

Source: Author's calculations from U.S. Census Bureau data.

a. Metro areas are CMSAs, MSAs, and (in New England) NECMAs, as defined in Census 2000. Names are abbreviated (full names appear in appendix B).

TABLE 1A - 2. Migration from Abroad and Net Domestic Migration, Metropolitan Areas with 2000 Population over 500,000, 1995–2000

Metropolitan area	Population in 2000	Totals (number of migrants) Migration from abroad	Net domestic migration	Rate[a] (percent) Migration from abroad	Net domestic migration
New York-Northern NJ-Long Island, NY-NJ-CT-PA CMSA	21,199,865	983,659	−874,028	4.97	−4.42
Los Angeles-Riverside-Orange County, CA CMSA	16,373,645	699,573	−549,951	4.63	−3.64
Chicago-Gary-Kenosha, IL-IN-WI CMSA	9,157,540	323,019	−318,649	3.81	−3.76
Washington-Baltimore, DC-MD-VA-WV CMSA	7,608,070	300,266	−58,849	4.23	−0.83
San Francisco-Oakland-San Jose, CA CMSA	7,039,362	373,869	−206,670	5.67	−3.14
Philadelphia-Wilmington-Atlantic City, PA-NJ-DE-MD CMSA	6,188,463	127,921	−83,539	2.21	−1.44
Boston-Worcester-Lawrence, MA-NH-ME-CT CMSA	6,057,826	196,042	−44,581	3.60	−0.82
Detroit-Ann Arbor-Flint, MI CMSA	5,456,428	108,975	−123,009	2.15	−2.42
Dallas-Fort Worth, TX CMSA	5,221,801	231,494	148,644	4.82	3.09
Houston-Galveston-Brazoria, TX CMSA	4,669,571	214,268	−14,377	4.99	−0.33
Atlanta, GA MSA	4,112,198	162,972	233,303	4.28	6.13
Miami-Fort Lauderdale, FL CMSA	3,876,380	299,905	−93,774	8.26	−2.58
Seattle-Tacoma-Bremerton, WA CMSA	3,554,760	122,766	39,945	3.69	1.20
Phoenix-Mesa, AZ MSA	3,251,876	135,017	245,159	4.50	8.17
Minneapolis-St. Paul, MN-WI MSA	2,968,806	66,120	34,207	2.40	1.24
Cleveland-Akron, OH CMSA	2,945,831	36,257	−65,914	1.32	−2.39
San Diego, CA MSA	2,813,833	108,822	−6,108	4.16	−0.23
St. Louis, MO-IL MSA	2,603,607	35,347	−43,614	1.45	−1.79
Denver-Boulder-Greeley, CO CMSA	2,581,506	93,970	93,586	3.92	3.90
Tampa-St. Petersburg-Clearwater, FL MSA	2,395,997	67,664	103,375	2.99	4.57
Pittsburgh, PA MSA	2,358,695	21,788	−57,997	0.98	−2.60
Portland-Salem, OR-WA CMSA	2,265,223	73,078	59,177	3.47	2.81
Cincinnati-Hamilton, OH-KY-IN CMSA	1,979,202	21,881	3,701	1.19	0.20
Sacramento-Yolo, CA CMSA	1,796,857	55,741	51,424	3.33	3.07
Kansas City, MO-KS MSA	1,776,062	31,490	16,079	1.91	0.98
Milwaukee-Racine, WI CMSA	1,689,572	27,525	−40,350	1.75	−2.56
Orlando, FL MSA	1,644,561	78,939	101,226	5.13	6.58
Indianapolis, IN MSA	1,607,486	23,675	20,954	1.59	1.41
San Antonio, TX MSA	1,592,383	39,952	5,674	2.72	0.39
Norfolk-Virginia Beach-Newport News, VA-NC MSA	1,569,541	34,990	−8,681	2.40	−0.59
Las Vegas, NV-AZ MSA	1,563,282	62,255	225,266	4.30	15.54
Columbus, OH MSA	1,540,157	31,434	33,774	2.20	2.36
Charlotte-Gastonia-Rock Hill, NC-SC MSA	1,499,293	41,485	93,505	2.98	6.71

New Orleans, LA MSA	1,337,726	15,283	-57,129	1.23	-4.58
Salt Lake City-Ogden, UT MSA	1,333,914	42,858	-18,135	3.53	-1.50
Greensboro–Winston-Salem–High Point, NC MSA	1,251,509	31,093	36,592	2.66	3.13
Austin–San Marcos, TX MSA	1,249,763	51,795	104,340	4.47	9.01
Nashville, TN MSA	1,231,311	25,173	45,606	2.20	3.98
Raleigh-Durham-Chapel Hill, NC MSA	1,187,941	47,710	91,272	4.31	8.25
Buffalo-Niagara Falls, NY MSA	1,170,111	15,487	-49,239	1.41	-4.48
Hartford, CT NECMA	1,148,618	31,740	-13,853	2.95	-1.29
Memphis, TN-AR-MS MSA	1,135,614	17,845	3,748	1.70	0.36
West Palm Beach-Boca Raton, FL MSA	1,131,184	46,706	61,001	4.37	5.70
Jacksonville, FL MSA	1,100,491	23,464	29,260	2.29	2.85
Rochester, NY MSA	1,098,201	17,471	-36,959	1.70	-3.59
Grand Rapids-Muskegon-Holland, MI MSA	1,088,514	18,029	12,609	1.79	1.25
Oklahoma City, OK MSA	1,083,346	23,081	6,289	2.29	0.62
Louisville, KY-IN MSA	1,025,598	13,373	-4,806	1.40	-0.50
Richmond-Petersburg, VA MSA	996,512	17,363	12,912	1.86	1.39
Providence-Fall River-Warwick, RI-MA NECMA	962,886	23,743	4,159	2.72	0.48
Greenville-Spartanburg-Anderson, SC MSA	962,441	15,219	35,786	1.69	3.98
Dayton-Springfield, OH MSA	950,558	9,310	-26,664	1.05	-3.00
Fresno, CA MSA	922,516	26,590	-31,734	3.14	-3.75
Birmingham, AL MSA	921,106	10,671	6,057	1.24	0.70
Honolulu, HI MSA	876,156	38,619	-69,866	4.71	-8.52
Albany-Schenectady-Troy, NY MSA	875,583	11,155	-19,426	1.36	-2.36
Tucson, AZ MSA	843,746	24,626	31,984	3.12	4.05
Tulsa, OK MSA	803,235	13,707	12,029	1.84	1.61
Syracuse, NY MSA	732,117	9,118	-31,851	1.33	-4.64
Omaha, NE-IA MSA	716,998	14,275	-3,172	2.15	-0.48
Albuquerque, NM MSA	712,738	14,837	-161	2.24	-0.02
Knoxville, TN MSA	687,249	6,873	21,894	1.06	3.39
El Paso, TX MSA	679,622	31,468	-47,790	5.06	-7.69
Bakersfield, CA MSA	661,645	21,867	-18,348	3.60	-3.02
Allentown-Bethlehem-Easton, PA MSA	637,958	10,648	-176	1.77	-0.03
Harrisburg-Lebanon-Carlisle, PA MSA	629,401	7,541	334	1.27	0.06
Scranton-Wilkes-Barre-Hazleton, PA MSA	624,776	3,430	-9,121	0.58	-1.54

(continued)

William H. Frey

TABLE 1A-2. Migration from Abroad and Net Domestic Migration, Metropolitan Areas with 2000 Population over 500,000, 1995–2000 (*continued*)

Metropolitan area	Population in 2000	Totals (number of migrants)		Rate[a] (percent)	
		Migration from abroad	Net domestic migration	Migration from abroad	Net domestic migration
Toledo, OH MSA	618,203	6,370	-12,924	1.10	-2.24
Springfield, MA NECMA	608,479	16,089	-963	2.81	-0.17
Baton Rouge, LA MSA	602,894	7,831	7,316	1.40	1.31
Youngstown-Warren, OH MSA	594,746	3,124	-14,645	0.56	-2.62
Sarasota-Bradenton, FL MSA	589,959	14,245	51,386	2.53	9.14
Little Rock-North Little Rock, AR MSA	583,845	8,223	9,625	1.51	1.77
McAllen-Edinburg-Mission, TX MSA	569,463	22,862	-13,249	4.47	-2.59
Stockton-Lodi, CA MSA	563,598	15,828	8,739	3.05	1.68
Charleston-North Charleston, SC MSA	549,033	9,130	14,029	1.78	2.74
Wichita, KS MSA	545,220	10,999	1,856	2.18	0.37
Mobile, AL MSA	540,258	6,487	2,419	1.29	0.48
Columbia, SC MSA	536,691	10,340	21,972	2.06	4.38
Colorado Springs, CO MSA	516,929	18,910	4,332	3.96	0.91
Fort Wayne, IN MSA	502,141	5,546	-5,267	1.19	-1.13
Metropolitan areas with net domestic in-migration	63,646,126	1,846,565	2,146,545	3.12	3.63
Metropolitan areas with net domestic out-migration	120,006,096	4,273,746	-3,075,569	3.83	-2.76

Source: Author's calculations from U.S. Census Bureau data.
a. Rate = (1995–2000 migration component) / (2000 population, ages 5 and over) × 100.

REFERENCES

Borjas, George J. 1999. *Heaven's Door: Immigration Policy and the American Economy.* Princeton University Press.

Borjas, George J., Richard B. Freeman, and Lawrence F. Katz. 1996. "Searching for the Effect of Immigration on the Labor Market." Working Paper 5454. Cambridge, Mass.: National Bureau of Economic Research.

California Department of Finance. 2003. "Updated Revised Historical County Population Estimates and Components of Change, July 1, 1990–1999." Sacramento.

Frey, William H. 1994a. "Immigration and Internal Migration 'Flight' from U.S. Metro Areas: 1990 Census Findings by Race, Poverty and Education." Research Report 94–304. Ann Arbor: University of Michigan Population Studies Center.

———. 1994b. "Immigration and Internal Migration: 1990 Census Findings for California." Research Report 94–306. Ann Arbor: University of Michigan Population Studies Center.

———. 1996. "Immigrant and Native Migrant Magnets." *American Demographics* 18 (12)(November): 37–40, 53.

———. 2002a. "Metro Magnets for Minorities and Whites: Melting Pots, the New Sunbelt and the Heartland." Research Report 02–496. Ann Arbor: University of Michigan Population Studies Center.

———. 2002b. "Census 2000 Reveals New Native-Born and Foreign-Born Shifts across U.S." Research Report 02-520. Ann Arbor: University of Michigan Population Studies Center.

Frey, William H., and Kao-Lee Liaw. 1998. "The Impact of Recent Immigration on Population Redistribution within the United States." In *The Immigration Debate: Studies on the Economic, Demographic and Fiscal Effects of Immigration,* by James P. Smith and Barry Edmonston. Washington: National Academy Press.

Kotkin, Joel. 1997 *California: A Twenty-First Century Prospectus.* Denver: Center for the New West.

Kritz, Mary M., and Douglas T. Gurak. 2001. "The Impact of Immigration on the Internal Migration of Natives and Immigrants." *Demography* 38 (1): 133–45.

Long, Larry. 1988. *Migration and Residential Mobility in the United States.* New York: Russell Sage Foundation.

Martin, Philip, and Elizabeth Midgley. 2003. "Immigration to the United States: Shaping and Reshaping America." *Population Bulletin* 58 (2).

Perry, Marc J., and Jason P. Schachter. 2003. "Migration of Natives and the Foreign Born: 1995–2000." Census 2000 Special Reports CENSR-11. Washington: U.S. Census Bureau.

Schachter, Jason P., Rachel S. Franklin, and Marc J. Perry. 2003. "Migration and Geographic Mobility in Metropolitan and Non-Metropolitan America: 1995–2000." Census 2000 Special Reports CENSR-9. Washington: U.S. Census Bureau.

Singer, Audrey. 2003. "At Home in the Nation's Capital: Immigrant Trends in Metropolitan Washington." Brookings.

———. 2004. "The Rise of New Immigrant Gateways." Brookings.

Suro, Roberto, and Audrey Singer. 2002. "Latino Growth in Metropolitan America: Changing Patterns, New Locations." Brookings.

Tilove, Jonathan. 2003. "Migration Patterns Point to a Nation of 'Three Americas.' " Newhouse News Service.

U.S. Census Bureau. 2003. *2000 Census of Population and Housing, Public Use Microdata Sample, United States: Technical Documentation.* Washington.

Wright, Richard A., Mark Ellis, and Michael Reibel. 1997. "The Linkage between Immigration and Internal Migration in Large Metropolitan Areas in the United States." *Economic Geography* 73: 234–54.

2

The Rise of New Immigrant Gateways
Historical Flows, Recent Settlement Trends

A U D R E Y   S I N G E R

The United States is in the midst of a wave of unprecedented immigration. Immigrants made up 11.1 percent of the U.S. population in 2000. During the 1990s the foreign-born population grew by 11.3 million (57.4 percent), bringing the Census 2000 count of immigrants to 31.1 million. The rapidity of this influx, coupled with its sheer size, means that American society will confront momentous social, cultural, and political change during the coming decades and generations.

Perhaps most importantly, immigrants' settlement patterns are shifting. Specifically, significant flows of the foreign-born are shifting from more traditional areas to places with little history of immigration. More than two-thirds of U.S. immigrants lived in just six states in 2000—California, New York, Texas, Florida, New Jersey, and Illinois. The share of the nation's immigrant population living in those states, however, declined significantly for the first time during the 1990s—from 72.9 percent of the total in 1990 to 68.5 percent in 2000. Thanks to "hot" job markets in their construction,

The author is grateful for the research assistance provided by Meghan McNally and Jill H. Wilson. She also thanks Mark Muro for his insightful editorial and substantive contributions and Amy Liu and Alan Berube for their generous contributions along the way. The author also benefited from the comments of reviewers of draft versions of this chapter, including those from Richard Alba, Caroline Brettell, Xav de Souza Briggs, Ivan Cheung, Katharine Donato, Samantha Friedman, Manuel Garcia y Griego, Michael Jones-Correa, Marie Price, Brian K. Ray, and Andrew Taylor. Also invaluable were the comments from participants in presentations given at the annual meetings of the Population Association of America, the Association of American Geographers, and the American Sociological Association.

services, manufacturing, and technology sectors, for example, states such as North Carolina, Georgia, and Nevada gained immigrants—who moved both from within the United States and directly from abroad—at rates not previously witnessed. Many of the areas with the highest growth during the 1990s have little twentieth-century history of receiving immigrants. The impact, particularly at the metropolitan level, has been great, as many cities and suburbs have had to adjust to new populations that place demands on schools and health-care systems, particularly with regard to language services.

In terms of absolute numbers the bulk of immigrants are still going to a handful of metropolitan areas. This explains why current research remains focused on the largest contemporary immigrant-receiving metropolitan areas: New York, Los Angeles, Chicago, Houston, and Miami.[1] A new research agenda, however, is suggested by the fact that metropolitan areas with few immigrants in 1980—such as Atlanta, Dallas, Fort Worth, and Las Vegas— are now seeing extraordinary growth in their immigrant populations. All four of these metropolitan areas saw their immigrant populations more than quadruple during the past twenty years.

This chapter analyzes the new geography of immigration during the twentieth century and highlights how immigrant destinations in the 1980s and 1990s differ from earlier settlement patterns. Historical U.S. Census Bureau data are used to develop a classification of urban immigrant "gateways" that describes the ebb and flow of past, present, and likely future receiving areas. Contemporary trends are examined to explore the recent and rapid settlement of the immigrant population in U.S. metropolitan gateways. Metropolitan areas that have seen little immigration to date may represent a new policy context for immigrant settlement and incorporation. This chapter takes an important first step in understanding how these changes are altering a range of receiving areas by examining the demographic, spatial, economic, and social characteristics of the immigrants that reside in them.

In sum the findings that follow confirm that the United States experienced unparalleled immigration in the 1990s that transformed many new destinations into emerging gateways and changed the character of established ones. Most large metropolitan areas across the country now need to meet the challenges of incorporating new immigrants with diverse backgrounds and needs.

BACKGROUND

The United States has a long and varied history of immigration; its twentieth-century flows can be seen in figure 2-1, which depicts both the number of

1. See Waldinger (2001); Foner (2002); Waldinger and Bozorgmehr (1996); Alba and others (1999b).

FIGURE 2-1. **Total Foreign-Born and Percent Foreign-Born in the United States, 1900–2000**

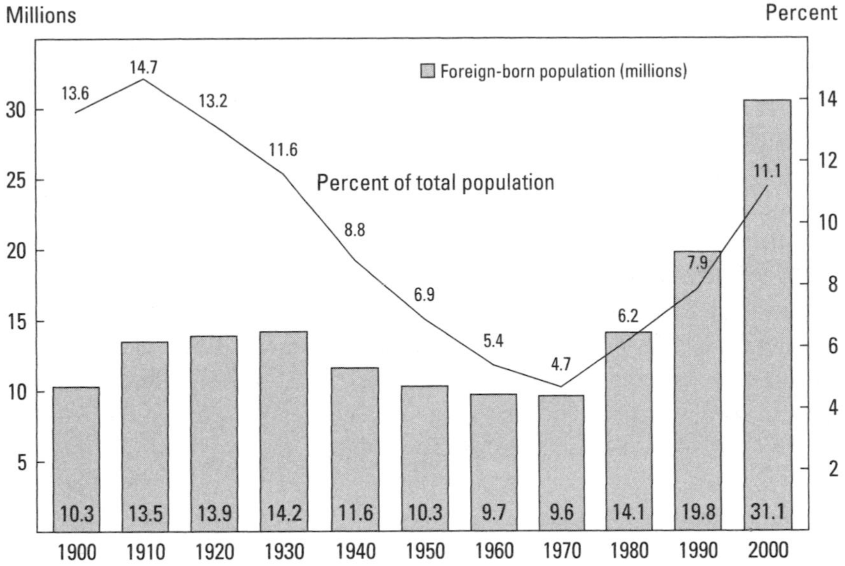

Millions   Percent

Source: U.S. Census Bureau.

immigrants and the share of the population that is foreign-born by decade. In 2000, the number of immigrants in the United States reached 31.1 million—a population three times larger than that in 1900. At the same time the 11.1 percent of the current population that is foreign-born remains proportionally smaller than the 13.6-percent 1900 figure.

Immigration ebbed and flowed during the last century. The immigrant population steadily increased during the first three decades of the twentieth century. Immigration stalled in the late 1930s during the Great Depression. Through the next four decades restrictive immigration policies instituted during World War II kept legal immigration levels low. These lower levels of immigration, combined with elevated fertility rates and the resulting "baby boom," depressed the proportion of the nation's population that was foreign-born during the 1950s and 1960s. But the Immigration and Nationality Amendments of 1965 (which went into effect in 1968) repealed national origin quotas, opening up immigration from regions other than Europe. This policy change, together with the mobility fostered by economic growth in many developing nations, combined to produce an immigration boom during the 1980s and 1990s. The immigrant population of the United States more than doubled during those twenty years—growing from 14.1 million to 31.1 million.

Not only did the tempo of immigration speed up, but the source countries shifted from Europe in the first three-quarters of the century to Latin America, the Caribbean, Asia, and Africa in the last quarter. During the first two decades of the century 85 percent of the 14.5 million immigrants admitted to the United States originated in Europe (largely southern and Eastern Europe). During the last two decades an equally large percentage of the two decades' 14.9 million immigrants hailed from the countries of Asia, Latin America, the Caribbean, and Africa.

Both periods—the beginning and the end of the century—saw broad restructuring of the nation's economy, from agriculture to industry in the early period and from manufacturing to services and information technology in the later period. Moreover, the social conflict and competition that accompanied the recent shift in immigrant origins to countries with different ethnic backgrounds, languages, religions, and political traditions resembles dynamics that unfolded in the earliest decades of the twentieth century.

Immigration was an enormous driver of population growth for the U.S. cities that developed in the nineteenth and early twentieth centuries. The burgeoning growth of manufacturing jobs in Northeastern and Midwestern cities attracted surplus labor from domestic rural areas, as well as from abroad. As the growth of industry and commerce in metropolitan areas continued through the 1950s, so did the rapid population growth of cities. At the same time many cities in the older industrial core began to lose population as their suburbs boomed and as metropolitan areas in the west developed. By the 1970s economic and population growth in the West and the Southwest began in earnest. Although some of the older Eastern cities maintained their status as immigrant gateway cities, others—mostly in the West and Southwest—became central destinations.

METHODOLOGY

This study uses decennial census data for the years 1900–2000 to describe the changing geography of immigration to the United States over the twentieth century. First, a typology of immigrant "gateway" types is determined by examining historical immigration flows to the nation's largest central cities, because cities dominated urban areas in the earlier part of the century. This typology of gateways anchors an examination of more recent immigrant settlement trends in forty-five U.S. metropolitan areas (including their suburbs).

The forty-five selected metropolitan areas represent a variety of experiences and conditions. Thirty-two of these forty-five metropolitan areas had at least 200,000 foreign-born residents in 2000, higher-than-average immigrant population shares, and faster-than-average growth in their immigrant populations.[2] Five other metropolitan areas had smaller populations but very fast immigrant population growth, whereas eight other immigrant destinations were studied for historical and comparative reasons. For the historical analysis, this chapter employs data for central cities that are comparable across the entire period.[3] The contemporary sections use data for metropolitan areas with consistent 2000 definitions for all decades. Immigrants residing in these forty-five metropolitan areas constitute 73 percent of the foreign-born population in the United States in 2000.

Definition of Immigrant

The terms "immigrant" and "foreign-born" are used interchangeably to describe all persons living in the United States who were born in another country (and were not born abroad to a U.S. citizen). In official parlance, the Bureau of Citizenship and Immigration Services (formerly the Immigration and Naturalization Service) uses the term "immigrant" to denote a person admitted to the United States for permanent residence. The Census Bureau considers anyone who is not born a U.S. citizen to be foreign-born. Although the U.S. Census contains a question on birthplace, it does not ask about a foreign-born person's legal status. Therefore it is not possible to determine whether a person born outside the United States is here, for example, as a legal permanent resident, a temporary worker or student, or if he or she is undocumented. Other relevant questions regarding the foreign-born determine place of birth, period of arrival, citizenship status, and English language proficiency.

Geographic Definitions

The cities studied in the historical portion of the analysis are based on an examination of the fifty largest urban places at each census.[4] The contemporary metropolitan areas analyzed are those defined by the Office of Management and Budget (OMB) as Metropolitan Statistical Areas (MSAs) and Primary Metropolitan Statistical Areas (PMSAs). Central cities for the contemporary section of the analysis are defined in this study as the largest city in the metropolitan area in combination with any other city of over 100,000

2. In three cases the 2000 foreign-born population was officially just under 200,000. These metropolitan areas—Fort Worth-Arlington, Orlando, and West Palm Beach-Boca Raton—have been classified as emerging because they meet all the other criteria and because the size of their immigrant populations set them apart from the pre-emerging gateways.

3. Historical data come from Gibson and Lennon (1999). These data show the nativity of the population for the fifty largest urban places for each decade, between 1870 and 1990.

4. As presented by Gibson and Lennon (1999).

(in 2000) that is named in the official MSA or PMSA.[5] Consolidated Metropolitan Statistical Areas (CMSAs) are not used as the unit of analysis, but their PMSA components are included if they qualify under the criteria stated in the accompanying box. The suburbs are the portion of the metropolitan area located outside the central city or cities.

Urban gateways serve as immigrants' residential entrance point to the United States. Immigrants settle in these places to live, work, and raise families. They also represent a phenomenon of consequence for the population residing in those places and for the institutions, services, and people that are affected by the movement of immigrants who may be culturally, socially, and linguistically different than the resident population. The word "gateway" also implies that the region functions as a symbolic destination. Such portals hold out opportunities for newcomers, and beckon to others as well-known centers populated by significant numbers of immigrants. As such, cities and localities become identified with immigrants, and their reputation may generate further settlement as social networks circulate information on employment, housing, and educational opportunities there. In this regard only the largest U.S. cities and metropolitan areas are considered in this study.[6]

FINDINGS

The findings that follow show that the United States experienced unparalleled immigration in the 1990s that transformed many new destinations into emerging immigrant gateways and changed the character of established ones.

U.S. Foreign-Born Population Grew and Dispersed in the 1990s

During the second half of the twentieth century, six states were the primary regions of immigrant settlement: California, Texas, New York, New Jersey, Illinois, and Florida. In 2000 more than two-thirds of all immigrants lived in these states. Twenty states had 1990s foreign-born growth rates that were lower than the national average (57.4 percent), including three of the largest

---

5. For example, the Minneapolis-St. Paul metropolitan area incorporates both named cities in its "central city," whereas the central city of Seattle-Bellevue-Everett consists only of Seattle and Bellevue (both cities with more than 100,000 population) but not Everett, which has a population of less than 100,000 people. Among the several exceptions to this rule, Orange County has no central city named in its PMSA title, but includes Anaheim, Irvine, and Santa Ana, each of which has a population of more than 100,000, and together, therefore, meet the definition of central city for this analysis. In addition, three PMSAs (Bergen-Passaic, Middlesex-Somerset-Hunterdon, and Nassau-Suffolk) have no identified central cities.

6. Many smaller cities and metro areas as well as rural areas are also experiencing booms in their immigrant populations. See, for example, McDaniel (2002) Hernández-León and Zúñiga (2000), and Kandel and Parrado (2004).

SIX IMMIGRANT GATEWAY TYPES, METROPOLITAN AREAS, 2000

Former	Continuous	Post-World War II
Above national average in percentage foreign-born 1900–30, followed by percentages below the national average in every decade through 2000.	*Above-average percentage foreign-born for every decade, 1900–2000.*	*Low percentage foreign-born until after 1950, followed by percentages higher than the national average for remainder of century.*
	Bergen-Passaic	
	Boston	
	Chicago	
Baltimore	Jersey City	Fort Lauderdale
Buffalo	Middlesex-Somerset-	Houston
Cleveland	Hunterdon	Los Angeles
Detroit	Nassau-Suffolk	Miami
Milwaukee	New York	Orange County
Philadelphia	Newark	Riverside-San Bernardino
Pittsburgh	San Francisco	San Diego
St. Louis		

Emerging	Re-emerging	Pre-emerging
Very low percentage foreign-born until 1970, followed by high proportions in the post-1980 period.	*Similar pattern to continuous gateways: Foreign-born percentage above national average 1900–30, below average after 1930, followed by rapid increase after 1980.*	*Very low percentage foreign-born for the entire twentieth century with high growth rates in the 1990s.*
Atlanta		Austin
Dallas	Denver	Charlotte
Fort Worth	Minneapolis-St. Paul	Greensboro-Winston-
Las Vegas	Oakland	Salem
Orlando	Phoenix	Raleigh-Durham
Washington, D.C.	Portland (OR)	Salt Lake City
West Palm Beach	Sacramento	
	San José	
	Seattle	
	Tampa	

All of the gateways have metropolitan populations greater than one million. Continuous, post–World War II, emerging, and re-emerging gateways have foreign-born populations greater than 200,000 and either foreign-born shares higher than the 2000 national average (11.1 percent) or foreign-born growth rates higher than the national average (57.4 percent) or both. Former gateways are determined through historical trends (see below).

The gateway definitions and selection are also based on the historical presence (in percentage terms) of the foreign-born in their central cities.

contemporary gateway states: California, New York, and New Jersey. For the first time in recent decades it appears that California's dominance as a destination is beginning to wane, as other states (including many that never attracted many immigrants) absorb more immigrants.

The 1990s saw unprecedented immigrant growth in many nontraditional areas. Thirty states saw their foreign-born growth rates outstrip the national average. These fast growers include the three other major destination states (Texas, Illinois, Florida), but they were not the fastest growers. Thirteen states had more than double the nation's immigrant growth rate. These states include several clustered in the West (Nevada, Arizona, Colorado, Utah, Idaho) and the Southeast (North Carolina, South Carolina, Georgia, Tennessee, Kentucky), as well as Minnesota, Nebraska, and Arkansas. Many of these states have not been major receivers of immigrants in the past few decades.

Six Major Types of U.S. Immigrant "Gateways"

Six basic types of immigrant gateways can be identified by examining trends in immigrant settlement in cities and metropolitan areas over the last century. The box accompanying this chapter defines these gateway types and lists the metropolitan areas included in the analysis. City-based immigration data were used to identify the gateway types; data on metropolitan areas were used to analyze contemporary trends.

"Former gateways"—such as Cleveland, Buffalo, and St. Louis—attracted immigrants in the 1900s, but no longer do. These cities appear in the 1900 panel of table 2-1, which lists the central cities that had the largest numbers of immigrant residents at each end of the twentieth century. The cities, along with others shown in figure 2-2, were important immigrant destinations at the beginning of the century, but saw their foreign-born populations decline throughout the remaining decades of the twentieth century. As figure 2-2 shows, all but Milwaukee had populations that were 95 percent native-born by 2000.

In contrast, a number of cities—such as New York, Chicago, and San Francisco—have always been dominant residential choices for immigrants. These cities appear in both the 1900 and 2000 panels of table 2-1 and can be identified as "continuous gateways." Like the former gateways these cities began the century with large shares of immigrants; like them, they saw such populations decline for two generations, reaching a nadir in 1970. Unlike former gateways continuous gateways registered high immigrant growth in the last three decades of the century. Figure 2-3 shows that by 2000 the foreign-born population shares in the continuous gateways had nearly reached the peak they registered in the early 1900s.

T A B L E   2 - 1 .   Central-City Immigrant Gateways, 1900 and 2000

		Foreign-born population	
Central city	Population	Number	Percent
1900			
New York	3,437,202	1,270,080	37.0
Chicago	1,698,575	587,112	34.6
Philadelphia	1,293,967	295,340	22.8
Boston	560,892	197,129	35.1
Cleveland	381,768	124,631	32.6
San Francisco	342,782	116,885	34.1
St. Louis	575,238	111,356	19.4
Buffalo	352,387	104,252	29.6
Detroit	285,704	96,503	33.8
Milwaukee	285,315	88,991	31.2
2000			
New York	8,008,278	2,871,032	35.9
Los Angeles	3,694,820	1,512,720	40.9
Chicago	2,896,016	628,903	21.7
Houston	1,953,631	516,105	26.4
San Jose	894,943	329,757	36.8
San Diego	1,223,400	314,227	25.7
Dallas	1,188,580	290,436	24.4
San Francisco	776,733	285,541	36.8
Phoenix	1,321,045	257,325	19.5
Miami	362,470	215,739	59.5

Source: U.S. Census Bureau.

F I G U R E   2 - 2 .   Percent Foreign-Born Population in Former Gateways, 1900–2000

Percent foreign-born

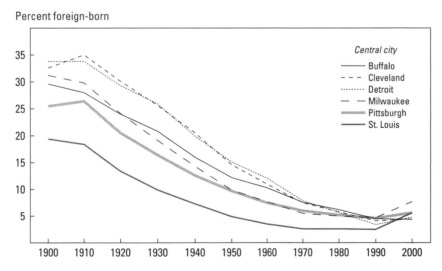

Source: U.S. Census Bureau.

FIGURE 2-3. **Percent Foreign-Born Population in Continuous Gateways, 1900–2000**

Percent foreign-born

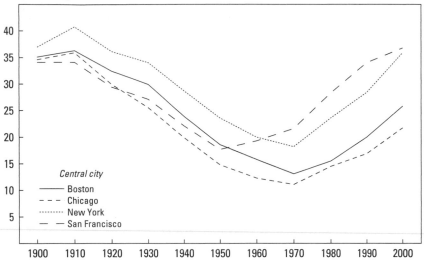

Central city
——— Boston
– – – Chicago
·········· New York
— — San Francisco

Source: U.S. Census Bureau.

Other cities became increasingly attractive for immigrants during the latter part of the twentieth century, a development that coincided with the liberalization of immigration from the Western hemisphere. Figure 2-4 depicts immigration flows to the large post–World War II gateways of Los Angeles, Miami, San Diego, and Houston. Los Angeles, San Diego, and Houston show similar patterns. Although on different scales, each city first witnessed dramatic immigration after 1970. By 2000 more than 40 percent of Los Angeles and more than 25 percent of both Houston and San Diego's population was foreign-born. Miami experienced the sharpest growth in its foreign-born population among the post–World War II gateway cities. The immigrant population there was nearly one in four persons in 1920, declined to 12 percent of the total in 1950, but then jumped significantly with an influx of Cuban refugees, climbing to 60 percent of the overall population in 2000.

These trends stand in contrast to those for the "emerging gateways." Figure 2-5 illustrates the degree to which these cities—Dallas, Washington, D.C., and Atlanta were some of the fastest-growing centers in the 1990s— experienced tremendous growth in their foreign-born populations in the last decade or two. These gateways saw their initially small immigrant

FIGURE 2-4. **Percent Foreign-Born Population in Post–World War II Gateways, 1900–2000**

Percent foreign-born

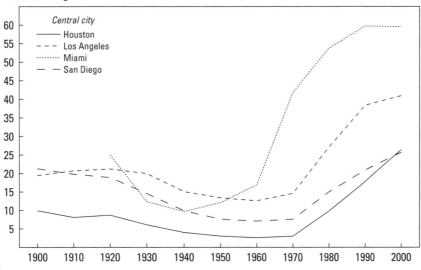

Source: U.S. Census Bureau.

FIGURE 2-5. **Percent Foreign-Born Population in Emerging Gateways, 1900–2000**

Percent foreign-born

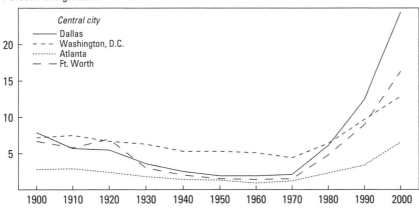

Source: U.S. Census Bureau.

FIGURE 2-6. Percent Foreign-Born Population in Re-Emerging
Gateways, 1900–2000

Percent foreign-born

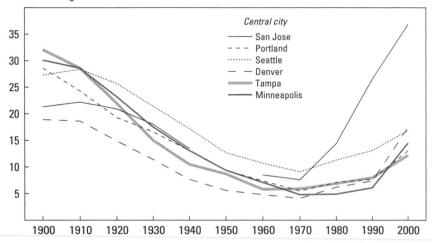

Source: U.S. Census Bureau.

populations rise from less than 10 percent to as much as 25 percent of their total populations during the past twenty years. Dallas's foreign-born population, for example, remained below 10 percent of its total population for most of the century, sagged to its lowest shares during the middle decades, and then rose significantly after the 1970s, reaching 24 percent of the total population in 2000.

Figure 2-6 shows the fifth pattern of foreign-born population growth: that of the "re-emerging gateways." These largely Western cities—such as Portland, San José, Denver, and Seattle—harbored high foreign-born shares in the early 1900s, saw them decline through the 1970s, and then saw a rebound of their foreign-born ratios in the 1990s. In the case of San José the 2000 share exceeded the city's peak in 1910. Should such growth continue, some of these places may soon reattain full gateway status.

These five gateway types, although identified by trends in their central cities, still hold when applied at the metropolitan level. A sixth category—the "pre-emerging gateway"—can be discerned only when one examines contemporary metropolitan area immigrant growth.[7] Pre-emerging gateways are places—such as Charlotte, Greensboro-Winston-Salem, and Salt Lake

7. For the most part these areas had so few immigrants that it is not meaningful to graph the share of the population that is foreign-born.

City—that had tiny immigrant populations in 1980 but experienced sudden, rapid growth in the 1990s. Charlotte's immigrant population, for example, numbered less than 15,000 in 1980 but jumped to 100,000 by 2000, a 315-percent growth rate over the twenty-year period.

In sum the changing geography of opportunity has altered the U.S. immigration map and has begun to reshuffle the nation's major immigrant destinations. Traditional gateways became former gateways; new gateways emerged; and even newer ones may still develop. Moreover this geography has been affected by the fact that Sun Belt and Southern cities (whose development postdated their Midwestern and Northeastern counterparts) lack long-term development of densely populated central cities and are more "suburban" in form. This has ensured that immigrant growth in these metropolitan areas has frequently occurred where most of the overall growth is taking place: outside the central cities and in the suburbs.

New Gateways Experience Rapid Growth; Established Ones See Slower Growth

Important relationships exist between regions' overall and foreign-born population growth, and underscore the critical role that immigration can play within larger population dynamics. Examining foreign-born growth in relation to overall growth can reveal the varying degrees to which immigrants contribute to metropolitan-wide population trends.

In the slow-growing former-gateway metropolitan areas immigration did not often contribute much to overall growth. Figure 2-7 shows that slow overall population growth (4.5 percent) prevailed among the former-gateway metropolitan areas. Absent the arrival of immigrants, these metropolitan areas would have still grown by 3.4 percent, suggesting that most of the growth in these metropolitan areas came from natural increase.[8] Such Rust Belt metropolitan areas as Buffalo, Cleveland, and Pittsburgh illustrate this dynamic. All lost overall metropolitan population during the 1980–2000 period, and all saw their foreign-born populations decline in both the 1980s and 1990s as well, as older immigrant cohorts aged and new immigrants settled elsewhere. Other former gateways, however, saw fairly large percentage gains in immigration. Baltimore led the way, doubling its immigrant population during the period to 146,000. Detroit and Philadelphia, meanwhile, retained larger immigrant populations in absolute terms, and also saw them grow considerably in the 1990s. If such trends continue these two

8. Schacter, Franklin, and Perry (2003) show net domestic out-migration for most of the former gateways.

FIGURE 2-7. **Population Growth in Metropolitan Areas by Gateway Type, 1980–2000**

Percent change

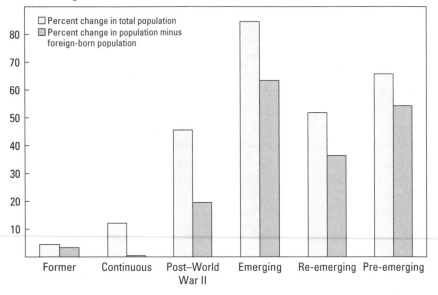

Source: U.S. Census Bureau.

metropolitan areas may soon attain re-emerging gateway status. (See table 2A-1 for total population and foreign-born population growth data for all forty-five metropolitan areas.)

Overall populations in the continuous gateways also grew relatively modestly during the last twenty years. On average these gateways' populations grew by 12.1 percent, with some metropolitan areas such as Newark (New Jersey), Jersey City, and Bergen-Passaic declining slightly during the 1980s but coming back stronger in the 1990s. Immigrant growth, however, remained strong across the entire period with nearly an 80-percent surge across all the continuous gateways. Collectively these metropolitan areas would have experienced little growth had it not been for their immigration gains (figure 2-7), and New York would have lost population were it not for its 1.3 million net immigrant newcomers.

Post–World War II gateways grew much faster by comparison. Taken together these seven metropolitan areas grew by nearly 50 percent overall during this period. At the same time their immigrant population increased by a collective 150 percent between 1980 and 2000—not surprising given that all of these gateways are in Florida, California, and Texas, three of the top immigrant-receiving states in the second half of the century. This growth, however, was neither evenly distributed across metropolitan areas nor across the time period. Riverside-San Bernardino and Houston, for example, saw their immigrant populations nearly quadruple over the two decades. Los Angeles's and Miami's populations "only" doubled, but they grew more quickly in the 1980s than the 1990s. Indeed, all of the individual post–World War II gateway metropolitan areas at least doubled their immigrant populations and all but Fort Lauderdale exhibited slower growth in the 1990s than in the 1980s. Moreover as figure 2-7 shows immigration drove much of these metropolitan areas' overall population growth, and Los Angeles and Miami would have grown little without the influx of immigrants.

Emerging gateways, for their part, saw their aggregate metropolitan population nearly double during the 1980s and 1990s. Immigrant populations in these metropolitan areas increased fivefold, from just over half a million to 2.7 million—a growth that nevertheless constituted only about one-third of the overall population growth. Las Vegas stands out as the only western metropolitan area in the group and for its simultaneous ultrafast growth in its total and immigrant populations (238- and 637-percent growth, respectively). In contrast to the continuous and post–World War II gateways, most of the emerging gateways experienced faster immigration during the 1990s than the 1980s. Orlando's immigrant population, for example, grew by 120 percent in the 1980s and by another 140 percent during the 1990s to reach 197,119 immigrants in 2000. Washington, D.C., is notable in that although it had virtually no immigration for most of its history, it has quickly climbed to the top of the immigrant destination list. Washington's 832,016 foreign-born residents place it seventh on the list of all metropolitan areas in 2000.[9] Indeed, Washington, D.C., may have actually already "emerged" as a leading immigrant gateway.

Although re-emerging gateways did not increase their overall populations as fast as emerging gateways during the past twenty years (their aggregate population grew 51.8 percent over the period), these reviving gateways were marked by steady immigration in both decades. These metropolitan areas tripled the size of their immigrant communities over the last two decades of the century. In addition, except for those in California, all re-emerging gateway metropolitan areas saw the pace of their immigration accelerate in the 1990s. Like the other gateway types, re-emerging gateways would have grown more slowly—by 30 percent—were it not for the newcomers from abroad.

9. Singer (2003).

Absent immigration, the Minneapolis-St. Paul and Portland metropolitan areas, for example, would have grown by only 20 percent.

Finally, the pre-emerging gateways include some of the fastest-growing smaller metropolitan areas in the country. Together these five metropolitan areas grew by some 66 percent, and grew more rapidly in the 1990s than the 1980s. But at the same time their foreign-born population increased by an aggregate 464 percent during the period. Three North Carolina metropolitan areas in this group—Charlotte, Greensboro–Winston-Salem, and Raleigh-Durham—averaged no less than 600-percent growth over the two decades. Moreover, the absolute size of the foreign-born population in the five pre-emerging gateways must now be taken into account. These areas' minuscule initial immigrant population (they collectively contained fewer than 100,000 immigrants in 1980) had by 2000 surged to 547,470 residents.

In sum immigration has slowed in the more established continuous and post–World War II gateways while it has accelerated in the emerging, re-emerging, and pre-emerging gateways. Certainly the continuous and post–World War II gateways will remain dominant due to the large numbers of immigrants residing in them and their continuing ability to attract newcomers. Job creation, however, in fast-growing metropolitan areas is simultaneously attracting both the native- and the foreign-born, raising sensitive issues of how to incorporate and accommodate the needs of a rapidly growing and rapidly diversifying population.

More Immigrants in Suburbs than in Cities

Calculations by the Louis Mumford Center for Comparative Urban and Regional Research indicate that 94 percent of the nation's immigrants lived in metropolitan areas in 2000, and that within those metropolitan areas 48 percent lived in central cities, whereas the remaining 52 percent resided in the suburbs.[10] This divide reflects a slight shift from 1990, when immigrants were nearly equally spread between suburbs and central cities. Moreover it foreshadows a more pronounced suburban tilt within the forty-five mostly larger gateway metropolitan areas examined in this study: In 1970, 54 percent of gateway immigrants favored central cities but by 2000 only 43 percent did. That meant that by 2000, 57 percent of immigrants in these metropolitan areas resided in suburban areas.

10. Accessed September 28, 2004, at mumford1.dyndns.org/cen2000/NewAmericans/NAdownload/profiles_download.xls. The Mumford Center's calculations utilize census definitions of central cities and suburbs and therefore differ slightly from those used in this analysis.

This marks a new development. For most of U.S. history, immigrants have been concentrated in central cities. Early waves of European immigrants initially located themselves in neighborhoods close to the factories, shops, and institutions that employed them. As immigrants became more upwardly mobile they moved out of immigrant enclaves to neighborhoods with better housing and schools—often in the suburbs. This classic scenario of European settlement was first described by the "Chicago school" of sociology and further elaborated on by social scientists who have found empirical support for the "spatial assimilation" of immigrants.[11] In this view immigrants initially clustered—often by national origin—in urban neighborhoods. Their movement to the suburbs was seen as an indicator of assimilation. More recently, though, Richard Alba and his colleagues used data from the 1990 Census to analyze suburban residential patterns among immigrants and found that: 1) immigrants were a growing presence in the suburbs; 2) immigrant suburbanization was related more to education and income and less to English language proficiency; 3) immigrant suburbanization reflects individual metropolitan areas' urban growth patterns; and 4) multiethnic suburbs were taking root in the 1990s.[12]

These developments have begun to define several distinctive patterns of immigrant settlement in different types of metropolitan areas. Most notably although the city-to-suburbs movement has been prevalent in the nation's historical immigration gateways, it has not occurred on the same scale in cities that began receiving immigrants in large numbers only recently. The central cities of continuous and former gateways, as well as of some of the re-emerging gateways, developed to their full urban scale earlier than the other gateway types, and so accommodated immigrants first in their cities. In these places, many immigrants moved to the suburbs as newer arrivals replenished central city neighborhoods, whereas immigration to the emerging and post–World War II gateways took place entirely in an era of metropolitan decentralization and suburbanization. These metropolitan areas are more suburban in form, with larger shares of their total populations living outside of central cities. It follows that metropolitan areas with more recent and extensive suburban development will have higher shares of their immigrants in the suburbs.

Contemporary data suggest that many immigrants are moving directly to the suburbs. The classic pattern of city to suburban migration no longer predominates. Table 2A-2 shows the changing reality by displaying city and

---

11. See Massey (1985); Alba and others (1999a, 1999b).
12. Alba and others (1999b).

suburban numbers and the varying percentages of immigrants in metropolitan areas for the 1970–2000 period. Keep in mind that the 1970 share of the national population that was foreign-born (4.7 percent) was at its lowest point of the twentieth century.

Table 2A-2 shows that a shift in residential preference, from central cities to suburbs, occurred across the forty-five metropolitan areas during this thirty-year period. In 1970 half a million more immigrants lived in cities than in suburbs. By 1980 the reversal had begun: In that year, approximately 100,000 more foreign-born resided in suburbs than in cities. Over the course of the next decade suburban immigrant growth continued. The suburbs gained 1 million more immigrant residents than the cities in the 1990s, and by 2000, more than three million more immigrants lived in suburban areas than in cities. Although immigrant settlement in cities in the 1990s expanded by a robust 43 percent, suburbs tallied 66-percent growth (see table 2A-3). Suburban areas in the gateway metropolitan areas now garner both absolutely greater numbers of immigrants and faster percentage growth as a group than cities. Yet the nature and degree of this suburbanization varies widely. To begin with, cities continue to attract large numbers of immigrants, retain greater foreign-born population shares, and continue to grow increasingly foreign-born.

Central cities in all gateway types but the emerging ones began the 1970–2000 period with higher percentages of their populations foreign-born than their suburbs and, across all types, ended the period that way. Moreover, the fact that an absolute majority of immigrants resided in suburbs by 2000 did not keep the percentage of the foreign-born in gateway cities from rising faster, and higher, than it did in gateway suburbs. In 2000 nearly one out of every four city residents was foreign-born—up from one in ten in 1970. By contrast, the corresponding immigrant share of the larger suburban population rose from 6 to 15 percent between 1970 and 2000.

In part these patterns reflect broad outflows of the general population from cities to suburbs during this period, which have helped elevate the proportional immigrant presence of many cities. Even so, the absolute growth of the immigrant population in central cities was sustained or grew over this period even as immigrant suburbanization came to the fore. Among the continuous gateways as well as in Los Angeles and Miami, the share of the central-city population that was foreign-born was in the double digits in 1970. Miami was particularly high at nearly 42 percent, and San Francisco was the next highest at approximately 22 percent. The remaining metropolitan areas in other gateways had smaller shares, ranging from an average of 2 to 3 percent for the emerging and pre-emerging gateways, to 6 percent for the re-emerging and former gateways. By 2000 the central cities of continuous and post–World War II gateways were on average approximately one-third foreign-born, whereas immigrants made up 18 percent, 20 percent, and 13 percent, respectively, of the emerging, re-emerging, and pre-emerging gateways' central cities. Miami's central-city immigrant growth stalled in the 1990s, however, and Los Angeles's was largely curtailed (see table 2A-3 for 1990s foreign-born growth rates).

A variety of different experiences of suburban immigrant growth can be discerned across the gateway types.[13] Few gateways, in fact, had large foreign-born presences in their 1970s suburban populations. Moreover in most former gateways tepid immigrant growth assured those presences remained modest—in the range of 2 to 8 percent. Nevertheless, the former gateways did see a higher share of their regions' immigrants residing in the suburbs. This is not surprising, given the extreme decentralization in these largely Midwestern and Northeastern metropolitan regions. With low levels of contemporary immigration, many of the foreign-born in these gateways represent an earlier immigrant cohort whose "spatial assimilation" followed a broader outward-migration to the suburbs beginning in the 1950s and 1960s.

Other gateway types exhibited more profound changes. Most continuous and post–World War II gateways began the 1970–2000 period with fairly large numbers and shares of immigrants in the suburbs, and then saw the presence of the foreign-born in their suburbs expand robustly during the following decades. Decades of steady immigration and assimilation followed and ensured that in 1970 more than 1.2 million immigrants made up about 8.5 percent of the suburban population in the continuous gateways.

In similar fashion the post–World War II gateways evolved from 8.5 percent foreign-born to more than 27 percent foreign-born between 1970 and 2000 as their collective foreign-born population increased from 750,000 to 4.8 million. Miami's suburbs were nearly 50 percent foreign-born by 2000 (compared to 17.9 percent in 1970), whereas Los Angeles's were one-third foreign-born by the later year, up from 9 percent in 1970. Suburban Houston began the period with just a 1.5-percent foreign-born presence and ended it 15.2 percent foreign-born—a percentage ten times higher.

As to their rates of growth, the solid 35- and 26-percent growth rates notched by the central-city immigrant populations in the continuous and post–World War II gateways during the 1990s were in each case significantly outpaced by the new suburban growth. Continuous-gateway suburbs saw

---

13. See www.brookings.edu/urban for maps of immigrant settlement for all forty-five gateway metropolitan areas.

their foreign-born populations grow by 55 percent; post–World War II gateways saw their foreign-born populations grow by 46 percent between 1990 and 2000.

In the case of Chicago the suburban growth of the foreign-born in the 1990s was nearly double the average across the continuous gateways. The suburbs came to house a majority of the area's immigrants, moving from 47 to 56 percent of the total during the 1990s. None of the other forty-five metropolitan areas saw greater absolute growth in its suburbs during the 1990s. By comparison, the continuous gateways of New York and San Francisco still house more immigrants in the city than the suburbs.

Big influxes of immigrants have also begun to reorient the emerging and re-emerging gateways' suburbs—especially in the 1990s. Emerging gateways' suburbs, for instance, absorbed almost the same absolute number of immigrants as the post–World War II gateways' (1.3 million compared to 1.5 million newcomers) in the 1990s, but their rate of foreign-born growth dwarfed that in the suburbs of the longer-standing gateways thanks to their small initial immigrant populations. These suburbs' foreign-born population soared by 131 percent compared to the 46-percent growth of the post–World War II gateway suburbs in the 1990s. During that decade Atlanta, Las Vegas, and Washington, D.C., notched 283-, 251-, and 76-percent increases in their suburban immigrant populations, respectively. That brought their suburban foreign-born presences to 10.7, 15.5, and 17.4 percent of their suburban populations, respectively.

Re-emerging gateways had metropolitan immigrant growth patterns that favored their suburbs—but only slightly. These gateways saw their collective suburban immigrant population grow by 100 percent (nearly 900,000 immigrants) during the 1990s. Foreign-born city populations in these gateways, however, also grew rapidly, as foreign-born populations surged by 94 percent, or 626,106 residents. As a result only 500,000 more immigrants resided in re-emerging gateway suburbs than in their central cities in 2000, as the two locales' populations reached 1.8 and 1.3 million respectively. It should be noted that this relatively balanced aggregate growth owes in part to the peculiar jurisdictional maps of metropolitan Phoenix and San José, whose central cities include vast quasi-suburban areas.[14]

Finally, large central cities in some of the pre-emerging gateways ensured that slightly more immigrants lived in cities than suburbs there—and both locales were growing rapidly in the 1990s. The pre-emerging gateways,

14. Fort Worth is an emerging gateway with a large central city. That central jurisdiction includes both Fort Worth and Arlington, and immigrant settlement patterns favor the central cities here too.

although small in population, experienced astounding suburban immigrant growth rates of nearly 250 percent, but their central cities also grew by 213 percent. This may reflect the nascent nature of the immigration to those areas. But it also reflects the larger central cities of places such as Austin, Greensboro, and Charlotte, which—like the central cities of the Phoenix and San José emerging gateways—encompass large swaths of essentially "suburban" territory.

Thus historical factors and broader population dynamics are important influences on the residential location of contemporary immigrants. The lack of historical immigrant neighborhoods in emerging and post–World War II gateways, for example, has a direct bearing on immigrants' settlement patterns.[15] Contemporary immigrants, like their earlier counterparts, frequently settle close to where the jobs are; however, this time, the jobs are mostly in the suburbs.[16] Moreover, many inner suburbs are distinguished by the affordability of their housing, especially as compared with dwindling options in many central city neighborhoods, particularly those experiencing gentrification.[17] This explains in part the sharp contrast between settlement patterns in

15. In the central cities of continuous gateways, long-standing immigrant and ethnic neighborhoods such as Chinatown in San Francisco, the Lower East Side in New York, and Pilsen/Little Village in Chicago have housed, employed, and otherwise incorporated large waves of successive immigrant groups. In Pilsen/Little Village, adjacent to the Loop in West Side Chicago, the source countries have shifted. In the nineteenth and early twentieth centuries this neighborhood was populated by European immigrants—largely Czech, German, and Polish. Since the 1950s, when Mexicans began settling in the area, Pilsen/Little Village has been transformed into a residential, commercial, and cultural center of Mexican life in Chicago. A majority of the neighborhood's residents are now Mexican and Mexican American, and Little Village has been dubbed *La Villita*.

Similarly, New York's Lower East Side once thronged with European Jewish immigrants. In its current incarnation, the neighborhood has been renamed "Loisaida" (Spanglish for Lower East Side), a reflection of the Puerto Rican and Dominican families that dominated the area in the latter half of the twentieth century. Central-city neighborhoods have served as major immigrant ports of entry within metropolitan areas for generations and helped to anchor and establish immigrant groups economically and residentially. For example, Washington, D.C., had some early immigrant residential enclaves such as Swampoodle, a neighborhood located near the U.S. Capitol and Union Station, which first housed Irish workers in the 1800s, followed by Italian immigrants in the 1900s. In many cities, few traces of these ethnic neighborhoods remain. Some early settlements tended to be temporary and offered inadequate housing. Temporary housing facilitated the settlement of immigrant workers, but as conditions and housing deteriorated, people found more desirable places to live. Often the work was transitory, as in the case of the Swampoodle immigrants who worked on the construction of the Capitol and other government buildings in Washington. Many early immigrants moved to the suburbs or moved on from Washington in search of opportunities in other cities. For more on Swampoodle, see Singer and Brown (2001).

16. Glaeser and Kahn (2001).

17. Wyly and Hammel (1999).

FIGURE 2-8. Share of Foreign-Born Population That Lives in the Suburbs, by Gateway Type, 1970–2000

Percent foreign-born

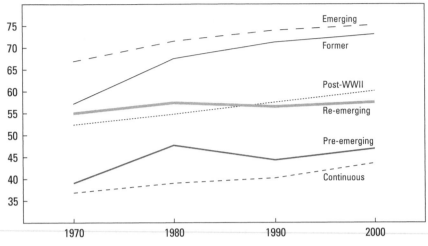

Source: U.S. Census Bureau.

continuous gateways (where more than half of the immigrants resided in central cities) and emerging gateways (where three-quarters of immigrants resided outside the central cities) in 2000 (see figure 2-8). In some emerging gateway metropolitan areas such as Atlanta and Washington, D.C., nearly all of the immigrants lived in the suburbs in 2000, whereas in 1970 only 55 percent of the areas' immigrants did.[18] In those metropolitan areas immigrant settlement patterns resemble those of the native-born population, so that similarly high shares of both populations reside in the suburbs.

Immigrants in Newest Gateways Fare Worse than Older Counterparts

In addition to the changing geography of immigration, variations in the characteristics of newer and older immigrant flows are also creating diverse challenges of incorporating large new populations.

18. To some extent suburban settlement patterns of the foreign-born reflect the overall likelihood of living in the suburbs within a metropolitan area. In all but the continuous gateways more than two-thirds of the total population resides in suburban areas. Emerging gateways top the list with 80 percent of their population suburban, followed by former (77 percent), post–World War II (70 percent), reemerging (70 percent), preemerging (67 percent), and continuous (63 percent).

Not only does the recentness of an immigrant cohort strongly influence the process of social and economic integration in a particular destination, so, too, do the particulars of a local immigrant flow's region of origin, English proficiency, affluence, and citizenship status. Some refugees from Southeast Asia, for example, are poor, have little formal education, and few aspirations beyond survival. Many recent Latin American immigrants spend part of the year in the United States and part in their home country, always with the intention of returning to their home communities. In view of that, Census data provide an important first look at the varying challenges gateway communities and their foreign-born residents face as they move into the twenty-first century.

The recentness of the phenomenally large immigrant influxes of the 1990s presents a first challenge. With more than 11 million new immigrants arriving in the United States in the 1990s, the impact of so many newcomers with heterogeneous backgrounds is being felt far and wide. The three categories of emerging gateways, not surprisingly, have the highest shares of the newest immigrants. The emerging gateways are particularly full of new arrivals: Just over half of immigrants living in these metropolitan areas reported entering the United States sometime during the 1990s. In the pre-emerging gateways the share is even higher (although smaller in absolute terms): Nearly two out of every three immigrants arrived in the 1990s. Even the foreign-born in re-emerging gateways, which represent a mixture of newcomers and older immigrants who have been aging in place, are also relatively recent: Some 47.5 percent of foreign-born residents in those metropolitan areas arrived during the 1990s. These trends contrast with the set of more established gateways. In the post–World War II metropolitan areas, for instance, only 37 percent of immigrants were recent arrivals. Forty-two percent of the foreign-born in continuous and former gateways arrived during the decade, which is on par with the national average.

These variations are important because newer immigrants—often possessing more limited language skills and weaker social networks than earlier arrivals—frequently encounter greater difficulty availing themselves of economic opportunity than longer-established newcomers. But they also point to the broader importance of human capital and employment skills in immigrant integration. Insights on these issues can be gained by exploring Census data on the national origins, language, income, and naturalization characteristics of the foreign-born by gateway type.

Table 2-2 displays the varying origin-region profiles of the six gateway types. The distinctive profile of the former and continuous gateways makes itself apparent: In these older gateways, there is a layering of immigrant

TABLE 2-2. **Region of Origin for the Foreign-Born Population, by Gateway Type, 2000**

Percent unless otherwise noted

Gateway type	Total foreign-born (number)	Region of origin					
		Europe	Asia	Africa	Latin America[a]	Mexico	Other
Former	887,634	35.1	37.7	4.7	10.3	6.6	5.6
Continuous	5,050,012	22.2	26.4	3.0	34.9	12.0	1.5
Post–World War II	5,772,798	6.2	23.6	1.4	28.4	38.6	1.8
Emerging	1,186,340	10.9	25.7	6.4	25.9	28.5	2.6
Re-emerging	1,539,902	15.0	38.9	3.1	8.3	29.8	4.9
Pre-emerging	166,662	12.5	22.5	4.2	13.1	43.3	4.4

Source: U.S. Census Bureau.

a. Excluding Mexico.

settlement and incorporation that includes the pre-1965 flows (largely European) as well as the post–1965 immigrant streams. Thus both types of gateways exhibit higher shares of European immigrants than any other gateway type, and lower shares of Mexican arrivals. In the case of the former gateways more than two-thirds of the foreign-population in 2000 hailed either from Europe or Asia, whereas just 6.6 percent of the aggregate foreign-born population came from Mexico.[19] There was also a dearth of Latin Americans, although 30 percent of Milwaukee's immigrants are from Mexico.[20] The continuous gateways (which are dominated by New York and environs) show greater diversity of national origins of immigrants, although they incorporate the second-highest share of European immigrants (22 percent). Together these gateways contain high overall shares of Caribbeans and non-Mexican Latin Americans, with nearly half of their newcomers originating from that region of the world. This gateway category also includes places like Boston with a fairly even distribution between Europeans, Asians, and non-Mexican Latin Americans and Caribbeans, as well as San Francisco, which is dominated by Asians (51 percent). In general, East Coast gateway metropolitan areas have heterogeneous populations and small Mexican populations (although this group is growing in the New York metropolitan area and surrounding metropolitan areas). For example, New York's largest

19. The use of "region" of origin categories, although easier to interpret, may also mask variations among gateways' various countries of origin. Asia is perhaps the most problematic case, with immigrants grouped together from the various countries of East Asia (China, Japan), Southeast Asia (Vietnam, Laos, Thailand), South Asia (India, Pakistan), and Western Asia (the countries of the Middle East). All of these national and subregional groups have different characteristics that might have a bearing on their social and economic incorporation.

20. See a list of the ten largest countries of birth for each metropolitan area at www.brookings.edu/metro.

group—immigrants from the Dominican Republic—constitutes just 12.2 percent of all immigrants, followed by China (6.8 percent), Jamaica (6.3 percent), Mexico (4.6 percent), and Guyana (4.2 percent). As in many of the East Coast continuous gateways, the ten largest immigrant groups make up only half of all immigrant groups.

The newer gateways look different—and not just because these regions contain smaller shares of European newcomers in their immigrant populations. Even more noticeable is the presence of Latinos. In the post–World War II gateways, for example, more than two-thirds of all immigrants hail from Latin America, with the largest group hailing from Mexico. Los Angeles and other California cities dominate this gateway category, with their huge Mexican-born populations. Miami, however, represents a departure: Although Miami is unmistakably Latin American and Caribbean at 91 percent (dominated by Cubans, followed by Nicaraguan, Colombian, Haitian, Dominican, Honduran, and Jamaican immigrants), it is not Mexican.

Flows into the other newer gateways have idiosyncratic national origins as well. In emerging gateways—the most mixed of all destinations by region of origin—the diversity of origin groups embraces even proportions of Asians, Mexicans, and Caribbean and other Latin Americans. Additionally, these gateways have the largest share of Africans in residence at 6 percent. Washington, D.C., and Atlanta stand out for their African immigrants: 8.7 percent of Atlanta's and 11.2 percent of Washington's immigrants come from African countries. Moreover, Washington's 93,000 African immigrants are second only to New York's 99,000, but in New York they only make up 3.2 percent of all immigrants. Among these metropolitan areas African immigrants' 14-percent share of Minneapolis-St. Paul's foreign population is the highest of any single metropolitan area. During the 1990s the resettlement of refugees from Somalia and other African nations boosted the Twin Cities' African population. Southeast Asian refugees also arrived in substantial numbers.

The re-emerging gateways are comparatively more Asian. Latin Americans make up only slightly more than one-third of all immigrants in these metropolitan areas, whereas Asians compose 39 percent. Not surprisingly Asians dominate the West Coast metropolitan areas in this category. They represent more than half of the immigrant population in San José, Seattle, and Oakland (although Mexican immigrants do predominate in Denver and Phoenix). At the same time the eastward spread of Mexican settlement at the end of the twentieth century is evident in the noticeable presence of Mexicans in the pre-emerging gateways. Mexicans and other Latin Americans dominate the pre-emerging gateways, where they constitute more than half of all immigrants.

TABLE 2-3. Selected Characteristics of the Foreign-Born, by Gateway Type, 2000

Percent

Gateway type	Entered in the 1990s	English proficiency		Poverty rate		
		Speaks well[a]	Does not speak well[b]	Native-born	Foreign-born	Naturalized
Former	41.7	82.6	17.4	10.5	13.7	50.6
Continuous	41.8	73.6	26.4	11.2	15.3	44.5
Post–World War II	37.0	65.3	34.7	13.2	19.7	39.0
Emerging	50.7	70.7	29.3	8.7	14.7	34.1
Re-emerging	47.5	72.5	27.5	8.3	16.1	38.6
Pre-emerging	61.0	65.8	34.2	8.9	18.5	26.9

Source: U.S. Census Bureau.
a. Speaks only English, or speaks it "very well" or "well."
b. Speaks English "not well" or "not at all."

In this regard the Mexicans' eastward dispersal in the 1990s marks a striking addition to that nationality's historical association with the U.S. Southwest. Mexico is now the fourth-largest immigrant source country in New York, where the region's 143,000 Mexicans are on par with re-emerging San José, Oakland, and Denver and significantly outnumber San Francisco's 80,000. In Atlanta 120,000 Mexicans rank as that gateway's largest immigrant group and represent more than five times the number of the next-largest immigrant group, Indians. Mexicans have also made inroads in other East Coast metropolitan areas as well as South Florida.

Language acquisition is another important indicator of integration that influences many facets of everyday life including community relations. Two-thirds or more of all immigrants in every gateway type reported that they spoke English "well" or "very well" (see table 2-3). These rates were highest in the more established gateways that include older immigrant cohorts such as the former, continuous and re-emerging gateways. Perhaps unexpectedly English proficiency rates are also relatively high in emerging gateways, where 71 percent of immigrants said they spoke English well. More troubling are the more than one-third of immigrants in post–World War II gateways and pre-emerging gateways that cannot speak English at all or do not speak it well.

Table 2-3 also shows the 2000 poverty rates of the native- and foreign-born by gateway type. Foreign-born poverty rates outstrip native-born rates in all gateway types. Native-born rates are all lower than the national average (11.3 percent) except in the post–World War II gateways. Foreign-born rates across gateway types are also lower than the national foreign-born average (17.7 percent) except in the post–World War II and pre-emerging gateways. Not surprisingly, a wider gap separates immigrant and native poverty rates in newer gateways (emerging, re-emerging, pre-emerging) than in the more established gateways. For instance, the average immigrant poverty rate of 19 percent in pre-emerging gateways was nearly double the native-born rate. Similarly the 14.7-percent foreign-born poverty rate in the emerging gateways remains two-thirds higher than the native-born rate, even though these metropolitan areas have the smallest share of immigrants living below the poverty rate among the various gateway types. These rates vary, however, across metropolitan areas within the gateway type. For example, the poverty rates in the emerging gateways of Dallas and Fort Worth are nearly twice as high (19 percent) as they are in Washington, D.C. (11 percent). Moreover, in re-emerging Denver and Seattle poverty rates for immigrants are twice that of natives, at 18 and 14 percent, respectively.

Yet the most disturbing immigrant poverty is in the post–World War II gateways where nearly one out of five immigrants lives in poverty. Unfortunately, this category encompasses three of the largest immigrant metropolitan areas in the country—Miami, Los Angeles, and Houston. In metropolitan Los Angeles more than one in five immigrants struggles with poverty, compared to about one in six native-born residents. In the continuous gateway of New York, by contrast, the immigrant and native poverty rates are nearly the same.

Naturalization status is also summarized in table 2-3 and has important bearing on the immigrant experience. For both immigrants and the broader community naturalization is often viewed as a traditional marker of integration into the U.S. society and polity. Although immigrants are encouraged to become U.S. citizens, they may live out their days in the United States without ever doing so. Generally the longer immigrants live in the United States, the more likely they are to naturalize. Citizenship status also frequently depends on home-country proximity to the United States (the closer the distance, the lower the rate), refugee status (which increases the propensity to naturalize), and other factors (such as origin-country literacy rates or English-language use).[21] In keeping with these factors, naturalization status varies across the gateway types. The average naturalization rate across all metropolitan areas is 40.5 percent. As might be expected, the continuous and former gateways have the highest rates, followed by the re-emerging gateways. These rates reflect the length of time many immigrants have resided in these metropolitan areas. Naturalization rates are lower in the newly emerging gateways due to the recentness of immigration to the area. It should be noted that the proportion of immigrants who have naturalized includes all

---

21. Jasso and Rosenzweig (1990).

immigrants, regardless of the amount of time they have spent in the United States and whether they are eligible for citizenship.

DISCUSSION

This chapter describes how the enormous in-flows of immigrants in recent decades are rearranging the United States's immigration map, transforming both new and old communities.

Huge flows of immigrants are still going to the largest, longest-established immigrant gateways, and changing them. New settlement areas, however, are appearing in new destinations, including unanticipated points across the South, as well as across numerous suburban areas that have long been bastions of the native-born.

Nor is such change coming without some signs of strain. Immigrant settlement is not always welcome or fully embraced. Some people feel immigrants take jobs away from U.S. citizens. Others feel immigrants work hard and contribute to the U.S. economy and culture. Some people worry that immigrants who do not speak English will dominate and denigrate U.S. culture. Others see themselves in immigrant and refugee newcomers who appreciate similar values of democracy and opportunity. Moreover President George W. Bush renewed public interest in the issue of immigrants in the U.S. economy and society with a call for a new temporary worker program and other changes to U.S. immigration policy. Like most national immigration policy decisions, the new proposal would alter the terms of admittance into the United States, but would not include provisions for facilitating immigrants' incorporation after arrival.

Nevertheless, the new reality of a growing immigrant population in new destinations invariably raises exactly that issue: integration and the policies to achieve it. Broadly speaking, integration refers to the movement of immigrants into the social, civic, and economic mainstream.[22] Implicit in this

22. Considerable debate now surrounds which term to use to describe this process. "Integration" is the current word of choice among those in immigrant policy circles, notwithstanding its somewhat awkward parallel to the language of the civil rights struggle. Disuse of the term "assimilation" reflects immigration scholars' questioning of the assumption that to move up the socioeconomic ladder immigrants have to adopt mainstream, middle-class, white sociocultural standards (Hirschman, Kasinitz, and DeWind 1999). These scholars observe that although the empirical evidence reports growing intermarriage and reductions of economic inequalities among European immigrants arriving around the turn of the twentieth century, the contemporary context is different (Alba and Nee 1997). Critiques of "straight-line" assimilation theory based on the experience of European immigrants frame their arguments around the characteristics of contemporary flows—namely, race and the number of generations residing in the United States. This point of view emphasizes mobility and incorporation rather than

term is the assumption that integration is a two-way process involving both immigrants and residents. This in turn implies that public policy responses should aid immigrants as they seek to facilitate integration.

Unfortunately, the work of easing immigrants' incorporation into U.S. communities is complicated by the fact that the federal government lacks any uniform or explicit set of policies and programs to aid that integration, notwithstanding the large numbers of immigrants and their families living in the United States. The federal government retains exclusive authority over immigrant and refugee admissions to the United States. However, thanks to the absence of a strong federal effort to help immigrants adapt to life in the United States, policies tend to be ad hoc, reactive, and localized.[23] States, counties, cities, and other municipalities play the de facto role of developing and maintaining policies and programs that help immigrants become part of communities where they live, and networks of nonprofit, faith-based, or community organizations have developed some capacity to fill in the gaps.

Also complicating the integration process has been the particular economic period during which recent waves of immigrants have arrived. Immigrants who entered the United States during the 1990s arrived during a decade of unprecedented growth that brought about a sharp reduction of unemployment by 2000—the year the Census was taken. These immigrants were attracted to a tight labor market that rewarded both low- and high-skilled labor with relatively higher wages. In the period since the Census was conducted, unemployment has risen and speculation abounds that the current economy may not be able to support the long-term economic mobility of contemporary immigrants and their children to the same degree it absorbed earlier European immigrants. Today's labor market, in short, may not offer stable paths to economic mobility or wages comparable to those that were available to lower-skill immigrants in earlier periods.[24]

In this context how local areas respond to the challenge of immigrant integration is of vital importance. Again, the swiftness, size, and geographical

---

assimilation into the "mainstream." It also acknowledges that downward mobility can occur, especially with second-generation immigrant youth. Latino and Asian immigrants generally have not been settled in the United States long enough to prove or disprove either theoretical position in the same way that European immigrants have. The "segmented" assimilation hypothesis, however, attempts to explain the uneven outcomes among and between contemporary immigrant groups. In this perspective the adaptation of second-generation immigrants may follow three alternative trajectories: (1) upward mobility; (2) downward mobility, particularly among second-generation youth in inner cities; and (3) upward mobility with a retention of ethnic culture (see Zhou 1997; Gans 1992).

23. See Fix, Zimmermann, and Passel (2001).

24. Sassen (1988).

reach of recent immigration poses distinctive challenges to every sort of immigrant gateway.

Established gateways such as New York, San Francisco, and Chicago are in many ways well positioned to receive and serve immigrant newcomers. Their long history of immigrant settlement has created an organizational, service-delivery, and advocacy infrastructure familiar with the needs of immigrants and their families. For many continuous and post–World War II gateways, moreover, immigration is part of their identity and a source of local cultural pride. A large share of the residents in these established gateways are first- or second-generation immigrants.[25] The predominance of the suburbs as the destination of choice in post–World War II gateways, however, and growing suburban trends in continuous gateways mean that many established gateways are experiencing immigration and integration issues akin to those in newer, emerging gateways. Moreover, the shift in national origins of immigrants and their growing diversity over the past thirty years has required a corresponding broadening of services as well as clientele in many of these metropolitan areas.

The picture is different in fast-growing emerging gateways such as Atlanta, Las Vegas, Denver, and Raleigh-Durham. Here immigrants are recent arrivals on a scene that is already stressed by the pressures of rapid population growth. Consequently, the institutional structures that can assist in the integration of immigrants—both community-based and governmental—are still being developed and strengthened. For example, in suburban Washington, D.C., enrollment in Montgomery County's adult English Speakers of Other Languages (ESOL) program last year rose by 58 percent, but only an estimated one-fourth of the demand could be met with classes offered by the county and smaller providers combined.[26] Moreover, many of the emerging and pre-emerging gateways are swiftly transforming from a black-white population to a multiethnic profile. Often immigrants and native-born African Americans are now competing for jobs, housing, and social services, meaning that racial and ethnic relations are changing with the arrival of immigrants, creating a more complex and competitive environment, and causing some degree of social conflict.

Given such differing realities, local policymakers and community leaders face a tall order as they seek to ease immigrants' incorporation into their communities. To even begin to meet that challenge, local leaders need to respond

25. The U.S. Census Bureau estimates that one out of every five persons living in the United States in 2000 had at least one foreign-born parent. See Schmidley (2001).
26. Branigin (2002).

sensitively to the changing composition of metropolitan neighborhoods and move to craft a welcoming environment that helps immigrants succeed in their new homes.[27] At least six major approaches are called for:

Understand Local Immigration Dynamics

The immigration context varies tremendously between metropolitan areas. Therefore it behooves every local government, community-based organization (CBO), and advocate to understand the characteristics of its local immigrant community. This chapter provides a preliminary picture of the changing geographic pattern and varying social and economic characteristics of immigrants in forty-five selected metropolitan areas. Nevertheless, more detailed information is often desirable—for example, neighborhood level data by country of origin. In rapidly changing emerging gateways, it can be challenging—if not impossible—to design service programs without understanding who is living in the community and what their needs may be. Indeed, many community-service and faith-based organizations are often "first responders" that have good knowledge about what is happening in their immediate neighborhood but may lack specific empirical data about their local service areas.

Census 2000 data can be used to understand local trends. For example, planners and CBOs can derive information on how many immigrants reside in their community, which countries they came from, the period in which they arrived in the United States, languages spoken and English language proficiency, their poverty status, and if they have become U.S. citizens. These basic data can be supplemented with other data such as school district data on students with limited proficiency in English, which can detect trends among the undocumented and serve as a leading indicator of immigrant growth. Other relevant data include health data (on births to immigrant mothers) and social service data on immigrant participation in public assistance programs. Several recent publications offer guidance on locating and using data for understanding local immigrant populations.[28]

Bring Cultural and Language Sensitivity to Service Delivery

Local entities, both private and public, connect immigrants to the broader gateway community—often in the context of service delivery. For many immigrant newcomers, however, limited English proficiency is a barrier to gaining information. Local governments in established gateways know that

27. See Fernandez (2003).
28. See, for example, Capps and others (2003b); Masters, Hamilton, and Wilson (2004).

the first step in overcoming this barrier is to develop the capacity to provide information and signage, deliver basic services, and provide public safety in the dominant languages of immigrant groups. If a single language such as Spanish predominates in a metropolitan area, as it does in many metropolitan areas with large settlements of Latin Americans, then it may be easier to provide services. More diverse, "layered" metropolitan areas may pose more difficult challenges.

Health-care delivery especially can be complicated not just by linguistic problems but by cultural differences between immigrants and U.S. health-care systems. Health-care providers in emerging gateways may be ill equipped to deal with the special needs of immigrant and refugee newcomers. For that reason some community health providers have opened clinics—or dispatched mobile medical clinics—that target particular ethnic populations, although many have not yet been able to do so. In particular, clinics focused on maternal health, domestic violence, and mental health treatment need to develop linguistic competency and cultural sensitivity.

Local and regional collaborations can be beneficial in this regard in helping to organize and disseminate local knowledge, and in promoting the duplication of what works well. In addition immigrant and ethnic communities themselves can be supportive of new arrivals in providing services, goods, and information in a familiar linguistic and cultural setting, thus somewhat easing the integration of immigrant newcomers. At the same time, these kinds of networks may be limited and fragmentary. For that reason, partnerships between community organizations and mainstream institutions to deliver services often work well: Mainstream institutions frequently have the ability to supplement the local knowledge and up-to-the-minute ideas of community organizations with resources and organizational capacity the community groups may lack.

Build English Language Capacity

The single most important issue for local communities and governments is the need for many immigrant newcomers to become proficient in the English language. Employers, governments, and immigrants themselves are concerned with basic communication on the job and in daily life. Local areas can improve immigrant adaptation by addressing the need for English language training in two ways.

First, schools have a responsibility to assist immigrant students to become proficient in English. They must do so, however, at the same time they are striving to have all students—native- and foreign-born—reach the same educational standards regardless of language competency. The challenges can be especially difficult in new areas of immigrant settlement and in localities with heterogeneous student populations. Those who provide instruction to non-English-speakers in such communities should look to the experiences of educators and administrators in established gateways to identify programs and policies that facilitate student achievement.

In confluences of multiple languages and cultures, schools face greater difficulties in addressing the needs of limited English proficient students. Shortages of appropriately trained teachers frequently hobble newer immigrant communities, though the problem also extends to recent settlement areas in established gateways. In suburban Chicago, for example, approximately 13 percent of the students in Schaumburg School District 54 are "English language learners" who speak forty-six languages collectively.[29] Other examples include North Carolina, where the number of limited English proficient students has more than quintupled since 1993.[30] Slightly more than half of the state's 20,000 public school children that do not speak English as their native language speak Spanish, but the rest speak 163 different languages.[31] One response to such challenges: DeKalb County in the Atlanta metropolitan area has recently created an international center to which all foreign-born students and a parent or guardian must first report in order to attend the county schools.[32] This center works to create linkages between parents and schools.

A second critical need is for adult language training. Adult language training is vital for success in the labor market. Immigrants themselves are quick to point out that English is essential; yet learning the language is often the most difficult challenge of life in the United States. In a recent survey of immigrants by Public Agenda two-thirds of those interviewed said they believe the government should require immigrants to learn English.[33] Education gaps in origin countries, however, coupled with limited opportunities to enroll in English classes for working immigrants in destination communities hamper the acquisition for many.

The private sector has also noticed that translation services are in greater demand, with more languages needed as immigrant and refugee flows change. For instance, a small Minneapolis-based firm, Asian Translations Inc., opened in 1996 focusing on translating, interpreting, and cultural training in a few Asian languages. In 2000 it was renamed International Translation Bureau in

---

29. Owens (2002).

30. Zhao (2002).

31. See *Ayudate,* a website produced in partnership with the North Carolina Governor's Office for Latino/Hispanic Affairs. Available at www.ayudate.org/ayudate/education.html.

32. Atiles and Bohon (2002).

33. Farkas and others (2003).

response to the expanding immigrant population with different language needs. The firm now employs translators that cover 100 languages.[34]

Innovative programs that teach adults English include those affiliated with schools that recognize the importance of parents learning English along with their student children, and employers who offer opportunities to learn English. Models exist among private sector firms, such as those in the construction industry where safety instruction is particularly important, that provide language training for immigrant workers, often in collaboration with community organizations.

Provide Workforce Support

Immigrant youth and adults also need programs that provide workforce development services. Many immigrant workers toil in low-skilled, low-paying occupations with little opportunity for mobility.[35] Many must contend with such barriers to employment as low educational attainment and weak English language competency. Eliminating such barriers requires strong intervention from community organizations to provide accessible services to help immigrants get the skills and education they need. Accepting day labor gathering sites and even providing skills building at those sites has been beneficial to immigrant workers in several communities. Other initiatives support immigrant business start-ups.

Community colleges are, in this respect, playing an increasingly important role in providing higher education to immigrants and the children of immigrants. Some have aligned their curriculum to fit the needs of post-secondary immigrant students. Many provide English classes and special programs on study skills and counseling for immigrant students. One example is Montgomery College in suburban Washington, D.C., which has a student population that is one-third foreign-born and hails from 170 countries, in a county that houses nearly half the foreign-born in Maryland. In recent years the college has received grants from the U.S. Departments of Education and State to strengthen and expand its international curriculum as well as to support faculty development in international issues including migration and globalization.

Create Linkages to Mainstream Institutions

Identifying, developing, and maintaining community partnerships and collaborations enhance capacity and can extend services that aid immigrants. For example, in both Austin, Texas, and suburban Prince George's County in metropolitan Washington, D.C., police departments have teamed up with

34. Nguyen (2002).
35. Capps and others (2003a).

local banks to encourage immigrants to open bank accounts as a way of reducing the robberies that have befallen vulnerable immigrant workers who lack formal banking experience and who are often reluctant to open accounts because they are undocumented. Many other police departments and banks have instituted policies to accept the *matricula consular,* an identification card issued by the Mexican government to Mexicans living in the United States, as a legitimate form of identification.

These police departments understand that initiating programs that link immigrants to banks promotes public safety in several ways. The primary aim is to reduce crime aimed at "unbanked" immigrants who are likely to carry cash and may be reluctant to report crime. These collaborations, however, also bring immigrants into a relationship with formal financial institutions that may facilitate longer-term financial integration. In addition, such partnerships open a dialogue about public safety and let immigrants know that local police do not exist to enforce immigration laws but are there to serve all members of the community and earn their trust. This matters because immigrants are more likely to seek protection from police when they feel such trust.

Encourage Civic Engagement

Ultimately, active participation in civic and community life is an important goal of immigrant integration. Such civic engagement may mean attending a parent-teacher conference, joining a community group that is organizing a neighborhood clean-up day, or attending a neighborhood association meeting. But it may also mean preparing to become a U.S. citizen, voting, or being elected to a political office. All of these activities are desirable as immigrants become more involved with their communities as well as with national issues.

Before immigrants are likely to become involved in their communities, immigrants must feel welcome and know where to turn for help in safety, education, and language training. Because these processes are intertwined, it is likely that as immigrants begin to integrate they will also be more likely to participate in civic life.

Organizations should therefore do all they can to promote interactions between immigrants and established residents—especially across generations. Building a stronger civic infrastructure that includes the collaboration of all residents, regardless of nativity status, will bolster such robust community relations. Such community building can be achieved through community events and projects that revolve around local issues such as public safety, public space and parks, sports teams, and schools.

Many organizations already have programs that assist immigrants in filling out tax forms, applying for naturalization, and registration drives to "get out the vote." For example, the New York Immigration Coalition has mounted several initiatives recently to encourage immigrants to vote. Such efforts have included the recruitment of bilingual poll workers, the distribution of voting instruction cards in multiple languages, and a series of new-citizen voter-education events.[36]

CONCLUSION

During 1970–2000 two broad changes have left an indelible mark on the U.S. landscape. The first is the deindustrialization, decentralization, and suburbanization that began after World War II and continue to the present time. Cities have become less dense as suburban areas have emerged as the locales where most Americans live and work.

The second change is the wave of immigration that began in the 1970s. These influxes have shifted the mix of immigrant source countries, as well as quickened the pace of immigration to more varied settlement areas. Along the way large flows of immigrants have followed the larger post–World War II out-migration from cities to settle in countless U.S. suburbs.

Moreover, the decade of the 1990s represents an even greater departure from historical trends. The scale of the immigration phenomenon has been unparalleled. New areas of settlement and growth have appeared in just the last ten years. And particularly in emerging gateways extraordinarily rapid growth in the foreign-born population has been accompanied by high rates of suburban settlement, diverse nations of origin, and large social challenges.

This chapter suggests that the process of immigrant incorporation depends heavily on the institutional capacity, resources, and experience of local communities. It also suggests that established and emerging gateways can learn from each other about policies and programs that facilitate the social, economic, and political incorporation of immigrants.

And they will need to. In the post–September 11 era, the question of how metropolitan areas and localities should deal with the arrival of new immigrants has gained new prominence—and complexity. As noted above President George W. Bush reopened the ongoing national discussion about immigration with his January 2004 announcement of a new immigration proposal. Thus new uncertainties now surround the fast-paced currents of immigration flow. Yet one thing remains certain. The future of social relations in the United States rests in large part on local communities' maintaining a receptive environment for immigrants and their children and meeting the challenges of incorporating newcomers.

36. See Carnegie Corporation of New York (2003).

TABLE 2A-1. Total and Foreign-Born Population, by Gateway Type, 1980–2000

Gateway type and metropolitan area	Number			Percent change		
	1980	*1990*	*2000*	*1980–90*	*1990–2000*	*1980–2000*
Total population						
Former						
Baltimore, MD PMSA	2,172,851	2,382,172	2,552,994	9.6	7.2	17.5
Buffalo-Niagara Falls, NY MSA	1,242,769	1,189,288	1,170,111	−4.3	−1.6	−5.8
Cleveland-Lorain-Elyria, OH PMSA	2,276,960	2,202,069	2,250,871	−3.3	2.2	−1.1
Detroit, MI PMSA	4,387,542	4,266,654	4,441,551	−2.8	4.1	1.2
Milwaukee-Waukesha, WI PMSA	1,396,889	1,432,149	1,500,741	2.5	4.8	7.4
Philadelphia, PA-NJ PMSA	4,780,357	4,922,175	5,100,931	3.0	3.6	6.7
Pittsburgh, PA MSA	2,411,763	2,394,811	2,358,695	−0.7	−1.5	−2.2
St. Louis, MO-IL MSA	2,392,828	2,511,698	2,626,411	5.0	4.6	9.8
Total	21,061,959	21,301,016	22,002,305	1.1	3.3	4.5
Continuous						
Bergen-Passaic, NJ PMSA	1,292,950	1,278,440	1,373,167	−1.1	7.4	6.2
Boston, MA-NH PMSA	3,147,521	3,227,633	3,406,829	2.5	5.6	8.2
Chicago, IL PMSA	7,139,852	7,410,858	8,272,768	3.8	11.6	15.9
Jersey City, NJ PMSA	556,341	553,099	608,975	−0.6	10.1	9.5
Middlesex-Somerset-Hunterdon, NJ PMSA	886,439	1,019,835	1,169,641	15.0	14.7	31.9
Nassau-Suffolk, NY PMSA	2,605,655	2,609,212	2,753,913	0.1	5.5	5.7
New York, NY PMSA	8,273,751	8,546,846	9,314,235	3.3	9.0	12.6
Newark, NJ PMSA	1,962,911	1,915,928	2,032,989	−2.4	6.1	3.6
San Francisco, CA PMSA	1,487,519	1,603,678	1,731,183	7.8	8.0	16.4
Total	27,352,939	28,165,529	30,663,700	3.0	8.9	12.1
Post–World War II						
Fort Lauderdale, FL PMSA	1,017,915	1,255,488	1,623,018	23.3	29.3	59.4
Houston, TX PMSA	2,753,541	3,322,025	4,177,646	20.6	25.8	51.7
Los Angeles-Long Beach, CA PMSA	7,473,005	8,863,164	9,519,338	18.6	7.4	27.4
Miami, FL PMSA	1,625,397	1,937,094	2,253,362	19.2	16.3	38.6
Orange County, CA PMSA	1,932,984	2,410,556	2,846,289	24.7	18.1	47.2
Riverside-San Bernardino, CA PMSA	1,557,989	2,588,793	3,254,821	66.2	25.7	108.9
San Diego, CA MSA	1,833,215	2,498,016	2,813,833	36.3	12.6	53.5
Total	18,194,046	22,875,136	26,488,307	25.7	15.8	45.6
Emerging						
Atlanta, GA MSA	2,015,703	2,959,950	4,112,198	46.8	38.9	104.0
Dallas, TX PMSA	1,956,740	2,676,248	3,519,176	36.8	31.5	79.8
Fort Worth-Arlington, TX PMSA	990,622	1,361,034	1,702,625	37.4	25.1	71.9
Las Vegas, NV-AZ MSA	463,056	852,737	1,563,282	84.2	83.3	237.6
Orlando, FL MSA	804,756	1,224,852	1,644,561	52.2	34.3	104.4
Washington, DC-MD-VA-WV PMSA	3,265,485	4,223,485	4,923,153	29.3	16.6	50.8
West Palm Beach-Boca Raton, FL MSA	576,720	863,518	1,131,184	49.7	31.0	96.1
Total	10,073,082	14,161,824	18,596,179	40.6	31.3	84.6
Re-emerging						
Denver, CO PMSA	1,428,658	1,622,980	2,109,282	13.6	30.0	47.6
Minneapolis-St. Paul, MN-WI MSA	2,141,007	2,538,834	2,968,806	18.6	16.9	38.7
Oakland, CA PMSA	1,758,693	2,082,914	2,392,557	18.4	14.9	36.0
Phoenix-Mesa, AZ MSA	1,599,727	2,238,480	3,251,876	39.9	45.3	103.3
Portland-Vancouver, OR-WA PMSA	1,297,332	1,515,452	1,918,009	16.8	26.6	47.8
Sacramento, CA PMSA	986,355	1,340,010	1,628,197	35.9	21.5	65.1
San Jose, CA PMSA	1,294,859	1,497,577	1,682,585	15.7	12.4	29.9
Seattle-Bellevue-Everett, WA PMSA	1,603,338	2,033,156	2,414,616	26.8	18.8	50.6
Tampa-St. Petersburg-Clearwater, FL MSA	1,568,374	2,067,959	2,395,997	31.9	15.9	52.8
Total	13,678,343	16,937,362	20,761,925	23.8	22.6	51.8

(continued)

T A B L E 2 A - 1. **Total and Foreign-Born Population, by Gateway Type, 1980–2000 (*continued*)**

Gateway type and metropolitan area	Number			Percent change		
	1980	*1990*	*2000*	*1980–90*	*1990–2000*	*1980–2000*
Total population (*continued*)						
Pre-emerging						
Austin-San Marcos, TX MSA	536,585	846,227	1,249,763	57.7	47.7	132.9
Charlotte-Gastonia-Rock Hill, NC-SC MSA	928,573	1,162,093	1,499,293	25.1	29.0	61.5
Greensboro–Winston-Salem–High Point, NC MSA	926,076	1,050,304	1,251,509	13.4	19.2	35.1
Raleigh-Durham-Chapel Hill, NC MSA	634,549	855,545	1,187,941	34.8	38.9	87.2
Salt Lake City-Ogden, UT MSA	910,127	1,072,227	1,333,914	17.8	24.4	46.6
Total	3,935,910	4,986,396	6,522,420	26.7	30.8	65.7
Total	94,296,279	108,427,263	125,034,836	15.0	15.3	32.6
Foreign-born population						
Former						
Baltimore, MD PMSA	73,759	87,653	146,128	18.8	66.7	98.1
Buffalo-Niagara Falls, NY MSA	69,355	52,220	51,381	−24.7	−1.6	−25.9
Cleveland-Lorain-Elyria, OH PMSA	129,421	100,005	114,625	−22.7	14.6	−11.4
Detroit, MI PMSA	282,674	234,479	335,107	−17.0	42.9	18.5
Milwaukee-Waukesha, WI PMSA	58,410	54,043	81,574	−7.5	50.9	39.7
Philadelphia, PA-NJ PMSA	244,063	252,505	357,421	3.5	41.6	46.4
Pittsburgh, PA MSA	81,200	57,708	62,286	−28.9	7.9	−23.3
St. Louis, MO-IL MSA	52,671	49,021	81,212	−6.9	65.7	54.2
Total	991,553	887,634	1,229,734	−10.5	38.5	24.0
Continuous						
Bergen-Passaic, NJ PMSA	180,211	236,938	352,592	31.5	48.8	95.7
Boston, MA-NH PMSA	307,005	364,632	508,279	18.8	39.4	65.6
Chicago, IL PMSA	746,081	885,081	1,425,978	18.6	61.1	91.1
Jersey City, NJ PMSA	133,534	169,434	234,597	26.9	38.5	75.7
Middlesex-Somerset-Hunterdon, NJ PMSA	76,492	126,653	243,406	65.6	92.2	218.2
Nassau-Suffolk, NY PMSA	230,508	273,522	396,939	18.7	45.1	72.2
New York, NY PMSA	1,832,396	2,285,996	3,139,647	24.8	37.3	71.3
Newark, NJ PMSA	220,907	266,466	385,807	20.6	44.8	74.6
San Francisco, CA PMSA	322,031	441,290	554,819	37.0	25.7	72.3
Total	4,049,165	5,050,012	7,242,064	24.7	43.4	78.9
Post–World War II						
Fort Lauderdale, FL PMSA	113,313	198,274	410,387	75.0	107.0	262.2
Houston, TX PMSA	215,352	440,321	854,669	104.5	94.1	296.9
Los Angeles-Long Beach, CA PMSA	1,664,472	2,895,066	3,449,444	73.9	19.1	107.2
Miami, FL PMSA	577,987	874,569	1,147,765	51.3	31.2	98.6
Orange County, CA PMSA	257,241	575,108	849,899	123.6	47.8	230.4
Riverside-San Bernardino, CA PMSA	134,950	360,650	612,359	167.2	69.8	353.8
San Diego, CA MSA	233,235	428,810	606,254	83.9	41.4	159.9
Total	3,196,550	5,772,798	7,930,777	80.6	37.4	148.1
Emerging						
Atlanta, GA MSA	46,166	116,624	423,105	152.6	262.8	816.5
Dallas, TX PMSA	90,612	234,522	591,169	158.8	152.1	552.4
Fort Worth-Arlington, TX PMSA	33,427	83,877	193,473	150.9	130.7	478.8
Las Vegas, NV-AZ MSA	35,062	74,304	258,494	111.9	247.9	637.2
Orlando, FL MSA	37,268	82,042	197,119	120.1	140.3	428.9

(*continued*)

T A B L E 2 A - 1 .   **Total and Foreign-Born Population, by Gateway Type, 1980–2000 (*continued*)**

Gateway type and metropolitan area	Number			Percent change		
	1980	*1990*	*2000*	*1980–90*	*1990–2000*	*1980–2000*
	Foreign-born population **(*continued*)**					
Washington, DC-MD-VA-WV PMSA	253,329	489,668	832,016	93.3	69.9	228.4
West Palm Beach-Boca Raton, FL MSA	58,004	105,303	196,852	81.5	86.9	239.4
Total	553,868	1,186,340	2,692,228	114.2	126.9	386.1
Re-emerging						
Denver, CO PMSA	65,023	81,334	233,096	25.1	186.6	258.5
Minneapolis-St. Paul, MN-WI MSA	70,908	88,093	210,344	24.2	138.8	196.6
Oakland, CA PMSA	186,956	337,435	573,144	80.5	69.9	206.6
Phoenix-Mesa, AZ MSA	86,588	161,830	457,483	86.9	182.7	428.3
Portland-Vancouver, OR-WA PMSA	65,646	88,072	208,075	34.2	136.3	217.0
Sacramento, CA PMSA	67,140	120,136	225,940	78.9	88.1	236.5
San Jose, CA PMSA	175,815	347,201	573,130	97.5	65.1	226.0
Seattle-Bellevue-Everett, WA PMSA	118,992	169,798	331,912	42.7	95.5	178.9
Tampa-St. Petersburg-Clearwater, FL MSA	106,017	146,003	233,907	37.7	60.2	120.6
Total	943,085	1,539,902	3,047,031	63.3	97.9	223.1
Pre-emerging						
Austin-San Marcos, TX MSA	22,459	56,154	152,834	150.0	172.2	580.5
Charlotte-Gastonia-Rock Hill, NC-SC MSA	14,452	24,041	99,760	66.4	315.0	590.3
Greensboro–Winston-Salem–High Point, NC MSA	9,932	15,318	71,565	54.2	367.2	620.5
Raleigh-Durham-Chapel Hill, NC MSA	13,445	29,374	108,803	118.5	270.4	709.2
Salt Lake City-Ogden, UT MSA	36,808	41,775	114,508	13.5	174.1	211.1
Total	97,096	166,662	547,470	71.6	228.5	463.8
Total	9,831,317	14,603,348	22,689,304	48.5	55.4	130.8

Source: U.S. Census Bureau.

T A B L E   2 A - 2 . **Foreign-Born Population in Metropolitan Areas, Central Cities, and Suburbs, by Gateway Type, 1970–2000**

Gateway type and metropolitan area	1970 Total	1970 Percent	1980 Total	1980 Percent	1990 Total	1990 Percent	2000 Total	2000 Percent
Metropolitan areas								
Former								
Baltimore, MD PMSA	57,374	2.8	73,759	3.4	87,660	3.7	146,128	5.7
Buffalo-Niagara Falls, NY MSA	86,836	6.4	69,355	5.6	52,220	4.4	51,381	4.4
Cleveland-Lorain-Elyria, OH PMSA	151,033	6.5	129,421	5.7	100,005	4.5	114,625	5.1
Detroit, MI PMSA	299,373	6.7	282,674	6.4	234,479	5.5	335,107	7.5
Milwaukee-Waukesha, WI PMSA	62,974	4.5	58,410	4.2	54,043	3.8	81,574	5.4
Philadelphia, PA-NJ PMSA	244,860	5.0	244,063	5.1	252,505	5.1	357,421	7.0
Pittsburgh, PA MSA	107,757	4.5	81,200	3.4	57,708	2.4	62,286	2.6
St. Louis, MO-IL MSA	48,418	2.0	52,671	2.2	49,021	2.0	81,212	3.1
Total	1,058,625	5.0	991,553	4.7	887,641	4.2	1,229,734	5.6
Continuous								
Bergen-Passaic, NJ PMSA	151,597	11.2	180,211	13.9	236,938	18.5	352,592	25.7
Boston, MA-NH PMSA	289,800	9.6	307,005	9.8	364,632	11.3	508,279	14.9
Chicago, IL PMSA	563,151	8.1	746,081	10.4	885,081	11.9	1,425,978	17.2
Jersey City, NJ PMSA	107,386	17.6	133,534	24.0	169,434	30.6	234,597	38.5
Middlesex-Somerset-Hunterdon, NJ PMSA	63,654	7.5	76,492	8.6	126,653	12.4	243,406	20.8
Nassau-Suffolk, NY PMSA	192,625	7.6	230,508	8.8	273,522	10.5	396,939	14.4
New York, NY PMSA	1,563,534	17.3	1,832,396	22.1	2,285,996	26.7	3,139,647	33.7
Newark, NJ PMSA	189,868	9.5	220,907	11.3	266,466	13.9	385,807	19.0
San Francisco, CA PMSA	229,936	15.6	322,031	21.6	441,290	27.5	554,819	32.0
Total	3,351,551	12.0	4,049,165	14.8	5,050,012	17.9	7,242,064	23.6
Post–World War II								
Fort Lauderdale, FL PMSA	49,613	8.0	113,313	11.1	198,274	15.8	410,387	25.3
Houston, TX PMSA	47,678	2.5	215,352	7.8	440,321	13.3	854,669	20.5
Los Angeles-Long Beach, CA PMSA	792,232	11.3	1,664,472	22.3	2,895,066	32.7	3,449,444	36.2
Miami, FL PMSA	307,387	24.3	577,987	35.6	874,569	45.1	1,147,765	50.9
Orange County, CA PMSA	84,766	6.0	257,241	13.3	575,108	23.9	849,899	29.9
Riverside-San Bernardino, CA PMSA	68,182	6.0	134,950	8.7	360,650	13.9	612,359	18.8
San Diego, CA MSA	91,108	6.8	233,235	12.7	428,810	17.2	606,254	21.5
Total	1,440,966	9.8	3,196,550	17.6	5,772,798	25.2	7,930,777	29.9
Emerging								
Atlanta, GA MSA	16,368	1.1	46,166	2.3	116,624	3.9	423,105	10.3
Dallas, TX PMSA	24,588	1.6	90,612	4.6	234,522	8.8	591,169	16.8
Fort Worth-Arlington, TX PMSA	9,459	1.2	33,427	3.4	83,877	6.2	193,473	11.4
Las Vegas, NV-AZ MSA	10,637	3.9	35,062	7.6	74,304	8.7	258,494	16.5
Orlando, FL MSA	13,262	2.5	37,268	4.6	82,040	6.7	197,119	12.0
Washington, DC-MD-VA-WV PMSA	130,328	4.5	253,329	7.8	489,668	11.6	832,016	16.9
West Palm Beach-Boca Raton, FL MSA	27,384	7.9	58,004	10.1	105,304	12.2	196,852	17.4
Total	232,026	3.0	553,868	5.5	1,186,339	8.4	2,692,228	14.5
Re-emerging								
Denver, CO PMSA	33,838	3.1	65,023	4.6	81,334	5.0	233,096	11.1
Minneapolis-St. Paul, MN-WI MSA	54,918	3.0	70,908	3.3	88,093	3.5	210,344	7.1
Oakland, CA PMSA	112,298	6.9	186,956	10.6	337,435	16.2	573,144	24.0
Phoenix-Mesa, AZ MSA	36,475	3.8	86,588	5.4	161,830	7.2	457,483	14.1
Portland-Vancouver, OR-WA PMSA	41,277	4.1	65,646	5.1	88,072	5.8	208,075	10.8
Sacramento, CA PMSA	35,691	4.7	67,140	6.8	120,136	9.0	225,940	13.9

(continued)

T A B L E   2 A - 2 .   **Foreign-Born Population in Metropolitan Areas, Central Cities, and Suburbs, by Gateway Type, 1970–2000 (*continued*)**

Gateway type and metropolitan area	1970 Total	1970 Percent	1980 Total	1980 Percent	1990 Total	1990 Percent	2000 Total	2000 Percent
Metropolitan areas (*continued*)								
San Jose, CA PMSA	82,464	7.7	175,815	13.6	347,201	23.2	573,130	34.1
Seattle-Bellevue-Everett, WA PMSA	86,245	6.1	118,992	7.4	169,798	8.4	331,912	13.7
Tampa-St. Petersburg-Clearwater, FL MSA	61,128	6.1	106,017	6.8	146,003	7.1	233,907	9.8
Total	544,334	5.1	943,085	6.9	1,539,902	9.1	3,047,031	14.7
Pre-emerging								
Austin-San Marcos, TX MSA	6,187	2.1	24,220	4.1	56,154	6.6	152,834	12.2
Charlotte-Gastonia-Rock Hill, NC-SC MSA	4,936	0.6	14,761	1.5	24,041	2.1	99,760	6.7
Greensboro–Winston-Salem– High Point, NC MSA	3,968	0.5	10,071	1.1	15,318	1.5	71,565	5.7
Raleigh-Durham-Chapel Hill, NC MSA	5,220	1.3	13,594	2.0	29,374	3.4	108,803	9.2
Salt Lake City-Ogden, UT MSA	23,200	3.4	36,805	4.0	41,775	3.9	114,508	8.6
Total	43,511	1.5	99,451	2.4	166,662	3.3	547,470	8.4
Total in metropolitan areas	6,671,013	7.8	9,833,672	10.4	14,603,354	13.5	22,689,304	18.1
Central city								
Former								
Baltimore, MD PMSA	28,710	3.2	24,667	3.1	23,467	3.2	29,638	4.6
Buffalo-Niagara Falls, NY MSA	35,252	7.6	22,025	6.2	14,741	4.5	12,856	4.4
Cleveland-Lorain-Elyria, OH PMSA	56,400	7.5	33,347	5.8	20,975	4.1	21,372	4.5
Detroit, MI PMSA	119,347	7.9	68,303	5.7	34,490	3.4	45,541	4.8
Milwaukee-Waukesha, WI PMSA	39,576	5.5	31,718	5.0	29,667	4.7	46,122	7.7
Philadelphia, PA-NJ PMSA	126,896	6.5	107,951	6.4	104,814	6.6	137,205	9.0
Pittsburgh, PA MSA	31,275	6.0	22,195	5.2	16,946	4.6	18,874	5.6
St. Louis, MO-IL MSA	16,260	2.6	11,878	2.6	10,034	2.5	19,542	5.6
Total	453,716	6.1	322,084	5.3	255,134	4.6	331,150	6.4
Continuous								
Bergen-Passaic, NJ PMSA	—	0.0	—	0.0	—	0.0	—	0.0
Boston, MA-NH PMSA	83,988	13.1	87,056	15.5	114,597	20.0	151,836	25.8
Chicago, IL PMSA	373,919	11.1	435,232	14.5	469,187	16.9	628,903	21.7
Jersey City, NJ PMSA	26,635	10.2	36,352	16.3	56,326	24.6	81,554	34.0
Middlesex-Somerset-Hunterdon, NJ PMSA	—	0.0	—	0.0	—	0.0	—	0.0
Nassau-Suffolk, NY PMSA	—	0.0	—	0.0	—	0.0	—	0.0
New York, NY PMSA	1,437,058	18.2	1,670,199	23.6	2,082,931	28.4	2,871,032	35.9
Newark, NJ PMSA	40,104	10.5	47,739	14.5	51,423	18.7	66,057	24.1
San Francisco, CA PMSA	154,507	21.6	192,204	28.3	246,034	34.0	285,541	36.8
Total	2,116,211	16.0	2,468,782	20.8	3,020,498	25.4	4,084,923	32.0
Post–World War II								
Fort Lauderdale, FL PMSA	8,890	0.0	15,228	9.9	25,963	17.4	32,938	21.7
Houston, TX PMSA	37,501	3.0	155,577	9.8	290,374	17.8	516,105	26.4
Los Angeles-Long Beach, CA PMSA	410,870	14.6	856,229	25.7	1,440,815	36.8	1,644,888	39.6
Miami, FL PMSA	140,207	41.8	186,280	53.7	214,128	59.7	215,739	59.5
Orange County, CA PMSA	23,284	0.0	100,889	20.8	249,808	37.3	349,786	43.3
Riverside-San Bernardino, CA PMSA	12,585	0.0	22,464	0.0	60,452	15.5	89,056	0.0
San Diego, CA MSA	52,977	7.6	130,906	15.0	232,138	20.9	314,227	25.7
Total	686,314	11.9	1,467,573	20.8	2,513,678	30.6	3,162,739	34.8

(*continued*)

T A B L E 2 A - 2 . **Foreign-Born Population in Metropolitan Areas, Central Cities, and Suburbs, by Gateway Type, 1970–2000 (*continued*)**

Gateway type and metropolitan area	1970 Total	1970 Percent	1980 Total	1980 Percent	1990 Total	1990 Percent	2000 Total	2000 Percent
Central city (*continued*)								
Emerging								
Atlanta, GA MSA	5,852	1.2	9,777	2.3	13,354	3.4	27,352	6.6
Dallas, TX PMSA	17,426	2.1	54,912	6.1	125,862	12.5	290,436	24.4
Fort Worth-Arlington, TX PMSA	5,939	1.5	24,603	4.5	60,306	8.5	138,031	15.9
Las Vegas, NV-AZ MSA	5,215	4.2	13,117	8.0	26,494	10.3	90,656	18.9
Orlando, FL MSA	3,298	3.3	6,641	5.2	11,436	6.9	26,741	14.4
Washington, DC-MD-VA-WV PMSA	33,562	4.4	40,559	6.4	58,887	9.7	73,561	12.9
West Palm Beach-Boca Raton, FL MSA	5,515	9.6	8,168	12.9	12,618	18.7	20,152	24.7
Total	76,807	2.8	157,777	5.5	308,957	9.6	666,929	17.6
Re-emerging								
Denver, CO PMSA	20,926	4.1	30,712	6.2	34,715	7.4	96,601	17.4
Minneapolis-St. Paul, MN-WI MSA	32,913	4.4	31,395	4.9	42,517	6.6	96,613	14.4
Oakland, CA PMSA	32,239	8.9	42,579	12.5	73,524	19.8	106,116	26.6
Phoenix-Mesa, AZ MSA	21,656	3.7	51,242	5.4	98,686	7.8	301,871	17.6
Portland-Vancouver, OR-WA PMSA	21,080	5.5	27,848	6.8	35,813	7.4	86,482	12.9
Sacramento, CA PMSA	17,489	6.9	27,708	10.0	50,569	13.7	82,616	20.3
San Jose, CA PMSA	33,962	7.6	90,914	14.4	207,041	26.5	329,757	36.9
Seattle-Bellevue-Everett, WA PMSA	48,423	9.1	62,432	11.0	79,284	13.1	121,734	18.1
Tampa-St. Petersburg-Clearwater, FL MSA	16,367	5.9	37,145	7.3	47,477	7.7	73,942	11.2
Total	245,055	6.0	401,975	8.4	669,626	11.9	1,295,732	19.5
Pre-emerging								
Austin-San Marcos, TX MSA	5,497	2.2	16,704	4.8	40,962	8.3	109,006	16.6
Charlotte-Gastonia-Rock Hill, NC-SC MSA	3,494	1.2	8,742	2.8	15,119	3.8	59,849	11.0
Greensboro–Winston-Salem– High Point, NC MSA	2,558	0.9	4,833	1.7	7,853	2.4	33,481	8.2
Raleigh-Durham-Chapel Hill, NC MSA	3,861	1.5	7,210	2.9	15,639	4.5	54,954	11.8
Salt Lake City-Ogden, UT MSA	11,107	6.3	14,489	6.6	13,258	8.3	33,252	18.3
Total	26,517	2.1	51,978	3.7	92,831	5.4	290,542	12.9
Total in central cities	3,604,620	10.4	4,870,169	14.3	6,860,724	18.9	9,832,015	24.7
Suburbs								
Former								
Baltimore, MD PMSA	28,664	2.5	49,092	3.5	64,193	3.9	116,490	6.1
Buffalo-Niagara Falls, NY MSA	51,584	5.8	47,330	5.3	37,479	4.4	38,525	4.4
Cleveland-Lorain-Elyria, OH PMSA	94,633	6.0	96,074	5.6	79,030	4.7	93,253	5.3
Detroit, MI PMSA	180,026	6.1	214,371	6.7	199,989	6.2	289,566	8.3
Milwaukee-Waukesha, WI PMSA	23,398	3.4	26,692	3.5	24,376	3.0	35,452	3.9
Philadelphia, PA-NJ PMSA	117,964	4.0	136,112	4.4	147,691	4.4	220,216	6.1
Pittsburgh, PA MSA	76,482	4.1	59,005	3.0	40,762	2.0	43,412	2.1
St. Louis, MO-IL MSA	32,158	1.8	40,793	2.1	38,987	1.8	61,670	2.7
Total	604,909	4.4	669,469	4.5	632,507	4.0	898,584	5.3
Continuous								
Bergen-Passaic, NJ PMSA	151,597	11.2	180,211	13.9	236,938	18.5	352,592	25.7
Boston, MA-NH PMSA	205,812	8.7	219,949	8.5	250,035	9.4	356,443	12.7
Chicago, IL PMSA	189,232	5.2	310,849	7.5	415,894	9.0	797,075	14.8
Jersey City, NJ PMSA	80,751	23.2	97,182	29.2	113,108	34.8	153,043	41.5

(*continued*)

TABLE 2A-2. **Foreign-Born Population in Metropolitan Areas, Central Cities, and Suburbs, by Gateway Type, 1970–2000 (*continued*)**

Gateway type and metropolitan area	1970 Total	1970 Percent	1980 Total	1980 Percent	1990 Total	1990 Percent	2000 Total	2000 Percent
Suburbs (*continued*)								
Middlesex-Somerset-Hunterdon, NJ PMSA	63,654	7.5	76,492	8.6	126,653	12.4	243,406	20.8
Nassau-Suffolk, NY PMSA	192,625	7.6	230,508	8.8	273,522	10.5	396,939	14.4
New York, NY PMSA	126,476	11.3	162,197	13.5	203,065	16.6	268,615	20.6
Newark, NJ PMSA	149,764	9.2	173,168	10.6	215,043	13.1	319,750	18.2
San Francisco, CA PMSA	75,429	9.9	129,827	16.1	195,256	22.2	269,278	28.2
Total	1,235,340	8.5	1,580,383	10.2	2,029,514	12.5	3,157,141	17.7
Post–World War II								
Fort Lauderdale, FL PMSA	40,723	8.5	98,085	11.3	172,311	15.6	377,449	25.7
Houston, TX PMSA	10,177	1.5	59,775	5.2	149,947	8.9	338,564	15.2
Los Angeles-Long Beach, CA PMSA	381,362	9.1	808,243	19.5	1,454,251	29.4	1,804,556	33.6
Miami, FL PMSA	167,180	17.9	391,707	30.6	660,441	41.8	932,026	49.3
Orange County, CA PMSA	61,482	5.6	156,352	10.8	325,300	18.7	500,113	24.5
Riverside-San Bernardino, CA PMSA	55,597	6.2	112,486	8.9	300,198	13.7	523,303	18.6
San Diego, CA MSA	38,131	5.9	102,329	10.7	196,672	14.2	292,027	18.4
Total	754,652	8.5	1,728,977	15.5	3,259,120	22.2	4,768,038	27.4
Emerging								
Atlanta, GA MSA	10,516	1.1	36,389	2.3	103,270	4.0	395,753	10.7
Dallas, TX PMSA	7,162	1.0	35,700	3.4	108,660	6.5	300,733	12.9
Fort Worth-Arlington, TX PMSA	3,520	0.9	8,824	2.0	23,571	3.6	55,442	6.6
Las Vegas, NV-AZ MSA	5,422	3.7	21,945	7.4	47,810	8.0	167,838	15.5
Orlando, FL MSA	9,964	2.4	30,627	4.5	70,604	6.7	170,378	11.7
Washington, DC-MD-VA-WV PMSA	96,766	4.5	212,770	8.1	430,781	11.9	758,455	17.4
West Palm Beach-Boca Raton, FL MSA	21,869	7.5	49,836	9.7	92,686	11.6	176,700	16.8
Total	155,219	3.1	396,091	5.5	877,382	8.0	2,025,299	13.7
Re-emerging								
Denver, CO PMSA	12,912	2.3	34,311	3.7	46,619	4.0	136,495	8.8
Minneapolis-St. Paul, MN-WI MSA	22,005	2.1	39,513	2.6	45,576	2.4	113,731	4.9
Oakland, CA PMSA	80,059	6.3	144,377	10.2	263,911	15.4	467,028	23.4
Phoenix-Mesa, AZ MSA	14,819	3.8	35,346	5.4	63,144	6.5	155,612	10.1
Portland-Vancouver, OR-WA PMSA	20,197	3.2	37,798	4.3	52,259	5.1	121,593	9.8
Sacramento, CA PMSA	18,202	3.7	39,432	5.5	69,567	7.2	143,324	11.7
San Jose, CA PMSA	48,502	7.9	84,901	12.8	140,160	19.6	243,373	30.9
Seattle-Bellevue-Everett, WA PMSA	37,822	4.2	56,560	5.5	90,514	6.3	210,178	12.1
Tampa-St. Petersburg-Clearwater, FL MSA	44,761	6.1	68,872	6.5	98,526	6.8	159,965	9.2
Total	299,279	4.5	541,110	6.1	870,276	7.7	1,751,299	12.4
Pre-emerging								
Austin-San Marcos, TX MSA	690	1.6	7,516	3.1	15,192	4.3	43,828	7.4
Charlotte-Gastonia-Rock Hill, NC-SC MSA	1,442	0.3	6,019	0.9	8,922	1.2	39,911	4.2
Greensboro–Winston-Salem–High Point, NC MSA	1,410	0.3	5,238	0.8	7,465	1.0	38,084	4.5
Raleigh-Durham-Chapel Hill, NC MSA	1,359	0.9	6,384	1.5	13,735	2.7	53,849	7.4
Salt Lake City-Ogden, UT MSA	12,093	2.4	22,316	3.2	28,517	3.1	81,256	7.1
Total	16,994	1.0	47,473	1.8	73,831	2.3	256,928	6.0
Total in suburbs	3,066,393	6.0	4,963,503	8.2	7,742,630	10.7	12,857,289	15.1

Source: U.S. Census Bureau.

TABLE 2A-3. Percent Change in Foreign-Born Population in Metropolitan Areas, Central Cities, and Suburbs, by Gateway Type, 1990–2000

Gateway type and metropolitan area	Metropolitan area	Central city	Suburbs
Former			
Baltimore, MD PMSA	66.7	26.3	81.5
Buffalo-Niagara Falls, NY MSA	−1.6	−12.8	2.8
Cleveland-Lorain-Elyria, OH PMSA	14.6	1.9	18.0
Detroit, MI PMSA	42.9	32.0	44.8
Milwaukee-Waukesha, WI PMSA	50.9	55.5	45.4
Philadelphia, PA-NJ PMSA	41.6	30.9	49.1
Pittsburgh, PA MSA	7.9	11.4	6.5
St. Louis, MO-IL MSA	65.7	94.8	58.2
Total	38.5	29.8	42.1
Continuous			
Bergen-Passaic, NJ PMSA	48.8	—	48.8
Boston, MA-NH PMSA	39.4	32.5	42.6
Chicago, IL PMSA	61.1	34.0	91.7
Jersey City, NJ PMSA	38.5	44.8	35.3
Middlesex-Somerset-Hunterdon, NJ PMSA	92.2	—	92.2
Nassau-Suffolk, NY PMSA	45.1	—	45.1
New York, NY PMSA	37.3	37.8	32.3
Newark, NJ PMSA	44.8	28.5	48.7
San Francisco, CA PMSA	25.7	16.1	37.9
Total	43.4	35.2	55.6
Post–World War II			
Fort Lauderdale, FL PMSA	107.0	26.9	119.1
Houston, TX PMSA	94.1	77.7	125.8
Los Angeles-Long Beach, CA PMSA	19.1	14.2	24.1
Miami, FL PMSA	31.2	0.8	41.1
Orange County, CA PMSA	47.8	40.0	53.7
Riverside-San Bernardino, CA PMSA	69.8	47.3	74.3
San Diego, CA MSA	41.4	35.4	48.5
Total	37.4	25.8	46.3
Emerging			
Atlanta, GA MSA	262.8	104.8	283.2
Dallas, TX PMSA	152.1	130.8	176.8
Fort Worth-Arlington, TX PMSA	130.7	128.9	135.2
Las Vegas, NV-AZ MSA	247.9	242.2	251.1
Orlando, FL MSA	140.3	133.8	141.3
Washington, DC-MD-VA-WV PMSA	69.9	24.9	76.1
West Palm Beach-Boca Raton, FL MSA	86.9	59.7	90.6
Total	126.9	115.9	130.8
Re-emerging			
Denver, CO PMSA	186.6	178.3	192.8
Minneapolis-St. Paul, MN-WI MSA	138.8	127.2	149.5
Oakland, CA PMSA	69.9	44.3	77.0
Phoenix-Mesa, AZ MSA	182.7	205.9	146.4
Portland-Vancouver, OR-WA PMSA	136.3	141.5	132.7
Sacramento, CA PMSA	88.1	63.4	106.0
San Jose, CA PMSA	65.1	59.3	73.6
Seattle-Bellevue-Everett, WA PMSA	95.5	53.5	132.2
Tampa-St. Petersburg-Clearwater, FL MSA	60.2	55.7	62.4
Total	97.9	93.5	101.2
Pre-emerging			
Austin-San Marcos, TX MSA	172.2	166.1	188.5
Charlotte-Gastonia-Rock Hill, NC-SC MSA	315.0	295.9	347.3
Greensboro–Winston-Salem–High Point, NC MSA	367.2	326.3	410.2
Raleigh-Durham-Chapel Hill, NC MSA	270.4	251.4	292.1
Salt Lake City-Ogden, UT MSA	174.1	150.8	184.9
Total	228.5	213.0	248.0
Total	55.4	43.3	66.1

Source: U.S. Census Bureau.

REFERENCES

Alba, Richard D., John R. Logan, Brian Stults, Gilbert Marzan, and Wenquan Zhang. 1999a. "Immigrant Groups in the Suburbs: A Reexamination of Suburbanization and Spatial Assimilation." *American Sociological Review* 64: 446–60.

Alba, Richard D., John R. Logan, Wenquan Zhang, and Brian Stults. 1999b. "Strangers Next Door: Immigrant Groups and Suburbs in Los Angeles and New York." In *A Nation Divided: Diversity, Inequality, and Community in American Society,* edited by Phyllis Moen, Henry Walker, and Donna Dempster-McClain. Cornell University Press.

Alba, Richard D., and Victor Nee. 1997. "Rethinking Assimilation Theory for a New Era of Immigration." *International Migration Review* 31: 826–74.

Atiles, Jorge H., and Stephanie A. Bohon. 2002. "The Needs of Georgia's New Latinos: A Policy Agenda for the Decade Ahead." Athens, Ga.: University of Georgia Carl Vinson Institute of Government.

Capps, Randolph, Michael E. Fix, Jeffrey S. Passel, Jason Ost, and Dan Perez-Lopez. 2003a. "A Profile of the Low-Wage Immigrant Workforce." Washington: Urban Institute.

Capps, Randolph, Jeffrey S. Passel, Dan Perez-Lopez, and Michael E. Fix. 2003b. "The New Neighbors: A User's Guide to Data on Immigrants in U.S. Communities." Washington: Urban Institute Press.

Carnegie Corporation of New York. 2003. "The House We All Live In: A Report on Civic Integration." New York.

Farkas, Steve, Ann Duffett, and Jean Johnson with Leslie Moye and Jackie Vine. 2003. "Now That I'm Here: What America's Immigrants Have to Say about Life in the U.S. Today." New York: Public Agenda.

Fernandez, Catherine. 2003. "Community Development in Dynamic Neighborhoods: Synchronizing Services and Strategies with Immigrant Communities." Washington: Neighborhood Reinvestment Corporation and Joint Center for Housing Studies of Harvard University.

Fix, Michael E., Wendy Zimmermann, and Jeffrey S. Passel. 2001. "The Integration of Immigrant Families in the U.S." Washington: Urban Institute Press.

Foner, Nancy. 2002. *From Ellis Island to JFK: New York's Two Great Waves of Immigration.* Yale University Press

Gans, Herbert J. 1992. "Second Generation Decline: Scenarios for the Economic and Ethnic Futures of the Post–1965 American Immigrants." *Ethnic and Racial Studies* 15 (2): 173–92.

Gibson, Campbell, and Emily Lennon. 1999. "Historical Census Statistics on the Foreign-Born Population of the U.S. States: 1850–1990." U.S. Census Bureau, Population Division Working Paper 29. Washington: U.S. Census Bureau.

Glaeser, Ed, and Matthew Kahn. 2001. "Decentralized Employment and the Transformation of the American City." *Brookings-Wharton Papers on Urban Affairs* 2.

Hernández-León, Rubén, and Víctor Zúñiga. 2000. " 'Making Carpet by the Mile': The Emergence of a Mexican Immigrant Community in an Industrial Region of the U.S. Historic South." *Social Science Quarterly* 81 (1): 49–66.

Hirschman, Charles, Philip Kasinitz, and Josh DeWind, eds. 1999. *The Handbook of International Migration: The American Experience.* New York: Russell Sage Foundation.

Jasso, Guillermina, and Mark R. Rosenzweig. 1990. *The New Chosen People: Immigrants in the U.S.* New York: Russell Sage Foundation.

Kandel, William, and Emilio Parrado. 2004. "Industrial Transformation and Hispanic Migration to the American South: The Case of the Poultry Industry." In *Hispanic Spaces, Latino Places: Community and Cultural Diversity in Contemporary America,* edited by Daniel D. Arreola. University of Texas Press.

Massey, Douglas S. 1985. "Ethnic Residential Segregation: A Theoretical Synthesis and Empirical Review." *Sociology and Social Research* 69 (3): 315–50.

Masters, Suzette Brooks, Kimberly Hamilton, and Jill H. Wilson. 2004. "Putting Data to Work for Immigrants and Communities: Tools for the D.C. Metro Area and Beyond." Washington: Migration Policy Institute.

McDaniel, Josh M. 2002. "Immigrants and Forest Industries in Alabama: Social Networks and Pioneer Settlements." Paper presented at Immigration and America's Changing Ethnic Landscapes Conference, Athens, Ga., April 12–14.

Sassen, Saskia. 1988. *The Mobility of Labor and Capital: A Study in International Investment and Labor Flows.* Cambridge University Press.

Schacter, Jason P., Rachel S. Franklin, and Marc J. Perry. 2003. "Migration and Geographic Mobility in Metropolitan and Nonmetropolitan America: 1995–2000." Census 2000 Special Reports CENSR-9. Washington: U.S. Census Bureau.

Schmidley, Diane A. 2001. "Profile of the Foreign-Born in the U.S., 2000." Current Population Reports, Series P23–206. Washington: U.S. Census Bureau.

Singer, Audrey. 2003. "At Home in the Nation's Capital: Immigrant Trends in Metropolitan Washington." Brookings.

Singer, Audrey, and Amelia Brown. 2001. "Washington, D.C." In *Encyclopedia of American Immigration,* edited by James Ciment. Armonk, N.Y.: M. E. Sharpe.

Waldinger, Roger, and Medhi Bozorgmehr. 1996. *Ethnic Los Angeles.* New York: Russell Sage Foundation.

Waldinger, Roger. 2001. *Strangers at the Gates: New Immigrants in Urban America.* University of California Press.

Wyly, Elvin K., and Daniel J. Hammel. 1999. "Islands of Decay in Seas of Renewal: Housing Policy and the Resurgence of Gentrification." *Housing Policy Debate* 10 (4): 711–71.

Zhou, Min. 1997. "Segmented Assimilation: Issues, Controversies, and Recent Research on the New Second Generation." *International Migration Review* 31 (4): 825–58.

3

The New Great Migration
Black Americans' Return to the South, 1965–2000

WILLIAM H. FREY

During the early part of the twentieth century black Americans left the U.S. South in large numbers. Several factors precipitated their "Great Migration" to northern cities.[1] First, the mechanization of Southern agriculture rendered many farm workers, including blacks, redundant. Second, the industrialization of the Northeast and Midwest created millions of manufacturing jobs for unskilled workers. Finally, the generally oppressive racial climate in the South acted as a "push" factor for many decades as blacks sought more tolerant communities in other regions. Even as whites migrated to the Sunbelt in large numbers at mid-century, black migration out of the South exceeded black in-migration as late as 1965–70.

Census migration data confirm that over the past three decades, the South has developed into a regional magnet for blacks more than for whites or the population as a whole. The South's appeal to blacks, especially those with higher education levels and from other parts of the country, provides additional evidence that the region's economic, amenity, and cultural "pull" factors now outweigh the "push" factors that predominated in past decades.

This chapter begins by examining the South's exchange of black migrants with other regions over the past four decennial censuses (1970, 1980, 1990, and 2000). It identifies shifts in the states and metropolitan areas over that period that gained and lost the most black residents due to internal (U.S.

The author is grateful to senior project programmer Cathy Sun and other support staff at the University of Michigan, as well as to Alan Berube for comments on this report.

1. Hamilton (1964); Lemann (1991).

domestic) migration. The chapter compares the rates at which black and white movers selected Southern destinations in the late 1990s, and looks at the educational attainment levels of those movers and the places experiencing the largest "brain gains" and "brain drains" of college graduates. Finally, the chapter examines California's reversal from a major recipient of black migrants from the South to a major "donor" state at the end of the century.

METHODOLOGY

This section briefly describes the geographic and census data that underpin this migration analysis.

Geographical Definitions

The four regions—Northeast, Midwest, South, and West—follow the definitions employed by the U.S. Census Bureau.[2] The metropolitan types analyzed include Consolidated Metropolitan Statistical Areas (CMSAs), Metropolitan Statistical Areas (MSAs), and New England County Metropolitan Areas (NECMAs) in the New England states, as defined by the U.S. Office of Management and Budget (OMB).[3]

This study differs from other Brookings census analyses in its use of CMSAs rather than their component parts, Primary Metropolitan Statistical Areas (PMSAs). CMSAs are metropolitan areas of 1 million or more people that are subdivided into two or more PMSAs. For example, four PMSAs exist within the Los Angeles-Riverside-Orange County CMSA: the Los Angeles-Long Beach, California, PMSA (consisting of Los Angeles County); the Orange County, California, PMSA (consisting of Orange County); the Riverside-San Bernardino, California, PMSA (consisting of Riverside and San Bernardino counties); and the Ventura, California, PMSA (consisting of Ventura County). This chapter uses CMSAs rather than PMSAs to reflect how migration patterns affect broad metropolitan regions, and to ensure that estimates

---

2. The regions are defined as follows: Northeast includes the states of Connecticut, Maine, Massachusetts, New Hampshire, New Jersey, New York, Pennsylvania, Rhode Island, and Vermont. Midwest includes Illinois, Indiana, Iowa, Kansas, Michigan, Minnesota, Missouri, Nebraska, North Dakota, Ohio, South Dakota, and Wisconsin. South includes Alabama, Arkansas, Delaware, the District of Columbia, Florida, Georgia, Kentucky, Louisiana, Maryland, Mississippi, North Carolina, Oklahoma, South Carolina, Tennessee, Texas, Virginia, and West Virginia. West includes Alaska, Arizona, California, Colorado, Hawaii, Idaho, Montana, Nevada, New Mexico, Oregon, Utah, Washington, and Wyoming.

3. This survey uses data from metropolitan areas defined by OMB as of June 30, 1999, and in effect for Census 2000. New metropolitan area definitions were announced by OMB in June 2003.

of domestic migration capture geographically significant changes in residence, rather than moves between two jurisdictions within the same region.

Data

The migration data analyzed in this chapter are drawn from the decennial census question, "Where did this person live five years ago?" Using the answers to this question, the chapter analyzes migration trends for 1995–2000 from Census 2000, and for 1985–90, 1975–80, and 1965–70 from the last three censuses. Net migration for a state or region is defined as the difference between the number of in-migrants to that area from elsewhere in the United States, minus the number of out-migrants from that area to other parts of the United States, for moves that took place over the five-year period. This chapter focuses solely on domestic migration, or movement within the fifty states (plus the District of Columbia), and thus does not take into account movement into the United States from abroad, or out-migration to other countries.

The migration data used in these analyses draw primarily from the "long form" sample of responses from the decennial censuses of 1970–2000. The data are based on an approximate 16 percent sample of all respondents in these censuses and are statistically weighted to represent 100 percent of the population. This chapter's analyses of metropolitan migration among black and white subpopulations, and by educational attainment, are based on weighted tabulations of 1995–2000 migration data from Census 2000 5-Percent Public Use Microdata Sample (PUMS) files.[4] As used here the term "blacks" refers to both Hispanic and non-Hispanic blacks in all census years. In 2000, blacks include those who identify black race alone, and whites include those who identify white race alone and non-Hispanic ethnicity.

FINDINGS

Analysis of data from the past four censuses confirms the South's emergence as a major magnet for a diverse group of black migrants from across the United States.

Black Migration out of the South Reversed by the 1990s

The period 1995–2000 completed a long-term reversal of the black population's historic out-migration from the South. Last observed in 1965–70 at the end of the "Great Migration," the historic pattern featured a considerable

4. U.S. Census Bureau (2003).

FIGURE 3-1. Black Net Migration, U.S. Regions, 1965–2000

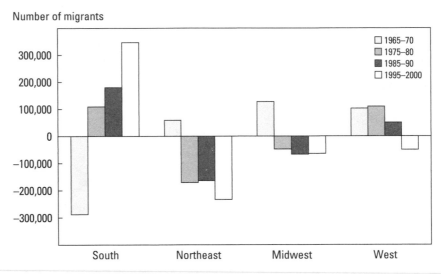

Number of migrants

Source: Author's analysis of 1970, 1980, 1990, and 2000 decennial censuses.

exodus of blacks from the South, as each of the three other regions of the United States gained black migrants (figure 3-1 and table 3A-1). During the late 1960s the fourteen states experiencing the greatest black out-migration were all located in the South, led by the "Deep South" states of Mississippi, Alabama, and Louisiana (table 3-1 and table 3A-2). At the same time the states with the greatest black migration gains during that period included those in the industrial Midwest and Northeast, as well as California. These states contained urban industrial centers that, at the time, attracted large numbers of less-skilled black laborers in search of employment.

This pattern began to shift in the late 1970s as industrial states—especially in the Northeast—sustained significant employment declines related to de-industrialization, and Southern employment prospects improved.[5] The South showed net gains of black migrants, whereas the Northeast and Midwest experienced net losses. Trends at the state level reflected this shift, as New York, Illinois, Pennsylvania, and Ohio ranked among those with the largest net black out-migration. Meanwhile new states were gaining blacks. Between 1975 and 1980, for example, no fewer than seven Southern states ranked among the top ten black migration gainers, whereas 1965–70 saw only one "border" Southern state (Maryland) among the top ten black migration gainers.

5. Frey and Speare (1988); Long (1988).

TABLE 3-1. Black Net Migration, States with Largest Gains and Losses, 1965–2000

1965–70		1975–80		1985–90		1995–2000	
Largest gains							
California	91,425	California	75,746	Georgia	80,827	Georgia	129,749
Michigan	63,839	Maryland	54,793	Maryland	59,966	North Carolina	53,371
Maryland	44,054	Texas	47,685	Florida	57,009	Florida	51,286
New Jersey	28,642	Georgia	29,616	Virginia	53,873	Maryland	43,549
Ohio	22,518	Virginia	22,295	North Carolina	39,015	Texas	42,312
Illinois	16,857	Florida	15,900	California	21,636	Virginia	29,149
Indiana	10,356	North Carolina	14,456	Minnesota	12,525	Nevada	19,446
Connecticut	9,845	Washington	10,216	Tennessee	11,297	Tennessee	19,343
Wisconsin	8,924	South Carolina	9,238	Nevada	10,143	South Carolina	16,253
Massachusetts	8,125	Colorado	8,861	Arizona	9,211	Minnesota	9,118
Largest losses							
Mississippi	−66,614	New York	−128,143	New York	−150,695	New York	−165,366
Alabama	−61,507	District of Columbia	−58,454	Illinois	−60,120	California	−63,180
Louisiana	−37,067	Illinois	−37,220	Louisiana	−46,053	Illinois	−55,238
North Carolina	−29,732	Pennsylvania	−25,849	District of Columbia	−43,727	New Jersey	−34,682
Arkansas	−27,594	Mississippi	−20,106	Mississippi	−19,522	District of Columbia	−34,118
South Carolina	−26,884	Ohio	−16,503	Michigan	−14,600	Louisiana	−18,074
Georgia	−23,363	Missouri	−10,428	Pennsylvania	−11,046	Pennsylvania	−18,024
Tennessee	−17,703	Arkansas	−9,236	New Jersey	−10,084	Michigan	−16,449
District of Columbia	−15,390	Alabama	−7,843	Arkansas	−8,931	Hawaii	−7,203
Virginia	−11,586	New Jersey	−6,462	Alabama	−8,332	Massachusetts	−6,538

Source: Author's analysis of 1970, 1980, 1990, and 2000 decennial censuses.

91

Black out-migration from the Northeast and Midwest and into the South continued in the late 1980s. California dropped from first to sixth among the states with the largest net gains of black migrants, surpassed by Georgia, Maryland, Florida, Virginia, and North Carolina.

By 1995–2000 the dominant black migration pattern was a full-scale reversal of the 1965–70 (and earlier) pattern. For the first time the West, as well as the Northeast and Midwest, contributed larger numbers of black migrants to the South than they received. Thus the positive contributions of black gains from the West, coupled with greater gains from the Northeast and Midwest, meant that the contribution of migration to the South's black population nearly doubled that from the late 1980s.[6]

Among states in the late 1990s California not only lost its status as one of the top black net migration gainers, but it became the second-largest loser of black migrants. At the same time Georgia far surpassed all other states in its net gain of black migrants. It and other "New South" states that now receive the most blacks (including North Carolina, Florida, Maryland, Virginia, and Tennessee) overlap only partially with the Deep South states that served as major donors of black out-migrants in the late 1960s (map 3-1).[7] These Southeastern states, as well as Texas, are locations for high-tech development, knowledge-based industries, recreation, and new urban and suburban communities. They are increasingly attractive to younger blacks as well as older "empty-nest" and retiree blacks with long-standing ties to the region.

The continued economic dynamism of the South, coupled with its improved racial climate, represents a different context for new generations of black migrants than the region their counterparts vacated in large numbers over thirty years ago.

Southern Metropolitan Areas Led the Way in Attracting Blacks

The thirty-five-year pattern of black movement back to the South also appears in an examination of the metropolitan areas that attracted—and lost—the most blacks over the 1965–2000 period.

At the metropolitan level dramatic changes in both the 1970s and 1980s characterize the reversal of the "Great Migration." The list of metropolitan areas that experienced the largest net losses of black migrants changed most abruptly between the late 1960s and late 1970s (table 3-2 and table 3A-3).

6. Although not specifically pictured in figure 3-1 net black migration from the Northeast to the South was 65,000 persons higher in 1995–2000 than in 1985–90; the comparable increase from the Midwest was 30,000.

7. It is noteworthy, however, that Alabama actually had a net gain of black migrants in the late 1990s, after experiencing the second largest net loss of blacks among the fifty states in the late 1960s (table 3A-3).

MAP 3-1. Top 10 States for Black Net Migration Gains, 1965–1970 and 1995–2000[a]

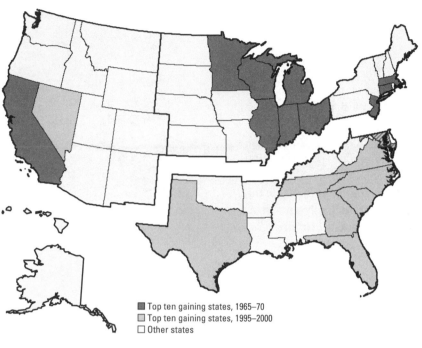

■ Top ten gaining states, 1965–70
▨ Top ten gaining states, 1995–2000
☐ Other states

Source: Author's analysis of 1970 and 2000 decennial census data.
a. Maryland was among the top ten states in both 1965–70 and 1995–2000.

With the exception of Pittsburgh, the ten largest net losses at the metropolitan level between 1965 and 1970 occurred in the South, and mostly in the Deep South areas, including three each in Alabama (Birmingham, Mobile, and Montgomery) and Louisiana (New Orleans, Lafayette, and Shreveport). In the late 1970s industrial shakeouts in the Northeast and Midwest fueled a new migration of blacks out of several metropolitan areas that were their major destinations in earlier decades. New York and Chicago led the new decliners, beginning a pattern of losses that continues to the present. In fact, only New Orleans—a metropolitan area that continues to lose black migrants today—represents the South on the "bottom ten" list in the late 1970s.

The pattern altered most radically in the late 1980s among the metropolitan areas that made the largest net gains from black migration. In the late 1970s the top destinations for blacks included three areas each in California and Texas. By the late 1980s, however, the top four gains accrued to metropolitan areas in the southeastern United States, and the large California

TABLE 3-2. Black Net Migration, Metropolitan Areas with Largest Gains and Losses, 1965–2000[a]

Largest gains

1965–70		1975–80		1985–90		1995–2000	
Los Angeles	55,943	Los Angeles	32,764	Atlanta	74,705	Atlanta	114,478
Detroit	54,766	Atlanta	27,111	Washington-Baltimore	29,904	Dallas	39,360
Washington-Baltimore	34,365	Houston	24,267	Norfolk-Virginia Beach	27,645	Charlotte	23,313
San Francisco	24,699	San Francisco	16,034	Raleigh-Durham	17,611	Orlando	20,222
Philadelphia	24,601	San Diego	15,621	Dallas	16,097	Las Vegas	18,912
New York	18,792	Dallas	12,460	Orlando	13,368	Norfolk-Virginia Beach	16,660
Dallas	16,384	Norfolk-Virginia Beach	10,141	Richmond	12,508	Raleigh-Durham	16,144
Houston	16,301	Washington-Baltimore	9,998	San Diego	12,482	Washington-Baltimore	16,139
Chicago	14,061	Killeen-Temple	9,959	Minneapolis-St. Paul	11,765	Memphis	12,507
Cleveland	10,914	Columbia	9,082	Sacramento	10,848	Columbia	10,899

Largest losses

1965–70		1975–80		1985–90		1995–2000	
Birmingham	−12,177	New York	−139,789	New York	−190,108	New York	−193,061
Memphis	−8,498	Chicago	−44,884	Chicago	−69,068	Chicago	−59,282
Mobile	−8,017	Philadelphia	−16,678	Detroit	−22,432	Los Angeles	−38,833
Pittsburgh	−5,003	Cleveland	−13,483	New Orleans	−17,395	San Francisco	−30,613
New Orleans	−4,886	St. Louis	−12,030	Los Angeles	−11,731	Detroit	−15,095
Montgomery	−4,635	Buffalo	−5,371	Cleveland	−11,553	New Orleans	−13,860
Charleston	−4,595	New Orleans	−4,889	St. Louis	−10,374	San Diego	−9,970
Jackson	−4,096	Boston	−4,576	San Francisco	−7,078	Miami	−7,772
Lafayette	−4,061	Pittsburgh	−3,022	Shreveport	−5,503	Pittsburgh	−7,425
Shreveport	−4,047	Kansas City	−2,795	Pittsburgh	−4,987	Boston	−7,018

Source: Author's analysis of 1970, 1980, 1990, and 2000 decennial censuses.

a. Metro areas are CMSAs, MSAs, and (in New England) NECMAs, as defined in Census 2000. Names are abbreviated.

metropolises of Los Angeles and San Francisco experienced black migration losses. Indeed the presence of the three non-Southern metropolitan areas among the top ten (San Diego, Minneapolis-St. Paul, and Sacramento) is explained in part by large migration flows out of their larger nearby areas (Los Angeles, Chicago, and San Francisco).

The 1995–2000 period solidified Southern metropolitan areas' dominance as magnets for black migrants while the nation's largest northern and western metropolises assumed the lead in the net out-migration of the black population. Atlanta was by far the largest migration magnet for blacks, with net migration nearly triple that of the second ranking area (Dallas). Charlotte, Memphis, and Columbia joined other Southeastern metropolitan areas on the list in the late 1990s. Only Las Vegas, catching some "spillover" from California, represented the non-South.

Meanwhile those areas witnessing the largest black net out-migration in the late 1990s reflect a familiar mix of non-Southern areas (New Orleans excepted), led by New York and Chicago. The fact that Los Angeles and San Francisco now rank third and fourth, with San Diego following close behind (seventh), underscores the changing role of California from a major black migration destination to a major migration origin.

Of the forty metropolitan areas gaining the largest number of black migrants (net) in each of four periods, only ten were located in the South in 1965–70, compared to twenty-two in 1975–80, twenty-six in 1985–90, and thirty-three in 1995–2000. A strong economic "push" from northern metropolitan areas, associated with the 1970s deindustrialization, marked the beginning of the black population's return to the South. In more recent years the increasing "pull" of economically vibrant and culturally familiar New South metropolitan areas—especially those in the Southeast—accentuated the prevailing pattern.

Blacks More Likely than Whites to Migrate to the South

The strong historical ties between blacks and the South, along with the critical mass of black professionals that reside in and around many Southern cities, are among several factors that may make black migrants from elsewhere in the United States more likely than their white counterparts to select Southern destinations.

The destinations of whites and blacks who relocated across regions in the late 1990s reveal a stronger preference among black migrants for Southern destinations. This pattern is evident for migrants leaving each region, especially the Northeast. Among black and white migrants residing in the Northeast in 1995,

85 percent of blacks headed South (as opposed to the Midwest or West), compared to only 64 percent of whites (figure 3-2). The share of black out-migrants moving to the South from the West and Midwest exceeded the comparable white out-migrant share by about 20 percentage points.

The top metropolitan destinations for migrants from outside the South from 1995–2000 also reflect this difference between whites and blacks (table 3-3). Both blacks and whites from the Northeast preferred Southern destinations, though white destinations tilted slightly toward south Florida retirement locations. In addition Los Angeles ranked among the top destinations for whites. Black and white migration patterns were even more distinct for migrants from the Midwest. The top three destinations for blacks were all in the South (Atlanta, Washington, and Dallas), whereas the top three destinations for whites were all western (Phoenix, Los Angeles, and Denver).

Among those leaving the West in the late 1990s differences among blacks and whites were more muted, as the groups shared four of the top five metropolitan destinations. Nevertheless there remained one constant across regions for black migrants: Atlanta and Washington, D.C., ranked as the top magnets. By contrast Atlanta was not among the top five destinations for whites from the Northeast, Midwest, or West. This underscores the importance of these two metropolitan areas, especially Atlanta, as premier destinations for black migrants from across the nation.

Black Migration to the South Highest among the College-Educated

Blacks migrating northward over much of the twentieth century did not score high on socioeconomic attributes. Generally South-to-North black migrants were less educated than their northern counterparts.[8] This largely reflected the "push" of eroding agricultural job prospects in the oppressive Southern racial climate, as well as heavy demand for manual labor in northern industrial states.

The new migration of blacks into the South turns this historical trend on its head. More educated blacks are now migrating to Southern destinations at higher rates than those with lower education levels. Figure 3-3 reflects this pattern, showing net rates of black migration per 1,000 black adult residents at each education level.[9] The rates are positive for every level of education,

8. Tolnay (1998).

9. For example, about 1.5 million black adult (age 25 and over) college graduates lived in the South in 2000. Between 1995 and 2000, a little over 90,000 black college graduates migrated into the South (61.4 for every 1,000), whereas about 55,000 black college graduates migrated out of the South (37.5 for every 1,000). Therefore net migration for black college graduates into the South was roughly 35,000 out of 1.5 million, or 23.9 per 1,000 (61.4 minus 37.5).

F I G U R E 3 - 2 . Regional Destinations for Out-Migrants, Blacks versus Whites, 1995–2000

From Northeast

Percentage selecting destination region

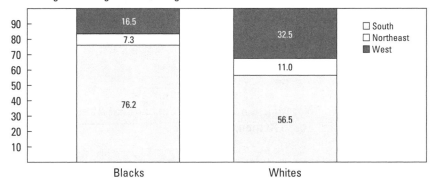

From Midwest

Percentage selecting destination region

From West

Percentage selecting destination region

Source: Author's analysis of Census 2000 data.

TABLE 3-3. Top Metropolitan Destinations, Black and White Migrants from Non-South Regions, 1995–2000[a]

Destination	Blacks	Destination	Whites
From Northeast region			
Washington-Baltimore	40,654	Washington-Baltimore	157,987
Atlanta	39,146	Miami	93,087
Miami	21,651	Tampa-St. Petersburg	89,385
Norfolk-Virginia Beach	19,188	Los Angeles	74,645
Orlando	11,402	West Palm Beach	71,066
From Midwest region			
Atlanta	30,853	Phoenix	124,203
Washington-Baltimore	12,444	Los Angeles	82,261
Dallas	9,891	Denver	76,846
Los Angeles	9,279	Dallas	74,240
Memphis	8,799	New York	70,025
From West region			
Atlanta	16,832	New York	89,323
Washington-Baltimore	13,663	Washington-Baltimore	88,570
Dallas	9,600	Dallas	83,882
Chicago	8,280	Chicago	68,387
New York	8,037	Boston	48,493

Source: Author's analysis of Census 2000 data.

a. Metro areas are CMSAs, MSAs, and (in New England) NECMAs, as defined in Census 2000. Names are abbreviated.

FIGURE 3-3. Net Migration Rates, by Educational Attainment, Blacks and Whites, South Region, 1995–2000

Per 1,000 population

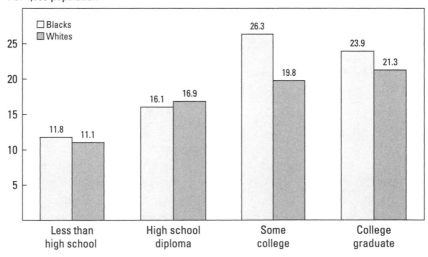

Source: Author's analysis of Census 2000 data.

TABLE 3-4. Top "Brain Gain" and "Brain Drain" States, Blacks and Whites, 1995–2000

State	Blacks	State	Whites
Largest net in-migration of college graduates			
Georgia	20,297	Florida	133,721
Texas	11,609	Arizona	69,159
Maryland	11,468	North Carolina	59,224
Florida	5,976	Colorado	51,847
North Carolina	4,016	Georgia	44,755
Tennessee	2,466	California	36,145
Arizona	2,420	Texas	36,102
Nevada	1,848	Washington	32,251
Virginia	1,018	Nevada	28,636
Delaware	888	Oregon	23,099
Largest net out-migration of college graduates			
New York	−18,573	New York	−134,103
Louisiana	−6,608	Illinois	−60,847
District of Columbia	−5,601	Pennsylvania	−55,093
Pennsylvania	−4,040	Ohio	−36,575
Alabama	−3,019	Michigan	−29,510
Mississippi	−2,947	Indiana	−28,496
Ohio	−2,875	Iowa	−25,094
Massachusetts	−2,389	New Jersey	−20,763
California	−2,173	Louisiana	−20,255
Oklahoma	−1,669	Utah	−15,143

Source: Author's analysis of Census 2000 data.

indicating that the South gained both less-educated and more-educated blacks through migration in the late 1990s. The net rates are highest for those with college degrees and those with at least some college. Thus black migration to the South over this period tended to raise the overall educational attainment level of Southern blacks.

This selective migration of "the best and the brightest" is consistent with conventional wisdom on interregional and interstate migrant flow across a national job market.[10] The pattern is mirrored in white migration to the South during the same period. As with the black population the South gained whites at all education levels, although net gains were larger for higher-educated whites.

State-level analysis provides a broader picture of "brain gain" and "brain drain" patterns for college graduate blacks. Table 3-4 shows net migration gains and losses for adult college graduates by state over the 1995–2000 period. Only sixteen states show net gains for black college graduates. Georgia, Texas, and Maryland lead all others, and four other Southeastern states rank among the top ten recipients. Arizona and Nevada, drawing some gains from

10. Long (1988).

California's out-flow, stand out as two migrant gainers in the West. The remaining states experiencing in-migration of blacks with college degrees attracted relatively small numbers of these individuals.

The major black "brain gain" states are distinct from those gaining the most white college graduates. Although Southern states such as Florida, North Carolina, Georgia, and Texas are among the largest white gainers, the top ten list also includes six Western states. Thus the South appears in comparison to exert a stronger "pull" on highly educated blacks than it does on their white counterparts.

Among the states that sustained the largest net losses of college graduate migrants, three ranked among the top ten for both blacks and whites: New York, Pennsylvania, and Ohio. What distinguished black "brain drain" states was the presence of economically stagnant Southern states (Louisiana, Alabama, Mississippi) that still contain large black populations. White "brain drain" states, by contrast, are located primarily in the Northeast and Midwest. Without these significant outflows of educated blacks from Deep South states, migration patterns would have increased black education levels in the region by an even greater degree. Nevertheless the recent trend represents a dramatic departure from that prevailing a few decades ago and contributed to the rise of a growing middle-class black population in Southern metropolitan areas.

California Reverses from Black "Magnet" to "Donor"

The reversal of the "Great Migration" did not occur solely across the Mason-Dixon Line. As shown earlier, California led all states in its net gains of black migrants in 1965–70 and 1975–80. Even in the late 1980s the state ranked sixth on this measure. During 1995–2000, however, California ranked second in the nation for black domestic migration losses. In part this can be attributed to California's declining economy over the course of the 1990s. The state's most severe economic decline, however, occurred during the early part of the decade, rather than the later period for which the census records migration data.[11]

California's in- and out-migration patterns for blacks over the last thirty-five years reflect a near mirror image of those in the South. In other words fewer blacks migrated to California from other states with each successive decade, especially in the late 1990s, as the number of blacks leaving California increased (figure 3-4). As a result the small black net in-migration occurring in the late 1980s gave way to a noticeable black migration loss in the late 1990s.

11. Kotkin (1997).

FIGURE 3-4. Black Migration Rates, California, 1965–2000

Per 1,000 population

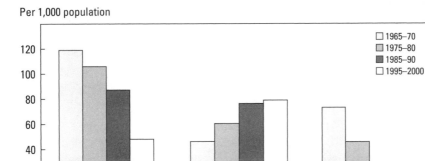

Source: Author's analysis of 1970, 1980, 1990, and 2000 decennial censuses.

Reviewing the particular origins and destinations of black migrants into and out of California helps illuminate how the state became an exporter of blacks over time. In each of the last four census periods, Texas ranked either first or second as an origin of in-migrants to California, and it was also the most popular destination of blacks migrating out of California (table 3-5). Louisiana shares a similar relationship with California, although it is not quite as consistent. Thus whether California gained or lost blacks in its exchanges with Texas and Louisiana bore heavily on its overall migration exchange with the rest of the United States. California lost more blacks to both states through migration in the late 1990s than it gained after three periods in which it experienced a net gain of black migrants from these two states.

The destination states for blacks migrating out of California have changed more markedly over time than have the origin states for blacks moving to California. Northern states—especially New York and Illinois—have long served as major feeders, with thousands of black residents of New York City and Chicago moving westward in each of the past four decades. Indeed, in 1995–2000, Texas, Illinois, and New York were still among the top origin states for black migrants to California. In the late 1960s and the late 1970s migrants from California—like in-migrants—were prone to select Texas and Louisiana, as well as Illinois, as part of the back-and-forth exchanges between these states. In the late 1980s, however, Georgia and Florida rapidly climbed

TABLE 3-5. Black Migration Exchange between California and Other States, 1965–2000

1965–70		1975–80		1985–90		1995–2000	
In-migration from							
Texas	19,193	New York	16,804	Texas	19,146	Texas	9,181
Louisiana	18,213	Texas	15,323	Louisiana	13,644	New York	6,743
Illinois	9,562	Illinois	14,344	New York	13,524	Illinois	5,913
Alabama	8,019	Louisiana	11,508	Illinois	13,376	Louisiana	5,529
Mississippi	7,804	Ohio	10,619	Michigan	7,529	Georgia	5,254
New York	7,536	Michigan	8,434	Ohio	7,301	Florida	4,259
Arkansas	6,034	Missouri	6,329	Florida	6,624	Washington	4,167
Ohio	5,593	Pennsylvania	6,217	Georgia	5,982	Arizona	3,850
Missouri	4,738	Alabama	5,831	Mississippi	5,192	Virginia	3,752
Michigan	4,658	New Jersey	5,447	Virginia	4,567	Nevada	3,446
Out-migration to							
Texas	8,153	Texas	14,804	Texas	15,874	Texas	17,590
Michigan	3,791	Louisiana	8,607	Georgia	7,974	Georgia	14,060
Louisiana	3,327	Washington	5,437	Florida	7,354	Nevada	13,704
Washington	2,746	Illinois	3,826	Illinois	6,915	Florida	8,371
Illinois	2,744	Georgia	3,746	Louisiana	6,719	Virginia	8,051
New York	2,617	Michigan	3,639	Nevada	6,646	Louisiana	7,882
Ohio	2,054	Florida	3,612	Virginia	6,626	Washington	6,816
Missouri	1,769	New York	3,363	New York	6,473	Arizona	6,135
Virginia	1,752	Virginia	3,302	Washington	6,451	North Carolina	5,123
Florida	1,749	Oklahoma	2,977	Ohio	5,674	Illinois	5,026

Source: Author's analysis of 1970, 1980, 1990, and 2000 decennial censuses.

the list to become the second- and third-most prominent destinations. By the late 1990s three of the top five destinations were Southeastern states, and the fourth was California's neighbor, Nevada.

In fact the increased flow of blacks from California to the South largely accounts for the West's transition from an "importer" to an "exporter" of blacks to the South over 1995–2000. California alone contributed 73 percent of the South's net migration gain of blacks from the West in the late 1990s.

Other states in the West have also begun to gain black population from California. In recent decades, substantial shares of California's white out-migrants located in surrounding states such as Nevada, Arizona, Oregon, and Washington. In fact some analysts have proposed that California's migration streams are part of two "migration systems": a nationwide exchange of high-skilled labor between all states and a "spillover" migration to neighboring Western states with more middle- and lower-level socioeconomic attributes.[12] The spillover migration reflects, in part, a movement away from the high cost of living in California metropolitan areas toward more affordable, less congested communities in nearby states. This out-migration pattern

12. Frey (1994); Frey (1999).

MAP 3-2. **California's Black Migration Exchange with Other States,
1995–2000**

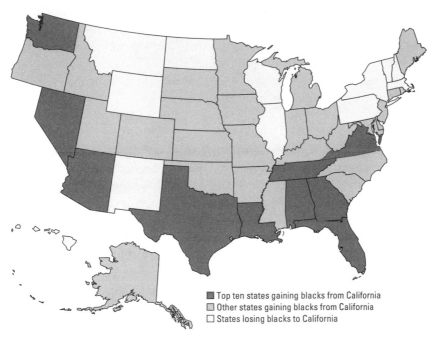

■ Top ten states gaining blacks from California
▨ Other states gaining blacks from California
☐ States losing blacks to California

Source: Author's analysis of Census 2000 data.

largely accounted for California's statewide loss of domestic migrants in the
late 1990s.[13]

California's blacks have joined in this "spillover" migration to surrounding states on a somewhat smaller scale. The state has lost black migrants (net)
in its exchange with Washington and Oregon since the late 1960s. The pattern expanded to include Nevada in the late 1970s, and Arizona in the late
1980s, even as California gained blacks (net) from other parts of the country.
As with California's out-migrants in general blacks moving to nearby states
in the late 1990s tended to have lower education levels than the black population at large.[14]

Overall California lost blacks in its migration exchange with 38 other
states between 1995 and 2000 (map 3-2). The states receiving the greatest
numbers of California's blacks included fast-growing Southeastern states

13. Associated Press, "Census Finds More Americans Flee than Find California Dream,"
New York Times, August 6, 2003, p. A12; Tilove (2003).
14. See Frey, chapter 1, this volume.

(such as Georgia, Virginia, and Florida), as well as traditional Southern destinations like Texas and Louisiana. The data also confirm a "spillover" of black out-migrants to nearby states in the West (Nevada, Washington, Arizona). The geographic breadth of this out-migration, and the long-term trend it culminates, suggest that California's net loss of blacks in the late 1990s reflects more than a symptom of the state's contemporary economic woes. It remains to be seen whether California will re-emerge as a major migration magnet for blacks in the future.

CONCLUSION

This analysis of Census 2000 migration data documents the full-scale reversal of black Americans' migration out of the South—a movement that dominated the better part of the twentieth century. Moreover the latest census is the first to show that the South experienced a net migration gain of blacks from the other three regions of the country. Overall the South's gains over 1995 2000 roughly doubled those recorded in the 1990 census, and tripled those recorded in the 1980 census.

Both economic and cultural factors help account for this long-term reversal of the Great Migration. The economic ascendancy of Southeastern states such as Georgia, Florida, Virginia, and the Carolinas made them primary destinations for black migrants to the region in recent decades. Texas also stands out for its continued appeal to black migrants. Improvements in the racial climate in these states over the past three decades helped create momentum for the return south, as many black Americans sought to strengthen ties to kin and to communities from which they and their forbears departed long ago. On their return south, however, blacks largely are not settling in the Deep South states that registered the greatest out-migration of blacks in the late 1960s. Atlanta, for instance, was by far the premier nationwide destination for blacks in the late 1990s.

The chapter also finds that when they relocate from the Northeast, Midwest, and West, blacks—particularly those with higher levels of education—are more likely than whites to head to the South. The black population's participation in an increasingly nationwide labor market, and its preference for Southern destinations, have fueled rising incomes and a growing black middle class and upper-middle class in several of the region's fast-growing metropolitan areas.[15] In turn these communities may be helping to attract

15. Frey (2003).

other educated black migrants who seek to draw on their emerging professional networks.

This cycle of black migration to the South has, however, drawn strength from the places blacks left in the greatest numbers. The Northeast and Midwest—particularly the New York and Chicago metropolises—lost increasing numbers of blacks to the South over the past three decades. By the late 1990s the West had been transformed from a receiver to a sender of black migrants to the South. As with large Northeast and Midwest states, such as New York and Illinois, California represented the West region's major destination for blacks leaving the South during the mid-twentieth century. California remained, on net, a destination for blacks even as Northern states started to lose black migrants in the 1970s and 1980s. In the most recent census, however, a plurality of blacks leaving California located in Southern states, at the same time that many black out-migrants followed other populations that "spilled out" into neighboring Western states. These trends confirm that a broad-based set of states and metropolitan areas have seen their more mobile, often more educated, black populations leave for the growing South.

With its demographic and geographic breadth, combined with the strong cultural and economic ties that the South holds for blacks, the "New Great Migration" has all the signs of a continuing trend. Although we have yet to fully appreciate its implications on economic, political, and race relations fronts, future research should examine the importance of this development not only for the South but also for the places that black Americans are leaving behind.

TABLE 3A-1. Black Migration, by Region, 1965–2000

Period	Northeast	Midwest	South	West
		In-migration		
1965–70	195,860	263,388	205,661	183,281
1975–80	117,224	190,038	439,367	236,560
1985–90	163,372	199,687	560,775	243,069
1995–2000	136,780	212,076	680,131	171,309
		Out-migration		
1965–70	137,086	136,373	493,101	81,630
1975–80	287,590	237,608	330,489	127,502
1985–90	326,586	266,502	380,800	193,015
1995–2000	369,665	276,090	333,585	220,956
		Net migration		
1965–70	58,774	127,015	−287,440	101,651
1975–80	−170,366	−47,570	108,878	109,058
1985–90	−163,214	−66,815	179,975	50,054
1995–2000	−232,885	−64,014	346,546	−49,647

Source: Author's analysis of 1970, 1980, 1990, and 2000 decennial censuses.

TABLE 3A-2. Black Net Migration, by State, 1965–2000

State	2000 black population	Percent of total population	Black net migration 1965–70	Black net migration 1975–80	Black net migration 1985–90	Black net migration 1995–2000
Alabama	1,155,930	26.0	−61,507	−7,843	−8,332	6,846
Alaska	21,787	3.5	60	653	405	−3,072
Arizona	158,873	3.1	246	2,239	9,211	8,909
Arkansas	418,950	15.7	−27,594	−9,236	−8,931	−2,192
California	2,263,882	6.7	91,425	75,746	21,636	−63,180
Colorado	165,063	3.8	5,593	8,861	2,084	−1,217
Connecticut	309,843	9.1	9,845	−3,012	−329	−5,810
Delaware	150,666	19.2	2,354	1,769	4,107	9,074
District of Columbia	343,312	60.0	−15,390	−58,454	−43,727	−34,118
Florida	2,335,505	14.6	−6,404	15,900	57,009	51,286
Georgia	2,349,542	28.7	−23,363	29,616	80,827	129,749
Hawaii	22,003	1.8	−724	2,874	−314	−7,203
Idaho	5,456	0.4	−87	355	405	−651
Illinois	1,876,875	15.1	16,857	−37,220	−60,120	−55,238
Indiana	510,034	8.4	10,356	−2,040	−1,007	6,192
Iowa	61,853	2.1	352	2,530	−264	−599
Kansas	154,198	5.7	454	4,215	1,093	−5,056
Kentucky	295,994	7.3	−5,556	5,550	−3,648	2,614
Louisiana	1,451,944	32.5	−37,067	−5,315	−46,053	−18,074
Maine	6,760	0.5	−516	−809	315	−861
Maryland	1,477,411	27.9	44,054	54,793	59,966	43,549
Massachusetts	343,454	5.4	8,125	−5,766	2,43	−6,538
Michigan	1,412,742	14.2	63,839	3,592	−14,600	−16,449
Minnesota	171,731	3.5	2,755	1,988	12,525	9,118
Mississippi	1,033,809	36.3	−66,614	−20,106	−19,522	−2,691
Missouri	629,391	11.2	1,572	−10,428	−3,362	2,334
Montana	2,692	0.3	−500	−572	−505	−435
Nebraska	68,541	4.0	−108	−221	−557	−414
Nevada	135,477	6.8	430	5,211	10,143	19,446
New Hampshire	9,035	0.7	−162	127	596	−696
New Jersey	1,141,821	13.6	28,642	−6,462	−10,084	−34,682
New Mexico	34,343	1.9	−1,256	−349	−1,287	−2,724
New York	3,014,385	15.9	5,250	−128,143	−150,695	−165,366
North Carolina	1,737,545	21.6	−29,732	14,456	39,015	53,371
North Dakota	3,916	0.6	−312	−493	−779	−726
Ohio	1,301,307	11.5	22,518	−16,503	−7,040	−2,313
Oklahoma	260,968	7.6	−1,497	7,192	−2,693	−317
Oregon	55,662	1.6	1,950	2,058	1,643	146
Pennsylvania	1,224,612	10.0	6,412	−25,849	−11,046	−18,024
Rhode Island	46,908	4.5	1,331	−411	970	111
South Carolina	1,185,216	29.5	−26,884	9,238	5,342	16,253
South Dakota	4,685	0.6	−192	46	−223	−554
Tennessee	932,809	16.4	−17,703	4,436	11,297	19,343
Texas	2,404,566	11.5	4,663	47,685	8,921	42,312
Utah	17,657	0.8	1,041	1,667	514	497
Vermont	3,063	0.5	−153	−41	363	−1,019
Virginia	1,390,293	19.6	−11,586	22,295	53,873	29,149
Washington	190,267	3.2	3,930	10,216	6,780	862
West Virginia	57,232	3.2	−7,614	−3,098	−3,152	392
Wisconsin	304,460	5.7	8,924	6,964	7,456	−309
Wyoming	3,722	0.8	−457	99	−661	−1,025

Source: Author's analysis of 1970, 1980, 1990, and 2000 decennial censuses.

TABLE 3A-3. Black Net Migration for Metropolitan Areas with Black Population over 50,000 in 2000, 1965–2000

Metropolitan area	2000 black population	Percent of total population	Black net migration			
			1965–70	1975–80	1985–90	1995–2000
New York–Northern New Jersey–Long Island, NY-NJ-CT-PA CMSA	3,637,778	17.2	18,792	−139,789	−190,108	−193,061
Washington-Baltimore, DC-MD-VA-WV CMSA	1,992,266	26.2	34,365	9,998	29,904	16,139
Chicago-Gary-Kenosha, IL-IN-WI CMSA	1,707,618	18.6	14,061	−44,884	−69,068	−59,282
Los Angeles-Riverside-Orange County, CA CMSA	1,245,039	7.6	55,943	32,764	−11,731	−38,833
Philadelphia-Wilmington-Atlantic City, PA-NJ-DE-MD CMSA	1,210,846	19.6	24,601	−16,678	−617	−5,479
Atlanta, GA MSA	1,189,179	28.9	10,135	27,111	74,705	114,478
Detroit-Ann Arbor-Flint, MI CMSA	1,149,331	21.1	54,766	−989	−22,432	−15,095
Miami-Fort Lauderdale, FL CMSA	790,518	20.4	4,984	6,106	10,401	−7,772
Houston-Galveston-Brazoria, TX CMSA	789,489	16.9	16,301	24,267	−4,661	9,633
Dallas-Fort Worth, TX CMSA	720,133	13.8	16,384	12,460	16,097	39,360
San Francisco-Oakland-San Jose, CA CMSA	513,561	7.3	24,699	16,034	−7,078	−30,613
New Orleans, LA MSA	502,251	37.5	−4,886	−4,889	−17,395	−13,860
Cleveland-Akron, OH CMSA	493,492	16.8	10,914	−13,483	−11,553	−6,948
Memphis, TN-AR-MS MSA	492,531	43.4	−8,498	−785	2,931	12,507
Norfolk-Virginia Beach-Newport News, VA-NC MSA	485,368	30.9	−1,333	10,141	27,645	16,660
St. Louis, MO-IL MSA	476,716	18.3	3,222	−12,030	−10,374	−2,481
Charlotte-Gastonia-Rock Hill, NC-SC MSA	307,886	20.5	121	2,725	7,497	23,313
Boston-Worcester-Lawrence-Lowell-Brockton, MA-NH NECMA	302,331	5.0	5,419	−4,576	2,235	−7,018
Richmond-Petersburg, VA MSA	300,457	30.2	3,643	8,110	12,508	8,355
Birmingham, AL MSA	277,083	30.1	−12,177	−1,158	−763	3,198
Raleigh-Durham-Chapel Hill, NC MSA	269,932	22.7	−1,100	5,774	17,611	16,144
Milwaukee-Racine, WI CMSA	254,810	15.1	8,389	5,528	4,305	−1,021
Greensboro–Winston-Salem–High Point, NC MSA	252,688	20.2	1,392	5,120	8,820	9,120
Tampa-St. Petersburg-Clearwater, FL MSA	244,457	10.2	2,350	1,788	1,807	6,965
Jacksonville, FL MSA	238,428	21.7	−2,647	−50	5,573	8,744
Cincinnati-Hamilton, OH-KY-IN CMSA	231,006	11.7	599	546	771	178
Orlando, FL MSA	227,868	13.9	−67	4,491	13,368	20,222
Kansas City, MO-KS MSA	226,503	12.8	3,529	−2,795	−963	−760
Indianapolis, IN MSA	223,974	13.9	5,072	2,373	3,538	7,889
Columbus, OH MSA	206,136	13.4	4,234	2,003	8,343	10,159
Jackson, MS MSA	201,027	45.6	−4,096	3,000	1,923	3,659
Baton Rouge, LA MSA	192,605	31.9	−1,871	3,960	−937	4,640
Nashville, TN MSA	191,876	15.6	965	2,954	6,476	6,048
Pittsburgh, PA MSA	190,511	8.1	−5,003	−3,022	−4,987	−7,425
Columbia, SC MSA	172,083	32.1	2,622	9,082	9,149	10,899

(continued)

107

TABLE 3A-3. Black Net Migration for Metropolitan Areas with Black Population over 50,000 in 2000, 1965–2000 (continued)

Metropolitan area	2000 black population	Percent of total population	Black net migration			
			1965–70	1975–80	1985–90	1995–2000
Charleston-North Charleston, SC MSA	169,079	30.8	-4,595	2,764	841	-674
Greenville-Spartanburg-Anderson, SC MSA	168,081	11.5	-3,032	203	1,394	2,409
Seattle-Tacoma-Bremerton, WA CMSA	165,938	4.7	4,131	8,925	6,411	821
Augusta-Aiken, GA-SC MSA	164,019	34.4	-467	6,250	4,123	1,732
San Diego, CA MSA	161,480	5.7	5,717	15,621	12,482	-9,970
Minneapolis-St. Paul, MN-WI MSA	157,963	5.3	2,861	2,807	11,765	7,585
West Palm Beach-Boca Raton, FL MSA	156,055	13.8	171	167	2,507	2,785
Mobile, AL MSA	147,909	27.4	-8,017	-809	-4,335	-823
Shreveport-Bossier City, LA MSA	146,686	37.4	-4,047	-818	-5,503	-1,921
Louisville, KY-IN MSA	142,760	13.9	1,303	-130	-2,425	1,358
Buffalo-Niagara Falls, NY MSA	137,049	11.7	1,692	-5,371	-844	-3,242
Dayton-Springfield, OH MSA	135,330	14.2	4,065	-752	-1,291	-1,834
Montgomery, AL MSA	129,653	38.9	-4,635	2,240	2,973	7,179
Sacramento-Yolo, CA CMSA	128,073	7.1	3,894	5,567	10,848	7,601
Little Rock-North Little Rock, AR MSA	127,737	21.9	-1,468	2,153	-453	3,937
Las Vegas, NV-AZ MSA	126,101	8.1	872	4,714	8,372	18,912
Macon, GA MSA	121,107	37.5	-1,826	196	367	2,833
Denver-Boulder-Greeley, CO CMSA	119,829	4.6	2,681	5,940	157	-170
Phoenix-Mesa, AZ MSA	119,509	3.7	996	2,197	7,414	10,895
Oklahoma City, OK MSA	114,351	10.6	-222	3,022	-984	1,367
Rochester, NY MSA	112,642	10.3	5,305	-107	-813	-3,440
Columbus, GA-AL MSA	110,874	40.4	-1,768	4,668	107	1,273

Hartford, CT NECMA	110,500	9.6	3,455	56	1,412	-1,245
Lafayette, LA MSA	108,573	28.2	-4,061	-368	-4,012	-1,258
Fayetteville, NC MSA	105,731	34.9	3,883	7,053	3,574	-1,342
San Antonio, TX MSA	105,618	6.6	1,288	1,285	-391	-2,237
Savannah, GA MSA	102,158	34.9	-1,357	1,545	1,618	-1,480
Austin-San Marcos, TX MSA	99,432	8.0	1,493	4,361	4,067	3,777
Beaumont-Port Arthur, TX MSA	95,494	24.8	-2,515	252	-2,601	1,009
Tallahassee, FL MSA	95,467	33.6	-1,432	3,904	4,423	6,519
Grand Rapids-Muskegon-Holland, MI MSA	79,335	7.3	1,886	719	2,345	1,507
Toledo, OH MSA	78,911	12.8	1,862	-786	-1,479	0
Huntsville, AL MSA	71,777	21.0	71	1,918	2,876	3,925
Tulsa, OK MSA	70,867	8.8	286	2,102	121	649
Biloxi-Gulfport-Pascagoula, MS MSA	70,350	19.3	-771	1,478	-1,338	51
Pensacola, FL MSA	68,010	16.5	-1,460	-1,636	1,380	1,141
Chattanooga, TN-GA MSA	66,229	14.2	-2,190	-1,280	-338	-526
Lakeland-Winter Haven, FL MSA	65,545	13.5	-939	231	1,182	1,206
Killeen-Temple, TX MSA	64,968	20.8	2,481	9,959	5,913	-791
Rocky Mount, NC MSA	61,613	43.1	-3,145	-1,368	-680	-876
Albany, GA MSA	61,600	51.0	-611	1,526	1,076	1,568
Youngstown-Warren, OH MSA	61,130	10.3	649	-2,151	-3,132	-846
Omaha, NE-IA MSA	59,447	8.3	642	-557	-1,333	-575
Portland-Salem, OR-WA CMSA	54,227	2.4	2,062	1,872	1,938	1,365
Albany-Schenectady-Troy, NY MSA	53,424	6.1	-256	-138	1,696	-458

Source: Author's analysis of 1970, 1980, 1990, and 2000 decennial censuses.

REFERENCES

Frey, William H. 1994. "Immigration and Internal Migration: 1990 Census Findings for California." Research Report 94–306. Ann Arbor: University of Michigan Population Studies Center.

———. 1999. "New Black Migration Patterns in the United States: Are They Affected by Recent Immigration?" In *Immigration and Opportunity: Race, Ethnicity, and Employment in the United States,* edited by Frank D. Bean and Stephanie Bell-Rose. New York: Russell Sage Foundation.

———. 2003. "Revival." *American Demographics.* October, pp. 27–31.

Frey, William H., and Alden Speare Jr. 1988. *Regional and Metropolitan Growth and Decline in the United States.* New York: Russell Sage Foundation.

Hamilton, C. Horace. 1964. "The Negro Leaves the South." *Demography* 1: 273–95.

Kotkin, Joel. 1997. *California: A Twenty-First Century Prospectus.* Denver, Colo.: Center for the New West.

Lemann, Nicholas. 1991. *The Promised Land: The Great Migration and How It Changed America.* New York: Knopf.

Long, Larry. 1988. *Migration and Residential Mobility in the United States.* New York: Russell Sage Foundation.

Tilove, Jonathan. 2003. "Migration Patterns Point to a Nation of Three Americas," Newhouse News Service.

Tolnay, Stewart E. 1998. "Educational Selection in the Migration of Southern Blacks, 1880–1990." *Social Forces* 77 (2): 489–514.

U.S. Census Bureau. 2003. *2000 Census of Population in Housing, Public Use Microdata Sample, United States: Technical Documentation.* Washington.

A Decade of Mixed Blessings

Urban and Suburban Poverty in Census 2000

4

ALAN BERUBE AND WILLIAM H. FREY

The 1990s was a decade of unprecedented economic growth in the United States. Real GDP grew at a blistering 4.3 percent annual pace from 1992 to 2000. The unemployment rate at the time of Census 2000 was 3.9 percent, the lowest in a generation. In the late 1990s the strong economy helped move millions of individuals from welfare to work, and lifted employment and earnings among such traditionally disadvantaged groups as high school dropouts.[1]

The percentage of people living below the federal poverty line declined from 13.1 percent to 12.4 percent between 1990 and 2000. Although the trend was positive it was a surprisingly small change in light of the nearly decade-long economic expansion.[2] Nevertheless the aggregate national trend obscured important variations in poverty changes across U.S. regions, metropolitan areas, cities, and suburbs.

This chapter examines data from Census 2000 on poverty for the nation's largest cities and their suburbs. It concludes that the outcomes were decidedly mixed in a decade widely regarded as one of the nation's most prosperous. Overall central-city and suburban poverty converged slowly, and half of central cities saw their poverty rates decline. Some of the largest decreases

The authors are grateful to senior project programmer Cathy Sun and other support staff at the University of Michigan Population Studies Center, to Mark Muro for editorial assistance, and to other staff at the Brookings urban center for their advice and contributions.

1. Blank (2002).

2. See Peter T. Kilborn and Lynette Clemenson, "Gains of '90s Did Not Lift All, Census Shows," *New York Times,* June 5, 2002, p. A1, and Cindy Rodriguez and Bill Dedman, "Welfare Plunged in '90s while Poverty Persisted," *Boston Globe,* June 5, 2002, p. A1.

occurred in cities that had very high poverty rates initially. The overall metropolitan poverty rate, however, was unchanged in the 1990s. By decade's end there were 2.5 million more people living in poverty in the nation's largest metropolitan areas than in 1990.

The slight overall poverty decline in the 1990s camouflaged sharper increases and decreases in certain parts of the nation. The region of the country in which a particular city or suburb was located appeared to be the best predictor of its poverty rate trend in the 1990s; rates dropped markedly in cities throughout the Midwest and South, whereas cities and suburbs in southern California and the Northeast experienced increases. The chapter also presents evidence that population change was not a good predictor of poverty change in the last decade—many cities that lost considerable population in the 1990s saw declines in their poverty rates.

METHODOLOGY

First, we describe the geographic areas considered in this chapter and how the census determines poverty status for families and individuals.

Metropolitan Area Definitions

This chapter evaluates poverty trends during the 1990s for the country's 102 largest metropolitan areas—those metropolitan areas with 500,000 or more inhabitants as reported in Census 2000. The metropolitan areas analyzed are those defined by the Office of Management and Budget (OMB) as Metropolitan Statistical Areas (MSAs) and Primary Metropolitan Statistical Areas (PMSAs), and defined in the New England states as New England County Metropolitan Areas (NECMAs).

Definition of Central City and Suburbs

The present analysis defines central cities and their suburbs (the portion of the metropolitan area located outside of the central city) largely in accordance with OMB definitions in effect for Census 2000. These definitions are applied consistently to both 1990 and 2000 census data. OMB standards sometimes combine multiple cities to form the official "central city" for a given metropolitan area.[3] These standards were modified slightly for pur-

---

3. The OMB designates the city with the largest population in each metropolitan area as a central city. Additional cities qualify for this designation if specified requirements are met concerning population size, commuting patterns, and employment/residence ratios. These standards, implemented after the 1990 Census, can be viewed at www.census.gov/population/www/estimates/mastand.html.

poses of this analysis, in that the largest or best-known city/cities in most large metropolitan areas have been designated as the "central city." Places listed in the official OMB metropolitan area name are generally treated as central cities. In the "Detroit, Michigan, PMSA," for example, OMB recognizes the cities of Detroit, Dearborn, Pontiac, and Port Huron as the combined "central city." This analysis includes only Detroit as the "central city," and the remainder of the Detroit PMSA is treated as suburbs. The official definition of "central city" has been modified in this manner for 56 of the 102 metropolitan areas in this study, identifying a total of 137 central cities in these metropolitan areas.[4]

Poverty Rates

The individual poverty rate is defined as the share of all family members and unrelated individuals in a particular place with incomes below the federal poverty threshold. Thresholds vary by family unit size, number of related children present, and the age of the householder. In 1999, the year for which income information was collected on the Census 2000 long form, the poverty threshold for a parent with one child under 18 years old was $11,483. For four people, including two children, the threshold was $16,895.[5]

The Census Bureau does not collect income information, nor make poverty calculations, for all persons. Institutionalized people, people in military group quarters, people living in college dormitories, and children under fifteen years old not living with relatives are excluded from the poverty rates presented here. The term "population," as used in this chapter, connotes those persons for whom poverty status is determined.

One other note: The poverty rate, although often used to assess the economic fortunes of a particular place, remains an admittedly imperfect tool for measuring the level of need among different urban populations. Although costs of living vary dramatically from place to place, poverty rates

4. We have excluded some officially designated central cities (in metropolitan areas with multiple central cities) to (1) include only central cities that are named in the metropolitan area name (thus omitting officially designated smaller cities that were not named); (2) include only one central city in the following multiple central-city metropolitan areas: Austin, TX; Buffalo, NY; Charlotte, NC; Cleveland, OH; Milwaukee, WI; Richmond, VA; Wilmington, DE; and Seattle, WA; and (3) designate only two central cities in the following metropolitan areas: Raleigh-Durham, NC; Allentown-Bethlehem, PA; and Scranton-Hazleton, PA. In four metropolitan areas in the greater New York area, no central city is named in the metropolitan area name, so these metropolitan areas are considered suburban. In the Orange County, CA, PMSA, Anaheim, Santa Ana, and Irvine are treated as central cities.

5. Poverty rates do not factor in the value of taxes and cash/in-kind government transfers, such as Food Stamps, subsidized health insurance, and the Earned Income Tax Credit.

are determined by a single set of thresholds that do not incorporate geographic differences.[6] Boston, Massachusetts, and Greenville, South Carolina, for instance, had the same 19.5 percent poverty rate in 2000, but the HUD Fair Market Rent for a two-bedroom apartment in 2001 was $539 in the Greenville area, and $979 in the Boston area.[7] The first part of this survey examines where poverty was highest and lowest in 2000, and thus does not control for the impact of these cost-of-living differences. The bulk of the analysis, however, focuses on how changes in poverty rates over the decade differed from place to place.[8]

FINDINGS

Census 2000 confirms that cities still exhibit higher poverty than their suburbs, but that broader regional economic dynamics left overall metropolitan poverty unchanged over the 1990s.

Central City Poverty Rate More than Double Suburban Rate

Census 2000 reveals that across the nation's largest metropolitan areas considerable disparities persist between cities and their suburbs in the percentage of individuals living in poverty. In central cities within the 102 largest metropolitan areas, nearly one in five individuals (18.4 percent) had incomes below the poverty level in 2000. In contrast, in the suburbs of these metropolitan areas only one in twelve (8.3 percent) people did. Overall the proportion of people living below poverty in cities was more than twice as high as in suburbs in 2000.

The disparity in the city-suburb poverty rate varied greatly among metropolitan areas, however, and strong regional patterns were evident (figure 4-1). In the Northeast and Midwest poverty rates in cities were more than triple those in the suburbs. In the South and West the gap between cities and suburbs was much smaller—central city poverty rates were less than twice suburban rates.

---

6. In 1995 a panel from the National Academy of Sciences issued a report that recommended recalculating the poverty thresholds to reflect differences in need by family size and geography, and to reflect changes in consumption patterns, household composition, and labor force patterns since poverty thresholds were first developed thirty years ago. See National Academy of Sciences (1996).

7. 186 *Federal Register* Vol. 66 (January 2, 2001).

8. For purposes of associating them with their corresponding decennial censuses, we refer to "1990" and "2000" poverty rates throughout this survey, though the income figures on which the rates are based are for the 1989 and 1999 calendar years. Where the poverty rate changed within +/−0.2 percentage points, we consider it to have been "stable" over the period.

FIGURE 4-1. Poverty Rates for Central Cities and Suburbs, 2000, Metro Areas with Population over 500,0000

Percentage of individuals in poverty

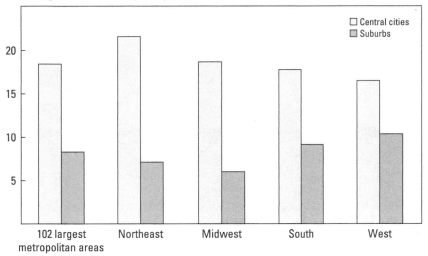

Moreover these regional differences disguise the fact that high city poverty rates could be found in every part of the country. Table 4-1 shows the location of the fifteen central cities and suburbs with the highest and lowest poverty rates in 2000. Cities with the highest poverty rates could be found in the "Rust Belt" extending from upstate New York through Ohio (Cleveland), Indiana (Gary), and Michigan (Detroit). High-poverty cities were also located in the Deep South and in central California. Cities with the lowest poverty rates could be found in the Southeast, Great Plains, and Northern California, but also in Indiana (Indianapolis and Fort Wayne), located near Midwestern cities of high poverty.

Suburban poverty, on the other hand, exhibited more distinct regional patterns in 2000. Fourteen of the fifteen suburbs with the highest poverty rates were located in either the South or the West (see table 4-1). Some of these suburbs were in metropolitan areas that are home to historically high levels of immigration and Hispanic population, such as Los Angeles, El Paso, Miami, and McAllen-Edinburg-Mission, Texas. In these metropolitan areas minority populations are more evenly distributed between cities and suburbs than in the rest of the United States.[9] High-poverty suburbs were also

9. Frey (2001).

TABLE 4-1. Central Cities and Suburbs with Highest and Lowest Poverty Rates, 2000

Highest		*Lowest*	
Central cities			
Hartford, CT	30.6	Colorado Springs, CO	8.7
Miami, FL	28.5	San Jose, CA	8.8
Newark, NJ	28.4	Ventura, CA	9.0
New Orleans, LA	27.9	Vallejo-Fairfield-Napa, CA	9.5
Syracuse, NY	27.3	Charlotte, NC	10.6
Buffalo, NY	26.6	Wichita, KS	11.2
Cleveland, OH	26.3	Omaha, NE	11.3
Fresno, CA	26.2	San Francisco, CA	11.3
Detroit, MI	26.1	Norfolk-Virginia Beach-Newport News, VA	11.5
Rochester, NY	25.9	Honolulu, HI	11.8
McAllen-Edinburg-Mission, TX	25.8	Seattle, WA	11.8
Gary, IN	25.8	Indianapolis, IN	11.9
Birmingham, AL	24.7	Las Vegas, NV	11.9
St. Louis, MO	24.6	Jacksonville, FL	12.2
Atlanta, GA	24.4	Fort Wayne, IN	12.5
Suburbs of central cities			
McAllen-Edinburg-Mission, TX	41.3	Milwaukee, WI	3.6
El Paso, TX	32.0	Minneapolis-St. Paul, MN	4.0
Bakersfield, CA	22.5	Omaha, NE	5.0
Fresno, CA	19.6	Kansas City, MO	5.2
Miami, FL	16.0	Fort Wayne, IN	5.2
Los Angeles-Long Beach, CA	14.6	Baltimore, MD	5.4
Albuquerque, NM	14.2	Middlesex-Somerset-Hunterdon, NJ	5.4
Riverside-San Bernadino, CA	14.2	Wichita, KS	5.5
Mobile, AL	13.6	Indianapolis, IN	5.5
Jersey City, NJ	13.5	Chicago, IL	5.6
New Orleans, LA	13.1	Hartford, CT	5.6
Stockton-Lodi, CA	12.2	Nassau-Suffolk, NY	5.6
Baton Rouge, LA	11.7	Allentown-Bethlehem, PA	5.6
Oklahoma City, OK	11.3	Salt Lake City-Ogden, UT	5.8
Charleston-North Charleston, SC	10.9	Washington, DC	5.8

found in Southern metropolitan areas with large black populations, such as Mobile, New Orleans, and Baton Rouge. In contrast the majority of low-poverty suburbs were located in the Northeast, Midwest, and Mid-Atlantic (Baltimore and Washington, D.C.) regions, where socioeconomic differences between cities and suburbs have historically been quite large.

Even though the city-suburb poverty gap varied widely across different parts of the nation in 2000, poverty remained far more of a city phenomenon than a suburban one. Fully 95 percent of large metropolitan areas retained higher poverty rates in their cities than their suburbs. Changes in the distribution of poverty between cities and suburbs in the last decade should thus be viewed with this larger context in mind.

FIGURE 4-2. Poverty Rates for United States, Large Metropolitan Areas (Including Central Cities and Suburbs), Smaller Metros, and Rural Areas, 1990 and 2000

Percent of people in poverty

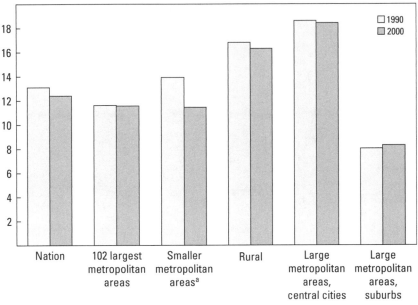

a. Metropolitan areas with population under 500,000 in 2000.

Poverty Rate Gap between Central Cities and Suburbs Narrowed Slightly

Census 2000 reveals that despite the decade's strong economic performance, the share of individuals living below poverty in the United States's largest metropolitan areas did not change between 1990 and 2000, holding steady at 11.6 percent (see figure 4-2). Several factors may account for the static overall poverty rate in large metropolitan areas, including, among other trends, international immigration and internal migration patterns; the effects of the early 1990s recession, particularly in California; and differences in birth rates and mortality rates between poor populations in metropolitan areas and elsewhere.

The stagnant poverty rate for large metropolitan areas nationally, however, masks subtle changes in this measure in central cities and suburbs over the decade. There was actually a small decline in the poverty rate among central cities of the 102 largest metropolitan areas between 1990 and 2000, from 18.6 to 18.4 percent (figure 4-2). In contrast the share of individuals

117

FIGURE 4-3. Poverty Rate Changes, 1990s versus 1980s, Central Cities of Metropolitan Areas with Population over 500,000

Percent of cities

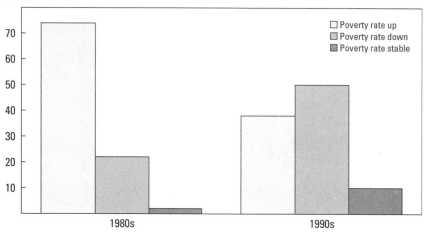

in suburbs living below the poverty line increased slightly during the same period—from 8.0 to 8.3 percent. Suburbs of large metropolitan areas were the only geographical category of those shown in figure 4-2 to see poverty increase over the decade; poverty rates fell not only in large central cities, but also in smaller metropolitan areas and rural areas.

These changes to aggregate city and suburban poverty rates in the 1990s were largely driven by the fact that poverty fell in a greater share of central cities than suburbs. A majority—51 percent (50 out of 98)—of central cities saw poverty decline over the decade. In contrast a slim minority of suburbs—46 percent (47 out of 102)—experienced a drop in their poverty rates. A slightly greater share of suburbs (42 percent) than central cities (39 percent) saw increases in poverty in the 1990s.[10] Thus the poverty rate trends for cities and suburbs in the aggregate were not dictated by the experiences of a few large metropolitan areas, but reflected poverty changes across the entire city-suburb spectrum.

The fact that poverty declined in the majority of cities in the 1990s represents a remarkable reversal of the trend in the 1980s.[11] During that decade poverty rates went up in three-fourths of central cities (74 out of 98) versus only 39 percent of central cities in the 1990s (figure 4-3). In part this pattern

10. In ten other central cities and twelve suburbs, poverty rates did not change by more than +/−0.2 percentage points.
11. Frey and Fielding (1995).

T A B L E   4 - 2 .   Poverty Rate Changes, Central Cities and Suburbs, 1990–2000ᵃ

	Central cities		Suburbs	
	Increasing poverty	Decreasing poverty	Increasing poverty	Decreasing poverty
Numberᵇ	38	50	43	47
Average change (percentage points)	2.2	−1.9	1.1	−1.8
Average population	717,682	518,721	1,519,511	863,231

Source: Authors' analysis of decennial census data.

a. Metropolitan areas with population over 500,000.

b. Poverty rates were largely unchanged in an additional ten central cities and twelve suburbs.

merely reflected the differing economic trends across the two decades—the national poverty rate rose from 12.5 percent to 13.1 percent between the 1980 and 1990 censuses, and then fell to 12.4 percent during Census 2000. Nonetheless the 1990s were clearly a better decade in many cities for those at the bottom of the economic ladder than the 1980s.

The slight narrowing of the overall "poverty rate gap" between cities and suburbs, and the fact that more cities than suburbs experienced poverty declines, together suggest that city and suburban poverty may have converged in most individual metropolitan areas during the 1990s. However, this was not the case. In fact the gap narrowed in only one-third of the 102 metropolitan areas; in more than half, it widened. As table 4-2 shows, this was attributable to the fact that in regions where poverty was on the rise, cities experienced faster poverty rate increases, but where it was on the decline, cities and suburbs shared equally in the trend. For instance, in Los Angeles, the poverty rate was up 3.6 percent in the city and 2.3 percent in the suburbs, but in Kansas City, poverty rates dropped by 1.0 percent in both city and suburbs.

As these examples indicate, even though aggregate city and suburban poverty rates moved in opposite directions in the 1990s, poverty rates moved in tandem within most metropolitan areas. In 80 percent of metropolitan areas (79 of 98) poverty rates moved in either a positive or negative direction in both the central city and the suburbs.[12] There were a few notable exceptions, however. Seven cities saw their poverty rates decline even as poverty increased in their suburbs. These included high-end cities like Chicago, Miami, San José, and Seattle, as well as Harrisburg, Jersey City, and Milwaukee. The first four cities may have seen poor families migrate to the suburbs, or new lower-income arrivals to those regions may have settled in

12. The overall correlation between city and suburb percentage-point changes in poverty rates was significant: 0.65.

the suburbs due to skyrocketing rents in the city. What might have accounted for the trend in the other three cities remains unclear. There was even less of a regional or economic pattern evident in the three metropolitan (Ann Arbor, Phoenix, and Oklahoma City) areas where city poverty rates rose while suburban rates fell. Nevertheless the broader trends of increasing and decreasing metropolitan poverty reflect important regional variations that we explore later.

Metropolitan Poor Split Evenly between Cities and Suburbs

The slight rise in the suburban poverty rate from 8.0 to 8.3 percent occurred during a decade in which the U.S. population decentralized at a considerable pace. One important implication of these trends is that a greater share of poor persons in metropolitan areas now lives in suburbs than a decade ago.

Cities and suburbs differed markedly in their overall population growth in the 1990s. Total population in the suburbs of the 102 largest metropolitan areas grew by 17 percent, compared to only 9 percent in the central cities. Moreover the city-suburb growth gap widened when it came to poor populations. Although the absolute number of people living below the poverty line increased by 8 percent in cities, the number of poor in suburbs grew by nearly 21 percent. As a result, over the decade the percentage of all poor individuals in large metropolitan areas living in the suburbs rose from 46 percent in 1990 to almost half (49 percent) in 2000.

It is worth emphasizing that this shift in the location of the poor occurred in the midst of overall growth in the number of poor people in both cities and suburbs. By decade's end there were more than 20 million people living in poverty in the 102 largest metropolitan areas—2.5 million more than in 1990. Over the 1990s cities gained 770,000 net new poor residents, and suburbs gained nearly 1.7 million.

By 2000 a greater share of metropolitan poor people lived in the suburbs despite the fact that increases in suburban poverty rates were generally modest. In large part this subtle suburbanization of the poor population was due to size differences between two types of suburbs. Among the forty-three suburbs in which poverty rates increased in the 1990s the average increase was a little over 1 percentage point (see table 4-2). During the same period, in suburbs where the rate declined the average decrease approached 2 percentage points. The suburbs in which poverty rates increased, however, were nearly twice as large on average as their decreasing-poverty counterparts. Many of these poverty-increasing locales were large, multiethnic metropolitan areas in the West; others were metropolitan areas in the Northeast with large suburban populations. In this fashion smaller poverty-rate increases in big suburbs outweighed larger declines in smaller suburbs, leading to a small increase in the overall suburban poverty rate, and a shift of the poor toward suburbs.

Nevertheless when viewed against the backdrop of other demographic trends, this shift in the location of the poor population is not enormous. The percentage of racial and ethnic minorities in large metropolitan areas that live in the suburbs, for instance, jumped from 19 to 27 percent over the decade—a considerably larger shift than that for individuals in poverty.[13] Nonetheless the fact that a growing share of the nation's poor lives in the suburbs underscores the increasing range of incomes in the suburbs, as well as the growing racial, ethnic, household, and age diversity to be found there.

Poverty Rate Changes Varied Significantly by U.S. Region

As with most demographic trends, national numbers on city-suburban poverty mask important geographical variation.

The cities that enjoyed the largest declines in poverty rates in the 1990s were in general situated in two very different regions: the Rust Belt, and southern Texas. The top panel of table 4-3 shows that among the ten cities with the largest poverty rate declines, five—Austin, El Paso, McAllen, Texas, New Orleans, and San Antonio—are located in the Deep South/Southwest. Another five—Akron, Dayton, Detroit, Gary, and Youngstown—are located in the industrial Midwest. The next ten form a similar group, with three additional cities in Ohio, and Atlanta, Memphis, and Baton Rouge in the South.

How did these contrasting sets of cities come to share the distinction of having the steepest declines in the poverty rate? A full answer demands more information from census long form data. Nevertheless it can be observed here that these cities struggled with poverty rates much higher than the central city average at the beginning of the decade. Perhaps because they had "nowhere to go but up" the strong national economy and federal/state policies to promote work may have reduced poverty in these cities by raising labor force participation and wages at the bottom of the labor pool. For example, Detroit, which had one of the highest poverty rates in the nation in 1990 (32.4 percent), registered one of the largest declines in the 1990s— 6.3 percentage points. Like Detroit, though, most of these cities are still home to high poverty; fourteen had poverty rates above the central city average of 18.4 percent in 2000.

The top panel of table 4-3 offers additional promising news for the cities that experienced the fastest poverty declines in the 1990s. Child poverty rates

13. Frey (2001).

T A B L E 4 - 3. **Central Cities with Greatest Declines and Greatest Increases in Poverty Rates, 1990–2000[a]**

Central cities of metropolitan areas	Poverty rate, all ages		Poverty rate, under 18	
	2000	1990–2000 change	2000	1990–2000 change
Greatest poverty rate declines				
McAllen-Edinburg-Mission, TX MSA	25.8	−8.1	34.0	−9.9
Detroit, MI PMSA	26.1	−6.3	34.8	−11.8
San Antonio, TX MSA	17.3	−5.4	24.6	−7.9
Dayton-Springfield, OH MSA	21.2	−3.7	30.1	−8.3
New Orleans, LA MSA	27.9	−3.7	40.5	−5.8
Gary, IN PMSA	25.8	−3.6	38.2	−4.7
Austin-San Marcos, TX MSA	14.4	−3.5	17.0	−4.4
Youngstown-Warren, OH MSA	22.8	−3.1	34.9	−6.1
El Paso, TX MSA	22.2	−3.1	30.1	−4.4
Akron, OH PMSA	17.5	−3.0	26.0	−5.2
Atlanta, GA MSA	24.4	−2.9	39.3	−3.6
Denver, CO PMSA	14.3	−2.8	20.8	−6.6
Miami, FL PMSA	28.5	−2.7	38.5	−5.5
Columbus, OH MSA	14.8	−2.4	19.0	−5.3
Cincinnati, OH-KY-IN PMSA	21.9	−2.4	32.5	−4.9
Memphis, TN-AR-MS MSA	20.6	−2.4	30.4	−4.5
Cleveland-Lorain-Elyria, OH PMSA	26.3	−2.4	38.0	−5.0
Baton Rouge, LA MSA	24.0	−2.2	31.7	−3.9
Colorado Springs, CO MSA	8.7	−2.2	11.3	−4.0
Chicago, IL PMSA	19.6	−2.0	28.5	−5.3
Greatest poverty rate increases				
Providence-Fall River-Warwick, RI-MA NECMA	20.1	5.1	29.4	6.0
Syracuse, NY MSA	27.3	4.6	35.4	2.2
Riverside-San Bernardino, CA PMSA	20.7	4.2	27.2	3.6
Allentown-Bethlehem-Easton, PA MSA	17.1	4.2	26.7	5.5
Albany-Schenectady-Troy, NY MSA	20.8	3.8	29.0	4.3
Los Angeles-Long Beach, CA PMSA	22.2	3.6	30.9	3.2
Honolulu, HI MSA	11.8	3.4	15.1	3.5
Washington, DC-MD-VA-WV PMSA	20.2	3.3	31.7	6.2
Wilmington-Newark, DE-MD PMSA	21.3	3.3	30.7	3.4
Hartford, CT NECMA	30.6	3.1	41.3	−2.5
Bakersfield, CA MSA	18.0	3.0	24.8	2.8
Stockton-Lodi, CA MSA	22.5	2.8	31.5	0.9
Sacramento, CA PMSA	20.0	2.8	29.9	1.3
Philadelphia, PA-NJ PMSA	22.9	2.6	31.6	1.3
Orange County, CA PMSA	15.6	2.4	19.9	3.1
Rochester, NY MSA	25.9	2.4	37.9	−0.5
Ventura, CA PMSA	9.0	2.3	12.7	2.6
Fresno, CA MSA	26.2	2.1	36.8	−0.1
Sarasota-Bradenton, FL MSA	15.2	2.1	26.0	3.9
Newark, NJ PMSA	28.4	2.1	36.9	−0.7

Source: Authors' analysis of decennial census data.

a. Metropolitan areas with population over 500,000.

in these cities actually dropped faster than overall poverty rates, by an average of 2.5 percentage points. The trend was especially pronounced in Midwestern cities such as Cincinnati, Dayton, Detroit, and Youngstown, where child poverty was particularly high in 1990.

Many of the cities that topped the list for poverty declines had suburbs that also experienced some of the fastest declines (see the top panel of table 4-4). Suburbs in a number of Texas metropolitan areas, as well as those around Southern cities like Memphis, Nashville, New Orleans, and Baton Rouge saw poverty decline substantially in the 1990s. The suburbs of the Midwestern cities in table 4-4 that had large poverty declines, however, did not follow their cities' trend. Poverty rates dropped by small amounts in most Midwestern suburbs, and were generally low enough at the outset that substantial declines were unlikely. By contrast nineteen out of twenty suburbs where poverty declined fastest had poverty rates above the national suburban average in 1990. It is also possible that some of the below-poverty city population in Midwestern metropolitan areas relocated to the suburbs in the 1990s, or to other regions of the U.S. Additional Census 2000 analysis could confirm whether intrametropolitan migration patterns contributed to these poverty trends.

On the other end of the spectrum, cities with the greatest increases in poverty rates were the geographical mirror image of their poverty-declining counterparts. As the bottom panel of table 4-3 shows, they were largely located in the Northeast (nine of the top twenty cities, if one includes Wilmington) and the West (also nine cities, eight in California). Cities from more than half of the Northeastern metropolitan areas and more than half of the California metropolitan areas make the list. Only seven of the twenty had above-average poverty rates in 1990, but now fourteen do—notably, the same number as among the top poverty decliners. In these places child poverty rates increased as well, though generally by smaller amounts than did overall poverty rates.

The evidence for the suburbs with the largest poverty changes is broadly consistent with the regional patterns that emerge for central cities. The suburbs with the largest poverty increases in the 1990s were also located in New England, the New York metropolitan area, and California (see the bottom panel of table 4-4). The suburbs of New York and Jersey City, as well as all four of the suburban New York/New Jersey metropolitan areas, experienced sizeable poverty rate increases. Most of their poverty rates, however, remain below the national suburban average of 8.3 percent.

These findings beg the question: What occurred in the Northeast and Southern California in the 1990s that caused poverty rates to go up?

T A B L E 4 - 4 . Suburbs with Greatest Declines and Greatest Increases in Poverty Rates, 1990–2000[a]

Suburbs of metropolitan areas	Poverty rate, all ages		Poverty rate, under 18	
	2000	1990–2000 change	2000	1990–2000 change
Greatest poverty rate declines				
Austin-San Marcos, TX MSA	7.4	−6.1	8.0	−7.7
El Paso, TX MSA	32.0	−5.5	38.6	−6.9
McAllen-Edinburg-Mission, TX MSA	41.3	−5.2	51.1	−6.1
Mobile, AL MSA	13.6	−4.6	18.6	−7.0
Memphis, TN-AR-MS MSA	8.5	−3.1	11.3	−4.2
Phoenix-Mesa, AZ MSA	9.5	−3.1	12.8	−5.1
Tucson, AZ MSA	9.7	−3.0	14.2	−5.0
Albuquerque, NM MSA	14.2	−2.8	19.3	−3.1
Colorado Springs, CO MSA	6.5	−2.6	8.7	−3.7
San Antonio, TX MSA	9.4	−2.5	13.4	−2.8
Tulsa, OK MSA	8.8	−2.4	11.0	−2.7
Knoxville, TN MSA	9.2	−2.1	11.8	−3.0
Baton Rouge, LA MSA	11.7	−2.1	14.4	−2.7
Youngstown-Warren, OH MSA	8.5	−2.0	12.3	−2.8
Ann Arbor, MI PMSA	6.3	−1.9	7.0	−3.3
New Orleans, LA MSA	13.1	−1.9	18.1	−2.5
Little Rock-North Little Rock, AR MSA	10.1	−1.8	12.8	−1.7
Salt Lake City-Ogden, UT MSA	5.8	−1.8	7.2	−2.2
Nashville, TN MSA	7.7	−1.7	9.0	−1.6
Charleston-North Charleston, SC MSA	10.9	−1.7	14.5	−1.8
Greatest poverty rate increases				
Bakersfield, CA MSA	22.5	4.7	30.2	4.2
Riverside-San Bernardino, CA PMSA	14.2	2.8	19.0	3.2
Los Angeles-Long Beach, CA PMSA	14.6	2.3	20.0	2.3
New York, NY PMSA	8.6	2.1	11.6	2.3
Ventura, CA PMSA	9.3	1.9	12.0	1.8
Honolulu, HI MSA	8.5	1.7	11.7	1.9
Fort Lauderdale, FL PMSA	10.9	1.6	14.5	1.5
Orange County, CA PMSA	8.2	1.6	10.6	1.7
Jersey City, NJ PMSA	13.5	1.5	18.5	−0.3
Bergen-Passaic, NJ PMSA	7.6	1.5	9.9	0.9
Hartford, CT NECMA	5.6	1.4	6.6	0.9
Syracuse, NY MSA	8.5	1.4	10.9	2.1
Nassau-Suffolk, NY PMSA	5.6	1.4	6.6	1.1
Fresno, CA MSA	19.6	1.3	27.0	0.2
Stockton-Lodi, CA MSA	12.2	1.3	15.4	0.7
Providence-Fall River-Warwick, RI-MA NECMA	8.3	1.3	10.8	1.8
Bridgeport, CT NECMA	7.2	1.2	9.3	0.3
Middlesex-Somerset-Hunterdon, NJ PMSA	5.4	1.2	6.0	0.8
Monmouth-Ocean, NJ PMSA	6.6	1.2	8.8	1.3
San Diego, CA MSA	10.8	1.1	14.7	1.1

Source: Authors' analysis of decennial census data.

a. Metropolitan areas with population over 500,000.

Further analysis is needed to determine the demographic and economic factors behind these increases. It is significant, however, that these cities are in regions of the country where the recession of the early 1990s hit especially hard. Southern California and some parts of New England underwent considerable economic restructuring in response to massive defense industry layoffs early in the decade. Many of the cities on this list returned to their prerecession unemployment rates only in the late 1990s.[14] As a result, the economic gains that these cities made in the last part of the decade may not have been large enough to make up for the increases in poverty they experienced earlier in the decade. In half of these cities, however, child poverty did not increase as fast as overall poverty, or actually declined even as overall poverty rose.

Demographic shifts may also have contributed to rising poverty in these regions. In the Northeast, for instance, recent research revealed that, during the 1990s, a net outflow of 2.7 million residents to other parts of the United States occurred, and that a large share of those residents were young and educated. During the same period the Northeast added 3.1 million foreign-born residents.[15] In California the share of the population that is foreign-born grew from 21.7 (in 1990) to 26.1 percent (in 2000). California immigrants—particularly those that arrived in the last two decades—were more likely to occupy the bottom of the income distribution than U.S.-born individuals.[16] The increasing presence of recent immigrants in these metropolitan areas could be another factor contributing to their poverty increases. Figure 4-4 shows how poverty rate increases and decreases differed by U.S. region:

—In the **Northeast,** poverty rose significantly in cities, and to a lesser extent, in suburbs. Poverty rate increases were widespread, occurring in 13 of 17 central cities, and 18 of 21 suburbs. By decade's end the poverty rate in Northeastern cities exceeded that in Midwestern cities by 3 percentage points. The cities with the largest jumps in poverty included Providence, a city widely thought to be in better shape than it was ten years before, as well as long-struggling, older industrial places like Syracuse and Allentown-Bethlehem. The suburbs of New York City, and suburbs in other New York-area metropolitan regions, saw poverty rates rise from 1 to 2 percent in the 1990s. The severity of the early 1990s recession, immigration, and the continued shift away from manufacturing to a lower-wage service economy in those metropolitan areas may all have contributed to the upward poverty trend in the Northeast.

---

14. Honolulu's economy suffered throughout the 1990s due to its close relationship with the Japanese economy.

15. Sum and others (2002).

16. Daly, Reed, and Royer (2001).

FIGURE 4-4. Central-City and Suburban Poverty Changes by Region, 1990–2000, Metropolitan Areas with Population over 500,000

Percentage of individuals in poverty

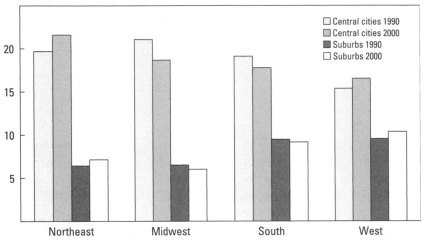

—In the **Midwest,** by contrast, poverty rates in cities fell by an even larger degree than they rose in Northeastern cities—by 2.4 percentage points overall. Poverty was off in Midwest suburbs by half a percentage point. As in the Northeast the poverty trend was consistent across the Midwest—twenty metropolitan areas, seventeen cities, and sixteen suburbs saw their poverty rates decrease. Unemployment rates throughout the Midwest were low in the 1990s, thanks in large part to a resurgence of manufacturing, particularly in the automotive industry.[17] Across the region the largest poverty declines occurred in the places that had the highest poverty rates in 1990 (see the Detroit example, above). Similarly Youngstown had the region's highest suburban poverty rate in 1990, and had the region's largest suburban poverty decline over the decade. Despite these improvements, though, the poverty-rate gap between Midwestern cities and suburbs remained high in 2000; overall, the central-city poverty rate remained more than three times as high as the suburban rate.

—Cities and suburbs in the **South** realized somewhat smaller poverty declines than their Midwestern counterparts in the 1990s; poverty rates there fell by 1.3 percentage points in central cities and just 0.4 percentage points in suburbs. Poverty reduction was also not as widespread, as rates fell in only nineteen central cities and twenty-three suburbs across the thirty-seven Southern metropolitan areas. Cities and suburbs in Texas fared well;

17. See Federal Reserve Bank of Chicago, *1996 Annual Report.*

the state was home to many of the cities and suburbs with the greatest poverty declines. On the other hand cities closer to the Northeast—Baltimore, Wilmington, Washington, D.C., and Richmond—saw their poverty rates increase over the decade. Otherwise no consistent geographic or demographic pattern described the places where poverty rose or fell in the South, although many places seemed to "revert to the mean." Where poverty was high— Atlanta, Miami, New Orleans, the Mobile suburbs—it often fell. Where poverty was low—Greensboro, Sarasota, West Palm Beach—it often rose.

—Poverty changes in the **West** largely split between southern/central California and everywhere else. Poverty rates fell in most Western New Sunbelt cities and suburbs like Colorado Springs, Denver, Salt Lake City, and Tacoma. These places attracted large numbers of domestic in-migrants and jobs in the 1990s.[18] In contrast, poverty rates rose in all nine of the cities and suburbs located in southern and central California—by 2 percentage points in the suburbs, and 3 percentage points in the cities. Outside of the Northeast and Washington, D.C., all of the cities and suburbs with the greatest poverty rate increases were located in California and Hawaii.

Some have attributed poverty increases over the decade in large multi-ethnic cities like New York, Washington, and Los Angeles to immigration trends.[19] The patterns analyzed here, although still preliminary in nature, hint that although immigration contributed to the picture, regional economic conditions and economic restructuring in the 1990s may have played an even greater role. To be sure, poverty rates in the Northeast, New York region, and Southern California might not have increased as much as they did in the absence of new immigration and births to immigrant families. Yet the fact that poverty rates fell in many cities and suburbs with high immigrant concentrations—all large Texas cities, as well as "new Latino destination" metropolitan areas—such as Atlanta, Charlotte, Nashville, and Portland— suggests that more than simple demographic trends were at work.[20]

Relationship between Population Change and Poverty Rate Change Not Straightforward

Early analysis of cities in Census 2000 has revolved around measuring urban health through simple indicators such as population growth. Population

18. Frey (2002).
19. See Janny Scott, "Census Finds Rising Tide, and Many Who Missed Boat," *New York Times,* June 17, 2002, p. B1, and Peter V. Hong, "Data Reflect Southland's Highs, Lows; People: Poverty and Education Levels Reflect Immigration Patterns, Demographer Says," *Los Angeles Times,* June 5, 2002, part 2, p. 1.
20. Suro and Singer (2002).

changes offer a look at where people choose to live, and that surely offers some insight into the well-being of a place. In general high population growth in a particular place reflects high demand to live there, and is thus treated as a sign of a healthy place.

Sample data from the Census long form offer a broad array of variables with which to measure the social and economic condition of a city's population, including education levels, incomes, immigration, housing costs, and employment. This chapter focuses on poverty rates as one indicator of cities' well-being, and suggests a more enigmatic relationship between population trends and local economic health than previous Census 2000 analysis has indicated.

Comparing poverty changes to population changes highlights the "stock" and "flow" factors that influence many demographic trends. A city might experience a declining poverty rate due to factors affecting its existing population. Improving economic conditions could be raising people above poverty, or there could be an excess of deaths over births among families in poverty. Alternatively the poverty rate could decline in response to shifts in the city's population. New arrivals could be disproportionately higher-income, more poor people might leave the city than enter, or the average size of poor families could decrease. In any given city these stock and flow factors combine to influence poverty in complicated ways. Improving economic conditions, for instance, could serve to attract new higher-income residents, or to convince young lower-income women to postpone childbirth in favor of employment. In theory a decline in poverty could occur in the midst of either increasing or decreasing population.

The evidence confirms that the relationship between population change and poverty change in the 1990s was not straightforward. Cities that lost population were nearly as likely to experience declining poverty rates as cities that gained population. Of the 28 cities that declined in population between 1990 and 2000, half displayed falling poverty rates (see figure 4-5). Similarly 33 of the 63 cities in which population increased experienced poverty rate declines. Just as falling population did not always signal increasing poverty, rising population was not always associated with poverty declines. About one-third of all cities that increased in population saw their poverty rates rise.

Cities with the largest population gains and losses in the 1990s serve to illustrate these trends (see table 4-5). Five of the ten cities with the sharpest population decline also experienced declines in their poverty rates. In each of those cities the number of people living below poverty dropped faster than total population. In Dayton-Springfield, for instance, the poor population fell at more than twice the rate as did the total population. All of the cities, with the exception of Syracuse, witnessed a drop in the size of their

FIGURE 4-5. Poverty Rate Change by Population Change, 1990–2000, Central Cities of Metropolitan Areas with Population over 500,000

Number of cities

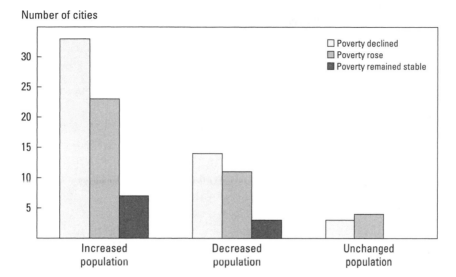

TABLE 4-5. Poverty Changes in Central Cities with Largest Population Losses and Gains, 1990–2000

Percent change

Central cities	Total population	Number of people in poverty	Poverty rate
Largest population losses			
Youngstown-Warren, OH MSA	−14.1	−24.5	−3.1
Baltimore, MD PMSA	−12.4	−8.2	1.1
Gary, IN PMSA	−12.2	−23.1	−3.6
St. Louis, MO-IL MSA	−12.2	−12.5	−0.1
Hartford, CT NECMA	−11.7	−1.8	3.1
Buffalo, NY MSA	−11.3	−7.9	1.0
Pittsburgh, PA MSA	−10.7	−15.0	−1.0
Dayton-Springfield, OH MSA	−10.0	−23.4	−3.7
Syracuse, NY MSA	−9.4	9.0	4.6
Cincinnati, OH-KY-IN PMSA	−9.2	−18.3	−2.4
Largest population gains			
Las Vegas, NV-AZ MSA	85.7	92.7	0.4
Austin, TX MSA	42.4	14.5	−3.5
Bakersfield, CA MSA	41.8	69.8	3.0
McAllen-Edinburg-Mission, TX MSA	40.8	7.0	−8.1
Portland-Vancouver, OR-WA PMSA	39.4	21.6	−1.9
Charlotte, NC-SC MSA	35.9	33.1	−0.2
Raleigh-Durham, NC MSA	35.7	34.0	−0.2
Phoenix-Mesa, AZ MSA	35.0	46.1	1.1
Colorado Springs, CO MSA	28.4	2.7	−2.2
Greensboro–Winston-Salem–High Point, NC MSA	25.1	29.3	0.4

Source: Authors' analysis of decennial census data.

poor populations. For some, however, that decline was not nearly as rapid as the decline in population generally. In Hartford the poverty rate rose by more than 3 percentage points because the number of people living below poverty fell at only a fraction of the rate that total population did. Regional differences in poverty are evident here as well: cities that lost population in the Midwest had declining poverty rates, whereas those in the Northeast (plus Baltimore) had increasing poverty rates.

All ten of the fastest-growing cities had increases in the size of their poor populations, but there were significant differences in how those gains compared to their overall population gains. In North Carolina, the central cities in the Charlotte, Raleigh-Durham, and Greensboro–Winston-Salem–High Point areas experienced comparable growth in their total populations and below-poverty populations. Migration magnets such as Austin, Colorado Springs, and Portland-Vancouver grew rapidly in size without rapid increases in the number of poor residents. In Phoenix-Mesa and Bakersfield, however, the share of population below the poverty line actually increased in the midst of a population boom. In-migrants to these cities may have been poorer on average, or employment opportunities and pay in the lower end of the labor market may have shrunk.[21] Again: The relationship between population change and poverty change in the 1990s does not appear straightforward.

All of this does not suggest that declining population can help a city's residents escape poverty, or that increasing population inevitably burdens a city with new poor residents. On the contrary, city population declines can create a host of problems besides poverty: struggling local businesses, vacant housing, falling property values, and negative market perceptions, to name a few. Conversely a city that has grown its resident population across the income spectrum may be able to tackle the added service challenges that accompany an increased poverty rate, and may create better opportunities in the future for its residents to lift themselves out of poverty. This comparison of city population and poverty changes reminds us that the determinants of poverty in place are numerous, and that the poverty rate is one of many tools that help us to understand a city's health and vitality.

CONCLUSION

Viewed from a national perspective, changes in poverty during the 1990s were subtle. During a period of prolonged economic growth, the national

---

21. Increases in the child poverty rate in these cities were no greater than overall poverty rate increases, but both cities experienced significant declines in male labor force participation between 1990 and 2000.

poverty rate fell only slightly. Equally noteworthy were the relatively modest shifts in poverty rates for residents of the nation's largest metropolitan areas detailed here. These shifts caused the city-suburb poverty gap to narrow overall, but the rift remains wide, to the point that city residents remain more than twice as likely to be poor as their suburban counterparts. Likewise the share of the poor population residing in the suburbs increased during the 1990s, though even so, half of all poor people in the United States's largest metropolitan areas still live in central cities.

Below the national level, however, the story was more varied. Poverty was on the decline in the 1990s in a majority of cities, in contrast to the 1980s, when three-fourths of all central cities experienced poverty rate increases. Cities where poverty decreased in the 1990s included places that traditionally had among the highest poverty rates. Poverty rates fell in Rustbelt cities (such as Detroit and Gary) and Southern cities (such as New Orleans and Atlanta)—in many cases by dramatic amounts. Poverty rates fell across the board in Texas. Children benefited most from the trend, as child poverty rates generally fell by greater amounts than overall poverty rates in these cities. At the same time, however, increases in poverty rates for many cities in California and the Northeast catapulted those places into the echelon of those with highest poverty levels. In many of these metropolitan areas, suburban poverty rates also increased appreciably.

These "mixed blessings" raise questions about how the various macroeconomic, policy, and demographic forces of the 1990s served as contributing factors. How much did the happenstance of a strong economy, coupled with welfare reform and other policies to promote work, contribute to the surprising declines in poverty rates in many Midwest inner cities? To what extent did demographic factors such as the selective migration from the Northeast to the Sunbelt, and new immigration to California and the Eastern Seaboard, contribute to the coastal gains in poverty rates? Most importantly, if the good economy of the mid-to-late 1990s was responsible for reversing much of the city poverty increase of the 1980s, what impact will the economic downturn and slow subsequent growth in the early part of this decade have on urban and suburban poverty in the 2000–10 period?

Data from Census 2000 allow researchers to explore many of these questions, as well as consider questions relating to other place-based measures of economic well-being: median income, per capita income, the size of the "middle-income" and "moderate-income" classes, and regional income inequality. The evidence on city and suburban poverty in the 1990s reminds us that beneath the national trends on many of these indicators lie important regional differences that reveal the shifting socioeconomic landscape of the United States's metropolitan geography.

TABLE 4A-1. Changes in Poverty Rate and Poverty Population, 1990–2000[a]

| | Poverty rates | | | | | | Poverty population | | |
| | Metropolitan area | | Central city | | Suburbs | | 1990–2000 change | | |
Metropolitan areas	2000	1990–2000 change	2000	1990–2000 change	2000	1990–2000 change	Metropolitan area	Central city	Suburbs
Midwest (20)									
Akron, OH PMSA	9.8	-2.3	17.5	-3.0	6.3	-1.5	-14.2	-17.0	-10.4
Ann Arbor, MI PMSA	8.2	-1.7	16.6	0.5	6.3	-1.9	-1.3	8.3	-6.3
Chicago, IL PMSA	10.5	-0.8	19.6	-2.0	5.6	0.6	4.0	-6.0	29.7
Cincinnati, OH-KY-IN PMSA	9.7	-1.9	21.9	-2.4	6.7	-1.0	-9.9	-18.3	-1.8
Cleveland, OH PMSA	10.8	-1.1	26.3	-2.4	6.7	-0.3	-7.8	-13.9	-0.4
Columbus, OH MSA	10.1	-1.8	14.8	-2.4	6.0	-1.2	-2.7	-2.6	-2.7
Dayton-Springfield, OH MSA	10.3	-1.6	21.2	-3.7	6.9	-0.4	-13.9	-23.4	-2.4
Detroit, MI PMSA	10.7	-2.4	26.1	-6.3	6.6	-0.5	-15.1	-26.0	0.8
Fort Wayne, IN MSA	8.2	0.5	12.5	1.0	5.2	-0.1	17.3	29.0	1.8
Gary, IN PMSA	10.8	-1.4	25.8	-3.6	7.8	-0.2	-7.8	-23.1	5.8
Grand Rapids-Muskegon-Holland, MI MSA	8.4	-1.2	15.7	-1.4	6.0	-0.8	1.4	-4.1	6.5
Indianapolis, IN MSA	8.6	-1.3	11.9	-0.7	5.5	-1.4	0.9	0.8	1.0
Kansas City, MO-KS MSA	8.5	-1.4	15.0	-1.0	5.2	-1.0	-3.1	-5.5	0.5
Milwaukee, WI PMSA	10.6	-1.0	21.3	-0.9	3.6	0.2	-4.0	-8.8	20.5
Minneapolis-St. Paul, MN-WI MSA	6.7	-1.4	16.4	-1.4	4.0	-0.9	-3.0	-3.9	-2.0
Omaha, NE-IA MSA	8.4	-1.1	11.3	-1.3	5.0	-1.1	-0.6	4.1	-11.3
St. Louis, MO-IL MSA	9.9	-0.8	24.6	-0.1	7.7	-0.5	-3.6	-12.5	1.4
Toledo, OH MSA	12.5	-1.4	17.9	-1.2	6.9	-0.7	-9.2	-12.1	-0.4
Wichita, KS MSA	9.1	-1.4	11.2	-1.3	5.5	-1.6	-2.3	1.9	-14.7
Youngstown-Warren, OH MSA	11.5	-2.7	22.8	-3.1	8.5	-2.0	-20.8	-24.5	-17.9
Northeast (21)									
Albany-Schenectady-Troy, NY MSA	9.4	0.7	20.8	3.8	6.1	0.0	9.5	14.4	5.0
Allentown-Bethlehem, PA MSA	8.7	1.3	17.1	4.2	5.6	0.3	25.0	33.4	16.5
Bergen-Passaic, NJ PMSA	7.6	1.5	b	b	7.6	1.5	34.0	b	34.0
Boston, MA-NH NECMA	8.6	0.4	19.5	0.8	7.5	0.4	11.6	6.9	12.9
Bridgeport, CT NECMA	8.1	1.2	18.4	1.3	7.2	1.2	22.3	6.2	26.6
Buffalo, NY MSA	11.9	-0.1	26.6	1.0	7.0	0.2	-2.7	-7.9	4.9
Harrisburg-Lebanon-Carlisle, PA MSA	8.1	0.3	20.4	-0.3	6.0	0.7	9.7	-6.5	22.0

Hartford, CT NECMA	8.3	1.2	30.6	3.1	5.6	1.4	19.5	-1.8	38.8
Jersey City, NJ PMSA	15.5	0.7	18.6	-0.3	13.5	1.5	14.8	3.6	27.0
Middlesex-Somerset-Hunterdon, NJ PMSA	5.4	1.2	b	b	5.4	1.2	48.3	b	48.3
Monmouth-Ocean, NJ PMSA	6.6	1.2	b	b	6.6	1.2	38.5	b	38.5
Nassau-Suffolk, NY PMSA	5.6	1.4	b	b	5.6	1.4	39.8	b	39.8
New York, NY PMSA	19.5	2.0	21.2	2.0	8.6	2.1	21.6	20.5	41.3
Newark, NJ PMSA	9.7	0.9	28.4	2.1	6.8	1.0	16.6	5.0	25.3
Philadelphia, PA-NJ PMSA	11.1	0.7	22.9	2.6	6.2	0.4	10.4	7.3	15.8
Pittsburgh, PA MSA	10.8	-1.3	20.4	-1.0	9.3	-1.2	-12.3	-15.0	-11.3
Providence-Fall River-Warwick, RI-MA NECMA	12.4	2.6	20.1	5.1	8.3	1.3	32.6	39.3	25.0
Rochester, NY MSA	10.3	0.7	25.9	2.4	6.4	0.7	10.6	4.7	17.3
Scranton-Hazleton, PA MSA	11.1	0.1	15.0	-0.3	10.5	0.2	-1.7	-9.1	-0.1
Springfield, MA NECMA	13.5	1.0	20.4	2.0	8.3	0.6	9.3	7.8	12.1
Syracuse, NY MSA	12.1	1.7	27.3	4.6	8.5	1.4	15.8	9.0	21.7
South (37)									
Atlanta, GA MSA	9.4	-0.7	24.4	-2.9	7.8	0.2	28.8	-6.5	47.5
Austin, TX MSA	11.1	-4.8	14.4	-3.5	7.4	-6.1	3.6	14.5	-14.1
Baltimore, MD PMSA	9.8	-0.3	22.9	1.1	5.4	0.6	4.4	-8.2	29.9
Baton Rouge, LA MSA	16.2	-2.6	24.0	-2.2	11.7	-2.1	-1.8	-5.2	2.6
Birmingham, AL MSA	13.1	-2.0	24.7	-0.1	9.0	-1.6	-5.0	-9.7	0.1
Charleston-North Charleston, SC MSA	14.0	-1.0	21.0	-0.7	10.9	-1.7	1.3	18.4	-10.1
Charlotte, NC-SC MSA	9.3	-0.3	10.6	-0.2	8.6	-0.3	25.8	33.1	21.1
Columbia, SC MSA	11.7	0.1	22.1	0.9	9.4	-0.1	20.0	24.8	17.6
Dallas, TX PMSA	11.1	-1.2	17.8	-0.2	7.7	-1.1	19.1	16.7	22.0
El Paso, TX MSA	23.8	-3.0	22.2	-3.1	32.0	-5.5	2.2	-3.6	30.4
Fort Lauderdale, FL PMSA	11.5	1.3	17.7	0.6	10.9	1.6	46.1	5.5	56.1
Fort Worth-Arlington, TX PMSA	10.3	-0.7	13.6	-0.4	6.9	-0.9	16.8	19.2	12.3
Greensboro-Winston-Salem-High Point, NC MSA	10.4	0.5	13.5	0.4	8.4	0.5	26.0	29.3	22.9
Greenville-Spartanburg-Anderson, SC MSA	11.8	0.2	19.5	-0.1	10.7	0.6	18.4	-5.9	26.5
Houston, TX PMSA	13.9	-1.2	19.2	-1.6	9.3	-0.4	15.8	10.8	25.9
Jacksonville, FL MSA	10.7	-1.2	12.2	-0.8	7.6	-1.6	10.0	9.6	11.2
Knoxville, TN MSA	12.0	-1.9	20.8	0.0	9.2	-2.1	1.7	5.7	-1.1
Little Rock-North Little Rock, AR MSA	12.1	-1.4	14.7	-0.6	10.1	-1.8	1.8	-0.9	4.7
Louisville, KY-IN MSA	10.9	-1.9	21.6	-1.0	7.4	-1.6	-8.0	-9.0	-7.0
McAllen-Edinburg-Mission, TX MSA	35.9	-6.0	25.8	-8.1	41.3	-5.2	26.8	7.0	35.2

(continued)

133

TABLE 4A-1. Changes in Poverty Rate and Poverty Population, 1990–2000[a] (*continued*)

| | Poverty rates | | | | | | Poverty population | | |
| | Metropolitan area | | Central city | | Suburbs | | 1990–2000 change | | |
Metropolitan areas	2000	1990–2000 change	2000	1990–2000 change	2000	1990–2000 change	Metropolitan area	Central city	Suburbs
Memphis, TN-AR-MS MSA	15.3	−3.1	20.6	−2.4	8.5	−3.1	−5.6	−4.5	−9.0
Miami, FL PMSA	18.0	0.0	28.5	−2.7	16.0	1.0	16.3	−8.4	28.0
Mobile, AL MSA	16.3	−3.6	21.2	−1.3	13.6	−4.6	−7.2	−4.6	−9.4
Nashville, TN MSA	10.1	−1.2	13.3	−0.1	7.7	−1.7	11.7	10.8	12.9
New Orleans, LA MSA	18.4	−2.9	27.9	−3.7	13.1	−1.9	−10.3	−13.9	−5.5
Norfolk-Virginia Beach-Newport News, VA-NC MSA	10.6	−0.8	11.5	−0.1	9.6	−1.6	1.7	2.9	0.0
Oklahoma City, OK MSA	13.5	−0.4	16.0	0.2	11.3	−0.9	9.6	14.5	4.1
Orlando, FL MSA	10.7	0.6	15.9	0.1	10.0	0.7	43.0	22.0	48.2
Raleigh-Durham, NC MSA	10.2	−0.4	12.9	−0.2	8.6	−0.4	35.2	34.0	36.4
Richmond, VA MSA	9.3	−0.5	21.4	0.5	6.3	−0.1	9.4	0.2	18.3
San Antonio, TX MSA	15.1	−4.4	17.3	−5.4	9.4	−2.5	−7.1	−6.5	−9.7
Sarasota-Bradenton, FL MSA	8.8	0.5	15.2	2.1	7.5	0.3	26.7	24.8	27.6
Tampa-St. Petersburg-Clearwater, FL MSA	11.2	−0.2	15.3	−0.4	9.6	0.0	13.7	4.6	20.0
Tulsa, OK MSA	11.4	−1.8	14.1	−0.9	8.8	−2.4	−2.1	0.7	−5.9
Washington, DC-MD-VA-WV PMSA	7.4	0.9	20.2	3.3	5.8	0.9	32.6	13.7	43.1
West Palm Beach-Boca Raton, FL MSA	9.9	0.6	13.0	1.9	9.4	0.4	39.9	43.0	39.3
Wilmington, DE-MD PMSA	8.2	0.7	21.3	3.3	6.4	0.6	24.8	17.6	28.5
West (24)									
Albuquerque, NM MSA	13.8	−1.2	13.5	−0.4	14.2	−2.8	11.1	12.7	8.6
Bakersfield, CA MSA	20.8	3.8	18.0	3.0	22.5	4.7	46.6	69.8	37.2
Colorado Springs, CO MSA	8.0	−2.3	8.7	−2.2	6.5	−2.6	2.0	2.7	0.0
Denver, CO PMSA	8.1	−1.6	14.3	−2.8	5.9	−0.9	8.2	−0.9	17.5

Metropolitan area[a]									
Fresno, CA MSA	22.7	1.7	26.2	2.1	19.6	1.3	30.8	32.0	29.5
Honolulu, HI MSA	9.9	2.4	11.8	3.4	8.5	1.7	39.7	43.0	36.4
Las Vegas, NV-AZ MSA	11.1	0.1	11.9	0.4	10.7	0.0	86.1	92.7	83.1
Los Angeles-Long Beach, CA PMSA	17.9	2.8	22.2	3.6	14.6	2.3	28.0	26.8	29.5
Oakland, CA PMSA	9.7	0.4	19.4	0.6	7.7	0.5	20.3	11.2	25.4
Orange County, CA PMSA	10.3	1.9	15.6	2.4	8.2	1.6	44.1	42.1	45.6
Phoenix-Mesa, AZ MSA	12.0	-0.9	14.2	1.1	9.5	-3.1	35.3	46.1	20.3
Portland-Vancouver, OR-WA PMSA	9.5	-0.4	12.9	-1.9	7.6	0.0	21.3	21.6	21.0
Riverside-San Bernardino, CA PMSA	15.0	2.9	20.7	4.2	14.2	2.8	55.8	42.1	59.3
Sacramento, CA PMSA	12.2	0.9	20.0	2.8	9.6	0.5	31.5	28.1	33.8
Salt Lake City-Ogden, UT MSA	7.7	-1.8	15.7	-0.8	5.8	-1.8	1.1	9.9	-4.0
San Diego, CA MSA	12.4	1.1	14.6	1.2	10.8	1.1	24.7	21.2	28.6
San Francisco, CA PMSA	8.4	-0.6	11.3	-1.3	6.0	0.0	0.6	-3.8	8.4
San Jose, CA PMSA	7.5	0.0	8.8	-0.5	6.0	0.5	13.4	8.7	22.2
Seattle, WA PMSA	7.9	0.3	11.8	-0.6	6.8	0.8	24.1	3.9	37.9
Stockton-Lodi, CA MSA	17.7	2.0	22.5	2.8	12.2	1.3	32.7	31.6	35.2
Tacoma, WA PMSA	10.5	-0.9	15.9	-0.9	8.4	-0.6	11.3	4.4	16.9
Tucson, AZ MSA	14.7	-2.5	18.4	-1.7	9.7	-3.0	8.0	9.1	5.1
Vallejo-Fairfield-Napa, CA PMSA	8.3	0.9	9.5	1.6	6.7	0.2	30.3	38.0	18.5
Ventura, CA PMSA	9.2	2.0	9.0	2.3	9.3	1.9	43.6	48.0	42.9

Source: Authors' analysis of decennial census data.

a. Metropolitan areas with population over 500,000. Pertains to MSAs, PMSAs, and (in New England) NECMAs, as defined in June 1999 by OMB with modifications for central cities. See text.

b. No OMB-defined central city exists for metropolitan area.

REFERENCES

Blank, Rebecca. 2002. "Welfare Reform and the Economy." In *Welfare Reform and Beyond: The Future of the Safety Net,* edited by I. Sawhill, K. Weaver, R. Haskins, and A. Kane. Brookings.

Daly, Mary C., Deborah Reed, and Heather N. Royer. 2001. "Population Mobility and Income Inequality in California." San Francisco: Public Policy Institute of California.

Frey, William H. 2001. "Melting Pot Suburbs: A Census 2000 Study of Suburban Diversity." Brookings.

———. 2002. "Metro Magnets for Minorities and Whites: Melting Pots, the New Sunbelt, and the Heartland." Research Report 02–496. Ann Arbor: University of Michigan Population Studies Center.

Frey, William H., and Elaine L. Fielding. 1995. "Changing Urban Populations: Regional Restructuring, Racial Polarization and Poverty Concentration." *Cityscape* 1 (2): 1–66.

National Academy of Sciences. 1996. *Measuring Poverty: A New Approach.* Washington: National Academy Press.

Sum, Andrew, Ishwar Khatiwada, Jacqui Motroni, and Nathan Pond. 2002. "Moving Out and Moving In: Out-Migration and Foreign Immigration in the Northeast Region and New England during the 1990s." Boston: Northeastern University Center for Labor Market Studies.

Suro, Roberto, and Audrey Singer. 2002. "Latino Growth in Metropolitan America: Changing Patterns, New Locations." Brookings.

5

Stunning Progress, Hidden Problems

The Dramatic Decline of Concentrated Poverty in the 1990s

PAUL A. JARGOWSKY

For many years the conditions of life in the poorest of poor neighborhoods have attracted the attention of filmmakers, journalists, and academic researchers. Each of these witnesses, in his or her own way, has provided stark evidence of the devastating effects impoverished environments can have on those unfortunate enough to dwell within them, and of how these effects spill over into society at large.

Poverty, in government statistics, is defined by a family's income relative to a standard meant to reflect the cost of basic necessities (the "poverty line"). This narrow conception of poverty, however, fails to capture the multiple ways in which poverty degrades the quality of life and limits the opportunities of those in its grip. One of the most important aspects of poverty not captured in the official statistics is its spatial dimension. In theory poor families and their children could be widely dispersed throughout the population. In fact they tend to live near other poor people in neighborhoods with high poverty rates. The problem is particularly acute for the minority poor, who are segregated by both race and income.

Why should we be concerned with the spatial organization of poverty? The concentration of poor families and children in high-poverty ghettos, barrios,

The author thanks J. D. Kim, Sonia Monga, and Karl Ho for research assistance and technical support. He also acknowledges participants in the Social Science Workshop at the University of Texas at Dallas, including Brian Berry, Don Hicks, and Dan O'Brien and others who asked questions and made helpful suggestions at an early stage of this research. Also helpful were reviewers from the Brookings Institution.

and slums magnifies the problems faced by the poor. Concentrations of poor people lead to a concentration of the social ills that cause or are caused by poverty. Poor children in these neighborhoods not only lack basic necessities in their own homes, but also they must contend with a hostile environment that holds many temptations and few positive role models. Equally important, school districts and attendance zones are generally organized geographically, so that the residential concentration of the poor frequently results in low-performing schools. The concentration of poverty in central cities also may exacerbate the flight of middle-income and higher-income families to the suburbs, driving a wedge between social needs and the fiscal base required to address them.

Between 1970 and 1990, the spatial concentration of the poor rose dramatically in many U.S. metropolitan areas.[1] The number of people living in high-poverty areas doubled; the chance that a poor black child resided in a high-poverty neighborhood increased from roughly one-in-four to one-in-three; and the physical size of the blighted sections of many central cities increased even more dramatically. By contrast, poverty measured at the family level—did not increase during this period. Thus there was not a change in poverty per se, but a fundamental change in the spatial organization of poverty. The poor became more physically isolated from the social and economic mainstream of society.

Two important factors contributed to the increasing concentration of poverty during the 1970s and 1980s. First, weaknesses in local or regional economies tended to disproportionately affect central cities. Second, exclusionary suburban development patterns contributed to increasing economic segregation.

Policymakers have been anxious to know how the spatial organization of poverty may have changed in the 1990s. For most metropolitan areas and the country as a whole, the decade was a period of unparalleled economic growth. Rapid suburban development continued, however, and perhaps even accelerated during this period. The net effect of these trends on the concentration of poverty in the 1990s is therefore ambiguous.

Only the decennial census provides sufficient detail at the neighborhood level to examine the concentration of poverty. With the release of Census 2000, we are now able to assess the net impact of the economy, suburban development, and other forces on the spatial dimension of poverty over the last decade.

---

1. For a thorough discussion of the trends in concentrated poverty between 1970 and 1990, see Jargowsky (1997), especially chapter 2.

Based on the trend of prior decades, one might have reasonably assumed that high-poverty neighborhoods were an unavoidable aspect of urban life and would continue to grow inexorably in size and population. The latest evidence contradicts this gloomy assessment. This chapter documents a dramatic decline in the 1990s in the number of high-poverty neighborhoods, their population, and the concentration of the poor in these neighborhoods. It also finds, however, several indications that poverty rose in the older suburbs of many metropolitan areas, even during a decade of economic expansion. The chapter concludes with a discussion of the meaning of these trends, and the more recent decline in economic conditions, for poor families and communities in the current decade.

METHODOLOGY

This chapter examines the changes in the concentration of poverty in the 1990s using sample data (the "long form") from the 1990 and 2000 decennial censuses.

For the purpose of this study poverty is defined using official U.S. poverty guidelines. An individual is considered poor if he or she lives in a family whose income is less than a specific threshold that varies by family size and composition. Although the official definition suffers from a number of known flaws and limitations, it is nevertheless widely accepted.[2] More importantly the Census Bureau provides data on poverty status based on the long form of the census.

THE FEDERAL POVERTY STANDARD

Developed by Mollie Orshansky of the Social Security Administration in the 1960s for use in the War on Poverty, the federal poverty standard has been criticized from every conceivable angle. Despite its imperfections it has endured as both an administrative tool to determine program eligibility and as a research tool. Persons are considered poor if they live in families whose total family income is less than a threshold meant to represent the cost of basic necessities. The thresholds vary by family size and are adjusted each year for inflation. In 2002 the poverty level was $15,260 for a typical family of three and $18,400 for a typical family of four. For more information, see Orshansky (1965), Fisher (1992), and the HHS poverty website: http://aspe.hhs.gov/poverty/poverty.shtml.

---

2. Ruggles (1990).

In everyday usage, one can talk about a neighborhood in general terms without specifying exact boundaries. For tabulation purposes, however, every household in the nation must reside in one and only one geographically specific neighborhood. In this study we use census tracts as proxies for neighborhoods. Census tracts are small, relatively homogeneous areas devised by the Census Bureau and local planning agencies, making use of bounding features such as major roads, railroad tracks, and rivers whenever possible. On average, they contain 4,000 persons, but in practice they vary widely in population. They also vary widely in geographic size due to differences in population density. When initially delineated, census tracts are meant to be relatively homogeneous with respect to social and economic characteristics and housing stock considerations. Although they may not always capture the mental map of neighborhoods that city residents have, they do divide the nation along geographic lines. In less dense rural areas one census tract may represent all or a substantial portion of a county.

As populations grow and change, census tracts may be split, merged, or modified in other ways. Contemporaneous tracts are used in this chapter. In other words 1990 census tract boundaries are used to interpret 1990 data, and 2000 census tract boundaries are used for the 2000 figures. Using contemporaneous boundaries is important because to do otherwise would invite a systematic bias into the analysis. If, for example, the 2000 census tract grid were superimposed on 1970 data, average neighborhood population would be far smaller in 1970 than in 2000. Defining neighborhoods differently over time would systematically bias the results of any analysis that is sensitive to the size of the neighborhood units.[3]

Combining the poverty dimension and the spatial dimension, a census tract is considered a high-poverty neighborhood if 40 percent or more of its residents are classified as poor using the federal poverty standard. Although any specific threshold is inherently arbitrary, the 40 percent level has become the standard in the literature and has even been incorporated into federal data analysis and program rules.[4] In addition to tabulating the number of high-poverty neighborhoods and the number and characteristics of their residents,

---

3. This is known as the Modifiable Areal Unit Problem, and has been studied extensively by geographers. See Openshaw and Taylor (1981). A consistent set of census tract boundaries, however, is employed for mapping purposes. That way it is possible to show how different areas changed over time. In view of that there is not an exact correspondence between the data used for the maps and the data used for the tables and figures presented in the text. For 1990 and earlier years these maps use data interpolated to the 2000 census tract grid by the Urban Institute and Geolytics, Inc.

4. Danziger and Gottschalk (1987); Jargowsky and Bane (1990); Kasarda (1993).

this paper examines the concentration of poverty—defined as the percentage of the poor in a city or region that resides in high-poverty neighborhoods.

These two concepts—the incidence of high-poverty neighborhoods, and the concentration of poverty—are not unrelated. In general the greater the number of high-poverty neighborhoods in a city or metropolitan area, the more likely poor residents of that place will be "concentrated" in those neighborhoods. Each measure, however, answers a different question. The former relates to the geographic footprint of very-low-income districts within a city or metropolitan area, which has important implications for economic development efforts and city planning. The latter captures the percentage of poor individuals who not only must cope with their own low incomes, but also with the economic and social effects of the poverty that surrounds them.

The figures presented below include all census tracts in the United States, including both metropolitan and nonmetropolitan areas, except as noted. A metropolitan area usually consists of one or more population centers (central cities) and the nearby counties that have close economic and commuting ties to them.[5] The Census Bureau defines several types of metropolitan areas. There are stand-alone Metropolitan Statistical Areas (MSAs) and Primary Metropolitan Statistical Areas (PMSAs). PMSAs are part of larger constructions called Consolidated Metropolitan Statistical Areas (CMSAs). In this chapter metropolitan areas are defined to include MSAs and PMSAs, not CMSAs. CMSAs are so large that they do not represent unified housing and labor markets, and so they are not considered in this analysis.[6]

The boundaries of metropolitan areas are adjusted over time like census tracts. New counties are added, and existing counties are deleted or moved to different metropolitan areas if there are changes in their demographics, in the commuting patterns of their residents, or if the Census Bureau changes the rules for allocating counties to metropolitan areas. In this chapter the definitions of metropolitan areas (including MSAs and PMSAs) in effect for Census 2000 are applied to both 1990 and 2000 data. Thus any changes in the figures for metropolitan areas shown below reflect actual changes in population demographics and not changes in boundaries or definitions.

---

5. New England metropolitan areas are built up from subdivisions of counties rather than whole counties. The U.S. Census Bureau also defines New England County Metropolitan Areas (NECMAs), which are composed of whole counties.

6. NECMAs are not considered for the same reasons. Nonmetropolitan areas were first completely divided into census tracts in 1990, so Census 2000 provides the first opportunity to conduct a nationwide study of the trends in concentrated poverty. For the purposes of this chapter, nonmetropolitan neighborhoods are grouped by state, but it should be noted that these areas are residuals and may or may not be contiguous.

To examine variation among racial and ethnic groups, population is divided first by Hispanic origin, and then non-Hispanics are further divided by racial group—black, white, American Indian, Asian, and people who indicated more than one race (in 2000) or "other race." Thus a reference to whites refers to non-Hispanic persons who indicated "White or Caucasian" as their sole racial group on the census form, a reference to blacks indicates non-Hispanic persons who chose "Black or African American" as their sole race, and so on.

A portion of this study analyzes levels and changes in high-poverty neighborhoods based on their location in central cities, suburbs, or rural areas. In practice, census tracts are subdivisions of counties, and thus often do not respect the municipal borders that define central cities.[7] In such cases the tract's poverty status is classified by the poverty rate for the entire tract. In other words there is only one poverty rate for each whole census tract, no matter how many ways the tract is split over city or metropolitan boundaries. Thus the count of persons residing in high-poverty areas is consistent, and systematic biases that would arise from the splitting of census tracts are avoided.

FINDINGS

Census 2000 highlights a welcome departure from past trends in concentrated inner-city poverty, but flags an area of growing concern in economically struggling suburbs.

Population Living in High-Poverty Neighborhoods Declined Dramatically in the 1990s

The strong economic conditions that prevailed throughout most of the 1990s appear to have dramatically altered long-term trends in the spatial organization of poverty. The number of high-poverty neighborhoods—census tracts with poverty rates of 40 percent or more—declined by more than one-fourth, from 3,417 in 1990 to 2,510 in 2000 nationwide. This is a stunning reversal of the trend between 1970 and 1990, as shown in figure 5-1.[8]

More importantly the total number of residents of high-poverty areas declined by 24 percent, from 10.4 million in 1990 to 7.9 million in 2000. The sharp decline does not merely reflect declines in overall poverty. In fact, despite the strong economy, the number of persons classified as poor in the

7. In New England, census tracts can even cross metropolitan area boundaries.

8. The data in figure 5-2 are for metropolitan areas only, as they existed at the time of each census. Nationwide data on neighborhood poverty are not available prior to 1990, because census tracts in nonmetropolitan areas were defined for the first time with the release of the 1990 census.

FIGURE 5-1. High-Poverty Neighborhoods and High-Poverty Neighborhood Population, U.S. Metropolitan Areas, 1970–2000

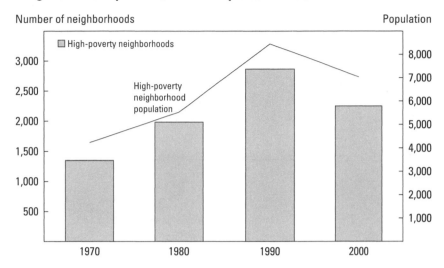

Source: Based on metropolitan areas as defined in year of census.

United States actually rose between 1990 and 2000, from 31.7 million to 33.9 million. The overall poverty rate did decline over the decade (from 13.1 percent to 12.4 percent), but by a much smaller degree than did the number of high-poverty neighborhoods. The implication is that there was a substantial change in the spatial organization of poverty during the 1990s. Poor neighborhoods, or at least the residents of high-poverty neighborhoods in 1990, benefited disproportionately from the boom.

Virtually the whole spectrum of racial and ethnic groups benefited from the decline in the number of persons residing in high-poverty neighborhoods. The number of white residents of these areas declined by 29 percent (from 2.7 to 1.9 million), and the number of black residents declined by an even faster 36 percent (from 4.8 million to 3.1 million). Despite this decline, however, blacks remained the single largest racial or ethnic group living in high-poverty neighborhoods.

The major exception to the pattern was Hispanics, whose numbers in high-poverty neighborhoods increased by 1.6 percent. At the same time the number of Hispanics in the United States increased dramatically in the 1990s—57.9 percent, compared to only 3.4 percent growth for whites and 16.2 percent for blacks. In the context of this rapid population growth, fueled by the immigration of many low-income persons from Central and South America, as well as births to immigrant families, a growth rate of only

FIGURE 5-2. Racial/Ethnic Composition of High-Poverty U.S. Neighborhoods, 1990–2000

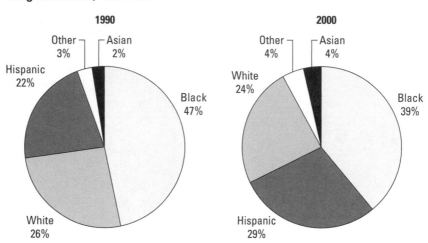

1.6 percent in the number of Hispanics in high-poverty neighborhoods could be viewed as a positive outcome.

Given that different racial and ethnic groups were growing at different rates, the composition of high-poverty zones changed over the period. Figure 5-2 shows how the population in high-poverty neighborhoods changed between 1990 and 2000 by race and ethnicity. Hispanic and Asian percentages increased, whereas those for whites and blacks declined; Hispanics now make up a larger share of high-poverty neighborhood residents than whites.

Midwest and South Experienced Steepest Declines in High-Poverty Neighborhoods

Earlier research indicated that the expansion of high-poverty ghettos and barrios was particularly acute in the Midwest, especially in central city neighborhoods. Now, however, the Midwest has exhibited the most rapid turnaround during the boom of the 1990s.

As shown in figure 5-3 population changes in high-poverty areas varied dramatically across regions of the country. In general places with the largest declines in the number of high-poverty neighborhoods also experienced the steepest drops in the number of people living in such areas.[9] The decline was

9. Exceptions included metropolitan areas such as Akron, Cleveland, Pittsburgh, and Youngstown, which despite double-digit decreases in the number of high-poverty neighborhoods, had declines of less than 30,000 people living in such neighborhoods.

FIGURE 5-3. Population of High-Poverty Neighborhoods by Region, 1990–2000

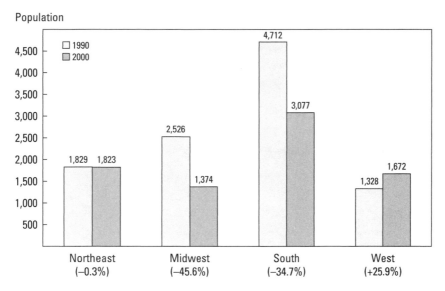

Population

largest in the Midwest where the population of high-poverty neighborhoods was nearly halved over the decade. There was also a substantial decline in the South, which nonetheless remained home to the largest number of high-poverty neighborhoods in 2000.

At the same time the number of high-poverty neighborhoods in the Northeast remained virtually the same in 2000 as in 1990, and the West saw a 26 percent increase in the population of these neighborhoods, albeit from a small base. In 1990 the population of high-poverty neighborhoods in the West was half that of the Midwest; by 2000 nearly 300,000 more people lived in high-poverty neighborhoods in the West than in the Midwest. This increase is explained almost entirely by an increase in the size and population of Hispanic barrios; the number of non-Hispanic persons in high-poverty areas in the West declined slightly.

Although only two out of four regions showed significant declines in the aggregate, the view at the state level is more positive. Map 5-1 shows the percentage change in high-poverty neighborhood population by state. Forty states had declines, with an average decline of 78,000 persons residing in high-poverty neighborhoods. Ten states, as well as the District of Columbia, had increases averaging 61,000 persons. Trends in the West as a whole are driven by California, which had an 87 percent increase in the population of high-poverty neighborhoods.

MAP 5-1. **Percentage Change in Population of High-Poverty Neighborhoods by State, 1990–2000**

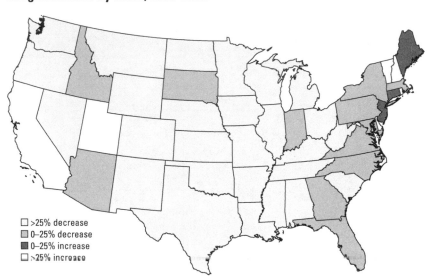

☐ >25% decrease
▨ 0–25% decrease
■ 0–25% increase
☐ >25% increase

Table 5-1 shows the fifteen metropolitan areas with the largest decreases in high-poverty-area population. The regional flavor is readily apparent. Without exception the metropolitan areas listed are located in the Midwest or in the South. Detroit's decline in the population of high-poverty neighborhoods was substantially larger than in any other metropolitan area. Chicago, however, experienced a comparable decrease in the number of high-poverty census tracts. All told 200 out of 331 metropolitan areas (MSAs and PMSAs) saw declines in the number of people living in high-poverty neighborhoods (table 5A-1 shows relevant data for all U.S. metropolitan areas, and non-metropolitan areas by state).

In most metropolitan areas high-poverty neighborhoods tend to be clustered in one or two main agglomerations located in the central city. In this way the United States differs markedly from most other nations of the world, in which poor neighborhoods are typically located on the periphery of the urban areas. As these zones of concentrated poverty increased in size between 1970 and 1990, they contributed to a general process of population deconcentration that generated "donut cities"—depopulating and impoverished urban cores surrounded by prosperous and growing suburbs. The 1990s, however, were a boon for central cities. Just as central cities bore the brunt of the fiscal, social, and economic burden of concentrating poverty in prior decades, they became prime beneficiaries of its reduction in the 1990s.

TABLE 5-1. Top Fifteen Metropolitan Areas by Decline in Population of High-Poverty Neighborhoods, 1990–2000

Metropolitan area	Decline in population		Decline in census tracts (number)
	Number	Percent	
Detroit, MI	313,217	74.4	97
Chicago, IL	195,075	43.1	73
San Antonio, TX	107,272	70.1	18
Houston, TX	77,662	47.8	27
Milwaukee-Waukesha, WI	63,357	45.0	16
Memphis, TN-AR-MS	61,924	43.6	11
New Orleans, LA	57,332	34.6	18
Brownsville-Harlingen-San Benito, TX	50,559	37.1	4
Columbus, OH	48,020	55.4	11
El Paso, TX	44,489	40.2	4
Dallas, TX	41,805	45.3	19
St. Louis, MO-IL	38,866	35.5	13
Lafayette, LA	33,978	54.8	10
Minneapolis-St. Paul, MN-WI	32,005	40.5	18
Flint, MI	31,631	61.2	6

A case in point is the Detroit metropolitan area. Map 5-2 shows the high-poverty zones in Detroit over three decades. From 1970 to 1990 there is a rapid growth in the number of neighborhoods with poverty rates of 40 percent or more. By 1990 nearly half the land area of the city of Detroit, the boundary of which is shown in black, had become a high-poverty zone. This trend is reversed between 1990 and 2000. The change is so dramatic it strains credulity. To some extent the maps may overstate the change, because many of Detroit's census tracts had all but emptied out by 1990. Thus a movement or change in poverty status of just a few families could serve to change the color of an entire census tract on the map. Even so the Detroit metropolitan area underwent an astonishing 74.4 percent reduction in the number of people residing in high-poverty zones between 1990 and 2000.

The growth of high-poverty zones between 1970 and 1990 and their subsequent declines were by no means limited to the Midwest. Map 5-3 shows the trend in the Dallas metropolitan area over the last three decades. The high-poverty areas of Dallas experienced their greatest expansion between 1980 and 1990, after the oil price "bust" hammered the region's economy. At the same time Dallas was also experiencing rapid suburban development. Plano, Texas, a "boomburb" just north of Dallas, was for years the fastest growing city in the nation.[10] After 1990, however, there was substantial

10. Lang and Simmons (2003).

MAP 5-2. Neighborhood Poverty Rates in Detroit, 1970–2000

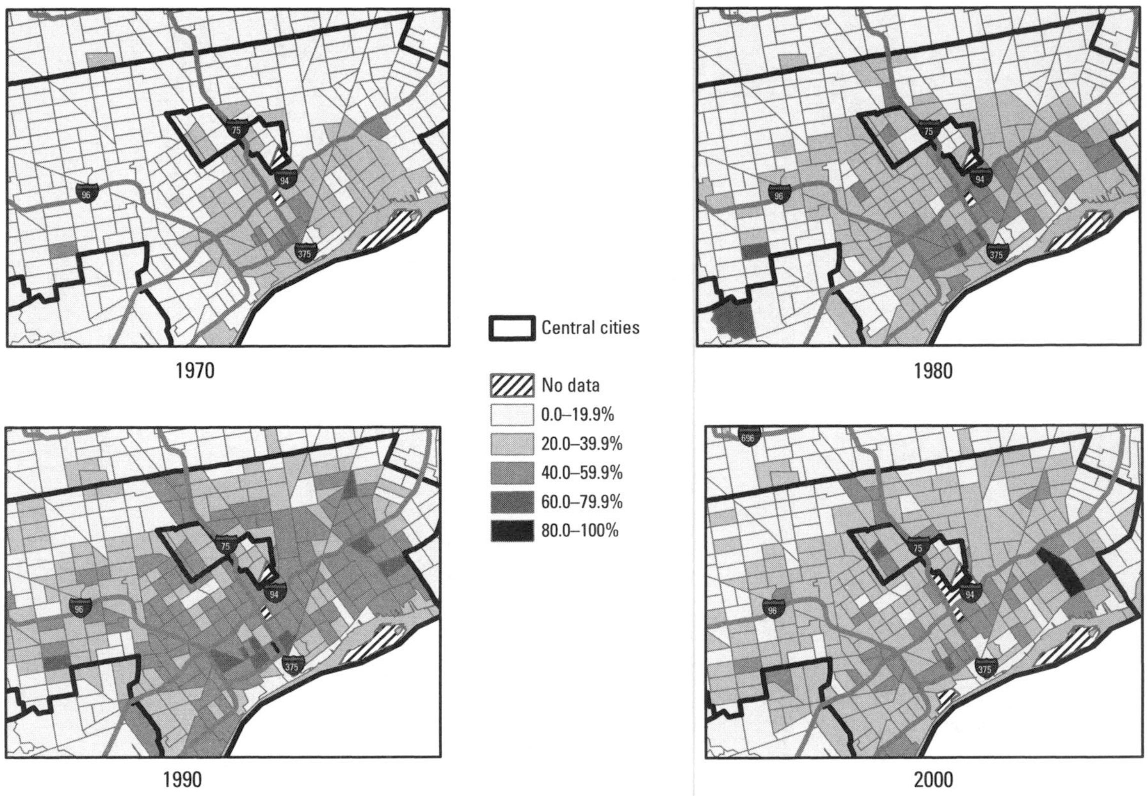

1980

2000

1970

1990

Central cities

No data
0.0–19.9%
20.0–39.9%
40.0–59.9%
60.0–79.9%
80.0–100%

MAPPING POOR NEIGHBORHOODS

The maps shown in these figures were produced using an interactive website. By visiting the website, users can easily produce maps such as these for any metropolitan area in the United States. The address for the website is www.urbanpoverty.net. Construction of the website was funded by the Brookings Institution Metropolitan Policy Program and the Bruton Center for Development Studies at the University of Texas at Dallas. Comments and suggestions about the website are welcome.

redevelopment of the downtown area, including condominium and apartment developments just north of downtown and along Interstate 45. The overall decline in the population of Dallas's high-poverty areas was 45 percent between 1990 and 2000.

The regional picture is quite different when we examine the metropolitan areas with the largest increases in high-poverty area population. Seven of the fifteen metropolitan areas in table 5-2 are located in one state— California—and six of those lie in either Southern California or the state's agricultural hub, the San Joaquin Valley. Other metropolitan areas include a handful in the Northeast (Providence, Wilmington, Rochester, and two suburban New Jersey metropolitan areas) and two smaller metropolitan

T A B L E 5 - 2 . Top Fifteen Metropolitan Areas, by Increase in Population of High-Poverty Neighborhoods, 1990–2000

| | Increase in population | | Increase in census tracts |
Metropolitan area	Number	Percent	(number)
Los Angeles-Long Beach, CA	292,359	109.2	81
Fresno, CA	60,005	68.7	12
Riverside-San Bernardino, CA	58,669	260.5	12
Washington, DC-MD-VA-WV	56,954	276.4	14
Bakersfield, CA	42,622	190.8	9
San Diego, CA	33,274	86.1	10
McAllen-Edinburg-Mission, TX	28,117	12.0	(1)
Providence-Fall River-Warwick, RI-MA	22,186	235.4	3
Chico-Paradise, CA	16,675	103.3	4
Middlesex-Somerset-Hunterdon, NJ	14,020	n.a.[a]	3
Wilmington-Newark, DE-MD	12,349	276.3	2
Bryan-College Station, TX	11,746	29.4	4
Visalia-Tulare-Porterville, CA	11,176	60.1	2
Rochester, NY	9,989	29.8	0
Monmouth-Ocean, NJ	9,114	318.3	(1)

a. Middlesex-Somerset-Hunterdon, NJ, had no census tracts with poverty rates of 40 percent or higher in 1990.

areas in Texas. Altogether a total of 91 out of 331 metropolitan areas had at least a nominal increase in persons living in high-poverty neighborhoods.

It is worth noting that the size of the population increase in high-poverty zones falls off rapidly as we read down the list. The fifteenth metropolitan area, Monmouth-Ocean, New Jersey, had a 9,000-person increase in its high-poverty neighborhood population, whereas the fifteenth metropolitan area in table 5-1 (Flint, Michigan) had a 32,000-person decline in its poverty-area population.

Map 5-4 illustrates the process in Los Angeles. The expansion of high-poverty neighborhoods (40 percent and above) is apparent. Also apparent is a considerable increase in the number of neighborhoods with moderate poverty rates (between 20 and 40 percent).

Los Angeles is notable for three factors that may explain its divergence from the national trend. First, the city experienced a destructive riot after the Rodney King verdict in 1992, and further heightening of racial tension due to the trial of O. J. Simpson in 1995. The riot and its aftermath almost certainly accelerated middle-class flight from the central city area, and the trial emphasized racial divisions in the region. Second, the Los Angeles region experienced tremendous immigration from Mexico and other Central and South American countries.[11] Riverside/San Bernardino, Fresno, and (to a lesser extent) San Diego also experienced a significant increase in low-income Hispanic population; the population of high-poverty neighborhoods increased in these areas as well. Third, the recession of the early 1990s was particularly severe in Southern California, and the economic recovery there was not as rapid as in other parts of California (such as the San Francisco/Silicon Valley area) that benefited from the Internet boom.

The other major exception to the trend was the Washington, D.C., metropolitan area. The number of high-poverty neighborhoods in the nation's capital more than doubled over the decade. The major factor at work here was likely the devastating fiscal crisis that plagued the District during the early and mid-1990s. The crisis undermined public confidence in the governance of the District and led to serious cutbacks in public services, including public safety. For this and other reasons there was a rapid out-migration of moderate- and middle-income black families, particularly into suburban Maryland counties to the east of the central city. The poor were left behind in economically isolated neighborhoods with increasing poverty rates. The late 1990s real estate boom in Washington seems not to have improved conditions in these neighborhoods.

11. During the 1990s Los Angeles County lost significant white population, at the same time that its Hispanic population grew by nearly 900,000.

MAP 5 - 3.   Neighborhood Poverty Rates in Los Angeles, 1970–2000

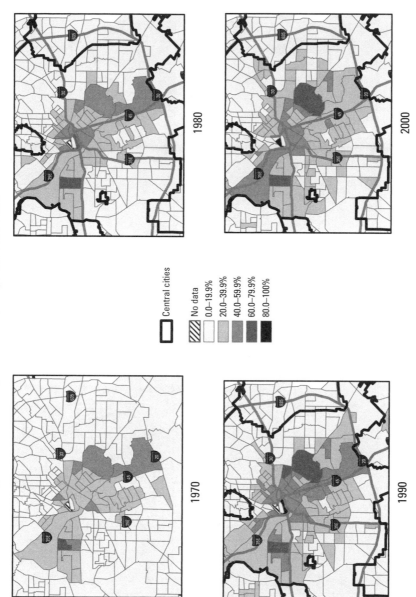

1980

2000

1970

1990

Central cities

No data
0.0–19.9%
20.0–39.9%
40.0–59.9%
60.0–79.9%
80.0–100%

MAP 5-4. Neighborhood Poverty Rates in Dallas, 1970–2000

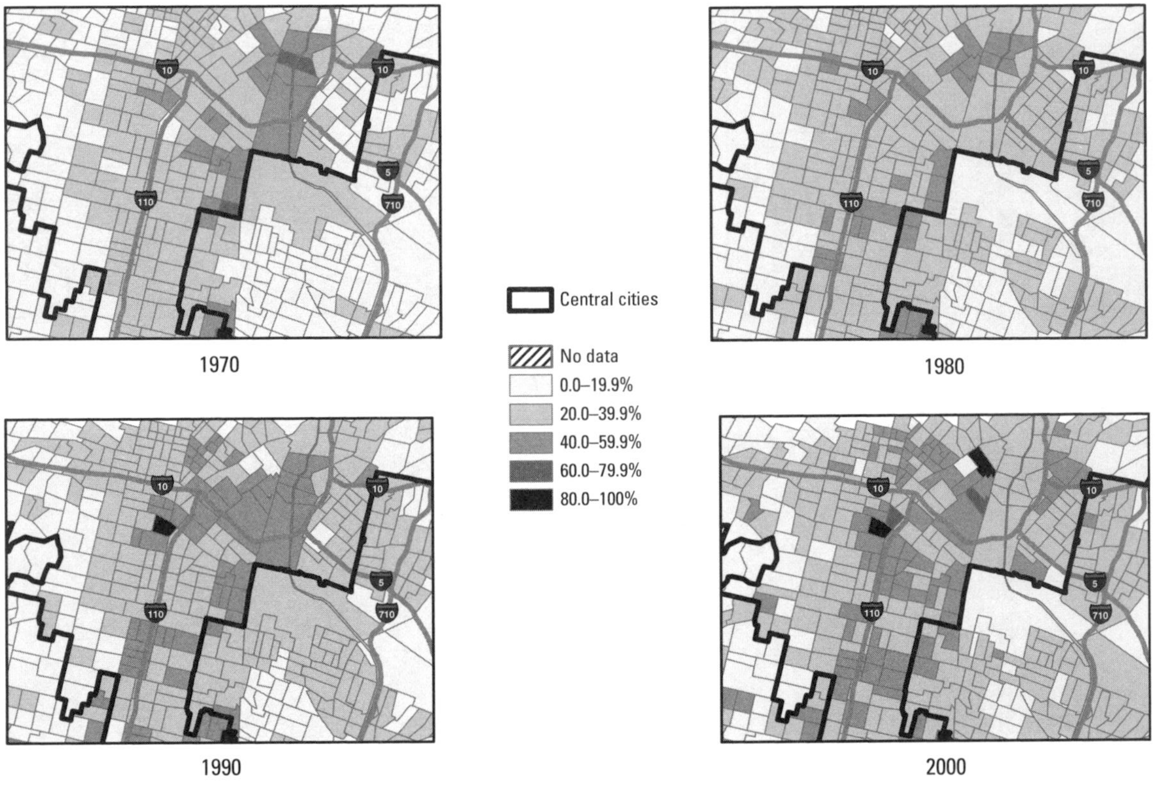

1980

2000

1970

1990

Central cities

No data
0.0–19.9%
20.0–39.9%
40.0–59.9%
60.0–79.9%
80.0–100%

Of course, these metropolitan areas and others in table 5-2 represent the exceptions to an overall decline in the number of high-poverty neighborhoods, and population of high-poverty neighborhoods, in the 1990s. Most areas of the United States saw improvements over the decade of greater magnitude than the deterioration that occurred in a minority of metropolitan areas.

Concentrated Poverty Declined among All Racial and Ethnic Groups

In the 1990s, consonant with the decline in high-poverty neighborhoods, the concentration of poverty—defined as the proportion of the poor in a given area in high-poverty zones—dropped across most of the nation. The number of poor persons living in high-poverty areas declined 27 percent, from 4.8 million to 3.5 million. In 1990 the share of poor individuals nationwide who lived in high-poverty areas (the concentrated poverty rate) was 15 percent. By 2000 that figure had declined to 10 percent.

These declines are both striking and gratifying. Between 1970 and 1990 the concentration of poverty grew steadily worse, especially for blacks. About one-fourth of the black poor lived in high-poverty areas in 1970; by 1990 the proportion had increased to one-third. The rate was even higher for black children, especially those in single-parent families. The economic and social isolation of these families and children prompted great concern among researchers investigating the opportunities and constraints facing low-income families in economically impoverished neighborhoods.[12]

Some have argued that poor persons may benefit from having poor neighbors. For example, they may share coping strategies and draw on geographically based support networks. Yet most researchers—and most of the general public—assume that the benefits of poor persons' living in high-poverty neighborhoods are outweighed by the extra hardships that such neighborhoods impose, including their deleterious effects on child development and the ability of poor adults to achieve self-sufficiency.

For those reasons, it is good news that all racial and ethnic groups shared in the deconcentration of poverty of the 1990s, as shown in figure 5-4. The decline was most significant for poor blacks; the percentage living in high-poverty neighborhoods declined from 30.4 percent in 1990 to 18.6 percent in 2000. American Indians experienced a similarly large decrease. Yet despite these substantial declines, blacks and American Indians still suffer the highest concentrated poverty rates, the former in highly segregated urban ghettos and the latter in remote rural reservations. The concentration of poverty

12. Wilson (1987); Mincy and Weiner (1993); Danziger and Gottschalk (1987).

FIGURE 5-4. **Percentage of Poor Living in High-Poverty Neighborhoods, by Race/Ethnicity, 1990–2000**

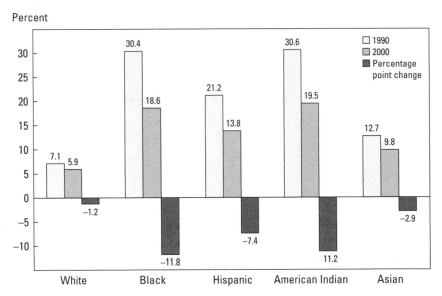

among non-Hispanic whites, low to start with, dropped by roughly one-sixth. The chances that a poor Hispanic lives in a high-poverty neighborhood dropped from more than one in five (21.2 percent) in 1990 to less than one in seven (13.8 percent) in 2000.[13]

The declines in concentrated poverty were not driven by a few large or unrepresentative metropolitan areas. Indeed substantial declines were the national norm. Of the 331 metropolitan areas in the United States in 2000, 227 (69 percent) saw the concentration of poor blacks decrease between 1990 and 2000; another 49 (15 percent) had no change; and only 55 (17 percent) had increases (table 5A-1). The story was similar for nonmetropolitan areas: The concentration of poor blacks in rural areas declined in twenty-nine of forty-nine states and remained the same in another eleven states.[14]

The numbers were similar, if not quite as positive, for Hispanics. More than half of all metropolitan areas had decreases in concentrated Hispanic

13. Unfortunately due to limitations in the collection of detailed ethnicity for Hispanic subgroups in Census 2000, it is not possible to examine the concentration of poverty among people of, for example, Cuban, Puerto Rican, or Mexican ancestry.

14. The fiftieth state is New Jersey, which does not have any nonmetropolitan areas, according to the official census definitions.

T A B L E 5 - 3 . Concentration of Black and Hispanic Poverty in the Twenty Largest Metropolitan Areas, 1990–2000[a]

Metropolitan area	Black 1990	Black 2000	Black Change	Hispanic 1990	Hispanic 2000	Hispanic Change
Detroit, MI	53.9	16.4	−37.5	36.1	6.9	−26.1
Minneapolis-St. Paul, MN-WI	33.3	13.0	−20.4	18.2	5.9	−12.3
Chicago, IL	45.3	26.4	−18.8	12.4	4.7	−7.7
St. Louis, MO-IL	39.1	23.8	−15.3	12.8	5.2	−7.6
Baltimore, MD	34.7	21.5	−13.2	9.7	3.5	−6.2
Dallas, TX	25.4	13.8	−11.6	12.8	3.5	−9.3
Tampa-St. Petersburg-Clearwater, FL	29.1	17.8	−11.4	7.3	4.7	−2.6
Houston, TX	28.0	17.1	−10.9	13.1	2.8	−10.3
Phoenix-Mesa, AZ	25.7	15.4	−10.3	21.3	12.2	−9.1
New York, NY	40.1	32.5	−7.6	40.9	32.2	−8.7
Philadelphia, PA-NJ	31.0	23.6	−7.5	61.6	49.5	−12.1
Boston, MA-NH	12.5	6.2	−6.3	10.7	8.1	−2.6
Atlanta, GA	26.6	20.5	−6.1	6.8	2.5	−4.2
Seattle-Bellevue-Everett, WA	6.8	3.4	−3.3	8.1	1.3	−6.8
San Diego, CA	15.4	13.0	−2.4	10.2	12.5	**2.3**
Nassau-Suffolk, NY	0.5	0.0	−0.5	0.0	0.0	0.0
Orange County, CA	0.0	0.0	0.0	0.0	0.1	**0.1**
Los Angeles-Long Beach, CA	17.3	21.3	**4.1**	9.1	16.9	**7.8**
Riverside-San Bernardino, CA	5.7	12.3	**6.6**	4.4	8.9	**4.5**
Washington, DC-MD-VA-WV	6.3	15.0	**8.7**	1.0	0.4	−0.6

a. Figures represent percentage of metropolitan-area-wide poor individuals in each racial and ethnic group living in census tracts with poverty rates of 40 percent or higher. Increases shown in bold.

poverty, eighty-seven (26 percent) had increases, and the remainder experienced no change.

The deconcentration of poverty for racial and ethnic minorities spread widely across the nation's largest metropolitan areas. Table 5-3 shows concentrated poverty rates among blacks and Hispanics in the twenty largest metropolitan areas, sorted by change in the concentrated black poverty rate between 1990 and 2000. Most of these areas experienced declines in the concentration of poverty for both groups. The largest declines for blacks were in Detroit (37.5 percentage points), Minneapolis-St. Paul (20.3), and Chicago (18.8). Four metropolitan areas had double-digit percentage point declines in the concentrated poverty rate for Hispanics: Detroit (29.1 percentage points), Minneapolis-St. Paul (12.3), Philadelphia (12.1), and Houston (10.3).

To be sure the percentage-point declines were generally largest in areas that had high rates of concentrated poverty to begin with; although the share of blacks living in high-poverty neighborhoods in the Seattle metropolitan area was halved in the 1990s, this represented a decline of only 3.3 percentage points. Nevertheless the extent of the decline in places like Detroit and Minneapolis-St. Paul is remarkable compared to an area like New York, which despite modest declines still has very high concentrated poverty rates for both groups.

Consistent with the data on the population of high-poverty areas, two areas of the country cut against the national trend. In Los Angeles-Long Beach and Riverside-San Bernardino, concentrated poverty increased among both the black and Hispanic poor; in San Diego, Hispanic concentrated poverty rose. In Washington, D.C., poor blacks became more spatially concentrated, but poor Hispanics did not.

One additional note on Western high-poverty neighborhoods: In that region, the increase in high-poverty neighborhoods owed almost entirely to an increase in the number of barrios (predominantly Hispanic high-poverty communities). Although increasing concentrated poverty among Hispanics in Southern California is certainly cause for concern, researchers have expended considerably greater effort studying the deleterious effects that high-poverty neighborhoods in the Midwest and Northeast have on the life chances of their residents, who are predominantly black. With their substantial immigrant populations Western inner-city barrios could represent more of a "gateway" to residential and economic mobility than inner-city ghettos in other areas of the country. Regardless, the rise in concentrated Hispanic poverty in California during the 1990s highlights a need to better understand how the opportunity structure in these communities may differ from that in other types of high-poverty neighborhoods.[15]

Number of High-Poverty Neighborhoods in Rural Areas and Central Cities Dropped; Little Change in Suburbs

This chapter has considered statistics on changes in high-poverty neighborhoods and the concentration of poverty at the national and metropolitan levels. These statistics obscure an important aspect of the trend in the 1990s that the maps help illuminate: Central cities, rather than suburbs, reaped the benefits of the decline. Not even the maps, however, reveal what transpired in the rural United States. This section examines changes within metropolitan areas, and outside them, in neighborhood poverty over the decade.

All neighborhoods—census tracts—nationwide can be classified as lying within the central cities of metropolitan areas, the suburbs—defined as the balance of metropolitan areas—or nonmetropolitan areas, which consist of rural areas and cities and towns too small or detached to be considered part of a metropolitan area. As shown in figure 5-5, the decline in high-poverty

---

15. For recent evidence exploring differences in job seeking in predominantly Hispanic versus predominantly black high-poverty communities, see Elliott and Sims (2001).

FIGURE 5-5. Population of High-Poverty Neighborhoods, by Location, 1990–2000

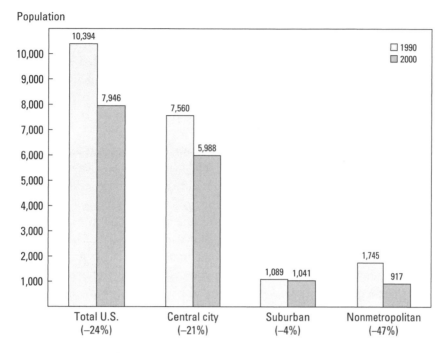

Population

area population was actually largest in nonmetropolitan areas, at nearly 50 percent. Central city areas, as indicated by the maps, also experienced a large decline of 21 percent.

It was the suburbs that had the slowest overall decline in poverty area residents—only 4.4 percent. As a result of these differing declines, by 2000 suburban United States was actually home to more neighborhoods of concentrated poverty than rural United States. Although the suburbs have more than twice the number of residents as nonmetropolitan areas, this finding is nonetheless striking given that the overall poverty rate outside metropolitan areas (14.6 percent) was considerably higher in 2000 than the poverty rate in suburbs (8.4 percent).

Moreover a careful inspection of the geography of suburban poverty during the 1990s reveals some disturbing trends. Not only did the number of neighborhoods of high poverty decline slowly in the suburbs, in addition poverty rates actually increased along the outer edges of central cities and in the inner-ring suburbs of many metropolitan areas, including those that saw dramatic declines in poverty concentration. In short poverty trends in these areas moved in the opposite direction from those in inner-city neighborhoods and booming suburbs at the metropolitan fringe.[16]

The economic decline of inner-ring suburbs, already evident in earlier decades, continued in the 1990s even as conditions were improving dramatically in most central cities.[17] The fact that inner-ring suburbs declined during this period is astonishing. Census 2000 was conducted in April of 2000, coinciding with the peak of a long economic boom. Unemployment rates nationwide were 4 percent, and lower in some of these metropolitan areas. The economy, in all likelihood, will never be stronger than it was during this period, at least not for any extended period of time.

A vigorous debate is under way concerning the role of suburban development in central city and older suburban decline and the concentration of poverty. There is, as yet, no consensus that rapid suburban development, characterized as "sprawl" by its opponents, exacerbates economic decline in the core. In fact some argue the contrary, and contend that these development patterns are a consequence of the economic and social disorder of the inner cities. These questions will continue to engender vigorous debate in the years ahead. It is clear from the data and maps presented here, however, that there is reason to be concerned about the prospects for inner-ring suburbs. If poverty in these areas rose during the strongest economy we can reasonably expect to enjoy, then they may well have a bleak future and develop many of the same fiscal and social concerns that plagued central cities in earlier periods.

CONCLUSION

The concentration of poverty is an important public policy concern because it has dynamic effects on income distribution, because it undermines the political and social fabric of the nation's major metropolitan areas, and—most importantly—because it restricts opportunity for some. Fortunately the excellent economy of the 1990s reversed several decades of increasing concentration of poverty and central city decline. With few exceptions metropolitan and rural areas across the United States saw a drop in concentrated poverty for all racial and ethnic groups.

16. For maps of neighborhood poverty rate change over time, see www.brookings.edu/metro/publications/jargowskypoverty.htm, or the interactive website, www.urbanpoverty.net.
17. Orfield (1996, 2002).

The extent to which some of these gains have already been erased by the downturn since the date of the Census is not known. Even at the height of the boom, however, troubling signs could be found that the pattern of metropolitan development, with rapid growth at the periphery, might be undermining other parts of metropolitan areas, particularly the inner ring of suburbs. This quiet erosion, largely unnoticed during the good times of the 1990s, leaves metropolitan areas in a weaker state and reduces their ability to cope with the less robust economic conditions that prevail today.

Although the reductions in concentration of poverty in the 1990s are certainly welcome news, it is difficult to be sanguine about the long-term picture. The snapshot of progress as of April of 2000 may be as misleading as the level of the NASDAQ on that date. If the inner-ring suburbs provide any indication, then the underlying development pattern that leads to greater neighborhood stratification was still at work in the 1990s, and is likely to have continued in the considerably weaker economic climate of the last three years. If so, greater concentration of poverty and more geographically stratified metropolitan areas could exacerbate social problems in a host of areas, from public safety to education to transportation. We should celebrate the gains made during the 1990s, to the extent that they have not already been erased, but we should not ignore the warning signs that U.S. society is still vulnerable to increasing concentration of poverty.

TABLE 5A-1. Population of High-Poverty Neighborhoods and Concentrated Poverty Rates, Metropolitan and Nonmetropolitan Areas, 1990–2000

Area	Total population, 2000	Number of high-poverty census tracts			Population in high-poverty census tracts			Concentrated poverty rate, total		
		1990	2000	Change	1990	2000	Change	1990	2000	Change
Metropolitan areas										
Abilene, TX	126,555	2	1	−1	1,536	581	−955	4.2	2.2	−2.0
Akron, OH	694,960	19	7	−12	48,632	22,268	−26,364	23.4	10.1	−13.3
Albany, GA	120,822	9	7	−2	23,725	18,700	−5,025	49.9	34.5	−15.4
Albany-Schenectady-Troy, NY	875,583	2	6	4	8,654	13,033	4,379	4.9	7.0	2.1
Albuquerque, NM	712,738	5	3	−2	12,523	10,999	−1,524	7.1	5.3	−1.8
Alexandria, LA	126,337	6	5	−1	15,204	11,854	−3,350	26.2	22.6	−3.6
Allentown-Bethlehem-Easton, PA	637,958	2	5	3	9,641	14,645	5,004	8.1	10.2	2.1
Altoona, PA	129,144	1	1	0	1,702	1,739	37	3.8	4.3	0.5
Amarillo, TX	217,858	7	2	−5	8,093	3,168	−4,925	12.7	4.3	−8.5
Anchorage, AK	260,283	0	0	0	0	0	0	0.0	0.0	0.0
Ann Arbor, MI	578,736	8	8	0	36,182	28,937	−7,245	24.4	25.2	0.8
Anniston, AL	112,249	3	2	−1	6,498	5,076	−1,422	17.9	10.5	−7.4
Appleton-Oshkosh-Neenah, WI	358,365	2	1	−1	7,348	5,614	−1,734	7.6	5.3	−2.3
Asheville, NC	225,965	3	2	−1	3,127	4,507	1,380	5.6	7.2	1.6
Athens, GA	153,444	7	8	1	23,651	31,425	7,774	33.2	40.5	7.3
Atlanta, GA	4,112,198	36	31	−5	92,053	92,039	−14	15.3	11.1	−4.2
Atlantic-Cape May, NJ	354,878	4	4	0	9,282	9,907	625	13.7	9.4	−4.3
Auburn-Opelika, AL	115,092	7	6	−1	22,357	23,876	1,519	50.6	44.4	−6.2
Augusta-Aiken, GA-SC	477,441	7	7	0	22,132	18,246	−3,886	17.6	12.3	−5.3
Austin-San Marcos, TX	1,249,763	12	7	−5	45,423	45,057	−366	14.4	12.3	−2.1
Bakersfield, CA	661,645	4	13	9	22,333	64,955	42,622	11.5	22.0	10.5
Baltimore, MD	2,552,994	38	33	−5	106,648	75,643	−31,005	22.5	13.5	−9.0
Bangor, ME	90,864	1	1	0	1,132	4,241	3,109	3.0	5.3	2.3
Barnstable-Yarmouth, MA	162,582	0	0	0	0	0	0	0.0	0.0	0.0
Baton Rouge, LA	602,894	16	9	−7	60,375	42,401	−17,974	28.3	17.6	−10.7
Beaumont-Port Arthur, TX	385,090	15	4	−11	23,311	7,858	−15,453	17.9	6.1	−11.8
Bellingham, WA	166,814	1	1	0	5,941	6,918	977	9.8	8.2	−1.5
Benton Harbor, MI	162,453	7	4	−3	15,716	9,690	−6,026	37.3	23.5	−13.8
Bergen-Passaic, NJ	1,373,167	3	5	2	5,483	11,755	6,272	3.0	4.9	1.9
Billings, MT	129,352	2	1	−1	4,088	3,592	−496	12.1	9.9	−2.2
Biloxi-Gulfport-Pascagoula, MS	363,988	4	2	−2	9,305	881	−8,424	8.4	0.1	−8.3
Binghamton, NY	252,320	2	3	1	4,366	5,446	1,080	7.0	7.3	0.3

Metropolitan area	Population									
Birmingham, AL	921,106	14	10	-4	54,871	33,631	-21,240	21.5	12.8	-8.7
Bismarck, ND	94,719	0	0	0	0	0	0	0.0	0.0	0.0
Bloomington, IN	120,563	4	6	2	23,622	32,689	9,067	32.0	50.1	18.1
Bloomington-Normal, IL	150,433	3	2	-1	11,689	10,706	-983	14.2	13.2	-1.0
Boise City, ID	432,345	2	0	-2	608	0	-608	1.3	0.0	-1.3
Boston, MA-NH	3,406,829	15	13	-2	31,757	32,643	886	5.0	4.2	-0.7
Boulder-Longmont, CO	291,288	1	2	1	5,530	6,806	1,276	10.3	11.7	1.4
Brazoria, TX	241,767	0	0	0	0	0	0	0.0	0.0	0.0
Bremerton, WA	231,969	1	0	-1	536	0	-536	1.3	0.0	-1.3
Bridgeport, CT	459,479	4	3	-1	6,086	6,317	231	10.9	7.8	-3.1
Brockton, MA	255,459	0	1	1	0	2,385	2,385	0.0	4.6	4.6
Brownsville-Harlingen-San Benito, TX	335,227	30	26	-4	136,312	85,753	-50,559	67.2	38.3	-28.9
Bryan-College Station, TX	152,415	6	10	4	39,934	51,680	11,746	44.3	51.6	7.3
Buffalo-Niagara Falls, NY	1,170,111	26	19	-7	72,230	51,303	-20,927	23.3	16.9	-6.4
Burlington, VT	169,391	0	1	1	0	3,935	3,935	0.0	10.9	10.9
Canton-Massillon, OH	406,934	5	2	-3	9,873	4,285	-5,588	11.0	6.2	-4.8
Casper, WY	66,533	0	0	0	0	0	0	0.0	0.0	0.0
Cedar Rapids, IA	191,701	1	0	-1	2,067	0	-2,067	5.5	0.0	-5.5
Champaign-Urbana, IL	179,669	4	4	0	24,536	22,482	-2,054	37.1	40.7	3.6
Charleston, WV	251,662	2	1	-1	3,847	1,426	-2,421	5.0	2.2	-2.8
Charleston-North Charleston, SC	549,033	13	11	-2	27,609	27,194	-415	17.8	15.5	-2.3
Charlotte-Gastonia-Rock Hill, NC-SC	1,499,293	10	4	-6	27,102	7,424	-19,678	10.7	2.1	-8.6
Charlottesville, VA	159,576	3	3	0	10,560	8,861	-1,699	29.2	25.8	-3.4
Chattanooga, TN-GA	465,161	7	4	-3	13,963	11,389	-2,574	14.4	11.7	-2.7
Cheyenne, WY	81,607	0	0	0	0	0	0	0.0	0.0	0.0
Chicago, IL	8,272,768	187	114	-73	412,853	234,945	-177,908	26.4	13.7	-12.8
Chico-Paradise, CA	203,171	3	7	4	16,140	32,815	16,675	18.7	35.0	16.3
Cincinnati, OH-KY-IN	1,646,395	31	23	-8	74,387	51,120	-23,267	24.4	16.1	-8.2
Clarksville-Hopkinsville, TN-KY	207,033	0	0	-1	3,050	0	-3,050	4.1	0.0	-4.1
Cleveland-Lorain-Elyria, OH	2,250,871	71	52	-19	102,494	76,146	-26,348	21.7	15.3	-6.4
Colorado Springs, CO	516,929	2	1	-1	1,640	1,739	99	1.7	1.6	-0.1
Columbia, MO	135,454	6	5	-1	21,049	17,149	-3,900	37.1	34.4	-2.7
Columbia, SC	536,691	11	8	-3	24,702	18,288	-6,414	18.2	9.8	-8.5
Columbus, GA-AL	274,624	13	10	-3	28,294	18,986	-9,308	33.7	24.0	-9.7
Columbus, OH	1,540,157	24	13	-11	86,657	38,637	-48,020	25.3	13.0	-12.3
Corpus Christi, TX	380,783	10	7	-3	41,066	22,462	-18,604	27.1	14.9	-12.2
Corvallis, OR	78,153	2	2	0	16,358	7,149	-9,209	43.8	21.3	-22.6
Cumberland, MD-WV	102,008	1	0	-1	534	0	-534	1.4	0.0	-1.4
Dallas, TX	3,519,176	36	17	-19	92,275	50,470	-41,805	13.8	5.4	-8.4
Danbury, CT	217,980	0	0	0	0	0	0	0.0	0.0	0.0

(continued)

TABLE 5A-1. Population of High-Poverty Neighborhoods and Concentrated Poverty Rates, Metropolitan and Nonmetropolitan Areas, 1990–2000 (continued)

Area	Total population, 2000	Number of high-poverty census tracts			Population in high-poverty census tracts			Concentrated poverty rate, total		
		1990	2000	Change	1990	2000	Change	1990	2000	Change
Danville, VA	110,156	1	0	−1	2,383	0	−2,383	5.7	0.0	−5.7
Davenport-Moline-Rock Island, IA-IL	359,062	7	2	−5	10,790	4,202	−6,588	11.7	5.4	−6.3
Dayton-Springfield, OH	950,558	18	8	−10	51,835	23,335	−28,500	21.5	7.2	−14.3
Daytona Beach, FL	493,175	3	2	−1	11,643	5,873	−5,770	10.2	3.7	−6.4
Decatur, AL	145,867	0	0	0	0	0	0	0.0	0.0	0.0
Decatur, IL	114,706	2	4	2	2,324	4,938	2,614	8.3	15.7	7.3
Denver, CO	2,109,282	11	2	−9	24,102	4,518	−19,584	7.6	1.5	−6.1
Des Moines, IA	456,022	2	0	−2	7,773	0	−7,773	9.2	0.0	−9.2
Detroit, MI	4,441,551	150	53	−97	420,739	107,522	−313,217	36.0	10.4	−25.6
Dothan, AL	137,916	3	0	−3	8,546	0	−8,546	18.0	0.0	−18.0
Dover, DE	126,697	1	0	−1	1,556	0	−1,556	2.0	0.0	−2.0
Dubuque, IA	89,143	0	0	0	0	0	0	0.0	0.0	0.0
Duluth-Superior, MN-WI	243,815	6	5	−1	9,090	6,948	−2,142	11.9	10.9	−1.0
Dutchess County, NY	280,150	0	1	1	0	1,963	1,963	0.0	4.1	4.1
Eau Claire, WI	148,337	2	1	−1	7,021	5,322	−1,699	18.9	16.3	−2.5
El Paso, TX	679,622	20	16	−4	110,735	66,246	−44,489	35.9	20.4	−15.5
Elkhart-Goshen, IN	182,791	0	0	0	0	0	0	0.0	0.0	0.0
Elmira, NY	91,070	1	2	1	2,445	2,713	268	11.8	8.8	−2.9
Enid, OK	57,813	0	0	0	0	0	0	0.0	0.0	0.0
Erie, PA	280,843	5	2	−3	13,082	4,311	−8,771	17.8	4.5	−13.3
Eugene-Springfield, OR	322,959	3	2	−1	11,900	9,509	−2,391	13.2	10.0	−3.1
Evansville-Henderson, IN-KY	296,195	1	0	−1	1,318	0	−1,318	2.0	0.0	−2.0
Fargo-Moorhead, ND-MN	174,367	2	1	−1	9,237	5,210	−4,027	9.0	5.2	−3.8
Fayetteville, NC	302,963	5	4	−1	8,952	7,196	−1,756	12.8	8.8	−4.0
Fayetteville-Springdale-Rogers, AR	311,121	1	1	0	5,254	3,214	−2,040	7.8	0.9	−7.0
Fitchburg-Leominster, MA	142,284	0	0	0	0	0	0	0.0	0.0	0.0
Flagstaff, AZ-UT	122,366	6	2	−4	22,622	3,085	−19,537	42.2	6.8	−35.4
Flint, MI	436,141	15	9	−6	51,714	20,083	−31,631	33.9	15.8	−18.1
Florence, AL	142,950	2	2	0	4,487	3,695	−792	11.7	9.5	−2.2
Florence, SC	125,761	2	1	−1	10,567	3,686	−6,881	20.0	7.9	−12.1
Fort Collins-Loveland, CO	251,494	1	1	0	5,297	7,819	2,522	3.9	14.8	10.9
Fort Lauderdale, FL	1,623,018	4	4	0	13,473	17,347	3,874	4.8	4.2	−0.5
Fort Myers-Cape Coral, FL	440,888	1	1	0	4,307	4,843	536	6.9	6.6	−0.3

Fort Pierce-Port St. Lucie, FL	319,426	3	3	0	13,459	11,423	-2,036	25.5	16.7	-8.7
Fort Smith, AR-OK	207,290	2	2	0	1,853	0	-1,853	2.6	0.0	-2.6
Fort Walton Beach, FL	170,498	0	0	0	0	0	0	0.0	0.0	0.0
Fort Wayne, IN	502,141	4	2	-2	5,080	2,371	-2,709	7.1	3.2	-3.9
Fort Worth-Arlington, TX	1,702,625	13	8	-5	34,385	17,997	-16,388	10.3	4.2	-6.0
Fresno, CA	922,516	15	27	12	87,293	147,298	60,005	25.1	33.6	8.4
Gadsden, AL	103,459	1	2	1	1,482	4,271	2,789	4.2	11.4	7.2
Gainesville, FL	217,955	7	7	0	45,583	44,894	-689	44.0	43.0	-1.0
Galveston-Texas City, TX	250,158	4	2	-2	6,890	4,466	-2,424	11.7	7.4	-4.3
Gary, IN	631,362	11	9	-2	21,408	18,631	-2,777	16.2	12.2	-4.0
Glens Falls, NY	124,345	0	0	0	0	0	0	0.0	0.0	0.0
Goldsboro, NC	113,329	1	1	0	495	560	65	1.1	1.2	0.1
Grand Forks, ND-MN	97,478	0	1	1	0	5,004	5,004	0.0	8.3	8.3
Grand Junction, CO	116,255	2	0	-2	1,423	0	-1,423	4.0	0.0	-4.0
Grand Rapids-Muskegon-Holland, MI	1,088,514	9	3	-6	19,281	5,826	-13,455	10.4	2.8	-7.6
Great Falls, MT	80,357	2	1	-1	2,540	721	-1,819	10.0	3.1	-6.9
Greeley, CO	180,936	3	1	-2	8,031	3,462	-4,569	12.4	6.1	-6.3
Green Bay, WI	226,778	0	1	1	0	1,949	1,949	0.0	0.1	0.1
Greensboro-Winston-Salem-High Point, NC	1,251,509	6	6	0	18,026	18,314	288	7.4	5.7	-1.7
Greenville, NC	133,798	1	3	2	8,564	17,290	8,726	15.9	28.7	12.7
Greenville-Spartanburg-Anderson, SC	962,441	9	8	-1	18,520	19,883	1,363	8.8	7.5	-1.2
Hagerstown, MD	131,923	0	0	0	0	0	0	0.0	0.0	0.0
Hamilton-Middletown, OH	332,807	4	2	-2	20,704	12,681	-8,023	24.9	15.9	-9.0
Harrisburg-Lebanon-Carlisle, PA	629,401	1	2	1	5,658	6,519	861	6.4	5.9	-0.4
Hartford, CT	1,183,110	11	8	-3	27,515	19,766	-7,749	18.2	10.0	-8.2
Hattiesburg, MS	111,674	5	4	-1	17,205	14,434	-2,771	33.5	23.1	-10.5
Hickory-Morganton-Lenoir, NC	341,851	0	0	0	0	0	0	0.0	0.0	0.0
Honolulu, HI	876,156	5	6	1	6,911	7,715	804	6.3	4.8	-1.5
Houma, LA	194,477	2	1	-1	9,521	2,493	-7,028	9.4	3.2	-6.3
Houston, TX	4,177,646	51	24	-27	162,487	84,825	-77,662	15.1	6.2	-8.9
Huntington-Ashland, WV-KY-OH	315,538	5	3	-2	12,063	5,437	-6,626	7.7	3.7	-4.0
Huntsville, AL	342,376	4	4	0	10,572	8,490	-2,082	16.8	11.8	-5.0
Indianapolis, IN	1,607,486	10	3	-7	24,384	5,341	-19,043	7.3	1.6	-5.7
Iowa City, IA	111,006	4	3	-1	14,638	14,124	-514	36.6	39.4	2.8
Jackson, MI	158,422	4	2	-2	8,438	3,850	-4,588	24.2	12.1	-12.2
Jackson, MS	440,801	17	8	-9	51,965	21,368	-30,597	33.4	12.9	-20.5
Jackson, TN	107,377	4	3	-1	9,829	7,721	-2,108	28.8	20.1	-8.7
Jacksonville, FL	1,100,491	12	7	-5	27,005	18,603	-8,402	11.8	6.8	-4.9
Jacksonville, NC	150,355	0	1	1	0	1,255	1,255	0.0	2.8	2.8

(continued)

163

TABLE 5A-1. Population of High-Poverty Neighborhoods and Concentrated Poverty Rates, Metropolitan and Nonmetropolitan Areas, 1990–2000 (continued)

Area	Total population, 2000	Number of high-poverty census tracts			Population in high-poverty census tracts			Concentrated poverty rate, total		
		1990	2000	Change	1990	2000	Change	1990	2000	Change
Jamestown, NY	139,750	3	0	-3	3,086	0	-9,086	14.7	0.0	-14.7
Janesville-Beloit, WI	152,307	1	0	-1	557	0	-557	1.7	0.0	-1.7
Jersey City, NJ	608,975	2	2	0	3,445	6,496	-1,949	4.8	3.3	-1.5
Johnson City-Kingsport-Bristol, TN-VA	480,091	1	1	0	53	2,042	1,989	0.0	0.1	0.1
Johnstown, PA	232,621	2	0	-2	3,948	0	-3,948	5.7	0.0	-5.7
Jonesboro, AR	82,148	0	1	1	0	5,629	5,629	0.0	16.1	16.1
Joplin, MO	157,322	0	0	0	0	0	0	0.0	0.0	0.0
Kalamazoo-Battle Creek, MI	452,851	9	4	-5	31,175	19,317	-11,858	21.4	11.2	-10.2
Kankakee, IL	103,833	2	0	-2	5,979	0	-5,979	24.6	0.0	-24.6
Kansas City, MO-KS	1,776,062	24	13	-11	31,896	16,576	-15,320	9.9	4.7	-5.2
Kenosha, WI	149,577	0	0	0	0	0	0	0.0	0.0	0.0
Killeen-Temple, TX	312,952	2	1	-1	5,396	1,730	-3,666	6.4	2.2	-4.2
Knoxville, TN	687,249	8	10	2	24,959	26,573	1,614	11.5	12.0	0.5
Kokomo, IN	101,541	1	0	-1	309	0	-309	1.4	0.0	-1.4
La Crosse, WI-MN	126,838	2	2	0	10,305	10,057	-248	26.5	23.8	-2.7
Lafayette, IN	182,821	6	4	-2	26,354	18,128	-8,226	38.2	33.4	-4.8
Lafayette, LA	385,647	16	6	-10	62,027	28,049	-33,978	30.2	15.4	-14.8
Lake Charles, LA	183,577	5	1	-4	11,988	1,820	-10,168	19.1	3.2	-15.9
Lakeland-Winter Haven, FL	483,924	1	2	1	2,650	2,833	183	2.5	2.5	-0.1
Lancaster, PA	470,658	2	1	-1	5,424	3,555	-1,869	7.4	4.0	-3.3
Lansing-East Lansing, MI	447,728	8	5	-3	19,368	18,676	-692	19.2	12.9	-6.4
Laredo, TX	193,117	13	9	-4	66,005	41,978	-24,027	64.8	34.1	-30.7
Las Cruces, NM	174,682	4	3	-1	24,945	18,551	-6,394	28.1	16.9	-11.2
Las Vegas, NV-AZ	1,563,282	5	2	-3	12,851	3,536	-9,315	7.0	0.8	-6.2
Lawrence, KS	99,962	2	2	0	11,941	12,698	757	25.0	23.4	-1.6
Lawrence, MA-NH	396,230	5	1	-4	12,656	1,818	-10,838	18.2	2.4	-15.8
Lawton, OK	114,996	1	2	1	2,410	2,510	100	8.7	5.8	-3.0
Lewiston-Auburn, ME	90,830	1	1	0	1,613	1,321	-292	7.3	6.1	-1.2
Lexington, KY	479,198	5	7	2	18,214	17,749	-465	10.3	12.3	2.1
Lima, OH	155,084	4	1	-3	6,771	1,648	-5,123	18.7	4.5	-14.3
Lincoln, NE	250,291	3	2	-1	3,674	5,257	1,583	8.8	0.2	-8.5
Little Rock-North Little Rock, AR	583,845	4	3	-1	13,167	4,808	-8,359	8.8	3.3	-5.4
Longview-Marshall, TX	208,780	3	0	-3	3,480	0	-3,480	4.3	0.0	-4.3

Los Angeles-Long Beach, CA	9,519,338	56	137	81	267,666	560,025	292,359	9.0	14.9	5.9
Louisville, KY-IN	1,025,598	11	12	1	35,277	38,160	2,883	17.4	17.9	0.6
Lowell, MA-NH	301,686	5	1	-4	12,768	2,754	-10,014	22.4	5.8	-16.5
Lubbock, TX	242,628	8	2	-6	19,428	5,625	-13,803	21.6	5.6	-16.1
Lynchburg, VA	214,911	3	2	-1	5,133	1,282	-3,851	7.9	0.8	-7.1
Macon, GA	322,549	11	9	-2	22,380	16,447	-5,933	20.7	14.9	-5.8
Madison, WI	426,526	4	3	-1	27,744	23,022	-4,722	29.7	25.1	-4.6
Manchester, NH	198,378	0	1	1	0	2,385	2,385	0.0	7.1	7.1
Mansfield, OH	175,818	3	0	-3	3,474	0	-3,474	7.1	0.0	-7.1
McAllen-Edinburg-Mission, TX	569,463	37	36	-1	234,467	262,584	28,117	74.5	60.6	-13.9
Medford-Ashland, OR	181,269	1	0	-1	1,904	0	-1,904	4.0	0.0	-4.0
Melbourne-Titusville-Palm Bay, FL	476,230	1	1	0	4,268	3,530	-738	5.8	3.4	-2.4
Memphis, TN-AR-MS	1,135,614	51	40	-11	142,060	80,136	-61,924	39.3	21.5	-17.8
Merced, CA	210,554	3	4	1	17,255	15,578	-1,677	21.1	16.6	-4.5
Miami, FL	2,253,362	33	31	-2	148,083	122,274	-25,809	20.7	14.2	-6.6
Middlesex-Somerset-Hunterdon, NJ	1,169,641	0	3	3	0	14,020	14,020	0.0	6.9	6.9
Milwaukee-Waukesha, WI	1,500,741	59	43	-16	140,825	77,468	-63,357	43.3	21.9	-21.4
Minneapolis-St. Paul, MN-WI	2,968,806	33	15	-18	79,048	47,043	-32,005	17.3	8.6	-8.7
Missoula, MT	95,802	1	1	0	2,268	2,083	-185	6.2	6.5	0.3
Mobile, AL	540,258	26	16	-10	59,438	35,798	-23,640	33.9	21.1	-12.8
Modesto, CA	446,997	3	2	-1	3,327	9,370	6,043	3.2	5.8	2.6
Monmouth-Ocean, NJ	1,126,217	4	3	-1	2,863	11,977	9,114	1.4	7.5	6.1
Monroe, LA	147,250	12	11	-1	34,782	26,612	-8,170	54.5	42.7	-11.9
Montgomery, AL	333,055	10	6	-4	33,347	17,779	-15,568	34.1	19.7	-14.4
Muncie, IN	118,769	4	4	0	11,175	13,893	2,718	27.8	26.7	-1.2
Myrtle Beach, SC	196,629	0	0	0	0	0	0	0.0	0.0	0.0
Naples, FL	251,377	2	2	0	7,956	8,087	131	27.8	14.2	-13.6
Nashua, NH	190,949	0	0	0	0	0	0	0.0	0.0	0.0
Nashville, TN	1,231,311	11	7	-4	32,834	22,064	-10,770	14.9	7.8	-7.1
Nassau-Suffolk, NY	2,753,913	2	1	-1	8,814	184	-8,630	0.5	0.0	-0.5
New Bedford, MA	175,198	0	2	2	0	4,344	4,344	0.0	8.5	8.5
New Haven-Meriden, CT	542,149	3	3	0	5,050	11,796	6,746	5.5	8.7	3.2
New London-Norwich, CT-RI	293,566	2	0	-2	328	0	-328	0.7	0.0	-0.7
New Orleans, LA	1,337,726	67	49	-18	165,751	108,419	-57,332	33.7	22.1	-11.6
New York, NY	9,314,235	279	253	-26	960,292	945,255	-15,037	31.3	24.9	-6.4
Newark, NJ	2,032,989	21	24	3	49,189	55,984	6,795	13.2	12.4	-0.8
Newburgh, NY-PA	387,669	3	2	-1	13,853	14,367	514	24.6	21.6	-3.0
Norfolk-Virginia Beach-Newport News, VA-NC	1,569,541	24	18	-6	61,274	45,544	-15,730	20.1	14.1	-6.1
Oakland, CA	2,392,557	9	12	3	29,610	33,725	4,115	6.0	6.4	0.3

(continued)

T A B L E 5 A - 1 . Population of High-Poverty Neighborhoods and Concentrated Poverty Rates, Metropolitan and Nonmetropolitan Areas, 1990–2000 (*continued*)

Area	Total population, 2000	Number of high-poverty census tracts			Population in high-poverty census tracts			Concentrated poverty rate, total		
		1990	2000	Change	1990	2000	Change	1990	2000	Change
Ocala, FL	258,916	2	1	-1	6,522	2,079	-4,443	11.0	2.6	-8.3
Odessa-Midland, TX	237,132	7	0	-7	22,320	0	-22,320	25.8	0.0	-25.8
Oklahoma City, OK	1,083,346	24	21	-3	39,420	35,085	-4,335	13.1	9.5	-3.7
Olympia, WA	207,355	0	0	0	0	0	0	0.0	0.0	0.0
Omaha, NE-IA	716,998	8	3	-5	16,825	7,400	-9,425	12.2	4.2	-7.9
Orange County, CA	2,846,289	1	2	1	95	2,974	2,879	0.0	0.7	0.7
Orlando, FL	1,644,561	5	5	0	16,773	19,740	2,967	6.5	5.3	-1.2
Owensboro, KY	91,545	1	0	-1	3,282	0	-3,282	10.6	0.0	-10.6
Panama City, FL	148,217	2	1	-1	4,600	1,680	-2,920	9.5	3.7	-5.8
Parkersburg-Marietta, WV-OH	151,237	0	1	1	0	724	724	0.0	1.4	1.4
Pensacola, FL	412,153	7	2	-5	14,132	6,525	-7,607	12.2	5.2	-7.0
Peoria-Pekin, IL	347,387	6	7	1	10,779	13,658	2,879	15.9	19.0	3.0
Philadelphia, PA-NJ	5,100,931	70	67	-3	241,863	240,926	-937	23.0	19.6	-3.4
Phoenix-Mesa, AZ	3,251,876	27	30	3	92,673	91,844	-829	15.2	10.5	-4.7
Pine Bluff, AR	84,278	5	2	-3	13,513	6,421	-7,092	30.0	14.4	-15.6
Pittsburgh, PA	2,358,695	42	26	-16	74,898	48,076	-26,822	13.3	8.5	-4.7
Pittsfield, MA	84,699	1	0	-1	32	0	-32	0.4	0.0	-0.4
Pocatello, ID	75,565	0	0	0	0	0	0	0.0	0.0	0.0
Portland, ME	243,537	2	0	-2	2,366	0	-2,366	5.9	0.0	-5.9
Portland-Vancouver, OR-WA	1,918,009	10	4	-6	15,304	8,189	-7,115	4.4	1.7	-2.7
Portsmouth-Rochester, NH-ME	240,698	0	1	1	0	7,564	7,564	0.0	8.2	8.2
Providence-Fall River-Warwick, RI-MA	1,188,613	5	8	3	9,425	31,611	22,186	3.5	9.6	6.1
Provo-Orem, UT	368,536	3	5	2	28,148	26,301	-1,847	30.0	28.9	-1.2
Pueblo, CO	141,472	5	1	-4	8,051	1,419	-6,632	14.1	0.5	-13.6
Punta Gorda, FL	141,627	0	0	0	0	0	0	0.0	0.0	0.0
Racine, WI	188,831	2	1	-1	4,602	623	-3,979	13.0	1.9	-11.1
Raleigh-Durham-Chapel Hill, NC	1,187,941	8	6	-2	23,369	20,621	-2,748	7.3	5.3	-2.0
Rapid City, SD	88,565	0	0	0	0	0	0	0.0	0.0	0.0
Reading, PA	373,638	2	4	2	7,076	14,023	6,947	12.4	18.8	6.4
Redding, CA	163,256	0	0	0	0	0	0	0.0	0.0	0.0
Reno, NV	339,486	0	0	0	0	0	0	0.0	0.0	0.0
Richland-Kennewick-Pasco, WA	191,822	1	0	-1	3,877	0	-3,877	8.1	0.0	-8.1

Richmond-Petersburg, VA	996,512	10	6	-4	24,415	19,308	-5,107	15.5	10.4	-5.1
Riverside-San Bernardino, CA	3,254,821	6	18	12	22,523	81,192	58,669	3.2	7.7	4.5
Roanoke, VA	235,932	2	3	1	4,929	4,053	-876	8.9	6.0	-2.8
Rochester, MN	124,277	1	0	-1	850	0	-850	0.1	0.0	-0.1
Rochester, NY	1,098,201	20	20	0	33,510	43,499	9,989	15.4	16.6	1.2
Rockford, IL	371,236	3	2	-1	9,676	6,463	-3,213	16.2	8.6	-7.6
Rocky Mount, NC	143,026	1	2	1	331	743	412	0.6	1.5	0.9
Sacramento, CA	1,628,197	5	6	1	18,294	26,602	8,308	5.3	5.4	0.1
Saginaw-Bay City-Midland, MI	403,070	10	6	-4	25,492	16,345	-9,147	22.6	16.1	-6.6
Salem, OR	347,214	0	1	1	0	3,388	3,388	0.0	0.5	0.5
Salinas, CA	401,762	0	0	0	0	0	0	0.0	0.0	0.0
Salt Lake City-Ogden, UT	1,333,914	6	4	-2	7,456	5,864	-1,592	3.8	2.7	-1.2
San Angelo, TX	104,010	2	1	-1	2,778	1,579	-1,199	8.7	4.9	-3.7
San Antonio, TX	1,592,383	31	13	-18	152,936	45,664	-107,272	28.9	8.0	-20.9
San Diego, CA	2,813,833	8	18	10	38,644	71,918	33,274	6.3	9.1	2.7
San Francisco, CA	1,731,183	4	1	-3	12,127	4,649	-7,478	3.7	1.7	-2.0
San Jose, CA	1,682,585	0	0	0	0	0	0	0.0	0.0	0.0
San Luis Obispo-Atascadero-Paso Robles, CA	246,681	1	3	2	9,292	9,598	306	13.0	12.1	-0.8
Santa Barbara-Santa Maria-Lompoc, CA	399,347	4	4	0	19,857	20,671	814	18.7	17.2	-1.5
Santa Cruz-Watsonville, CA	255,602	0	0	0	0	0	0	0.0	0.0	0.0
Santa Fe, NM	147,635	0	0	0	0	0	0	0.0	0.0	0.0
Santa Rosa, CA	458,614	0	0	0	0	0	0	0.0	0.0	0.0
Sarasota-Bradenton, FL	589,959	0	0	0	0	0	0	0.0	0.0	0.0
Savannah, GA	293,000	11	8	-3	15,060	10,121	-4,939	20.9	13.0	-7.9
Scranton—Wilkes-Barre—Hazleton, PA	624,776	2	2	0	3,483	8,568	5,085	2.2	3.7	1.5
Seattle-Bellevue-Everett, WA	2,414,616	9	4	-5	24,775	14,646	-10,129	5.0	2.4	-2.6
Sharon, PA	120,293	3	2	-1	4,363	2,407	-1,956	13.5	8.7	-4.7
Sheboygan, WI	112,646	0	0	0	0	0	0	0.0	0.0	0.0
Sherman-Denison, TX	110,595	1	0	-1	325	0	-325	1.2	0.0	-1.2
Shreveport-Bossier City, LA	392,302	18	18	0	59,130	40,741	-18,389	35.4	25.2	-10.2
Sioux City, IA-NE	124,130	2	1	-1	4,517	51	-4,466	13.6	0.2	-13.3

(continued)

T A B L E 5 A - 1 . Population of High-Poverty Neighborhoods and Concentrated Poverty Rates, Metropolitan and Nonmetropolitan Areas, 1990–2000 (continued)

Area	Total population, 2000	Number of high-poverty census tracts			Population in high-poverty census tracts			Concentrated poverty rate, total		
		1990	2000	Change	1990	2000	Change	1990	2000	Change
Sioux Falls, SD	172,412	1	0	−1	1,252	0	−1,252	5.2	0.0	−5.2
South Bend, IN	265,559	1	0	−1	1,525	0	−1,525	3.0	0.0	−3.0
Spokane, WA	417,939	6	1	−5	5,766	2,203	−4,563	5.9	2.0	−3.8
Springfield, IL	201,437	2	1	−1	4,000	1,818	−2,182	10.8	5.9	−5.0
Springfield, MA	591,932	11	11	0	43,814	34,957	−8,857	28.7	21.7	−7.0
Springfield, MO	325,721	4	2	−2	13,163	6,046	−7,117	11.2	3.6	−7.6
St. Cloud, MN	167,392	3	1	−2	12,172	1,102	−11,070	22.9	1.1	−21.8
St. Joseph, MO	102,490	2	0	−2	4,132	0	−4,132	12.7	0.0	−12.7
St. Louis, MO-IL	2,603,607	39	26	−13	109,516	70,650	−38,866	20.5	13.0	−7.5
Stamford-Norwalk, CT	353,556	0	0	0	0	0	0	0.0	0.0	0.0
State College, PA	135,758	5	6	1	23,679	28,955	5,276	52.1	49.5	−2.6
Steubenville-Weirton, OH-WV	132,008	4	2	−2	5,756	3,330	−2,426	12.5	8.2	−4.4
Stockton-Lodi, CA	563,598	5	7	2	25,858	34,504	8,646	15.2	15.5	0.3
Sumter, SC	104,646	3	0	−3	13,545	0	−10,545	22.1	0.0	−22.1
Syracuse, NY	732,117	14	12	−2	33,150	34,670	−3,480	20.4	16.9	−3.5
Tacoma, WA	700,820	5	3	−2	12,688	8,180	−4,508	10.0	4.7	−5.4
Tallahassee, FL	284,539	10	9	−1	35,036	43,439	7,403	34.2	39.8	5.6
Tampa-St. Petersburg-Clearwater, FL	2,395,997	16	11	−5	40,956	29,465	−11,491	9.1	5.5	−3.5
Terre Haute, IN	149,192	2	2	0	3,006	5,501	2,495	6.5	5.9	−0.5
Texarkana, TX-Texarkana, AR	129,749	2	3	1	4,587	8,327	3,740	12.2	16.2	4.0
Toledo, OH	618,203	20	9	−11	53,392	23,381	−30,011	25.1	10.6	−14.5
Topeka, KS	169,871	0	0	0	0	0	0	0.0	0.0	0.0
Trenton, NJ	350,761	1	2	1	5,110	4,829	−281	7.9	7.6	−0.3
Tucson, AZ	843,746	13	8	−5	52,879	28,962	−23,917	21.1	8.5	−12.6
Tulsa, OK	803,235	11	6	−5	29,066	14,328	−14,738	13.3	6.7	−6.5
Tuscaloosa, AL	164,875	6	3	−3	26,988	10,712	−16,276	34.6	16.1	−18.5
Tyler, TX	174,706	4	0	−4	10,105	0	−10,105	18.1	0.0	−18.1
Utica-Rome, NY	299,896	4	6	2	3,094	9,165	6,071	4.6	10.7	6.2
Vallejo-Fairfield-Napa, CA	518,821	1	1	0	96	1,096	1,000	0.2	0.2	0.0
Ventura, CA	753,197	0	0	0	0	0	0	0.0	0.0	0.0
Victoria, TX	84,088	2	0	−2	4,373	0	−4,373	15.6	0.0	−15.6
Vineland-Millville-Bridgeton, NJ	146,438	0	0	0	0	0	0	0.0	0.0	0.0
Visalia-Tulare-Porterville, CA	368,021	4	6	2	18,606	29,782	11,176	11.6	14.4	2.8

Area											
Waco, TX	213,517	9	7	-2	33,038	24,695	-8,343	40.8	30.8	-10.0
Washington, DC-MD-VA-WV	4,923,153	10	24	14	20,609	77,563	56,954	3.3	7.6	4.3
Waterbury, CT	228,984	1	1	0	253	4,788	4,535	0.7	9.1	8.4
Waterloo-Cedar Falls, IA	128,012	2	1	-1	3,461	8,170	4,709	9.3	11.1	1.8
Wausau, WI	125,834	0	0	0	0	0	0	0.0	0.0	0.0
West Palm Beach-Boca Raton, FL	1,131,184	6	7	1	16,018	19,762	3,744	9.0	7.8	-1.2
Wheeling, WV-OH	153,172	0	3	3	0	3,066	3,066	0.0	6.3	6.3
Wichita Falls, TX	140,518	6	0	-6	8,398	0	-8,398	20.5	0.0	-20.5
Wichita, KS	545,220	6	2	-4	15,104	5,598	-9,506	13.3	4.9	-8.4
Williamsport, PA	120,044	1	1	0	2,326	2,140	-186	8.7	6.1	-2.7
Wilmington, NC	233,450	5	2	-3	9,120	4,317	-4,803	17.5	6.2	-11.3
Wilmington-Newark, DE-MD	586,216	3	5	2	4,470	16,819	12,349	5.3	13.4	8.1
Worcester, MA-CT	511,389	4	5	1	8,413	8,585	172	10.2	7.9	-2.3
Yakima, WA	222,581	4	2	-2	21,179	12,439	-8,740	23.5	11.5	-12.0
Yolo, CA	168,660	1	1	1	6,330	6,619	289	8.6	6.1	-2.5
York, PA	381,751	0	0	0				0.0	0.0	0.0
Youngstown-Warren, OH	594,746	19	6	-13	35,651	7,582	-28,069	20.2	4.3	-15.8
Yuba City, CA	139,149	0	0	0	0	0	0	0.0	0.0	0.0
Yuma, AZ	160,026	3	1	-2	9,574	4,713	-4,861	19.6	7.3	-12.3
Nonmetropolitan areas of										
Alabama	1,338,141	33	14	-19	102,111	43,746	-58,365	17.1	6.9	-10.2
Alaska	366,649	1	0	-1	1,522	0	-1,522	1.9	0.0	-1.9
Arizona	603,632	22	19	-3	91,119	81,934	-9,185	45.1	32.1	-12.9
Arkansas	1,352,381	22	6	-16	94,024	25,490	-68,534	15.6	4.2	-11.3
California	1,121,254	3	3	-4	9,207	15,553	6,346	2.7	3.6	0.9
Colorado	693,605	4	0	0	5,043	0	-5,043	2.9	0.0	-2.9
Connecticut	148,665	0	0	0	0	0	0	0.0	0.0	0.0
Delaware	156,638	0	0	0	0	0	0	0.0	0.0	0.0
Florida	1,144,881	2	1	-1	4,831	3,908	-923	1.5	0.9	-0.6
Georgia	2,519,789	13	13	0	52,027	48,303	-3,724	5.4	5.2	-0.3
Hawaii	335,381	2	1	-1	370	147	-223	0.6	0.1	-0.4
Idaho	786,043	2	2	0	11,443	10,977	-466	5.6	5.7	0.1
Illinois	1,877,585	9	7	-2	41,191	23,361	-17,830	5.3	5.0	-0.4
Indiana	1,690,582	1	0	-1	1,028	0	-1,028	0.3	0.0	-0.3
Iowa	1,600,191	3	1	-2	12,678	3,307	-9,371	2.5	1.0	-1.4
Kansas	1,167,355	2	3	1	9,027	12,203	3,176	1.9	3.2	1.3
Kentucky	2,068,667	52	15	-37	136,283	36,732	-99,551	13.6	4.1	-9.5
Louisiana	1,098,766	43	20	-23	175,906	76,485	-99,421	27.3	13.2	-14.1
Maine	808,317	1	0	-1	15	0	-15	0.0	0.0	0.0

(continued)

TABLE 5A-1. Population of High-Poverty Neighborhoods and Concentrated Poverty Rates, Metropolitan and Nonmetropolitan Areas, 1990–2000 (continued)

Area	Total population, 2000	Number of high-poverty census tracts			Population in high-poverty census tracts			Concentrated poverty rate, total		
		1990	2000	Change	1990	2000	Change	1990	2000	Change
Maryland	385,446	1	0	-1	1,595	0	-1,595	1.7	0.0	-1.7
Massachusetts	247,672	0	0	0	0	0	0	0.0	0.0	0.0
Michigan	1,768,978	10	4	-6	34,562	20,761	-13,801	4.7	3.1	-1.6
Minnesota	1,456,119	2	2	0	11,363	11,072	-291	2.3	2.5	0.3
Mississippi	1,820,996	77	30	-47	315,974	120,899	-195,075	31.2	13.4	-17.8
Missouri	1,800,410	8	4	-4	21,546	14,898	-6,648	3.1	1.7	-1.3
Montana	596,684	7	8	1	19,500	12,161	-7,339	10.0	6.0	-4.0
Nebraska	811,425	0	1	1	0	47	47	0.0	0.0	0.0
Nevada	250,521	0	0	0	0	0	0	0.0	0.0	0.0
New Hampshire	496,087	0	0	0	0	0	0	0.0	0.0	0.0
New Mexico	783,991	29	15	-14	90,945	52,403	-38,542	27.9	14.2	-13.7
New York	1,503,399	9	4	-5	20,900	10,692	-10,208	2.8	2.7	-0.1
North Carolina	2,612,257	10	6	-4	35,012	18,136	-16,876	4.0	2.1	-2.0
North Dakota	358,234	6	3	-3	18,100	1,059	-17,041	14.3	1.1	-13.1
Ohio	2,139,364	3	4	1	19,186	15,620	-3,566	2.4	2.4	0.0
Oklahoma	1,352,292	15	3	-12	34,710	9,124	-25,586	5.5	1.2	-4.3
Oregon	919,033	0	0	0	0	0	0	0.0	0.0	0.0
Pennsylvania	1,889,525	2	4	2	12,497	18,576	6,079	1.8	3.2	1.4
Rhode Island	61,968	0	0	0	0	0	0	0.0	0.0	0.0
South Carolina	1,205,050	4	1	-3	10,445	2,570	-7,875	2.2	0.6	-1.6
South Dakota	493,867	11	19	8	38,227	30,257	-7,970	22.6	21.4	-1.2
Tennessee	1,827,139	5	2	-3	5,931	5,260	-671	0.9	0.8	-0.1
Texas	3,159,940	51	26	-25	210,746	109,885	-100,861	16.0	9.0	-7.0
Utah	524,673	1	4	3	3,495	17,709	14,214	4.1	11.9	7.7
Vermont	439,436	1	0	-1	7	0	-7	0.0	0.0	0.0
Virginia	1,550,447	4	3	-1	22,258	22,778	520	2.9	6.2	3.3
Washington	994,967	5	4	-1	17,111	18,051	940	4.7	5.2	0.5
West Virginia	1,042,776	10	6	-4	33,300	19,636	-13,664	5.5	4.0	-1.4
Wisconsin	1,723,367	4	0	-4	12,676	0	-12,676	2.9	0.0	-2.9
Wyoming	345,642	2	1	-1	7,412	3,345	-4,067	8.1	1.5	-6.6
U.S. total	281,421,906	3,417	2,510	-907	10,393,954	7,946,291	-2,447,663	15.1	10.3	-4.8

REFERENCES

Danziger, Sheldon H., and Peter Gottschalk. 1987. "Earnings Inequality, the Spatial Concentration of Poverty, and the Underclass." *American Economic Review* 77: 211–15.

Elliott, James R., and Mario Sims. 2001. "Ghettos and Barrios: The Impact of Neighborhood Poverty and Race on Job Matching among Blacks and Latinos." *Social Problems* 48 (3): 341–61.

Fisher, Gordon M. 1992. "The Development and History of the Poverty Thresholds." *Social Security Bulletin* 55: 3–14.

Jargowsky, Paul A. 1997. *Poverty and Place: Ghettos, Barrios, and the American City.* New York: Russell Sage Foundation.

Jargowsky, Paul A., and Mary Jo Bane. 1990. "Ghetto Poverty: Basic Questions." In *Inner-City Poverty in the United States,* edited by L. E. Lynn and M. G. H. McGeary. Washington: National Academy Press.

Kasarda, John D. 1993. "Inner-City Poverty and Economic Access." In *Rediscovering Urban America: Perspectives on the 1980s,* edited by J. Sommer and D. A. Hicks. Washington: U.S. Department of Housing and Urban Development.

Lang, Robert E. and Patrick A. Simmons. 2003. "Boomburbs: The Emergence of Large, Fast-Growing Suburban Cities." In *Redefining Urban and Suburban America: Evidence from Census 2000,* edited by Bruce Katz and Robert E. Lang. Brookings.

Mincy, Ronald B., and Susan J. Weiner. 1993. *The Under Class in the 1980s: Changing Concepts, Constant Reality.* Washington: Urban Institute Press.

Openshaw, S., and P. J. Taylor. 1981. "The Modifiable Areal Unit Problem." In *Quantitative Geography: A British View,* ed. N. Wrigley and R. J. Bennett. London: Routledge.

Orfield, Myron. 1996. *Metropolitics: A Regional Agenda for Community and Stability.* Brookings.

———. 2002. *American Metropolitics: The New Suburban Reality.* Brookings.

Orshansky, Mollie. 1965. "Counting the Poor: Another Look at the Poverty Profile." *Social Security Bulletin* 28: 3–29.

Ruggles, Patricia. 1990. *Drawing the Line: Alternative Poverty Measures and Their Implications for Public Policy.* Washington: Urban Institute Press.

Wilson, William Julius. 1987. *The Truly Disadvantaged: The Inner-City, the Underclass and Public Policy.* University of Chicago Press.

6

The Trajectory of Poor Neighborhoods in Southern California, 1970–2000

SHANNON McCONVILLE AND PAUL ONG

Growing economic inequality remains one of this nation's most pressing problems. After controlling for the effects of the business cycle, there is a clear, long-term trend of a "widening divide" between rich and poor.[1] Several factors have contributed to this trend, including global competition, rapid technological change, industrial restructuring, increasing returns to education, and demographic shifts in the workforce, including high levels of immigration.

The impact of rising inequality has not affected people or places evenly. Residential and economic segregation in most metropolitan areas often results in the poor being constrained to high-poverty neighborhoods—with poverty rates greater than 20 percent—and often disproportionately composed of minority groups and immigrants. These poor neighborhoods may have few institutional and social resources, and neighborhood poverty may have deleterious effects on a number of health and social outcomes.[2]

The authors thank Douglas Miller, Douglas Houston, Jordan Rickles, Troy Strange, Julia Heintz-Mackoff, and Jennifer Wang for their assistance with this research. We would also like to thank the Southern California Association of Governments (SCAG), the Los Angeles Metropolitan Transit Authority (MTA), and the Southern California Air Quality Management Board (AQMB), who collaborated with us on this project. This project was supported by the Brookings Metropolitan Policy Program and the UCLA Ralph and Goldy Lewis Center for Regional Policy Studies. The authors alone are responsible for the content and any errors.

1. For national studies, see Ilg and Haugen (2000); Primus and Greenstein (2000). For California studies, see Reed, Haber, and Mameesh (1996); Legislative Analysts Office (2000); Ong and Zonta (2001); Daly, Reed, and Royer (2001). For Southern California studies, see Ong (2003).

2. Pearl, Braverman, and Abrams (2001); Ross and Mirowsky (2001); Boardman and others (2001); Zeiler and others (2000); Ainsworth (2002).

Researchers have documented that "concentrated poverty" in metropolitan areas—that is, the number and population of neighborhoods where at least 40 percent of people live below the poverty line—increased during the 1970s and 1980s, but declined dramatically in the 1990s.[3] Southern California, however, failed to share in this recent improvement. Most studies that examine poor neighborhoods are based on metropolitan areas in the Northeast and Midwest. Given the different physical and economic growth trends that prevail in the western United States, these analyses likely fail to capture the dynamics of neighborhood poverty in the Greater Los Angeles region.

With these differences in mind this chapter analyzes the changing spatial distribution of poverty in greater Los Angeles over the past thirty years, focusing on trends in Los Angeles, Orange, Riverside, San Bernardino, and Ventura counties. We examine the location of poor neighborhoods across the five-county region between 1970 and 2000, and pinpoint where poor neighborhoods have grown the most quickly. We explore the changing demographic characteristics of poor neighborhoods, including the factors associated with changes to neighborhood poverty levels. We also investigate the extent to which continued immigration to the region is associated with the emergence of concentrated poverty over the period. By better understanding the characteristics and dynamics of poor neighborhoods in Greater Los Angeles, the region's policymakers and community leaders can formulate more effective interventions to address the problems facing residents of disadvantaged neighborhoods.[4]

BACKGROUND

There are several factors that distinguish Southern California from other parts of the United States. The following five factors drive our interest in poverty trends in this region.[5]

Significant Population Growth

Unlike many metropolitan areas in the Northeast and Midwest, the five-county Los Angeles region experienced significant population growth between

---

3. Wilson (1987); Jargowsky, chapter 5, this volume; Kingsley and Pettit (2003).
4. Mincy, Sawhill, and Wolf (1990).
5. We use "Southern California," "Greater Los Angeles," and "Los Angeles region" interchangeably to refer to the five-county area that includes Los Angeles, Orange, Riverside, San Bernardino, and Ventura counties. San Diego and Imperial counties are also located in Southern California but are not included in this analysis because, unlike the five-county region, they do not share common employment and population centers.

1970 and 1990. Greater Los Angeles grew by 46 percent during that time, more than twice the rate of population growth nationally, and roughly ten times that in the Northeast and Midwest. Growth in the region slowed somewhat in the 1990s, although it still kept pace with the nation's 13 percent growth over the decade. Today over 16 million people live in Greater Los Angeles, more than in the entire state of Florida.

Substantial Racial-Ethnic Diversity

In contrast to metropolitan areas in the Northeast and Midwest that are characterized by largely white and black populations, Southern California has significant numbers of Latinos and Asians, as well as whites and blacks. Roughly 40 percent of the five-county population identifies as Latino, 39 percent as white, 10 percent as Asian, and 7 percent as black. Although residential segregation levels are high, the region's suburban areas (those outside the City of Los Angeles) are home to similarly high proportions of ethnic Latinos and Asians. As a result, in 1980 and 1990 poverty was less concentrated in the urban core than in other major metropolitan areas, and poor neighborhoods were more ethnically diverse.[6]

Continued Immigration

Southern California emerged as a new "Ellis Island" in the latter half of the twentieth century. From 1970 to 2000 the number of immigrants in greater Los Angeles increased by more than 4 million, and by 2000, 31 percent of the region's population was foreign-born, compared with 11 percent nationally. As of 2000 one-third of foreign-born individuals in the five-county area had lived in the United States for fewer than ten years.

Increasing Poverty

Although the national poverty rate remained relatively steady over the past thirty years (between 12 and 14 percent), the poverty rate in Southern California rose from 10 percent in 1970 to over 15 percent in 2000. This translates to 1.5 million more people in poverty in the five-county region since 1970. Los Angeles County drove much of this rise; home to 60 percent of the region's total population, the county saw a substantially higher poverty rate from 1980 onward than other counties in the region (table 6-1).

6. Grant (2000).

TABLE 6-1. **Poverty Rates, Los Angeles Region versus California and United States, 1970–2000**

Percent

County	1970	1980	1990	2000
Los Angeles	10.7	13.4	15.1	17.9
Orange	6.4	7.3	8.5	10.3
Riverside	13.2	11.4	11.5	14.2
San Bernardino	11.7	11.1	12.6	15.8
Ventura	9.0	8.0	7.3	9.2
Southern California	10.4	11.8	13.1	15.6
California	11.1	11.4	12.5	14.2
United States	13.7	12.4	13.1	12.4

Increasing Concentration of Poverty

As noted earlier, although the share of the nation's poor who live in high-poverty neighborhoods declined rather dramatically during the 1990s, this was not the case in the Los Angeles region. In fact, Los Angeles and Washington, D.C., were the only two major U.S. areas in which poverty became more concentrated over the decade. California's trend may be explained, in part, by the protracted recession that the region suffered during the early 1990s, when closures in the aerospace industry resulted in the loss of many high-paid, blue-collar jobs. The economic recovery that occurred in the later part of the 1990s may have been insufficient to reverse the increased concentration of poverty that occurred during the first part of the decade.

METHODOLOGY

To analyze the dynamics of neighborhood poverty in the Los Angeles region, we use decennial census data from 1970 to 2000.[7] Essential characteristics of the method follow.

Defining Neighborhoods

We treat census tracts as neighborhoods. The U.S. Census Bureau defines census tracts as "relatively homogenous areas with respect to population characteristics, economic status and living conditions." Census tracts in urban areas typically contain 4,000 to 5,000 people, and although tracts do not always

---

7. Specifically the analysis draws on data from the 1970 Second Count and Fourth Count machine-readable files, and the 1980, 1990, and 2000 Census of Population, *Summary Tape Files 1A and 3A.*

replicate neighborhoods as they are understood by urban dwellers, they serve as good approximations.[8]

Measuring Poverty

We use poverty rates to classify neighborhoods. A neighborhood's poverty rate is defined as the total number of persons living in families and non-families with annual incomes below the federal poverty level, as a percentage of the total population for whom poverty status is determined.[9]

Classifying Neighborhoods

We classify neighborhoods in the greater Los Angeles area into one of three categories: "nonpoor," "poor," and "very poor." Other research provides guidelines for assessing neighborhood distress based on poverty concentrations. The U.S. Census Bureau uses poverty rates of at least 20 percent to designate "poverty areas," and we adopt that criterion to define "poor" neighborhoods.[10] In his seminal work, *The Truly Disadvantaged*, William Julius Wilson defines "urban underclass" as those residing in neighborhoods with poverty rates of at least 40 percent.[11] That threshold defines "very poor" neighborhoods in this analysis. The remainder of the region's neighborhoods are referred to as nonpoor, although nearly all contain at least some people living below the poverty line.

Other research uses composite measures that combine poverty with several other indicators, such as joblessness and welfare receipt, to categorize neighborhoods.[12] Rather than using these factors to construct the measure of distress, we examine similar outcomes within poor neighborhoods over time.

If poor individuals were evenly distributed across the region, there would be no neighborhoods with poverty rates above 20 percent. In reality the poor

8. Small and Newman (2001); Kasarda (1993).

9. In 1999, the year for which Census 2000 captured income information, the federal poverty threshold for a family of four was annual income of $17,029; for a family of three it was $13,290. Poverty status is not determined for people in military barracks, institutional group quarters, or for unrelated individuals under age 15 (such as foster children). These groups are considered neither "poor" nor "nonpoor" and thus are not included in this analysis of poverty. For 1970 we calculated the total number of persons in poverty by combining aggregate persons in families below poverty and unrelated individuals below poverty, and we calculated the population for whom poverty status was determined by subtracting the institutionalized population from the total population. In all other years we used the total number of persons in poverty divided by the poverty universe to calculate the poverty rates.

10. U.S. Census Bureau (1995).

11. Wilson (1987).

12. Mincy, Sawhill, and Wolf (1990).

are distributed unevenly across regions, particularly in Southern California, creating areas of concentrated poverty. Concentrated poverty, in turn, creates additional barriers that stem from the nature of the institutional and social structures available in high-poverty neighborhoods.

City versus Suburbs

To quantify changes in poverty concentrations between "suburbs" and "city," we face the thorny task of delineating the central city of Los Angeles. The Los Angeles region differs from many Northeastern and Midwestern metropolitan areas because it does not adhere to a simple central city-suburb dichotomy. Rather the region has several distinct areas, some of which look more like central cities and others that look more like suburbs.[13] Using the City of Los Angeles boundary alone to define inner-city Los Angeles is problematic because areas such as the San Fernando Valley are contained within the city limits but are far more comparable from a physical and demographic standpoint with suburban areas. Likewise there are cities apart from Los Angeles that surround the downtown area, such as Compton and East Los Angeles, that share more characteristics with the central city than with suburbs.

To portray the city-suburb distinction in the Los Angeles region, we rely on Pastor's classification of 1990 PUMAs (Public Use Microdata Areas) in Los Angeles County. He uses various demographic and economic characteristics to construct a geographic definition of inner-city Los Angeles.[14] In addition to several neighborhoods in the City of Los Angeles, this inner-city classification also includes the following areas outside the city: unincorporated East Los Angeles, Huntington Park, Carson, Bell Gardens, Bell, Commerce, Cudahy, Maywood, Vernon, and Compton. We refer to these areas as "inner-city Los Angeles." Likewise the definition excludes areas of the city such as Bel Air, Pacific Palisades, Westwood-West Los Angeles, and the San Fernando Valley. These and other parts of Los Angeles County outside the inner city we classify as "Los Angeles County suburbs," and the remainder of the five-county region as "other suburbs."

Neighborhood Transitions

In addition to identifying poor neighborhoods in each decade, we also analyze the changing status of neighborhoods between decennial censuses, from non-

---

13. Stoll and Raphael (2000).

14. Public Use Microdata Areas (PUMAs) used to define inner-city Los Angeles include: East Los Angeles, Huntington Park/Florence, Carson, Bell Gardens/Commerce, Compton, Eagle Rock, Downtown, South Central, Adams-Crenshaw, Vermont, Miracle Mile, Hollywood, Silverlake-Chinatown, and Harbor City-San Pedro. See Pastor (2001).

poor to very poor and vice versa. Because census tract boundaries change to reflect population changes, we reconcile census tract boundaries across decades by matching 1990 data to 2000 data; 1980 data to 1990 data; and 1970 data to 1980 data. We examine each decade separately so that neighborhood transitions in the 1970s represent changes that occurred between 1970 and 1980, transitions in the 1980s signify changes occurring between 1980 and 1990, and transitions in the 1990s represent changes occurring between 1990 and 2000.[15]

We classify neighborhood transitions into one of four categories: poor and very poor neighborhoods that remained the same ("stayed poor"); poor and very poor neighborhoods that improved ("got better"); poor and very poor neighborhoods that declined ("got worse"); and neighborhoods that remained nonpoor ("stayed nonpoor"). (In the findings below we discuss the various mechanisms by which a neighborhood's poverty rate may increase or decrease.) We only identify transitions in which the neighborhood changed poverty classification and in which the poverty rate changed by at least 3 percentage points over the ten-year period.[16]

FINDINGS

Analysis of decennial census data from 1970 to 2000 reveals a growing and shifting pattern of poverty and distress in the Greater Los Angeles area.

Southern California's Poor Have Become More Geographically Concentrated

The percentage of neighborhoods with high levels of poverty grew dramatically in the Los Angeles region between 1970 and 2000. Figure 6-1 shows the neighborhoods across the five counties that were poor and very poor in each decade, and the percentage of the region's population, and total poor population, living in those neighborhoods.

One consequence of this expansion is that poor individuals and families became more concentrated in neighborhoods of extreme poverty. In 1970 and 1980 fewer than 2 percent of neighborhoods regionwide were very poor (with

15. For the transition analysis we reconcile tract boundaries between the two years bounding the decade so that the same geographic area is used to calculate poverty rates and other changes in neighborhood composition.

16. This methodology does not, for example, identify a neighborhood in which the poverty rate fell from 35 to 25 percent as having "gotten better" because it did not change poverty classification even though its economic circumstances may have improved noticeably. In effect this approach attempts to capture changes in neighborhood poverty levels associated with the threshold effects that the literature identifies at 20 and 40 percent poverty rates.

FIGURE 6-1. Population Distribution, by Neighborhood Poverty Status, Los Angeles Region, 1970–2000

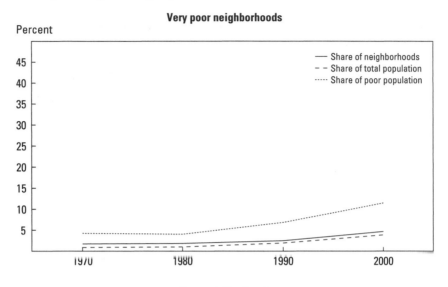

Very poor neighborhoods

Percent

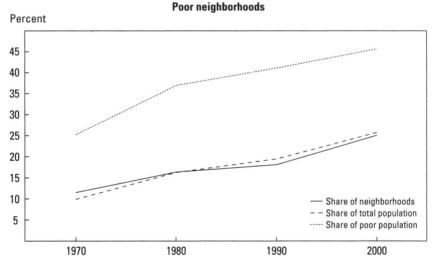

Poor neighborhoods

Percent

poverty rates of at least 40 percent), and only 4 percent of the region's poor lived in those neighborhoods. By 2000 nearly 5 percent of neighborhoods were very poor, and nearly 12 percent of the poor population resided there. The largest jump in neighborhood poverty concentrations occurred in the 1990s, when the proportion of the region's poor individuals residing in very poor neighborhoods increased by about 5 percent.

As very poor neighborhoods grew in number, so too did poor neighborhoods—those with poverty rates between 20 and 40 percent. Slightly more than one in ten neighborhoods were poor in 1970, but by 2000, one in four neighborhoods in the region was poor. Likewise the proportion of the region's poor residing in poor neighborhoods steadily increased from 25 percent in 1970 to more than 45 percent in 2000, although the increase was most significant in the 1970s.

Overall the percentage of the region's population living in poor and very poor neighborhoods doubled between 1970 and 2000, from 29 to 57 percent. This increase reflects, in part, the rise in the regional poverty rate during this period, from 10 to 16 percent. It is worth reiterating that if the region's poor were distributed evenly across neighborhoods, no poor people would live in neighborhoods where the poverty rate was 20 percent or higher. Instead, more than half live in poor or very poor neighborhoods. Such a dramatic rise in this proportion over thirty years reflects a large-scale spatial reorganization of poverty in the Los Angeles region.

How do trends in Southern California over the past decade compare to those nationwide? Jargowsky finds that the population of very poor neighborhoods declined by 24 percent nationwide between 1990 and 2000.[17] By contrast the Los Angeles region saw the number of people living in very poor neighborhoods more than double in the 1990s. In 2000 the percentage of poor in the five-county Los Angeles region who lived in very poor neighborhoods was higher than that in three-fourths of the nation's largest metropolitan areas.

Similarly across the nation, the proportion of poor individuals residing in poor and very poor neighborhoods declined by about 10 percentage points in the 1990s, from nearly 65 percent to about 54 percent. The Los Angeles region, meanwhile, experienced an increase of 9 percentage points. As a result, in 2000, a poor individual was more likely to live in a poor or very poor neighborhood in the Los Angeles region than in the rest of the country.

Suburbs Experienced the Most Rapid Increases of Poor Neighborhoods

As poor individuals became more concentrated in neighborhoods throughout the Southern California region, the locus of growth in poor neighborhoods shifted. Table 6-2 charts the growing suburbanization of poverty in the region over the 1970–2000 period.

17. Jargowsky, chapter 5, this volume.

TABLE 6-2. Neighborhoods, Total Population, and Poor Population, by Neighborhood Poverty Status and Location, Los Angeles Region, 1970–2000[a]

	Neighborhoods			Total population			Poor population		
Neighborhood	Very poor	Poor	Non-poor	Very poor	Poor	Non-poor	Very poor	Poor	Non-poor
2000									
Los Angeles County–inner-city	96	333	147	376,090	1,456,329	653,429	172,777	437,717	85,304
Los Angeles County–suburbs	41	301	1,123	161,161	1,552,935	5,149,827	76,311	406,209	496,281
Other suburbs	20	208	1,088	82,481	1,130,678	5,506,339	38,916	302,609	493,986
1990									
Los Angeles County–inner-city	45	256	168	209,018	1,441,658	767,737	97,118	415,024	96,900
Los Angeles County–suburbs	11	111	1,054	42,471	759,557	5,461,637	20,346	201,313	477,554
Other suburbs	7	93	803	21,497	565,053	4,960,333	9,863	149,457	395,699
1980									
Los Angeles County–inner-city	32	239	202	93,196	1,116,886	842,999	45,410	315,965	107,331
Los Angeles County–suburbs	8	84	1,060	13,481	410,812	4,861,086	5,896	106,489	403,707
Other suburbs	2	53	707	40	219,860	3,721,890	35	55,254	294,452
1970									
Los Angeles County–inner-city	29	156	286	80,170	584,696	1,217,379	39,976	157,959	151,266
Los Angeles County–suburbs	7	49	1,043	4,287	180,392	4,822,941	2,963	46,999	353,380
Other suburbs	2	49	575	834	198,438	2,671,739	368	51,536	213,469

a. See text for definitions of "inner-city" and "suburbs" for Los Angeles County.

In 1970 very poor neighborhoods were almost completely confined to Los Angeles County, and located predominantly in inner-city Los Angeles.[18] As in subsequent decades, poor neighborhoods typically surrounded very poor neighborhoods, creating large contiguous areas of poverty. Poor neighborhoods were found in downtown Los Angeles, and the port areas of San Pedro and Long Beach also contained pockets of poor neighborhoods. A large area of poor neighborhoods also existed in the southern part of the city of San Bernardino.

During the 1970s the ring of poverty around downtown Los Angeles expanded, with more poor neighborhoods developing in South Los Angeles and East Los Angeles. Poor neighborhoods also emerged in Orange County in Santa Ana, whereas the number of poverty tracts in Riverside, San Bernardino, and Ventura counties remained relatively steady. Still the majority (271 of 418, or 65 percent) of the region's poor and very poor neighborhoods were located in inner-city Los Angeles in 1980.

During the 1980s poverty began to shift to the suburbs. Several poor neighborhoods sprouted up in the San Fernando Valley north of inner-city

18. The few very poor neighborhoods outside inner-city Los Angeles in 1970 all contained large institutionalized populations. In subsequent years these populations are not included in the poverty universe, and those neighborhoods are no longer classified as very poor.

Los Angeles. Poverty areas also began to expand eastward, from East Los Angeles along Interstate 10 (I-10) toward Pomona and San Bernardino County. Very poor neighborhoods developed for the first time outside Los Angeles County, around the city of San Bernardino. The city of Santa Ana in Orange County saw the number of poor neighborhoods continue to grow, and new poverty pockets began to emerge in Anaheim.

In the 1990s concentrated poverty affected every part of the region. Downtown Los Angeles and the Long Beach port area saw many poor neighborhoods worsen, becoming very poor neighborhoods, and the inner-city ring of poverty further expanded into the cities of Inglewood and Hawthorne. At the same time the San Fernando Valley witnessed a sizable increase in concentrated neighborhood poverty, as did Lancaster and Palmdale in northern Los Angeles County. This reflected a continued expansion of poverty eastward from inner-city Los Angeles into Pomona and stretching across county boundaries into San Bernardino. Very poor neighborhoods also began to emerge in Riverside, Santa Ana, and Anaheim.

Not only had poverty widened by the 1990s, but the areas responsible for its growth had shifted outward, to the suburbs. The number of people living in very poor neighborhoods in suburban Los Angeles County nearly quadrupled, and the number living in poor neighborhoods more than doubled (table 6-2). By 2000 nearly as many people lived in poor and very poor neighborhoods in suburban Los Angeles County (1.7 million) as in the inner city (1.8 million). Meanwhile, in Orange, Riverside, San Bernardino, and Ventura counties, the population of poor and very poor neighborhoods more than doubled in a decade's time, from 600,000 in 1990 to over 1.2 million in 2000.

In fact in 2000, more of the region's poor individuals lived in the four suburban counties (840,000) than in inner-city Los Angeles (700,000). Nevertheless the more severe concentrations of poverty (40 percent and above) remain largely an inner-city Los Angeles phenomenon, whereas the majority of neighborhoods with concentrations ranging from 20 to 40 percent are located outside the inner city.[19]

The rise of concentrated poverty in the Los Angeles suburbs is, to an extent, consistent with national trends. Jargowsky finds that during the 1990s concentrated poverty declined in most central cities but remained stable in suburbs. He also finds that poverty rates rose in the inner suburbs of most metropolitan areas, although to levels below 40 percent. Nevertheless the Los Angeles region is notable for its rapid increases in very poor neighborhoods

19. Maps of poor neighborhoods in the Los Angeles region, by decade, are available at www.brookings.edu/metro/publications/20031124_ong.htm.

over the past decade and the degree to which the city and suburbs have converged on measures of poverty concentration over time.

Immigration Changed the Demographics of Poor Neighborhoods

Geography aside, the demographic characteristics of the region's poor changed markedly between 1970 and 2000.[20] Figure 6-2 compares the five-county poor population with the population below the poverty line by race and immigration status. Immigration, particularly from Latin American countries, has transformed the makeup of both poor neighborhoods and the region as a whole. The Latino share of the region's population increased dramatically, from 14 percent in 1970 to 37 percent in 2000, as did its share of the poor population, from 22 to 54 percent. The proportion of Asian/Pacific Islanders (API) in the region more than quintupled over the period, from 2 to 11 percent, and their proportion of the poor population increased in tandem. By 2000 Latinos and APIs accounted for almost two-thirds of the regional poor population, up from less than one-fourth in 1970.

As noted, these increases resulted in large part from immigration, as the foreign-born share of the region's adult population rose from 13 percent in 1970 to 44 percent in 2000. Immigrants, both new (arriving within the past ten years) and established (arriving ten or more years before), are disproportionately represented among the poor population, constituting 61 percent of the region's adult poor. As in 1970 new immigrants in 2000 were roughly twice as likely as adults throughout the region to be poor.

Returning to the geography of poverty in the region the demographic shifts in the poor population translated into a dramatic change in the racial-ethnic composition of poor and very poor neighborhoods (figure 6-3).[21] Whereas blacks made up a majority of very poor neighborhoods in 1970, Latinos did so (65 percent) in 2000. The large decline in black representation in very poor

20. The Census Public Use Microdata Sample (PUMS) provides information on individuals rather than aggregated geographic entities such as census tracts. The 1970 estimates use the 5 percent sample. The 2000 estimates are from the PUMS version of the Census 2000 Supplementary Survey (C2SS).

21. We construct mutually exclusive race categories for each year. In 1970, Latinos are people of "Spanish origin or descent" taken from the 1970 Fourth Count (Item 24). The remaining racial-ethnic counts come from the Second Count data. Non-Hispanic whites are defined as whites minus Latinos; blacks are defined as Negroes; Latinos are all persons of Spanish origin or descent; Asians/Pacific Islanders are those identifying as Japanese, Chinese, Filipino, Korean, and Hawaiian; Others include Indian and other categories. In 1980, 1990 and 2000, we used the Summary (Tape) File 1A to construct the racial and ethnic categories. Non-Hispanic whites are whites not of Hispanic origin; Latinos are whites and others of Hispanic origin; blacks are blacks; Asians/Pacific Islanders are Japanese, Chinese, Filipinos, Koreans, Asian Indians, Vietnamese, Hawaiians, Guamanians, and Samoans; and Others are American Indians and others.

FIGURE 6-2. Total Population and Poor Population, by Race/
Ethnicity and Nativity Status, Los Angeles Region, 1970 and 2000

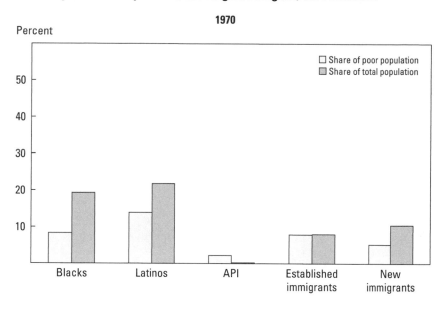

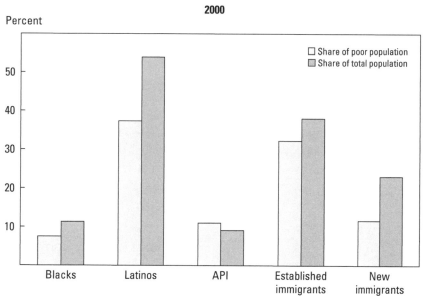

FIGURE 6-3. Neighborhood Composition, by Race/Ethnicity, Nativity Status, and Poverty Status, Los Angeles Region, 1970–2000

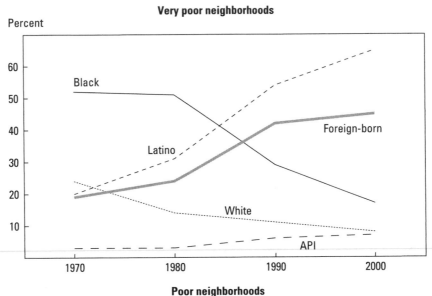

Very poor neighborhoods

Percent

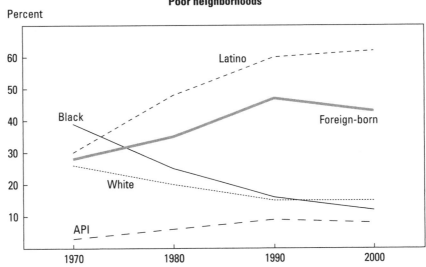

Poor neighborhoods

Percent

neighborhoods may reflect both the migration of Latinos to those neighborhoods and a redistribution of black population to other neighborhoods within the region. Overall the black share of the population throughout the region did not change considerably over the thirty-year period.

In 1970 blacks dominated the region's poorest neighborhoods, most of which were located in inner-city Los Angeles. Whites populated the few poor neighborhoods in suburban areas, particularly in San Bernardino and Riverside counties. In 1980, inner-city neighborhoods that were poor or very poor were nearly equally likely to be majority Latino as majority black. By 1990 poor black communities had been supplanted by poor Latino communities, and Latino growth in the San Fernando Valley eastward to San Bernardino and to the south in Santa Ana and Anaheim coincided with the rise in newly poor neighborhoods. In downtown Los Angeles and the San Gabriel Valley, poor API communities also began to appear. By 2000 Latinos would come to dominate most poor neighborhoods in all six areas of the region. The few exceptions include traditionally black neighborhoods in Watts, Compton, and Inglewood, poor API neighborhoods in the San Gabriel Valley just east of downtown and near Santa Ana, and several predominantly white poor neighborhoods in northern Los Angeles and San Bernardino counties.

Examining the share of the population in poor neighborhoods that is foreign-born reveals that the impacts of immigration on neighborhood poverty are most pronounced in the 1980s, when poor and particularly very poor neighborhoods witnessed large increases of foreign-born residents (figure 6-3). Those increases—12 percentage points in poor neighborhoods and 18 percentage points in very poor neighborhoods—were steeper than the 9 percentage point increase in foreign-born population share in nonpoor neighborhoods. New immigrants to the region were significantly more likely to be poor than other individuals (as shown in figure 6-2), and they often located in neighborhoods with high levels of poverty.

By contrast the proportion of foreign-born individuals in poor and very poor neighborhoods changed little in the 1990s, even though their representation in nonpoor neighborhoods continued to increase. In fact the proportion of the population that is foreign-born actually fell slightly in poor neighborhoods in the 1990s.

More Neighborhoods Became Poor in the 1990s than in Prior Decades

A neighborhood's poverty rate, and thus its classification as poor or very poor, may change as the result of several factors. Incomes among residents living in the neighborhood may decline or increase. Poor people may move out of a neighborhood, or wealthier people may move in. Conversely poor people may move into neighborhoods because of employment opportunities or affordable housing. Families already in the neighborhood may grow or shrink in size, adding or subtracting residents associated with their above- or below-poverty incomes. Each of these factors may redistribute the poor population and contribute to the changing status of neighborhoods. Although it is therefore difficult to generalize about the factors that led to greater concentrations of poverty in the Los Angeles region over the past thirty years, we examine the dynamic processes that underlay neighborhood changes in poverty status.

In the 1970s the majority of neighborhood changes occurred within inner-city Los Angeles, although declining conditions were evident in some parts of the San Fernando Valley, the San Gabriel Valley, and Orange County. During the 1980s the San Fernando Valley and the I-10 corridor east toward San Bernardino saw several neighborhoods fall into poverty, and San Bernardino and Orange counties also saw worsening neighborhood poverty in a few areas. Improvements in neighborhood poverty were largely limited to inner-city Los Angeles, where changes were fairly common overall.

The most widespread changes occurred in the 1990s, when a far greater number of neighborhoods across the region worsened or improved than in past decades. Compared with prior decades, suburban areas increasingly saw newly poor or very poor neighborhoods develop, particularly in the San Fernando Valley, areas just west of inner-city Los Angeles, northern Los Angeles County communities such as Palmdale and Lancaster, and southern San Bernardino and northern Riverside counties.[22]

Clearly, as table 6-3 shows, conditions in the 1990s were much more volatile than in the 1980s or 1970s. Between 1990 and 2000 the poverty status of 16 percent of the region's neighborhoods either worsened or improved compared with 9–11 percent in the prior decades. In 2000 nearly twice as many people as in 1990 lived in neighborhoods whose poverty status worsened. Moreover the chances that a changing neighborhood experienced increased poverty were much higher in the 1990s than in the 1970s or 1980s. Although in each decade there were more neighborhoods whose poverty status worsened than improved, the 1990s saw more than five times as many neighborhoods worsen than improve; in the 1970s the ratio was only three to one.

Column 5 in table 6-4 (change in foreign-born population) explores the relation between immigration and poverty changes. In the 1970s and 1980s

---

22. Maps of neighborhood poverty transitions in the Los Angeles region, by decade, are available at www.brookings.edu/metro/publications/20031124_ong.htm.

T A B L E   6 - 3 . Neighborhood Poverty Transitions, by Decade, Los Angeles Region, 1970–2000[a]

Poverty transition	Number of neighborhoods	Percentage of neighborhoods	Total population	Total poor population	Change in foreign-born population (percent)	Change in less-than-HS population (percent)
1990s						
Stayed poor	552	16.5	2,637,021	814,938	0.8	0.7
Got worse	449	13.4	2,191,313	617,943	4.8	5.5
Got better	87	2.6	342,402	73,102	0.1	−3.9
Stayed nonpoor	2,263	67.5	10,897,826	1,004,117	4.8	−0.3
1980s						
Stayed poor	333	13.1	1,973,733	584,439	12.9	4.1
Got worse	184	7.3	1,076,340	304,726	14.6	3.7
Got better	47	1.9	186,709	35,001	7.3	−1.7
Stayed nonpoor	1,971	77.8	10,986,738	937,380	7.3	−2.3
1970s						
Stayed poor	204	8.6	884,030	272,478	17.5	−4.4
Got worse	196	8.3	902,960	236,673	19.8	−1.5
Got better	66	2.8	281,161	45,878	7.7	−14.9
Stayed nonpoor	1,909	80.4	9,204,847	779,100	6.7	−9.8

a. Population figures reflect those recorded in the next census (for example, figures for 1990s represent 2000 population).

neighborhoods that remained poor or became poor experienced significantly larger increases in their foreign-born population than nonpoor or improving neighborhoods. This suggests that new immigration probably contributed significantly to the concentration of poverty in the region over those decades.

In the 1990s the proportion of the population that was foreign-born increased by a much smaller degree across all types of neighborhoods. In contrast to previous decades neighborhoods that stayed poor in the 1990s experienced only a minimal increase in their foreign-born share of population. Moreover neighborhoods with worsening poverty and those remaining nonpoor experienced the same increase in foreign-born (5 percent). The relationship between foreign-born growth and changes in poverty also appears considerably weaker than the relation between low education and poverty. In the 1990s residents of neighborhoods with worsening poverty were increasingly more likely to have less than a high school education, whereas neighborhoods that stayed nonpoor saw a slight decrease in their residents without high school degrees.

These simple statistics by no means disprove a link between increasing poverty concentration and immigration in the 1990s. In fact the continued increases in poor and very poor neighborhoods throughout the 1990s likely result, in part, from increasing numbers of children born to immigrant

TABLE 6-4. Neighborhood Profile, by Poverty Status, Los Angeles Region, 1970–2000

Indicator	Very poor neighborhoods				Poor neighborhoods				Nonpoor neighborhoods			
	1970	1980	1990	2000	1970	1980	1990	2000	1970	1980	1990	2000
Educational attainment												
Less than high school	65	57	60	62	60	53	54	49	39	24	21	19
High school only	21	25	18	18	25	25	19	20	34	32	22	20
Labor and employment												
Labor force participation	39	43	54	51	52	59	63	56	60	66	67	61
Employment ratio—male	37	40	52	49	59	64	66	56	74	74	73	64
Employment ratio—female	28	31	37	34	36	43	45	42	41	51	56	50
Unemployment rate	14	16	17	17	10	10	12	11	7	6	6	6
Job density (number per capita)	n.a.	1.9	1.5	0.9	n.a.	0.7	0.6	0.5	n.a.	0.5	0.6	0.6
Family												
Single parent	35	38	33	30	18	21	21	22	8	12	10	11

n.a. Not available.

families. These native-born children share their parents' economic circumstances, which may blur the line between poverty among immigrants and nonimmigrants. The statistics do, however, remind us that a complex set of factors led to worsening poverty in the region over the last decade. They also suggest that the changes are influenced by broader conditions in the labor market, selective in- and out-migration of certain workers, and an emerging population of children born to immigrant parents.

Employment in Poor Neighborhoods Increased; Single Parenthood Declined

Other analyses of urban distress rely on composite measures of disadvantage in neighborhoods, including low levels of work and education, and high levels of single parenthood.[23] As we identify distress based on a poverty measure alone, it is instructive to examine the degree to which poor neighborhoods have exhibited characteristics associated with the "urban underclass."

Along these dimensions the condition of very poor neighborhoods improved considerably between 1970 and 2000 (table 6-4). In 1970 39 percent of working-age residents of very poor neighborhoods were in jobs or looking for work. The proportion increased somewhat in the 1970s, but then jumped dramatically in the 1980s, such that by 1990 54 percent were in the labor force. Although the percentage slipped to 51 percent by 2000 this likely reflects difficult labor market conditions throughout the region; labor force

23. Mincy, Sawhill, and Wolf (1990).

participation in nonpoor neighborhoods declined by an even greater amount in the 1990s. These thirty years effectively narrowed the gap between labor force participation rates in very poor neighborhoods and nonpoor neighborhoods by half, from 21 percentage points in 1970 to 10 percentage points in 2000. The same pattern held for male employment although the gap remains wider in 2000 than for overall labor force participation.

The labor market gains made by residents of poor neighborhoods in the Los Angeles region are even more noteworthy in light of the trends in education among adults in these neighborhoods (table 6-4). Education gaps, in fact, stand out amid the neighborhood characteristics. More than half (50–60 percent) of adults in poor areas lack a high school diploma compared with only 19–39 percent of adults in nonpoor areas. Indeed the percentage of adults in very poor neighborhoods who have not completed high school was virtually the same in 2000 as it was in 1970, whereas the proportion of adults in nonpoor neighborhoods with such low attainment declined by half. Residents of poor neighborhoods made gains over the thirty-year period, but remain at a significant educational disadvantage compared with their counterparts in higher-income neighborhoods.

At the same time female employment in very poor neighborhoods continues to lag that in the rest of the region by a significant degree, and unemployment levels remain much higher (table 6-4). These gaps may reflect a decline in job opportunities in and around very poor neighborhoods. Although in 1980 very poor neighborhoods contained roughly two jobs for every resident, as extreme poverty spread into less dense parts of inner-city Los Angeles, suburban Los Angeles County, and surrounding suburban counties, the average number of jobs per resident fell to less than one. In nonpoor areas, by contrast, job density—although lower overall—increased over the same period. Therefore, job access, in addition to job readiness and labor market effort, may have contributed to the increasing unemployment rate in very poor neighborhoods during the three decades.

Consonant with the increases in labor force participation, the decline in single-parent families as a percentage of all households was also largest in very poor neighborhoods. In contrast single-parent families made up a larger share of the population in poor and nonpoor neighborhoods in 2000 than in 1970.

CONCLUSION

The Los Angeles region has changed dramatically in the past thirty years from demographic, social, and economic perspectives. Perhaps the most troubling change is the growing geographical concentration of poverty in the region, particularly during the 1990s.

Several factors contributed to the long-term increase in neighborhood poverty in Southern California. The first factor is immigration and the economic assimilation of immigrant children. Immigrants experience high poverty for a variety of reasons, including issues of acculturation, English language ability, and low skill and education levels that translate into lower earnings and lower economic mobility. The continued increase in neighborhoods with concentrated poverty in the 1990s, in part, may reflect increasing numbers of second-generation immigrants—native-born children with foreign-born parents—who continue to live in poverty. These second-generation immigrants attain higher levels of education than their parents, but continue to lag native-born whites overall. Their experiences in the region's public school systems have not provided them with the gains in human capital that will allow them to fare better than their parents over time.

The second contributing factor also relates to the influx of immigrants, but operates at the labor-market level. A large supply of less-skilled workers has depressed wages and created more competition at the bottom end of the labor market, which is disproportionately composed of minorities, immigrants, and second-generation workers.[24] The result is slow wage growth and limited economic mobility for the region's lower-skilled workers.

A third factor concerns industrial restructuring and demand-side forces. For a long time, the Los Angeles labor market offered aerospace and other well-paid manufacturing jobs, thereby creating a solid "middle rung" on the economic mobility ladder. In the 1990s, many of these jobs disappeared and were not replaced. Job competition at the bottom end of the labor market intensified, and today there may be fewer routes to the middle class. In addition, this sector's competition with developing countries has adversely affected employment and wages.

What can be done to stem the current trends in concentrated poverty in Southern California? In some respect future prospects are brighter than the current situation because of intergenerational economic mobility. Economic assimilation, however, appears to be slower in Los Angeles than in other large metropolitan areas such as New York.[25] Increasing economic mobility for second and subsequent generations of immigrants through education is the region's critical challenge. Los Angeles and surrounding areas must ensure that public schools provide the human capital necessary to move future generations of immigrants out of the bottom end of the labor market. At the same time the region must focus economic development efforts to help rebuild labor demand for a middle class.

24. Ong and Valenzuela (1996).
25. Ong (2003).

The increases in employment levels and labor force participation rates in impoverished neighborhoods over the past few decades are promising, but they must be accompanied by increases in real wages at the bottom end of the labor market and opportunities for middle-class jobs and economic mobility. This will, in turn, reduce concentrated poverty by increasing earnings and promoting true residential mobility for lower-income families.

REFERENCES

Ainsworth, James. 2002. "Why Does It Take a Village? The Mediation of Neighborhood Effects on Educational Achievement." *Social Forces* 81 (1): 117–52.

Boardman, Jason D., and others. 2001. "Neighborhood Disadvantage, Stress and Drug Use among Adults." *Journal of Health and Social Behavior* 42 (2): 151.

Daly, Mary C., Deborah Reed, and Heather N. Royer. 2001. "Population Mobility and Income Inequality in California." San Francisco: Public Policy Institute of California.

Grant, David M. 2000. "A Demographic Portrait of Los Angeles County, 1970 to 1990." In *Prismatic Metropolis: Inequality in Los Angeles,* edited by L. Bobo and others. New York: Russell Sage Foundation.

Ilg, Randy, and Steven E. Haugen. 2000. "Earnings and Employment Trends in the 1990s." *Monthly Labor Review* 123 (3): 21.

Jargowsky, Paul. 2003. "Stunning Progress, Hidden Problems: The Dramatic Decline of Concentrated Poverty in the 1990s." Brookings.

Kasarda, John D. 1993. "Inner-City Concentrated Poverty and Neighborhood Distress: 1970 to 1990." *Housing Policy Debate* 4 (3): 253–302.

Kingsley, G. Thomas, and Kathryn L. S. Pettit. (2003). "Concentrated Poverty: A Change in Course." Washington: Urban Institute.

Legislative Analysts Office. 2000. "California's Changing Income Distribution." Sacramento.

Mincy, Ronald B., Isabel V. Sawhill, and Douglas A. Wolf. 1990. "The Underclass: Definition and Measurement." *Science* 248 (4954): 450–53.

Ong, Paul M. 2003. "Intergenerational Economic Mobility in Los Angeles and New York." Unpublished analysis. Los Angeles: UCLA Ralph and Goldy Lewis Center for Regional Policy Studies.

Ong, Paul M., and Abel Valenzuela. 1996. "The Labor Market: Immigrant Effects and Racial Disparities." In *Ethnic LA,* edited by Roger Waldinger and Mehdi Bozorgmehr. New York: Russell Sage Foundation.

Ong, Paul M., and Michaela Zonta. 2001. "Trends in Earnings Inequality." In *State of California Labor,* edited by Paul M. Ong and J. Lincoln. Los Angeles and Berkeley: UCLA Institute of Industrial Relations and UC Berkeley Institute of Industrial Relations.

Pastor, Manuel. 2001. "Looking for Regionalism in All the Wrong Places: Demography, Geography, and Community in Los Angeles County." *Urban Affairs Review* 36 (6): 747–82.

Pearl, Michelle, Paula Braverman, and Barbara Abrams. 2001. "The Relationship of Neighborhood Socioeconomic Characteristics to Birthweight among Five Ethnic Groups in California." *American Journal of Public Health* 91(11): 1808–15.

Primus, Wendell, and Ronald Greenstein. 2000. "Analysis of 1999 Census Poverty and Income Data." Washington: Center on Budget and Policy Priorities.

Reed, D., M. Haber, and L. Mameesh. 1996. "The Distribution of Income in California." San Francisco: Public Policy Institute of California.

Ross, Catherine E., and John Mirowsky. 2001. "Neighborhood Disadvantage, Disorder, and Health." *Journal of Health and Social Behavior* 42 (3): 258.

Small, Mario L., and Katherine Newman. 2001. "Urban Poverty after *The Truly Disadvantaged:* The Rediscovery of the Family, the Neighborhood, and Culture." *Annual Review of Sociology* (annual): 23–38.

Stoll, Michael, and Steven Raphael. 2000. "Racial Differences in Spatial Job Search Patterns: Exploring the Causes and Consequences." *Economic Geography* 76 (3): 201–15.

U.S. Census Bureau. 1995. "Poverty Areas." Statistical Brief. (www.census.gov/population/socdemo/statbriefs/povarea.html [August 30, 2003]).

Wilson, William J. 1987. *The Truly Disadvantaged: The Inner City, the Underclass, and Public Policy.* University of Chicago Press.

Zeiler, Sally, and others. 2000. "Economic Deprivation and AIDS Incidence in Massachusetts." *American Journal of Public Health* 90 (7): 1064.

7

The Shape of the Curve

Household Income Distributions in
U.S. Cities, 1979–99

ALAN BERUBE AND THACHER TIFFANY

The notion of cities as centers of the American melting pot is well rooted in our nation's history and popular consciousness. As much as places where people of different races and ethnicities mix, cities have long been portrayed as bringing the wealthy, the middle class, and the poor together within their borders.[1]

Of course just because individuals of different means have lived in cities does not mean that they have necessarily interacted. Poor Eastern European immigrants reaching Ellis Island at the turn of the twentieth century, and blacks moving to the Northeast during the Great Migration, did not move in next door to J. P. Morgan. Indeed sharp contrasts between pockets of poverty and wealth characterize most cities.

In fact over the latter part of the twentieth century, the number of extremely poor communities in the United States rose dramatically, with most concentrated within central cities.[2] This trend owed to policies and economic and social forces that confined growing poor, mostly black, populations to urban centers, including: the physical concentration of subsidized housing in

The authors thank Jared Bernstein, Matthew Fellowes, William Frey, Amy Liu, Janet Pack, Kathleen Short, Audrey Singer, and Rebecca Sohmer for advice and comments, and Mark Muro for his editorial and substantive contributions.

1. Sir Peter Hall notes, "It is not just that big cities have more people living in them; it is that they contain so many different kinds of people, different in birthplace and race and social class and wealth, different indeed in every respect that differentiates people at all, living in almost infinitely complex social relationships" (1998).

2. Jargowsky (1997).

the urban core; exclusionary zoning and racial discrimination that impeded the movement of lower-income and minority families into the suburbs; stagnating wages for less-skilled urban workers; and the economic distress accompanying rising rates of single parenthood in inner cities.[3] The resulting conditions, it is argued, helped prompt the "flight" of many middle- and upper-income, mostly white, families to rapidly developing suburbs and beyond.[4]

Nevertheless recent trends have not rendered cities home to the poor alone. Although poverty rates in central cities remain higher than those elsewhere, some of the nation's wealthiest households inhabit places like San Francisco's Pacific Heights, Boston's Beacon Hill, and Manhattan's Upper East Side.[5] Downtowns across the nation are newly crowded with luxury housing and amenities tailored for higher-income residents.[6] Meanwhile the number of extremely poor communities dropped significantly during the 1990s, most dramatically in central cities.[7]

Amid the turbulence at the high and low ends of the scale, however, most observers agree that a steady decline in the size of the urban middle class has occurred in recent decades. As early as 1961, author Jane Jacobs observed: "To be sure, cities are losing their middle-class populations."[8] In subsequent decades, a growing chorus of urban researchers has echoed this concern.[9] Without these households, it is argued, struggling city neighborhoods lack positive role models for children; public schools labor to educate an increasingly disadvantaged population; and key middle-income workers like police officers, nurses, and teachers lose connections to the communities they serve. Middle-income earners may form an important part of a city's fiscal base by contributing revenues that the poor cannot, while allowing the city to keep tax rates on wealthier households and businesses competitive with those in surrounding jurisdictions. They may also bolster civic engagement, providing a bridge between the concerns of lower-income and higher-income residents. Finally the presence of poor and wealthy households, and a lack of middle-income households, may lead to higher prices for all city consumers.[10]

---

3. Wilson (1987); Massey and Denton (1993).

4. Frey and Fielding (1995).

5. See Berube and Frey, chapter 4, this volume.

6. Haya El Nasser, "Downtowns Make Cities Winners." *USA Today,* May 27, 2001, p. 3A.

7. See Jargowsky, chapter 5, this volume.

8. Jacobs (1961).

9. Leone (1976); Ladd (1993); McMahon, Angelo, and Mollenkopf (1998); Michael Hill, "Is It Too Late for Cities?" *Baltimore Sun,* December 8, 2002, p. 1F.

10. Frankel and Gould (2001); Pack (1998).

In these ways a more balanced distribution of households by income likely benefits places and their residents. Indeed city residents themselves tend to express a preference for such diversity in neighborhood satisfaction surveys.[11] Nevertheless little research has examined income distributions and income diversity at the city level. Researchers generally prefer to analyze income inequality across a metropolitan geography.[12] They argue that because metropolitan areas approximate labor markets, and most income is derived from labor market activities, one must analyze inequality at that scale.

Yet cities—rather than metropolitan areas—remain critical gathering points of economically diverse residents. Moreover the incomes of city residents crucially affect the fiscal and social health of local jurisdictions. Adding to the interest of city-level income distributions is the question of whether those distributions resemble the nation's. Overall the income profile of metropolitan areas closely mirrors the national profile, because a majority of the nation's population lives in large metropolitan areas. At the same time, though, the income distribution in large cities could diverge more widely from the national distribution, with greater attendant consequences for those cities.

For these reasons this analysis focuses on recent trends in the distribution of households by income in cities. Data from the 1980 and 2000 censuses are employed to investigate the changing distribution of household incomes in the nation's 100 largest cities. First, after an explanation of the report's methodology, the chapter examines the overall distributional pattern in 1999, and identifies common types of income distributions that occur across cities.[13] It then examines how these distributions changed across the 1980s and 1990s, looking especially at increases and declines in the presence of low-income and high-income households in different types of cities.[14] Finally, suburban income distribution and household fortunes are compared historically to those of their central cities.

The chapter asserts that the nation's cities can—and should—provide a suitable living environment for individuals and families from across the

---

11. Brower (1996).

12. Madden (2000); Cloutier (1997).

13. Income data in the decennial census are collected for the prior year, so that respondents to Census 2000 reported income for calendar year 1999, and respondents to the 1980 census reported income for 1979.

14. The analysis does not control for city boundary changes that occurred over the two-decade period. Some of the changes in city household income distributions may result from cities' annexing formerly suburban areas and their households. Although such changes do not reflect migration or income growth/decline among existing city residents, which are arguably better indicators of a city's economic health, they do tend to positively affect a city's fiscal base, an important motivation for this research. See Pack (2002) for further discussion.

income spectrum. Along the way, the study assesses which cities exhibit this type of diversity, where the gaps exist, and how the obstacles to creating truly mixed-income places differ markedly across urban America.

METHODOLOGY

This chapter measures the distribution of households by income in the 100 largest U.S. cities. The data on household income were collected on the decennial census "long form" and reported on census summary files. Households report their income for the prior year in each census; thus 1980 census statistics reflect income in 1979, 1990 census statistics reflect 1989 income, and Census 2000 statistics reflect 1999 income.[15]

About the Data

As with most census "long form" topics, data on household income are available for small levels of geography—down to the block group (averaging 1,500 people). Privacy considerations thus obligate the Census Bureau to report these income data categorically. This means that for any given geography summary file data provide the number of households within predetermined income ranges.[16] For 2000 the Census Bureau provides the number of households in each of sixteen income categories. Households in the first category had incomes between 0 and 9,999 dollars in 1999, the second between 10,000 and 14,999, and so on. Income categories, unfortunately, are not the same size across the income spectrum (ranges become wider at higher income levels), or across censuses (1980 had seventeen categories, and 1990 had twenty-five). In the interest of examining places with significant populations that act as economic centers for their regions, the analysis is limited to the 100 largest cities as of 2000. New York City is largest with a population of

15. The decennial census asks respondents to report on a wide range of income sources, including: earnings, self-employment, passive income (such as interest and dividends), Social Security or Railroad Retirement payments, Supplemental Security Income, public assistance (welfare) payments, pensions, and other regular payments (for example, child support, Veteran's Administration payments, unemployment, or alimony). Respondents are not asked to report on their receipt of in-kind payments such as food stamps and housing subsidies, or on tax refunds, which for some lower-income individuals can increase overall income (primarily through the Earned Income Credit).

16. Data from the long form provide better estimates of city-level incomes than census Public Use Microdata Areas (PUMAs) because the latter represent a smaller sample of households, and because the geographies for which PUMAs are available do not coincide with municipal boundaries in most cities.

8 million and more than 3 million households. The smallest city, Irving, Texas, had 193,000 residents and 76,000 households in 2000.[17]

Median versus Distribution

Why look at the entire distribution of income, rather than a simpler measure like median income, which indicates the "middle" income above and below which 50 percent of households lie? For cities at the extremes the median tells one much about the distribution. Buffalo, with a median household income of just $24,500 in 1999, is likely to see its households cluster at the bottom of the distribution. The opposite surely holds in San José, where the median was over $70,000.

For cities between the extremes, though, examining the median alone can obscure important differences between distinct places. For instance the median household income in both Atlanta and Oklahoma City ran about $35,000 in 1999. Atlanta, however, had many more households at the extremes—24 percent earned less than $15,000, and 15 percent earned more than $100,000. By contrast, the corresponding figures for Oklahoma City were 19 and 8 percent. Although poverty and wealth are no doubt apparent in both places, Atlanta may resemble a city of haves and have-nots to a much greater degree than Oklahoma City. These differences are apparent only when one examines the full spectrum of households by income.

Households versus Families

Any study on income involves a choice among numerous "units of analysis." In other words a study may examine how income is distributed among people or places; within places it may examine individuals or groups of individuals. Many studies use per capita income—total income divided by population—to examine differences across places and across time.[18] For purposes of examining changes in the distribution of income in a particular

---

17. By examining the 100 largest cities as of 2000, and looking backward to their income distributions in 1980, the analysis may be somewhat biased toward fast-growing cities in the South and West that were not the population centers twenty years ago they are today. Plano, Texas, for instance, had only 22,000 households in 1980, a far cry from the 81,000 living there in 2000. Nevertheless this approach is preferred to one that analyzes the 100 largest cities as of 1980, a number of which have suffered serious economic decline in recent decades and are no longer among the nation's largest (for example, Syracuse, New York; Worcester, Massachusetts; Kansas City, Kansas; and Flint, Michigan). The 100 largest cities of their respective census years could have been examined, but a changing set of cities across the period would have limited our ability to track trends in specific places.

18. Pack (2002); Nelson (1988).

place, per capita measures are not useful, because they average total income across all residents.[19]

Because this chapter uses census-based income data, an important choice is whether to focus on families or households, because the census provides data for both groupings. Looking at families—defined as two or more related people living together—may better control for the diversity of income-earning units. Families typically do not include young singles, senior citizens living alone, or nonrelated group living situations where individuals may have different incomes or expenses than other household types. A major disadvantage of looking at families, however, is that doing so excludes a substantial portion of city populations. If families were used in this analysis, it would effectively exclude four out of every ten households in the 100 largest cities.[20] Households, on the other hand, include the majority of city population.[21]

Because we are interested in establishing general trends in city-dweller incomes, we opt for inclusivity, and focus on households. If we were interested in issues that specifically concerned families, such as how the presence of an urban middle class affects city schools, families might be a more appropriate measure.[22]

Creating Income Groups

To provide a consistent measure of how income is distributed across cities and across time, household income data were used to create five "income groups" for each city, in each census year. These income groups reflect the national household income distribution in the given year, so that each

19. Although census household income data are not adjusted for household size, as are official poverty figures, we note that average household size in the 100 largest cities in 2000 (2.56 persons) roughly equaled that in the nation as a whole (2.59 persons). Individual cities, of course, do deviate more widely from these averages. Most income distribution analyses, however, do not attempt to control for these household or family-size differences across time or place.

20. Nonfamily households are even more prevalent in cities than in the United States as a whole; in 2000, 39 percent of households in the 100 largest cities were nonfamilies, compared to 32 percent nationwide. The Census Bureau began reporting household income data in 1967 to provide more comprehensive analysis, and today it considers households its main demographic unit of income analysis. Jones and Weinberg (2000).

21. People living in group quarters, such as nursing homes or college dormitories, are excluded from household data.

22. In order to ensure that the use of household data did not unduly bias our results, we compiled data for families as well. Both the static distribution and the trends over time for families in large cities resemble those identified for households. The primary difference, not surprisingly, is that fewer middle-income families than households reside in cities.

income group contains 20 percent of all U.S. households.[23] By this method income "cutoffs" were established for each group. For instance in 1999 census data indicate that 20 percent of U.S. households had incomes under $18,320.[24] For each of the 100 largest cities categorical income data were used to estimate the number and proportion of households with income in the $0 to $18,320 range (though adjustments were made to these estimates for regional cost differences (see "Accounting for Regional Cost Differences" below). These figures represent the size of the low-income household population for each city.

We apply the same method to derive the size of the other four income groups—"lower-middle income," "middle income," "upper-middle income," and "high-income"—in each large city in 1999. Similarly we use household income data from the 1980 census to create income groups that reflect the national distribution of household income in that year. Thus the ceiling for the low-income group in 1979 was $7,107.

Of course the allocation of income across groups has shifted over the last two decades, as the highest earners have garnered an increasing share of the nation's income.[25] Although cities surely shared in this overall trend, the Census Bureau does not report income data in a way that sheds light on equity trends at the city level. For that reason this chapter instead assumes that the income distribution of the nation's households can help shape fundamental notions of who is "low-income" or "middle income," and the degree to which these groups are over- or underrepresented in the nation's large cities.

Interpreting the Data

Cities' income distributions were assessed primarily by analyzing the shares of their households that fit within each of the five income brackets. These shares were calculated for the 100 largest cities in the aggregate, and for each

23. In 2000 about one in five U.S. households lived in one of the 100 largest cities. Thus how households distribute by income in the 100 cities does influence the overall distribution of income nationally, but by a small enough amount to render the comparison meaningful. For a similar analysis with family units, see Frankel and Gould (2001).

24. The other national category cutoffs for 1999 are lower middle income, up to $33,835; middle income, up to $51,857; upper middle income, up to $79,356. These compare closely to Current Population Survey–based estimates for the same year (www.census.gov/hhes/income/histinc/h01.html [June 2004]). Other research examining households by income quintile includes tax analyses published by organizations such as the Congressional Budget Office (2003) and the Urban-Brookings Tax Policy Center (Gale and Orszag [2004]), and income analyses published by the U.S. Census Bureau (2003).

25. Mishel, Bernstein, and Boushey (2003).

of the cities individually.[26] These data show, for a given year, how a given city's households compare by income to all of the nation's households. Therefore even if a city's household income distribution changes over time, the data may reflect little transition if those changes mirrored changes occurring at the national level.

For a city with a perfectly balanced income distribution, by our measures, 20 percent of all households would fall within each of the five income brackets—in other words its households' incomes would mirror those earned by all U.S. households. As the proportion of households in any income group trends away from 20 percent (in either a positive or negative direction), it diverges from the nation as a whole. Together the five income groups' shares must total 100 percent, but in some cities households tend to bunch into a narrow part of the distribution curve.

For example, in 1999, middle-income households in both Austin and El Paso, Texas, represented about 20 percent of all households. In other words the size of the middle-income household population in these cities mirrored the size of that group nationally. Yet in other parts of the income distribution, these cities differed significantly. In Austin no single income group captured more than 22 percent of households, or less than 19 percent of households. By contrast El Paso had twice as many low-income households (26 percent) as high-income households (13 percent) in 1999. These differences among cities, and between large cities and the nation generally, motivate our analysis.[27]

26. Some analyses use percentile measures to understand how relationships among income groups shift over time. For instance, in Los Angeles, the household at the eightieth percentile in that city's income distribution made $115,000 in 1999, and $77,000 in 1989. One could examine how this income growth compared to that experienced by households at that city's twentieth and fortieth percentiles. The approach in this chapter, by contrast, applies a uniform set of "quintiles" across all 100 cities (adjusted for regional cost differences) to examine changes in the percentage of households in the five income groups. We feel that this approach better reflects the dynamic nature of income distribution at the city level, as households move across income groups, and in and out of cities themselves.

27. A city with an income distribution mirroring the nation's is not necessarily an egalitarian place. Secular growth in income inequality at the national level has meant increases in the incomes of those in the uppermost brackets, even as incomes at the lower end have stalled. One could argue that instead of striving to house representative numbers of households at all income levels, cities should aim to increase, through attraction or retention strategies, the number of households earning at least a middle income. Although we would applaud such an outcome, especially if it reflects economic mobility for lower-earning households, we nonetheless remain interested in the degree to which cities remain centers of income diversity and house residents from across the income spectrum. This requires us to find some objective way to measure income diversity, for which we turn to national census figures. (One could also compare each city to the 100-city aggregate, rather than a national aggregate; however, this might imply

Accounting for Regional Cost Differences

Wide variations in the prevailing cost of living characterize the nation's largest cities. Any analysis that compares incomes in different areas of the country must somehow account for the large differences in the bundle of goods and services that households with the same income can purchase in, for example, San Francisco, California, versus Birmingham, Alabama. The median San Francisco household in 1999, for example, made $55,221, whereas the median Birmingham household made $26,735 (nationwide, median household income was $41,994). At the same time vast differences in the cost of housing, insurance, food, and other services characterize each locale. Given these differences it does not seem appropriate to use the same income range to identify "middle-income" households in these two cities.

Because no standard published indicator reports these regional price differences the chapter uses a "metropolitan price index" to adjust for such differences among the 100 cities, and changes in those costs across the two decades. The index reflects fair market rent prices collected and published by the U.S. Department of Housing and Urban Development, and methodology the U.S. Census Bureau has used to derive experimental poverty measures.[28] We use this index to adjust the cutoffs for each national income group to the prevailing costs in each city. For example, a San Francisco household is considered middle-income if it made between $44,102 and $67,591 in 1999, whereas a Birmingham household only needed to earn between $31,504 and $48,282 to receive that designation (table 7-1). To qualify as "high-income" a household must have earned $30,000 more annually in San Francisco than in Birmingham.

By adjusting for regional price differences we can define a smaller number of households as high-income, and a larger number of households as low-income, in expensive cities. In inexpensive cities the reverse pattern holds. Because metropolitan areas are overall more expensive than the national

---

that large cities themselves represent a more optimal mix of household incomes than national averages. As the present analysis demonstrates the aggregate income profile of the 100 largest cities differs sharply from that of the nation as a whole—and in a negative direction.) In addition although the top fifth of earners has enjoyed greater income growth nationally than other groups in recent decades, the even more extraordinary increases enjoyed by the highest-income households (for example, the top 1 percent) do not distort our comparisons to the nation, because they are merely part of the broader top income quintile. See Mishel, Bernstein, and Boushey (2003).

28. See technical appendix for a detailed explanation of how this index was derived, and the rationale for using it.

TABLE 7-1. Household Income Ranges, by Group, United States versus Selected Cities, 1999

Income group	United States	San Francisco (index = 1.30)	Birmingham (index = 0.93)
Low-income	Under $18,320	Under $23,878	Under $17,057
Lower-middle-income	$18,320 to $33,835	$23,878 to $44,101	$17,057 to $31,503
Middle-income	$33,836 to $51,857	$44,102 to $67,591	$31,504 to $48,282
Upper-middle-income	$51,858 to $79,356	$67,592 to $103,433	$48,283 to $73,885
High-income	Over $79,356	Over $103,433	Over $73,885

Source: Brookings calculations from Census 2000 and HUD Fair Market Rent data.

average, and because central cities within metropolitan areas are examined, the aggregate totals for the 100 cities reflect a marginal "high cost" effect.[29]

Timing and Business Cycles

Economists often examine "secular" changes from one peak of the business cycle to the next when they study long-term income trends. This is a useful technique because it compares incomes at similar stages in the overall economy. The analysis is limited to one year each decade, as it examines city-level data using the decennial census. It is thus reassuring that business cycle peaks have correlated almost perfectly with the decennial census during the last two decades, occurring in 1979, 1989, and 2000.[30] Although the data examined here are now about four years old, our interest in city income trends independent of the business cycle make these data useful and compelling. Future enhancements to the American Community Survey may enable researchers to track these city-level trends more closely on an intercensal basis.[31]

29. The average fair market rent in the 100 largest cities in 1999 was $636, compared to the national average of $608. Thus income quintile cutoffs have been adjusted slightly upward from where they occur nationally. At the same time exactly half of the 100 largest cities had a metropolitan price index under 1.00 in 1999, so the income cutoffs shift lower in 50 cities. Note that this method assumes that the relative fair market rents among cities mirror those among their metropolitan areas.

30. The National Bureau of Economic Research, the group that dates recessions, identifies January 1980, July 1990, and March 2001 as the peak quarters for the last three business cycles. Because GDP began to decline in these years, the ideal peak-to-peak year for income is prior to each of these dates—1979, 1989, and 2000. For more information see www.nber.org/cycles/cyclesmain.html.

31. We experimented with tracking recent changes in household incomes for the sixty-four large cities that appear in the Census 2000 Supplementary Survey and the 2002 American Community Survey. Large differences, however, between the results from these two surveys (which employ similar survey methodologies), and between these surveys and Census 2000, in the number of overall households counted, and the median incomes of those households, suggested that city-level estimates had too high a degree of error to include in this analysis.

FINDINGS

Analysis of decennial census data from 1980, 1990, and 2000 indicates that cities overall lack a balanced set of household incomes. At the same time, cities themselves are quite diverse in their income profiles.

Disproportionate Numbers of Large-City Households Occupy the Bottom Tiers of the National Income Distribution

Low-income individuals who seek proximity to employment centers and inexpensive housing have always populated cities. Some also argue that the poor are more likely to live in cities because they seek greater access to public transit or more generous welfare policies.[32] Even in 1967, before the significant increases in urban poverty that followed, the Census Bureau recorded a 15-percent poverty rate in central cities, 4 percentage points higher than in the nation as a whole. This gap widened by the mid-1990s to 7 percentage points, before it narrowed slightly in the 1990s.

It may therefore come as no surprise that the nation's largest cities today contain a disproportionate number of households that, judged by national standards, have low incomes. Across the 100 cities in the aggregate, about one-quarter of households occupied the bottom fifth of the national income distribution in 1999 (figure 7-1). Although the exact dollar amount these households earned varied from city to city (reflecting adjustments for regional price differences), these households' incomes generally fell below about $19,150 for the year.[33] The largest cities also contained an above-average share of lower-middle-income households. These households accounted for 21.5 percent of households overall.

Along with containing more than their share of lower-income households the largest 100 cities also contained fewer than their share of high-income households. Such households—which on average made more than $83,000 in 1999—accounted for only one-sixth of large-city households (again, compared to one-fifth nationally). In a reverse image of the lower-income end of the scale, upper-middle-income households also made up less than one-fifth of large-city households. Although some cities contain highly sought-after housing and neighborhoods, higher-income households are underrepresented in large cities.

The 100 largest cities include a wide range of places, however, and their household income profiles reflect this diversity. Table 7-2 describes the income continuum across the largest cities. It shows that, in fact, lower-income house-

32. Glaeser, Kahn, and Rappaport (2000).
33. This figure represents the national ceiling for the low-income quintile in 1999 ($18,320) multiplied by the household-weighted average of the cost index for the 100 largest cities (1.045).

FIGURE 7-1. **Proportion of Households, by Income Category, 100 Largest Cities, 1999**

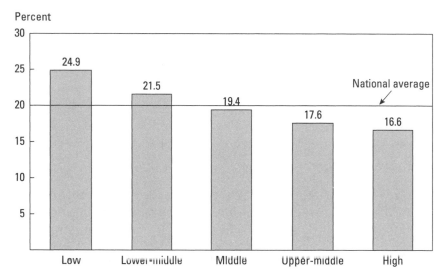

Source: Authors' analysis of Census 2000 data.

holds do not concentrate in every city. In Plano, Texas, a fast-growing city in the suburbs of Dallas, nearly 46 percent of households occupied the highest-income quintile in 1999.[34] Miami, however, displayed an exactly opposite pattern, with 43 percent of its households residing in the lowest national quintile.

For middle-income households, however, the variance among cities is less extreme. The leading city for middle-income households, Aurora, Colorado, has just 24 percent of its households in that segment. By contrast, Miami and Plano count roughly 15 percent of their households in this category. Although middle-income households are slightly underrepresented in large cities overall, more cities hover close to the national average for this segment of the distribution than for the others.

As the overall pattern demonstrates, though, city households tend to cluster toward the bottom of the income distribution. Roughly one-third or more of the households in the ten cities with the largest proportions of low-

34. Although many urban scholars might not consider Plano to be much of a "city," its rapid growth over the past four decades has catapulted it to the ranks of the seventy-eighth-largest city in the United States, ahead of well-recognized places like Akron, OH; Montgomery, AL; and Richmond, VA. Robert Lang and Patrick Simmons identify Plano as the second-fastest-growing "Boomburb" in the nation. Arlington, Garland, and Irving, all among the top 100 cities, also qualify as "Boomburbs" in the Dallas region and typify the fast-growing, geographically large, suburban-style cities that occur throughout the South and Southwest. Lang and Simmons (2003).

T A B L E 7 - 2 . Cities with Largest Shares of Households in Low-, Middle-, and High-Income Categories, 1999

City	Households in quintile	Total households	Percent of households
Largest low-income shares			
Miami, FL	57,208	134,344	42.6
Newark, NJ	37,423	91,366	41.0
Buffalo, NY	45,369	122,671	37.0
Cleveland, OH	69,350	190,725	36.4
Rochester, NY	31,438	89,092	35.3
New Orleans, LA	65,251	188,365	34.6
Philadelphia, PA	198,737	590,282	33.7
Birmingham, AL	32,975	98,748	33.4
Detroit, MI	111,370	336,483	33.1
St. Louis, MO	48,389	147,286	32.9
Largest middle-income shares			
Aurora, CO	25,703	105,526	24.4
Virginia Beach, VA	36,753	154,636	23.8
Irving, TX	18,218	76,373	23.9
Santa Ana, CA	17,009	72,993	23.3
Mesa, AZ	34,566	146,700	23.6
Fort Wayne, IN	19,179	83,416	23.0
Des Moines, IA	18,228	80,621	22.6
Garland, TX	16,819	73,279	23.0
Grand Rapids, MI	16,169	73,337	22.0
Jacksonville, FL	62,476	284,660	21.9
Largest high-income shares			
Plano, TX	37,022	81,179	45.6
Fremont, CA	26,626	68,303	39.0
Scottsdale, AZ	31,167	90,602	34.4
San Jose, CA	82,267	276,408	29.8
Anchorage, AK	23,788	95,081	25.0
Charlotte, NC	55,250	215,803	25.6
Chesapeake, VA	16,136	69,836	23.1
Arlington, TX	28,708	124,851	23.0
San Francisco, CA	77,656	329,850	23.5
Raleigh, NC	25,424	112,727	22.6

Source: Authors' analysis of Census 2000 data.

income households lie in that category. On the other hand, the tenth city on the high-income list registers just 23 percent of its households in the top category. In this way the aggregate statistics reflect that the large numbers of low-income households in poorer cities outweigh the presence of high-income households in wealthy cities.

The Largest Cities Exhibit Six Basic Household Income Distribution Patterns

The 100 largest cities exhibit a wide variety of household incomes, and not all cities follow the average pattern. Miami and Plano remain outliers. Numerous cities, however, share common features that can illuminate where and how certain household types cluster, and how cities have changed in recent decades.

At least six prominent types of city household income profiles can be described based on the relative number of households in each part of the income scale.

Four of them simply reflect where the most households reside along the income continuum:

—In *balanced cities,* the household income distribution largely mirrors the national distribution. The number of households in any one category does not exceed that in any other by more than 25 percent.[35]

—*Divided cities* have a "u-shaped" income distribution, such that both high-income and low-income households outnumber middle-income households.

—*Middle-class cities* have their largest number of households in one of the three central categories—lower middle income, middle income, or upper middle income.

—In *higher-end cities,* more households reside in the top income category than in any other.

The remaining cities have their largest number of households in the lowest-income quintile. Notwithstanding the enormous diversity that exists even among these cities, two additional types of cities can be discerned:

—*Stressed cities* have at least twice as many households in the bottom two categories combined (lower middle and middle income) as in the top two categories combined (upper middle and high income).

—*Low-moderate cities* include those that remain. Their income distribution slopes downward (in other words, each successive income category contains fewer households) but not as steeply as in stressed cities.

The resulting typology of cities is displayed in table 7-3 with the overall distribution for each city type displayed in figure 7-2. As with any typology this one pivots on certain numeric thresholds that place similar cities in different categories. The household income distribution in Oklahoma City, for example, closely resembles that in Tulsa (see table 7A-1 for data on all 100 cities). Yet Tulsa is labeled *middle-class* because it has 700 more lower-middle-income households than low-income households, whereas Oklahoma City is labeled *low-moderate* because its low-income households outnumber

35. By definition, then, no category contains fewer than 17.8 percent of the city's households, and none contains more than 22.2 percent.

TABLE 7-3. 100 Largest Cities, by Household Income Distribution Type, 1999[a]

Balanced (n=13)	Divided (n=7)	Higher-end (n=8)	Middle-class (n=29)	
Riverside, CA	Atlanta, GA	Plano, TX	Aurora, CO	Glendale, AZ
San Diego, CA	Baton Rouge, LA	Fremont, CA	Santa Ana, CA	Nashville, TN
Lexington-Fayette, KY	Washington, DC	Scottsdale, AZ	Garland, TX	St. Paul, MN
Seattle, WA	Los Angeles, CA	San Jose, CA	Irving, TX	Portland, OR
Bakersfield, CA	San Francisco, CA	Charlotte, NC	Virginia Beach, VA	St. Petersburg, FL
Austin, TX	Yonkers, NY	Anchorage, AK	Mesa, AZ	Madison, WI
Honolulu, HI	Glendale, CA	Arlington, TX	Des Moines, IA	Fort Worth, TX
Indianapolis, IN		Raleigh, NC	Fort Wayne, IN	Kansas City, MO
Greensboro, NC			Anaheim, CA	San Antonio, TX
Omaha, NE			Lincoln, NE	Albuquerque, NM
Phoenix, AZ			Colorado Springs, CO	Denver, CO
Las Vegas, NV			Grand Rapids, MI	Minneapolis, MN
Wichita, KS			Chesapeake, VA	Dallas, TX
			Columbus, OH	Tulsa, OK
			Jacksonville, FL	

	Low-moderate (n=29)		Stressed (n=14)
	Montgomery, AL	Toledo, OH	Louisville, KY
	Tacoma, WA	Mobile, AL	New Orleans, LA
	Oklahoma City, OK	New York, NY	Detroit, MI
	Corpus Christi, TX	Lubbock, TX	Baltimore, MD
	Houston, TX	Memphis, TN	Tucson, AZ
	Sacramento, CA	Spokane, WA	Philadelphia, PA
	Chicago, IL	El Paso, TX	St. Louis, MO
	Oakland, CA	Shreveport, LA	Birmingham, AL
	Stockton, CA	Akron, OH	Rochester, NY
	Long Beach, CA	Norfolk, VA	Buffalo, NY
	Jersey City, NJ	Pittsburgh, PA	Hialeah, FL
	Tampa, FL	Milwaukee, WI	Cleveland, OH
	Fresno, CA	Richmond, VA	Newark, NJ
	Boston, MA	Cincinnati, OH	Miami, FL
	Augusta-Richmond, GA		

Source: Authors' analysis of Census 2000 data.

a. See text for explanation of city types.

its lower-middle-income households by about 300. Each category should be viewed as a continuum in which the cities at the bottom of one category overlap slightly with those at the top of the next.[36]

36. Cities are ordered within each category by the size of the relevant income category, and how closely they resemble adjoining categories. For example, Aurora, CO, is ordered first among middle-class cities because it has the largest middle-income segment as a proportion of all households. Montgomery, AL, is first among low-moderate cities because its low-income category is only slightly larger than its lower-middle-income category. Note also that some cities occupying the same category have somewhat different income profiles. For example, compared to Minneapolis, Aurora has few low-income households. Nevertheless both qualify as middle-class cities because one of their middle-income categories predominates.

FIGURE 7-2. **Proportion of Households by, Income Category and City Type, 100 Largest Cities, 1999**

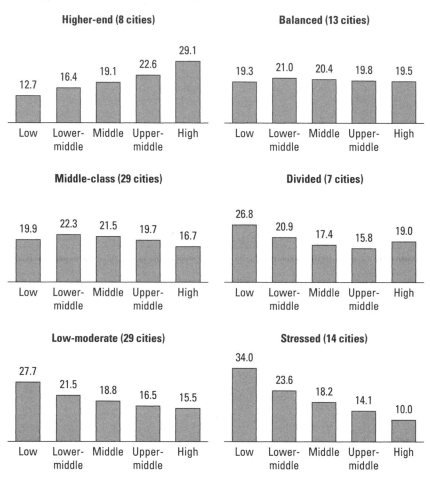

Higher-end (8 cities)

12.7	Low
16.4	Lower-middle
19.1	Middle
22.6	Upper-middle
29.1	High

Balanced (13 cities)

19.3	Low
21.0	Lower-middle
20.4	Middle
19.8	Upper-middle
19.5	High

Middle-class (29 cities)

19.9	Low
22.3	Lower-middle
21.5	Middle
19.7	Upper-middle
16.7	High

Divided (7 cities)

26.8	Low
20.9	Lower-middle
17.4	Middle
15.8	Upper-middle
19.0	High

Low-moderate (29 cities)

27.7	Low
21.5	Lower-middle
18.8	Middle
16.5	Upper-middle
15.5	High

Stressed (14 cities)

34.0	Low
23.6	Lower-middle
18.2	Middle
14.1	Upper-middle
10.0	High

Source: Authors' analysis of Census 2000 data.
See text for explanation of categories.

Several observations bear making about the classification system:

A surprising number of cities boast significant middle-income popula-tions. Despite the perception that relatively few middle-class households reside in cities, it is noteworthy that more than one-quarter of the 100 largest cities contain abundant numbers of middle-tier households. These twenty-nine middle-class cities divide nearly evenly between three regions of the country—the South (eleven), the Midwest (nine), and the West (nine). As figure 7-2 shows, roughly 20 percent or more of these cities' households reside in each of the three middle-income categories. High-income households, by contrast, represent just over one-sixth of all households, the same proportion as in the 100 cities generally.

These cities are by no means homogeneous. They range from those with concentrations of lower-middle-income households, like Dallas, to those with large numbers of upper-middle-income households, like Chesapeake, Virginia. Yet all place at least one-fifth of their households squarely in the middle-income bracket. Their middle-income orientation may owe to a variety of factors. Many lie in Sunbelt metropolitan areas that have recently attracted significant numbers of families and educated workers.[37] Several are Midwestern cities, such as Columbus, Kansas City, and Fort Wayne, which have expanded their borders over time through annexation, thereby incorporating more middle-income households.[38] Moreover other cities, such as Irving, Mesa, and Glendale, are themselves suburban in design and demography, and have emerged as full-fledged cities only in the last twenty or thirty years.[39]

What is more, several other prominent U.S. cities—among them Dallas, Denver, Minneapolis and St. Paul, and Portland, OR—manage to rank among those with a decent-sized middle-income population even without enjoying such regional or temporal advantages. These cities' natural amenities and/or robust employment growth seem to have fueled their success in attracting and retaining younger households and families that disproportionately occupy the middle rungs of the distribution.

Relatively few cities hew closely to the national distribution. Out of the 100 largest cities, only 13 displayed a balanced income distribution. These cities are distinguished by their large geographical size—ten encompass more than 100 square miles—and their location—ten sit in the southern or western regions of the United States. Many of these cities, like Phoenix, Las Vegas, Bakersfield, and Riverside, experienced rapid in-migration in recent years of both higher-income and lower-income households. At the same time some used their "elastic" borders to incorporate once-suburban communities within central-city borders, boosting their overall income diversity.[40]

37. See Frey, chapter 1, this volume.
38. Two southern cities, Nashville and Jacksonville, are consolidated with their counties and rank among the largest cities in the United States geographically.
39. A couple of cities in the middle-class category, including Santa Ana and Anaheim, may reside there thanks to their larger-than-average households; on a per-person basis, they might look more like low-moderate cities.
40. Rusk (2003).

Only seven cities encompass large numbers of both low-income and high-income households. Among the 100 largest cities, only 7 appear to contain larger-than-average numbers of both poor and rich households. The broader perception that this is a common feature of cities may be shaped by the fact that these divided cities include some of the nation's largest and most recognizable centers, including Los Angeles, Atlanta, San Francisco, and Washington, D.C. As Figure 7-2 shows, these cities collectively count only 17 percent of their households in the middle-income category, a smaller proportion than in the other five city types. For the most part, however, their income distribution is more "ski jump–shaped" than "u-shaped" because many more of their households have low incomes (27 percent) than high incomes (19 percent). Large demographic and economic disparities by race and ethnicity characterize most of these cities. For example, the incomes and education levels of black households in Atlanta and Washington and Latino households in Los Angeles and San Francisco substantially trail those of their white counterparts, contributing to the large divides in their cities' income distributions.[41]

A few cities—including several "Boomburbs"—are havens for mostly higher-income residents. Most of the eight places in the higher-end category are fast-growing cities in the southern and western United States. Lang and Simmons identify four of these eight cities as "Boomburbs."[42] These cities have experienced rapid growth in recent decades but have largely retained their suburban character, thanks in part to the master-planned–community development that has fueled their growth. The wealthy profile of other cities in this category—including San José, Charlotte, Raleigh, and Anchorage—owes to their geographically expansive borders and strong economic growth in recent years.

Low-income households predominate in forty-three cities, although some cities are better off than others. The 100 cities' overall downward-sloping income distribution implies that in a large number of these cities low-income households represent the largest group. Because fully forty-three cities meet this criterion, it makes sense to distinguish between those cities where the income distribution skews just slightly toward the low end, and those where lower-income households predominate.

41. Brookings Institution Center on Urban and Metropolitan Policy (2003b).
42. Lang and Simmons (2003). The "Boomburbs" in this category include Arlington, Texas; Fremont, California; Plano, Texas; and Scottsdale, Arizona. Several others figure prominently in the middle-class category.

The first group, labeled low-moderate cities, consists of twenty-nine places that include some of the largest in the nation, such as Houston, Chicago, Boston, and New York. Although they still contain a fairly diverse set of households by income—in fact, the aforementioned cities all have significant numbers of higher-income households—a good number still confront familiar urban problems associated with a lower-income profile: above-average poverty, low-performing public schools, slow population growth or decline, and segregated neighborhoods. Like divided cities, these cities contend with significant gaps between white and minority populations, although the magnitude of the separation remains smaller. Overall a little under half of households in these twenty-nine cities occupy the bottom two income categories. That suggests that the great amounts of wealth held by their highest-income households—rather than any large surplus of such households—accounts for popular notions of cities like New York and Boston as high-end havens.

Yet these low-moderate cities remain much better positioned to address their challenges than the fourteen stressed cities. The stressed list includes places struggling with larger problems that include the long-term transition away from a manufacturing-dominated economy, extreme racial segregation, and migration out of the northern United States to southern and western states. As figure 7-2 shows, more than one in three households in these fourteen cities occupies the lowest income category. Northeastern cities on this list—including Newark, Philadelphia, and Rochester—are "hemmed in" by incorporated jurisdictions that forestall their ability to annex suburban territory. At the same time a number of Sunbelt cities with high rates of black or Hispanic poverty—ranging from Miami (and its neighboring city, Hialeah) and Birmingham to New Orleans and Tucson—also fall into this category.[43]

In sum households in the lowest national income bracket make up a high concentration of the household count in a plurality of large U.S. cities. Most cities, to be sure, are not without higher-earning households, but a handful of cities in struggling regions of the United States face daunting challenges associated with high concentrations of households living on low incomes. At the same time, a significant number of middle-class cities dot the Southeast, Southwest, and Midwest. Many of these cities have expansive borders and include suburban-like development, whereas others of more traditional design seem to appeal to younger middle-income populations. A few cities show high levels of inequality, or heavy tilt toward upper-income households. Finally,

43. Louisville resides in this category based on its 1999 household income characteristics, but pursuant to the city's consolidation with surrounding Jefferson County, Kentucky, in 2003, the Regional City of Louisville likely has a much more diverse income profile. Brookings Institution Center on Urban and Metropolitan Policy (2002).

only about one in eight cities resembles the nation as a whole, with roughly equal numbers of households within each segment of the income scale.

Households with High Incomes Declined in Most Large Cities

Far from immutable, the income distribution within U.S. big cities has shifted during the last twenty years.

At the outset, it bears noting that declines or increases in different parts of the income distribution can occur for a variety of reasons. A rise in a city's share of low-income households, for instance, may owe to that segment's either growing faster or shrinking more slowly than other segments, whether thanks to in- or out-migration or other causes. Similarly, economic growth may bolster the earnings of middle-income households, advancing them into the upper-middle-income category. Alternatively, the demographics of aging, through their influence on household formation patterns, may influence a city's income profile over time. For example, as households age into retirement, their incomes may decrease even though they maintain a comparable standard of living by drawing on accumulated assets. In like fashion a city may trade lower-income households for higher-income ones as singles form households and combine earnings.[44]

Given the variety of these potential influences on city income distribution, this assessment makes no attempt to identify empirically the various factors at play in particular cities. The discussion does, however, offer some speculation as to why some cities experienced large changes in their income distributions, based on larger demographic, economic, and physical growth trends prevailing over the two decades.

Looking at the 100 largest cities as a group, it is not always clear whether cities overall have more lower-income, middle-income, or higher-income households than they did twenty years ago. Places like Detroit and Cleveland that lost significant population and decent-paying jobs in recent decades are undoubtedly home to poorer households than before. Fast-growing cities in the South and West, however, may have offset that trend by absorbing more middle- and high-income households. Within metropolitan areas, decentralizing development and exploding exurbs seem to have lured higher-income households farther away from the urban core. Yet low- and moderate-income households populate suburbs in growing numbers, too, especially as immigrants increasingly bypass cities altogether in certain U.S. regions.[45]

---

44. See Madden (2000) for further discussion on the role of household formation trends on metropolitan-level income inequality in the 1980s.

45. See Jargowsky, chapter 5, this volume; and Singer, chapter 2, this volume.

FIGURE 7-3. **Proportion of Households, by Income Category, 100 Largest Cities, 1979–1999**

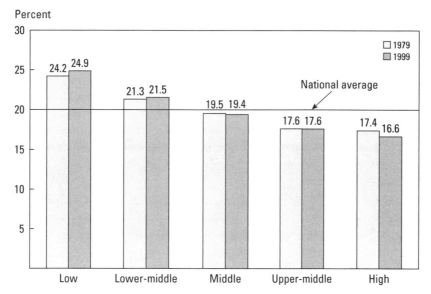

Source: Authors' analysis of 1980 and 2000 decennial censuses.

Notwithstanding these divergent trends, the income distribution of households in the 100 cities appears to have changed only slightly between 1979 and 1999.[46] The number of households in each part of the income distribution grew in the 100 largest cities over the twenty-year period. Yet because higher-income households grew at a significantly slower rate than other types, their share of all households in the 100 largest cities declined by three-quarters of a percentage point (figure 7-3).[47]

These small changes at the aggregate level, however, have not precluded other more substantial forces that pulled individual cities in countervailing directions over the two decades. The most salient changes emerged along regional lines and by city size:

Most cities saw their shares of households with high incomes decline over the two decades. Fully 79 of the 100 largest cities saw the share of their

46. The focus is primarily on the aggregate twenty-year trend because large shifts in the income distribution in a few large cities in both the 1980s and 1990s tend to skew the decade-by-decade results for all 100 cities.

47. Had the number of high-income households increased at the same rate as all other households in large cities during the 1980s and 1990s, the 100 cities combined would have had an additional 194,000 high-income households in 1999.

households in the top income quintile decline between 1979 and 1999. Places as diverse as Los Angeles, Indianapolis, Virginia Beach, and Baton Rouge all watched the relative size of their high-income household population shrink.

Given how many cities shared in this pattern, those cities that actually saw growth in their high-income shares over the twenty-year period merit examination (table 7-4). Many of these cities are identified with industry sectors that enjoyed considerable success in the 1980s and 1990s, including technology and high-end financial services. More generally, nearly all are home to significant concentrations of "knowledge workers" whose income growth in recent decades has propelled them into the high-earner category. Nevertheless they represent a variety of income types, from higher-end places like Fremont and Scottsdale to more middle-class places like Minneapolis and Tampa-St. Petersburg.

So where did this leave the other seventy-nine cities? The cities experiencing the largest declines over the two decades in their high-income brackets include some that suffered ongoing losses of manufacturing jobs, such as Toledo and Milwaukee (table 7-4). Some like Houston, Corpus Christi, Tulsa, and Mobile are located in the "oil patch" that endured a dramatic oil price bust during the late 1980s. Either way these economic developments may have slowed income growth for wealthier households, put the brakes on higher-income households' in-migration, or perhaps caused high-income households to relocate. As a result many formerly higher-end or balanced cities assumed a low-moderate income profile by 1999.

Nevertheless places like Aurora, Garland, Anchorage, and Irving all figure prominently on this list. All of these cities also had large numbers of high-income households at the beginning of the period. Indeed of the twenty cities that had the highest proportion of their households in the top income bracket in 1979, seventeen saw that high-income segment decline over the twenty-year period. These declines reflect that many of these places changed from suburban enclaves into full-fledged cities. In so doing, they acquired a more diverse income profile, and attracted large middle-income and lower-middle-income populations that transformed their 1979 higher-end designation into a middle-class one by 1999 (figure 7-4).

Three-quarters of the 100 largest cities saw their household income distribution tilt toward the low end. By definition, as one part of the income distribution shrinks, another expands. Consequently an increase in the proportion of households with low incomes accompanied the drop in high-income households in most large cities. Some of the largest increases, not surprisingly, occurred in cities such as Houston and Mobile where high-income

T A B L E 7 - 4 . Cities with Fastest Growth and Fastest Decline in High-Income Household Share, 1979–99

City	High-income households, 1979		High-income households, 1999		Percentage change 1979–99	City type	
	Number	Percent	Number	Percent	1979–99	1979	1999
Fastest growth							
Atlanta, GA	22,395	13.7	33,261	19.8	6.0	Stressed	Divided
Fremont, CA	14,760	33.4	26,626	39.0	5.6	Higher-end	Higher-end
Austin, TX	19,226	14.3	51,698	19.5	5.1	Low-moderate	Balanced
Charlotte, NC	24,575	20.7	55,250	25.6	4.9	Balanced	Higher-end
San Francisco, CA	56,381	18.8	77,656	23.5	4.7	Low-moderate	Divided
Tampa, FL	13,052	12.3	20,039	16.1	3.7	Low-moderate	Low-moderate
Boston, MA	24,999	11.4	36,031	15.0	3.6	Stressed	Low-moderate
Chesapeake, VA	7,513	20.5	16,136	23.1	2.6	Middle-class	Middle-class
San Diego, CA	60,623	18.9	96,590	21.4	2.6	Balanced	Balanced
New York, NY	380,494	13.6	483,779	16.0	2.4	Low-moderate	Low-moderate
San Jose, CA	57,711	27.5	82,267	29.8	2.3	Higher-end	Higher-end
San Antonio, TX	34,881	13.5	63,799	15.7	2.3	Low-moderate	Middle-class
St. Petersburg, FL	12,103	11.6	15,117	13.8	2.2	Low-moderate	Middle-class
Scottsdale, AZ	11,175	32.6	31,167	34.4	1.8	Higher-end	Higher-end
Oakland, CA	22,089	15.5	26,098	17.3	1.8	Low-moderate	Low-moderate
Fastest decline							
Aurora, CO	16,417	28.0	18,133	17.2	-10.9	Higher-end	Middle-class
Garland, TX	13,430	29.3	13,823	18.9	-10.4	Middle-class	Middle-class
Anchorage, AK	20,903	34.4	23,788	25.0	-9.3	Higher-end	Higher-end
Toledo, OH	27,060	20.3	15,822	12.3	-8.0	Balanced	Low-moderate
Anaheim, CA	20,302	25.5	17,228	17.8	-7.7	Higher-end	Middle-class
Milwaukee, WI	42,140	17.4	22,965	9.9	-7.5	Balanced	Low-moderate
Irving, TX	10,039	25.0	13,392	17.5	-7.5	Higher-end	Middle-class
Lubbock, TX	13,200	21.6	11,082	14.3	-7.4	Balanced	Low-moderate
Houston, TX	150,144	24.9	129,118	18.0	-6.9	Higher-end	Low-moderate
Santa Ana, CA	12,387	19.3	9,392	12.9	-6.4	Middle-class	Middle-class
Mobile, AL	14,842	20.7	11,548	14.7	-6.0	Balanced	Low-moderate
Wichita, KS	25,836	23.4	24,256	17.4	-6.0	Higher-end	Middle-class
Tulsa, OK	33,321	23.0	28,418	17.1	-5.8	Higher-end	Middle-class
Corpus Christi, TX	16,545	21.6	15,560	15.8	-5.8	Balanced	Low-moderate
Arlington, TX	16,742	28.6	28,708	23.0	-5.6	Higher-end	Higher-end

Source: Authors' analysis of 1980 and 2000 decennial censuses.

FIGURE 7-4. Number of Cities, by Household Income Distribution Type, 100 Largest Cities, 1979 and 1999

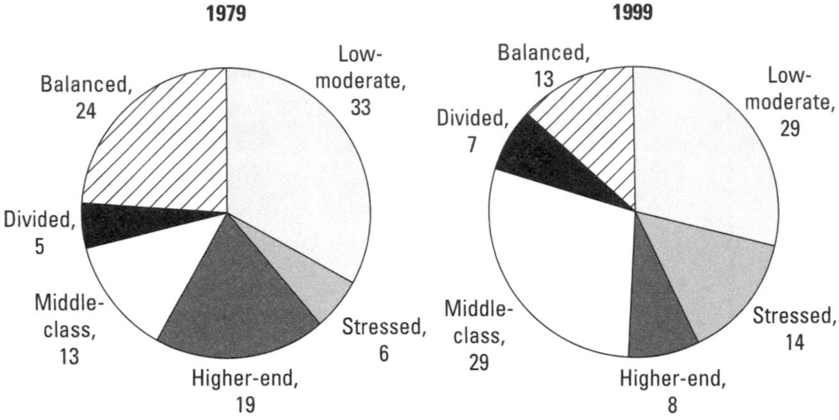

Source: Authors' analysis of 1980 and 2000 decennial censuses.

households dropped most precipitously. Overall, low-income households grew by 21 percent in the 100 largest cities, outpacing the overall household growth rate of just under 18 percent. The share of all households they represented grew by about two-thirds of a percentage point (table 7A-1).

The disproportionate growth in households at the lower end of the distribution largely accounts for an increase in cities with a stressed income profile (figure 7-4). Struggling Rust Belt cities like Detroit, Cleveland, Philadelphia, and Baltimore lost large numbers of middle- and higher-income households. At the same time, their regions grew more segregated, as economic and residential decentralization further isolated their central city minority populations from economic opportunity. As a result, such places changed from low-moderate cities in 1979 to stressed cities by 1999. Only three cities—Miami, St. Louis, and Newark—had a stressed designation at both points in time.

Did immigration play a large role in these changes? It may well have contributed to the growth of low-income households in cities over the 1980s and 1990s, but closer scrutiny reveals a more complicated story. Across the 100 largest cities, the foreign-born share of the population increased from under 12 percent in 1980 to over 20 percent in 2000. As immigrants tend to arrive in the United States with lower levels of education and skills than their native-born counterparts, we might expect that cities with high levels of immigration experienced more rapid increases in low-income households than other cities.[48] In fact many cities that experienced especially large increases in the foreign-born share of their populations, including most in Southern California, as well as Dallas and its suburban cities, did show larger-than-average increases in the percentage of households with low incomes. Yet cities that registered a much smaller-than-average climb—or loss—in foreign-born population, such as Buffalo, Rochester, Toledo, and Lubbock, showed even larger jumps in low-income households. Thus immigration may help explain the proliferation of low-income households in certain cities, but it cannot alone account for the fairly consistent rise in the share of households with low incomes in most large cities.

Middle-income households dwindled in big cities and Northeastern cities, but proliferated in other places, especially the Midwest. The nation's largest cities experienced the most pronounced declines in the relative numbers of middle-income households. Fully eight of the ten largest cities saw middle-income households dwindle as a proportion of all households, compared to fewer than half of the other eighty cities (table 7A-1).[49] Among the big cities, declines in the size of the middle-income segment loomed largest in New York and San Diego. Other big cities outside the top ten, including Washington, D.C., and San Francisco, also experienced significant decreases in middle-income households that created or exacerbated their divided household income profiles. The relative decline of the middle-income population in these big coastal cities may have owed to several factors affecting families, including a limited supply of affordable homes, low perceived quality of public schools, or crime.

Yet the middle-income slide did not affect all cities. In fact several cities emerged as middle-income destinations. The middle-income share of households rose notably in Grand Rapids, Michigan; Tacoma, Washington; and Des Moines, Iowa, among other places. Figure 7-4 shows that the number of middle-class cities with concentrations of households in the central part of the income distribution more than doubled between 1979 and 1999. Some of this resulted from higher-end suburban-like cities such as Aurora, Colorado, and Irving, Texas, growing and diversifying over the twenty-year period. Other large cities, however, graduated upward. San Antonio, Jacksonville, and Columbus had low-moderate distributions in 1979, but gained enough middle-income households over the two decades that households in their

---

48. Martin and Midgley (2003).
49. The correlations between city population and change in lower-middle-income and middle-income household shares (larger cities experienced larger losses) are much stronger than those for the other three income groups.

center segment dominated by 1999. The ascendancy of the middle-class in these places accompanied, not surprisingly, large increases in the percentages of their populations holding at least a high school diploma.[50]

The divide between the rise and fall of urban middle-income households broke along regional lines as well (table 7A-1). All nine cities in the Northeast experienced a drop in the proportion of their households that had middle incomes. Collectively, middle-income households in the nine cities accounted for 17.7 percent of households in 1999, down from 19.4 percent in 1979. Meanwhile fifteen of the twenty Midwestern cities enlarged their middle-income segment. Even cities in that region with fast-declining high-income segments, like Milwaukee, Kansas City, and Wichita, managed to retain—and in some cases attract—a larger middle-income population over the twenty-year period.

In short, the most common income trend affecting large cities over the past twenty years was not decline in the middle-class population, but loss of high-income households, paired with disproportionate growth in low-income households in many places. A handful of large cities, especially in the Northeast, did lose middle-income households. At the same time growth of the middle class in a number of Midwestern and Sun Belt cities somewhat offset those changes. The most worrying developments occurred in Rust Belt cities that already had a lower-income orientation in 1979. Over the subsequent twenty years these centers lost middle- and higher-income households at a rapid pace.

Suburban Income Distribution Inverts City Distribution

The suburbs of the largest 100 cities also experienced significant change.[51]

Households living in the 82 suburban areas containing the 100 largest cities invert, in the aggregate, the income structure of their cities. In fact they

50. Among adults age 25 and over, the percentage holding a high school diploma rose from 66 to 82 percent in Jacksonville, from 69 to 84 percent in Columbus, and from 59 to 75 percent in San Antonio, between 1980 and 2000.

51. For purposes of this analysis, suburbs make up the remainder of the metropolitan areas (MSAs and PMSAs) containing the 100 largest cities after those cities are netted out. Metropolitan areas are used as they were defined by OMB in 1999 (for Census 2000) to analyze income information from both the 1980 and 2000 decennial censuses. Thus the analysis of income in suburbs in 1979 may include households living in counties not then considered part of metropolitan areas. Holding the boundaries of these metropolitan areas constant, however, avoids spurious results that might stem from the redefinition of metropolitan areas by OMB, rather than from real change in household income composition over time. Overall the analysis includes the 81 suburban areas containing the 100 largest cities. The city of Anchorage, Alaska, is coincident with its metropolitan area, and therefore is not associated with any suburbs. The income "cutoffs" for regional cost differences are adjusted here in the same way as for cities, because the cost index is a metropolitan-level measure.

FIGURE 7-5. Proportion of Households, by Income Category, Suburbs of 100 Largest Cities, 1979–1999

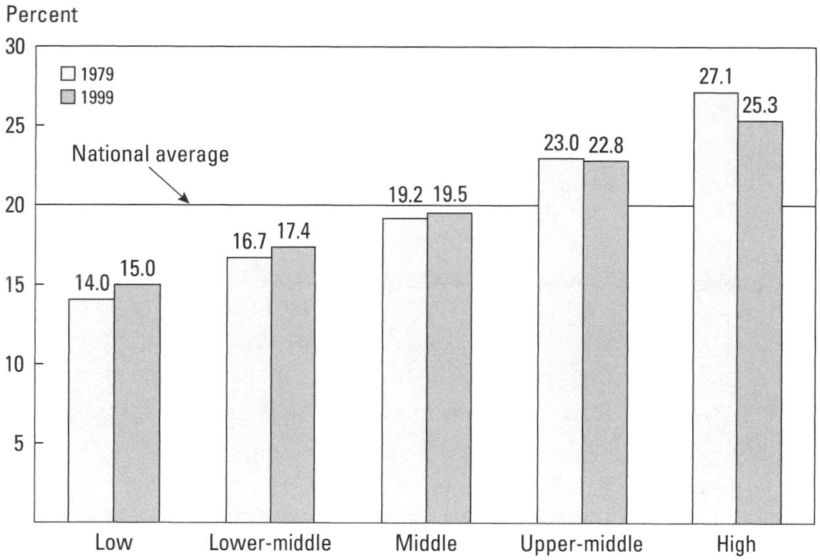

Percent

Source: Authors' analysis of 1980 and 2000 decennial censuses.

concentrate to a somewhat greater degree in the higher-income brackets than large-city households do in the lower-income brackets. In 1999 more than one-fourth of households in these suburbs had high incomes, and another 23 percent had upper-middle incomes (figure 7-5).

That these suburbs have an upward-sloping household income distribution is not surprising, given that they and their cities together contain more than half the nation's households. As metropolitan areas, they account for the better part of the national income distribution. Yet higher-income households are overrepresented in the nation's largest metropolitan suburbs to a striking degree. The suburbs of Chicago, Washington, D.C., Baltimore, San Francisco, Oakland, San José, New York, and Newark, New Jersey, all count 30 percent or more of their households in the highest-income category. All of these metropolitan areas do contain lower-income, older-suburban jurisdictions close to their urban cores, but for the most part their suburbs remain better-off communities dominated by single-family housing and households containing multiple earners.

Despite their higher-income orientation today, during 1979–99, most of these suburbs—like their cities—actually saw high-income households decline as a proportion of all households. In 1979 27 percent of suburban

TABLE 7-5. Cities and Suburbs, by Income Category Change, 1979–99

	Increase in category size			Decrease in category size		
Category	Cities	Suburbs	Percentage	Cities	Suburbs	Percentage
Low-income	75	41	54.7	25	20	80.0
Lower-middle-income	64	48	75.0	36	25	69.4
Middle-income	55	40	72.7	45	24	53.3
Upper-middle-income	33	22	66.7	67	38	56.7
High-income	21	15	71.4	79	53	67.1

Source: Authors' analysis of 1980 and 2000 decennial census data.

households had high incomes, but that proportion dropped to 25 percent by 1999. The largest declines were apparent in two types of places. First, the nation's major metropolitan centers—including many of those mentioned above—attracted a more economically diverse group to their suburbs in recent decades than lived there in 1980. The suburbs of Chicago, Washington, D.C., Seattle, Houston, and Denver experienced much faster growth in lower- and middle-income households than high-income households (tables 7A-2 and A-3). Although these suburbs remain relatively wealthy places today, they include a wider array of household types and racial and ethnic groups than they did a generation ago.[52]

Second, Rust Belt suburbs such as those surrounding Cleveland, Detroit, Milwaukee, Toledo, and Pittsburgh also saw large declines in the proportion of their households with high incomes. Although these suburbs still contain above-average shares of households in the top income category, these declines did not necessarily owe to the economically diverse in-migration occurring in other metropolitan centers. Rather, it may be that the fiscal and social stress emerging in suburbs close to their urban cores, combined with increased out-migration from these regions in response to economic restructuring, effectively shifted the distribution of households by income downward.

These Rust Belt trends point to the fact that overall, most suburbs experienced changes in their household income distribution similar to those occurring in their cities over the 1980s and 1990s. Their parallel experiences reflect evidence of an economic interdependence between cities and suburbs in the 1980s and 1990s.[53] Table 7-5 shows that, for each income category, more than half the cities that gained household share in that segment were located in suburbs that also gained share in that segment. Likewise, majorities of cities

52. Frey and Berube (2002); Frey (2001); Singer, chapter 2, this volume.
53. See, for example, Voith (1994).

and suburbs shared in decreases—for instance, among the seventy-nine cities that saw their high-income share decline, fifty-three were located in suburbs also experiencing a relative decline in that segment. In general it is too simplistic to suggest that middle-income or high-income households abandoned central cities for suburbs over the past decades. The increased mobility of U.S. households, and the maturation of the suburban Baby Boomers over this time period, suggest that relocation is more likely to occur from the suburbs of one metropolitan area to another, rather than from a city to its own suburbs (or vice versa). Instead it appears that recent city household income trends often reflected broader economic changes occurring at the metropolitan level.

Yet despite the similar trends playing out in cities and their suburbs over this period, in most metropolitan areas, cities and suburbs remain far apart in the mix of household incomes they exhibit. Regional economic trends alone cannot explain why one-third of St. Louis's households occupy the lowest-income bracket, whereas its suburbs resemble the national average. Policy choices, racial and ethnic disparities, and the effects of concentrated poverty have all contributed to the low-income profile of cities like St. Louis.

DISCUSSION

Conventional wisdom holds that U.S. cities lost much of their middle class in recent decades, but this study's assessment somewhat contradicts that notion. Some large cities did indeed lose disproportionate numbers of middle-income households in the 1980s and 1990s, and today several places, such as Los Angeles, Washington, D.C., San Francisco, and Atlanta, have a "missing middle." Over those decades, however, the middle class also expanded in geographically large cities in the Sunbelt and Midwest. Thus it seems that middle-income households did not abandon urban America so much as shift regions over the past twenty years.

Cities did, however, experience a relative loss of higher-income households over this time period. The trend was by no means exclusive to the central cities—many of their suburbs also saw high-income households decline as a share of the population—but in cities, those losses exacerbated a household-income profile already weighted toward the bottom of the distribution. The perception that cities lost middle-class households may owe in part to the expansive way that Americans define the middle class—specifically, that it contains many households and families who actually have high incomes, but perhaps exhibit lifestyle or consumption patterns also associated with middle-income families.[54]

Whether cities lost middle-income or high-income residents in recent decades, the fact remains that most lack a mix of households reflective of the nation's true income diversity. To the extent that large cities seek to provide a suitable living environment for households across the income spectrum, our findings suggest that no one national urban policy could achieve that goal, given the variety of household income distributions that characterize large cities.[55] Philadelphia and Phoenix, and Chicago and Charlotte, have witnessed different changes in their income mix over the past two decades, and start from different places in the current decade.

City and regional leaders themselves must therefore understand the "shape of the curve" in their own places in order to craft regionally specific responses. In particular, the typology developed here may help urban leaders to identify their income peers, thus facilitating policy learning and exchange. With this in mind, a number of different approaches to achieving a more balanced household mix suggest themselves for cities occupying different segments of the household-income typology.

Higher-End Cities

In one sense these cities might seem blessed. Their concentrations of upper-income households provide them the means to offer higher-quality public services, and help them to attract private sector investment in residential and commercial development. At the same time, however, many still contain substantial shares of lower-income households. In places such as Charlotte, Raleigh, and San José, these households are spatially clustered in neighborhoods within the city's core. In addition, they struggle to afford the higher costs of living in these cities, especially the cost of housing. Across the eight higher-end cities, 52 percent of households with incomes under $50,000 in 1999 paid at least 30 percent of their income for rent—the threshold beyond which a household is typically recognized as facing a rent burden. By con-

---

54. House Republicans reportedly sought to extend the federal child tax credit in 2004 to families with incomes up to $300,000 because it would "bring tax relief to families that do not consider themselves rich." Jonathan Weisman, "House Votes to Keep Tax Credit for Children," *Washington Post*, May 21, 2004, p. A3. In general income is not the only determinant of "middle-class" status. Chris Baker, "What Is Middle Class?" *Washington Times*, November 30, 2003, p. A1.

55. Nevertheless the fact that large cities overall contain disproportionate numbers of low-income households suggests that policies to maintain high levels of employment economy-wide, which lead to rising wages and incomes for low earners, would benefit cities disproportionately. Bernstein and Baker (2003).

trast, only 38 percent of households nationwide at that income level faced such a burden. For these places, then, ensuring that the city's neighborhoods contain an affordable mix of housing—for both renters and homeowners—may be critical for reducing key service-sector workers' cost burdens, and retaining those workers over time.

Stressed Cities

At the other end of the spectrum lie the stressed cities. These cities have been hardest hit by economic transition and metropolitan decentralization over the past two decades. Their higher-income households suburbanized in large numbers, often in search of bigger and better housing than was available in the central city.[56] Today they (and many of their older suburbs) strain to provide a decent level of public services, from schools to safety to basic infrastructure, even as a cycle of private sector disinvestment continues to afflict their neighborhoods. What is more, most of these cities are "hemmed in" by surrounding jurisdictions, unable to annex close-in suburban development that might enhance their income diversity.

How can these cities surmount such a severe set of obstacles? No simple answer exists, of course. The idea of consolidation with surrounding counties has attracted recent attention. Louisville completed a merger with surrounding Jefferson County, Kentucky, in 2003, and the resulting jurisdiction has a much more balanced income profile than the city as of 1999.[57] The city of Buffalo and surrounding Erie County, New York, are actively debating a similar step.[58] Not all of these cities even have the luxury of considering such an option, however.

In considering priorities, stressed cities might first focus on how best to increase the population of higher-income residents who can bolster their heavily eroded fiscal bases. Because their rents tend to be lower, and many of their neighborhoods contain significant levels of vacant and abandoned housing, these cities may be able to attract higher-income households without contributing significantly to problems of housing affordability.[59] Many have significant assets, however, in their downtowns, waterfronts, and historic housing stock that could make them attractive places to live for

56. Bier (2001).

57. Brookings Metropolitan Policy Program (2002).

58. Robert J. McCarthy, "Consolidation Panel Faces Difficult Task," *Buffalo News,* May 15, 2004, p. B1.

59. Existing housing affordability problems in these places seem to stem largely from the low incomes earned by residents, and not from escalating rents or house prices. See, for example, Brookings Metropolitan Policy Program (2003a).

younger unmarried households (such as those graduating from local universities) and older "empty nester" households. Such strategies may have relevance not only for the fourteen cities identified as stressed, but also for the low-moderate cities that could be headed in this direction (for example, Pittsburgh, Richmond, and Cincinnati).

Indeed, Atlanta and Boston, both of which contended with a stressed profile in 1979, seem to have succeeded over the past two decades in attracting higher-income households and rebuilding downtown neighborhoods in the process. Their resulting income profiles come with their own set of challenges, of course. No city should chase after wealthier households to the exclusion of addressing basic public service issues that could improve prospects for the bulk of its population. Nevertheless by bringing back some of the higher-income households that departed in droves over the past few decades, stressed cities would surely be better positioned to offer higher-quality services within a functioning marketplace that appeals to middle-income households, and provides lower-income households real opportunities to move up the income ladder.

At the same time, these cities should be strong advocates for regional policies that give lower-income households, especially minority households living in segregated neighborhoods, access to opportunities beyond inner-city neighborhoods alone. The fact that incomes in Rust Belt suburbs and cities tended to move in the same direction over the 1980s and 1990s suggests that regional collaboration—rather than intrametropolitan competition—on housing, economic development, and workforce planning could help grow the tax base in both types of jurisdictions.

Divided Cities

The few divided cities like Atlanta, San Francisco, and Washington, D.C., best fit the perception that big cities are home to the rich and poor, and not much in between. Attracting the middle class back to these cities, and retaining the middle class households still there, belongs high on their priority list for the many reasons noted above.

Some cities have taken specific steps to counter middle-class flight and foster a new urban middle class.[60] California cities, including Los Angeles, San José, and Oakland, have subsidized housing specifically for public school teachers and public safety workers.[61] Other cities have focused their efforts on

60. Researchers in Atlanta recognize their city's bifurcated income distribution in a 1997 report, and recommend several policy options for attracting and retaining middle-class residents. Research Atlanta (1997). For additional background on these strategies, see Varady (1994).
61. Legislative Analyst Office (2003).

reforming public schools to keep more middle-income families in the city once their children reach school age. Middle-class retention also provided much of the impetus for Mayor Richard Daley's takeover of Chicago's public schools in 1995.[62] Likewise, Washington, D.C., a city that lost vast numbers of middle-income families in the last few decades, is seeking to increase the city's population by 100,000, a strategy designed to rebuild Washington's middle class and enhance its fiscal position over the long term.[63]

Beyond rebuilding the middle class, however, divided cities face serious challenges in preserving housing affordability for existing low-income and moderate-income residents. Gentrification may be a real concern in these cities. Their concentrations of high-income residents, especially in and around traditionally lower- and middle-income neighborhoods, can place upward pressure on rents and make those neighborhoods unaffordable for households of moderate means. Therefore, alongside strategies to attract and retain middle-income residents, these cities might consider inclusionary zoning, targeted tax relief, and infill strategies to minimize displacement and maximize income diversity.[64]

Low-Moderate Cities

Finally, the low-moderate cities seem poised at a transition point. Of the cities that had this profile in 1979, about half had moved to a different part of the income typology by 1999. Detroit, Baltimore, Cleveland, and Birmingham, among other cities, lost large numbers of middle- and upper-income households and consequently became stressed cities. Several others, however, including Columbus, Portland, Oregon, and both of the Twin Cities (Minneapolis and St. Paul), became more middle-class places. In most cases the latter group achieved the transition by growing the number of households in the middle of the distribution, not simply by attracting high-income households.

To be sure, estimating the degree to which these changes owe to policy choices—as opposed to broader economic and demographic forces—remains impossible. For the most part the stressed cities were home to manufacturing and other heavy industries that have suffered the greatest job losses over the past two decades. Nonetheless, it bears noting that the cities located within the Portland, Oregon, and Twin Cities regions, home to some of the most active growth management policies in the nation, moved "up" the typology

---

62. John Kass, "Daley Gets Behind Plan to Cut City School Board," *Chicago Tribune,* April 1, 1995, p. 5.

63. Rivlin and others (2003).

64. Kennedy and Leonard (2001).

over the twenty years.[65] Indeed, some have credited Portland's growth management strategies with enhancing that city's economic diversity.[66] Future research should investigate the degree to which such policies made central cities more attractive to middle-income households, or whether they fostered income growth for lower-income households.

With that said, low-moderate cities would particularly benefit from helping more of their lower-income households to climb the income ladder. Although national economic conditions such as unemployment and inflation exert perhaps the greatest influence on income growth, local and regional policymakers can play a vital role in promoting economic success for lower earners. Investment in education, particularly postsecondary education and training through community colleges, can help to raise earnings for lower-skilled workers over time.[67] At the same time, improving workers' ability to access new jobs throughout the region can lead to faster earnings growth.[68] In addition, some cities might tailor strategies to assist particular demographic groups that are overrepresented in the lower-income population, such as immigrants.[69] The potential benefits of these policies are by no means confined to low-moderate cities; the significant numbers of lower-middle-income households in many middle-class cities would gain from locally tailored strategies to further grow the urban middle class from within. Such strategies are consistent with Jane Jacobs's observation that, in order to truly expand the middle class, cities must consider their people "valuable and worth retaining, right where they are, before they become middle class."[70]

CONCLUSION

In the end, cities should become informed and strategic in their efforts to provide a suitable living environment for all types of households. A balanced mix of incomes can contribute to improved fiscal, political, and social outcomes for cities and their residents. Large-scale economic forces such as globalization and technological innovation, as well as national decisions around monetary and fiscal policy, will undoubtedly continue to play significant roles in shaping the incomes of residents in both cities and suburbs.

65. For further information on these policies, see Nelson and others (2002); and Mondale and Fulton (2003).

66. Betsy Hammond, "Income Groups Intermingle," *Oregonian,* May 15, 2002, p. A1.

67. Brookings Metropolitan Policy Program (2004).

68. Andersson, Holzer, and Lane (2003).

69. Bowles and Kotkin (2003).

70. Jacobs (1961).

By setting the right priorities at the local level, however, city leaders can position themselves better to attract and retain households that form a truly diverse mix, and to realize the promise of the city as economic melting pot.

TECHNICAL APPENDIX

This appendix explains the methodology employed in this paper for calculating each group's income range (in other words, low income, lower middle income, and so forth) nationally, and for estimating the proportions of city and suburban households occupying each of those categories. It includes an explanation of how and why we derived our metropolitan price index to adjust "cutoffs" for the income quintiles by city.

National Quintiles

We identify income quintile "cutoffs" ("upper limits") using linear interpolation below national household median income, and Pareto interpolation above that amount. We use a combination of approaches because income distributions tend to have even densities below the median and decreasing densities above.[71] In both cases the variables listed and defined below are used.

Y = income at percentile of interest
P = percentile of interest
a = the income value at the lower limit of the category containing P
b = the income value at the upper limit of the category containing P
P_a = proportion of the distribution that lies below the lower limit
P_b = proportion of the distribution that lies below the upper limit

Because they are below the median (by definition) we identify the upper limits for the first and second quintiles using this equation:

$$Y = \frac{(P - P_a)}{(P_b - P_a)} \times (b - a) + a.$$

Because they are above the median we identify the cutoffs (or upper bounds) of the third and fourth quintiles using the set of equations below.[72]

71. Miller (1966).
72. The equations used for Pareto estimation are derived from a technical document prepared for the Lewis Mumford Center by Brian J. Stults (mumford1.dyndns.org/cen2000/CityProfiles/Profiles/MHHINote.htm [May 2004]).

The upper limit for the fifth quintile is, of course, undefined and not relevant for our analysis.

$$Y = \left(\frac{k}{(1 - P)^{\frac{1}{\Theta}}} \right)$$

$$k = \left(\frac{P_b - P_a}{\left(\frac{1}{a^{\Theta}} - \frac{1}{b^{\Theta}} \right)} \right)^{\frac{1}{\Theta}}$$

$$\Theta = \left(\frac{\log(1 - P_a) - \log(1 - P_b)}{\log(b) - \log(a)} \right)$$

For example, the first quintile would be calculated using linear interpolation as follows. In 1999 the first income category provided by the census, 0 to 10,000 dollars, is 9.5 percent of the population. Adding the second category brings it to only 15.8 percent, but adding the third group puts the total over 20 percent. We know that the first cutoff exists somewhere between 15,000 and 19,999 dollars—the range of the third group. By applying the linear equation above, we can locate the income cutoff within this range. In this example, P is 0.2, a is \$15,000, b is \$19,999, P_a is 0.16, and P_b is 0.22. Solving for Y, the resulting first quintile cutoff (in other words, the twentieth percentile) is estimated to be \$18,320.

The third and fourth quintile cutoffs, because they are above the median, are calculated using the Pareto distribution. We use the same variables to solve first for *theta*, then for k, and use these values to solve for Y.

City and Suburban Income Group Shares

Once the national income quintiles are established, we then investigate the number and share of households within each quintile at the city level. We use the same assumptions about the nature of the income distribution as when estimating the quintile cutoffs, but in this case we calculate the share of households below a given dollar amount (P) rather than a dollar amount below which a certain share of households lie (Y).

As in calculating the national quintile cutoffs, we assume a linear distribution below the median and a Pareto distribution above it. In this case, however, the determination of when to use which method requires a bit more thought. City and suburban median incomes differ, and national quintiles change from place to place because we adjust them for regional cost-of-living differences (see below for methodology).

We calculate median household incomes from the following equation, using *theta* and *k* as defined in the previous section (although SF3 provides median household income for cities, we use this method for both cities and suburbs to maintain consistency):

$$median = k\left(2^{\frac{1}{\theta}}\right).$$

If the quintile of interest is below the median then the following linear equation is used:

$$P = \frac{(Y - a)}{(b - a)} \times (P_b - P_a) + P_a.$$

If the quintile of interest is above the median then the following Pareto equation is used:

$$P = 1 - \left(\frac{k}{Y}\right)^{\Theta}.$$

Because *P* in both equations is a percentile (or cumulative share), to arrive at the actual share within the income group we subtract the *P* value for the previous group from the *P* in the group of interest. The fifth income group has a value of 100 for *P* so its share is calculated by simply subtracting the fourth group's *P* value from 100. To arrive at the actual number of households within any of these income groups for a particular place, we multiply the share by the total number of households.

In Detroit, for example, median household income in 1999 based on the method above was $29,544 (compared to a similar $29,536 from SF3). The national cutoffs for the first and second quintiles in 1999, adjusted for regional price differences, are $18,578 and $34,311. Therefore we derive the share of people in the first income group using the linear method, and the share of people in all other groups using the Pareto method. Conversely, in a place like Scottsdale, the high median household income of $57,769 obligates us to use linear interpolation for the first, second, and third income groups (all below $52,587), and the Pareto method is used only for the fourth group.

Although we believe that the use of both linear and Pareto interpolation improves our estimates, compiling the data using linear estimates exclusively indicates that our findings are not particularly sensitive to this methodological choice.

Metropolitan Price Index

Our metropolitan price index is based on data collected by the U.S. Department of Housing and Urban Development (HUD) on Fair Market Rents for two-bedroom units. U.S. Census Bureau researchers have used these rents to create a price index that shifts poverty thresholds depending on the state in which a family is located and whether or not it is in a metropolitan area.[73] We used this method to create a metropolitan-level index for 1979, 1989, and 1999. Our calculation is fairly simple:

$$\text{index} = m/n * 0.33 + 0.67.$$

where m is the metropolitan fair market rent, and n is the average national fair market rent. HUD does not report an average national rent; we calculate it as a household-weighted average of the rents in every metropolitan area and non-metropolitan county. (In 1979, only metropolitan FMRs are available, so we use an adjusted weighted average for that year.) We multiply the index by 0.33 because the average household spent 33 percent of its income on housing-related costs in Census 2000. We note that this index thus holds nonhousing costs constant. This is a modest assumption given that housing and other costs are correlated, and likely leads our index to understate the difference in prices across metropolitan areas. This method is preferred, however, to using private-sector estimates, such as those compiled by ACCRA, because this method is not specific to salaried workers and it relies solely on publicly available data.[74]

The economic literature is admittedly skeptical as to whether regional cost-of-living adjustments are always appropriate. First, there is no officially recognized governmental index on regional, subregional, or metropolitan prices. Second, to a certain degree, consumption patterns adjust to incomes. The median household in Birmingham may choose lower-quality housing than the median household in San Francisco, so that comparing median rents between the two cities would offer a somewhat skewed view of the cities' cost-of-living differential. Third, differences in incomes may reflect real differences in the amenities and quality-of-life available to households in different places. A San Francisco household making $40,000, even if it can purchase fewer goods and services than a Birmingham household making that amount, could still achieve a similar level of well-being if living in San Francisco provided it with access to higher-quality goods, services, and amenities that com-

73. Short (2001a).
74. For ACCRA data, see www.costofliving.org. To learn more about the Fair Market Rent survey, see www.huduser.org/datasets/fmr.html. To view values for our metro index in 1979 and 1999, see our website at www.brookings.edu/metro.

pensated it for the consumption gap. Many researchers have coped with these issues by developing "hedonic" pricing models that value the effects of urban amenities (and/or unpleasantness) on wages, rents, or other goods.[75]

Although we recognize the empirical and conceptual challenges associated with adjusting for regional price differences, we have chosen to make these adjustments for a few reasons. First, scholars have noted that the magnitude of price differentials across regions suggests that poverty thresholds should be revised to take account of these differences.[76] Although measuring poverty is not exactly analogous to measuring household incomes across the income spectrum, we similarly seek to adjust nationally calculated thresholds (for income quintiles) for the large price differences that prevail across cities. Second, the particular method we choose to adjust for cost-of-living differences, using HUD Fair Market Rents, is based closely on a method used by a National Academy of Sciences Panel and Census Bureau researchers to derive experimental poverty estimates.[77] Short further notes that using housing data was among a few methodologies that experts surveyed by the GAO agreed showed at least moderate promise for capturing geographic cost-of-living differences.[78] Third, our metropolitan index is relatively conservative in its adjustments, multiplying national income quintile cutoffs by a factor of between 0.89 and 1.24 in 1979, and between 0.92 and 1.30 in 1999. By comparison, metropolitan hedonic model price indexes developed by Bureau of Labor Statistics (BLS) economists for 1988–89 range from 0.7 to 1.8.[79] The primary effect we observe upon employing our index is a reduction in the number of households in expensive cities—New York, San Francisco, Boston, Los Angeles—who occupy the high-income category. On practical grounds, we are satisfied that households in these cities earning, say, $90,000 are not living a "high-income" lifestyle. Finally, we hope that by using this index, this analysis will provoke methodological discussion, critique, and needed further inquiry into geographic cost adjustments that might not otherwise occur. (We suspect that an analysis that did not attempt at all to adjust for these geographic differences would attract at least as much criticism on these grounds.)

75. See, for example, Blomquist, Berger, and Hoehn (1998).

76. Ruggles (1990); Citro and Michael (1995). The need to adjust these thresholds across geographical areas is also reflected in the growing literature on "family self-sufficiency" budgets. See Brocht (2001).

77. Citro and Michael (1995); Short and Garner (2002).

78. Short (2001b).

79. Kokoski, Cardiff, and Moulton (1994). The Bureau of Labor Statistics subsequently updated these indexes with 1995 data, reducing the spread from least expensive to most expensive metropolitan area to approximately the range reflected in our index. Bureau of Labor Statistics (1997).

TABLE 7A-1. Households, by Income Category, 100 Largest Cities, 1979 and 1999

City	Region	Percentage by income category, 1979						Percentage by income category, 1999					
		Low	Lower-middle	Middle	Upper-middle	High	City type, 1979	Low	Lower-middle	Middle	Upper-middle	High	City type, 1999
Chicago, IL	MW	25.78	19.93	19.07	17.72	17.50	Low-moderate	26.15	20.77	19.76	17.21	16.11	Low-moderate
Detroit, MI	MW	29.62	19.68	18.57	16.87	15.26	Low-moderate	33.10	23.02	17.85	14.95	11.08	Stressed
Indianapolis, IN	MW	17.36	19.32	20.18	21.27	21.88	Higher-end	18.70	21.32	21.10	20.64	18.24	Balanced
Columbus, OH	MW	21.97	21.96	21.05	19.14	15.88	Low-moderate	20.71	21.78	21.25	20.95	15.32	Middle-class
Milwaukee, WI	MW	20.75	20.23	20.24	21.40	17.38	Balanced	27.35	24.63	21.07	17.07	9.89	Low-moderate
Cleveland, OH	MW	31.67	20.34	18.21	17.19	12.59	Low-moderate	36.36	25.08	18.14	13.30	7.12	Stressed
Kansas City, MO	MW	20.83	20.39	19.60	19.68	19.51	Balanced	21.52	21.89	20.67	19.52	16.41	Middle-class
Omaha, NE	MW	19.58	20.05	20.43	20.37	19.57	Balanced	18.85	22.16	21.06	20.12	17.81	Balanced
Minneapolis, MN	MW	25.32	22.92	20.29	17.22	14.24	Low-moderate	22.81	22.98	20.41	17.80	16.00	Middle-class
St. Louis, MO	MW	31.31	24.22	18.41	15.22	10.84	Stressed	32.85	24.11	18.68	14.16	10.19	Stressed
Wichita, KS	MW	15.75	18.57	20.58	21.71	23.39	Higher-end	18.60	21.32	21.23	21.42	17.43	Balanced
Cincinnati, OH	MW	28.40	22.25	19.33	15.99	14.04	Low-moderate	30.82	23.41	18.01	14.45	13.31	Low-moderate
Toledo, OH	MW	21.51	18.96	18.23	21.00	20.31	Balanced	26.75	22.42	19.72	18.84	12.28	Low-moderate
St. Paul, MN	MW	21.73	21.55	21.01	19.43	16.29	Low-moderate	21.87	23.16	20.82	19.20	14.96	Middle-class
Lincoln, NE	MW	15.92	19.81	20.21	22.53	21.53	Middle-class	17.33	21.44	21.51	22.11	17.61	Middle-class
Akron, OH	MW	23.77	21.51	20.44	19.43	14.84	Low-moderate	26.68	24.56	20.20	17.94	10.63	Low-moderate
Madison, WI	MW	19.68	20.09	19.43	20.03	20.78	Balanced	20.01	20.19	21.78	20.71	17.31	Middle-class
Fort Wayne, IN	MW	18.43	22.26	21.78	21.21	16.32	Middle-class	19.81	22.95	22.99	20.54	13.71	Middle-class
Des Moines, IA	MW	19.17	20.56	21.47	21.24	17.56	Balanced	19.21	22.85	22.61	21.70	13.64	Middle-class
Grand Rapids, MI	MW	20.58	21.00	19.68	20.81	17.93	Balanced	21.50	22.13	22.05	20.18	14.14	Middle-class
Midwest cities (n=20)		*24.24*	*20.51*	*19.53*	*18.68*	*17.04*		*25.06*	*22.22*	*20.16*	*18.06*	*14.51*	
New York, NY	NE	29.99	22.10	19.36	14.92	13.63	Low-moderate	30.32	20.30	17.56	15.81	16.01	Low-moderate
Philadelphia, PA	NE	29.79	22.13	19.57	16.21	12.29	Low-moderate	33.67	22.93	18.61	14.93	9.87	Stressed
Boston, MA	NE	30.68	24.17	19.52	14.21	11.41	Stressed	29.19	20.42	18.40	16.95	15.04	Low-moderate
Pittsburgh, PA	NE	27.87	21.74	19.23	16.76	14.41	Low-moderate	31.41	22.72	17.78	15.11	12.98	Low-moderate
Buffalo, NY	NE	31.70	22.40	18.30	15.89	11.71	Low-moderate	36.98	23.95	16.79	12.99	9.28	Stressed
Newark, NJ	NE	39.55	23.42	17.30	12.35	7.38	Stressed	40.96	21.96	16.30	13.35	7.43	Stressed
Jersey City, NJ	NE	28.54	22.34	19.03	15.95	14.15	Low-moderate	27.67	20.96	18.86	17.12	15.40	Low-moderate
Rochester, NY	NE	27.80	22.21	20.33	16.98	12.67	Low-moderate	35.29	24.05	18.04	13.65	8.97	Stressed
Yonkers, NY	NE	19.88	18.87	21.03	19.61	20.60	Balanced	25.46	19.24	17.96	18.80	18.55	Divided
Northeast cities (n=9)		*29.97*	*22.19*	*19.35*	*15.25*	*13.24*		*31.10*	*20.94*	*17.75*	*15.64*	*14.57*	
Houston, TX	S	15.84	18.84	20.17	20.27	24.88	Higher-end	23.06	22.82	19.72	16.44	17.96	Low-moderate
Dallas, TX	S	18.69	21.92	20.57	17.70	21.12	Balanced	22.66	24.57	20.26	15.75	16.76	Middle-class
San Antonio, TX	S	24.49	23.82	21.09	17.14	13.46	Low-moderate	22.55	22.56	20.75	18.42	15.72	Middle-class

City													
Jacksonville, FL	S	22.32	21.93	19.92	18.65	17.17	Low-moderate	19.13	21.24	21.95	20.75	16.94	Middle-class
Austin, TX	S	24.46	23.82	20.64	16.76	14.32	Low-moderate	19.53	21.53	20.24	19.23	19.47	Balanced
Baltimore, MD	S	30.01	22.57	18.82	16.04	12.55	Low-moderate	32.75	22.92	18.55	14.86	10.93	Stressed
Memphis, TN	S	25.11	21.03	18.68	17.67	17.51	Low-moderate	26.58	22.87	20.06	16.84	13.65	Low-moderate
Washington, DC	S	22.19	21.10	19.69	15.80	21.22	Divided	26.59	20.82	17.36	15.49	19.74	Divided
El Paso, TX	S	22.84	23.90	20.26	17.66	15.34	Middle-class	26.68	23.47	19.62	16.81	13.42	Low-moderate
Nashville, TN	S	19.98	21.38	21.05	19.77	17.82	Balanced	20.55	22.78	21.53	18.99	16.16	Middle-class
Charlotte, NC	S	17.09	20.99	21.19	19.98	20.75	Balanced	14.28	18.72	20.04	21.37	25.60	Higher-end
Fort Worth, TX	S	21.17	22.44	20.89	18.16	17.35	Middle-class	21.92	22.77	21.08	18.53	15.70	Middle-class
Oklahoma City, OK	S	19.49	20.51	19.66	19.74	20.59	Balanced	22.40	22.26	20.51	18.46	16.37	Low-moderate
New Orleans, LA	S	32.28	21.45	16.43	13.99	15.85	Low-moderate	34.64	21.99	16.85	13.23	13.30	Stressed
Virginia Beach, VA	S	11.49	17.92	21.35	24.52	24.72	Higher-end	10.40	18.65	23.77	25.33	21.85	Middle-class
Atlanta, GA	S	33.54	23.20	16.87	12.65	13.74	Stressed	30.16	20.39	15.65	14.05	17.13	Divided
Tulsa, OK	S	17.45	20.36	19.68	19.56	22.96	Higher-end	22.60	23.05	20.39	16.84	17.12	Middle-class
Miami, FL	S	37.39	25.12	17.80	10.95	8.75	Stressed	42.58	23.04	14.82	10.08	9.48	Stressed
Arlington, TX	S	11.20	16.32	19.29	24.60	28.59	Higher-end	13.56	18.66	21.80	22.99	22.99	Higher-end
Tampa, FL	S	29.31	23.74	19.08	15.53	12.34	Low-moderate	25.62	22.83	19.54	15.93	16.08	Low-moderate
Corpus Christi, TX	S	18.59	19.63	18.99	21.23	21.56	Balanced	23.86	21.42	19.99	18.98	15.75	Low-moderate
Raleigh, NC	S	16.69	20.76	19.71	19.55	23.29	Higher-end	15.62	20.03	20.73	21.07	22.55	Higher-end
Lexington-Fayette, KY	S	19.37	20.96	20.14	18.54	20.98	Balanced	20.59	20.28	19.03	19.41	20.69	Balanced
Louisville, KY	S	29.33	21.57	18.81	15.90	14.38	Low-moderate	30.70	23.65	19.01	14.57	12.07	Stressed
St. Petersburg, FL	S	28.77	26.76	18.55	14.33	11.58	Stressed	23.51	24.59	20.90	17.21	13.79	Middle-class
Birmingham, AL	S	30.46	22.43	18.26	15.80	13.05	Low-moderate	33.39	23.77	18.98	14.14	9.71	Stressed
Norfolk, VA	S	26.90	26.36	19.80	15.35	11.59	Low-moderate	26.78	25.17	21.04	15.67	11.33	Low-moderate
Baton Rouge, LA	S	25.24	20.90	17.59	16.38	19.88	Divided	29.84	21.24	16.63	14.95	17.34	Divided
Hialeah, FL	S	23.15	23.84	24.64	17.60	10.77	Middle-class	32.34	26.57	20.43	13.60	7.05	Stressed
Greensboro, NC	S	18.20	21.52	20.65	18.96	20.67	Balanced	18.88	22.20	20.89	19.39	18.64	Balanced
Plano, TX	S	5.84	8.06	12.99	24.87	48.24	Higher-end	6.34	10.67	14.71	22.67	45.61	Higher-end
Garland, TX	S	7.44	13.55	20.31	29.42	29.28	Middle-class	12.70	21.11	22.95	24.38	18.86	Middle-class
Montgomery, AL	S	20.94	19.64	19.30	18.64	21.48	Balanced	23.64	20.98	19.72	17.89	17.77	Low-moderate
Shreveport, LA	S	23.39	19.43	18.95	18.21	20.01	Divided	28.80	22.72	18.34	15.52	14.62	Low-moderate
Augusta-Richmond, GA	S	24.83	23.34	20.44	16.95	14.45	Low-moderate	25.67	22.34	21.32	17.19	13.47	Low-moderate
Lubbock, TX	S	18.20	20.60	20.28	19.27	21.65	Balanced	27.26	22.39	19.43	16.64	14.27	Low-moderate
Chesapeake, VA	S	14.81	18.40	21.72	24.52	20.54	Middle-class	12.73	16.25	21.29	26.63	23.11	Middle-class
Mobile, AL	S	22.46	19.95	18.46	18.42	20.71	Balanced	29.10	21.02	18.31	16.86	14.70	Low-moderate
Richmond, VA	S	25.48	23.96	20.38	16.10	14.08	Low-moderate	29.71	23.92	18.79	14.56	13.01	Low-moderate
Irving, TX	S	10.05	17.69	22.32	24.92	25.01	Higher-end	14.06	23.43	23.85	21.12	17.53	Middle-class
South cities (n=40)	S	*22.62*	*21.49*	*19.64*	*17.85*	*18.40*		*23.56*	*22.08*	*19.83*	*17.56*	*16.98*	

(continued)

235

TABLE 7A-1. Households, by Income Category, 100 Largest Cities, 1979 and 1999 (continued)

City	Region	Percentage by income category, 1979					City type, 1979	Percentage by income category, 1999					City type, 1999
		Low	Lower-middle	Middle	Upper-middle	High		Low	Lower-middle	Middle	Upper-middle	High	
Los Angeles, CA	W	23.46	21.54	18.52	15.89	20.58	Divided	27.59	21.83	17.57	15.29	17.72	Divided
Phoenix, AZ	W	17.25	20.75	21.30	20.99	19.71	Balanced	18.73	22.03	21.38	19.49	18.37	Balanced
San Diego, CA	W	20.14	22.34	20.69	17.98	18.85	Balanced	19.41	20.03	19.38	19.78	21.41	Balanced
San Jose, CA	W	12.69	15.80	19.14	24.87	27.49	Higher-end	13.28	15.07	18.66	23.23	29.76	Higher-end
San Francisco, CA	W	23.07	21.49	19.91	16.72	18.80	Low-moderate	22.32	18.28	17.61	18.25	23.54	Divided
Seattle, WA	W	20.86	21.07	19.15	18.37	20.56	Balanced	19.32	20.06	19.62	19.40	21.59	Balanced
Denver, CO	W	20.94	21.82	20.60	18.18	18.46	Balanced	21.31	22.40	20.83	18.11	17.34	Middle-class
Portland, OR	W	22.64	22.14	19.33	17.95	17.94	Low-moderate	20.88	21.86	21.15	19.71	16.39	Middle-class
Tucson, AZ	W	22.84	24.12	20.95	18.45	13.64	Middle-class	27.51	26.88	20.78	15.21	9.62	Stressed
Las Vegas, NV	W	18.12	20.96	20.81	20.72	19.40	Balanced	18.08	21.15	21.54	20.76	18.47	Balanced
Long Beach, CA	W	23.90	21.90	19.52	17.56	17.11	Low-moderate	26.68	21.95	18.07	16.89	16.41	Low-moderate
Albuquerque, NM	W	17.34	19.98	19.88	20.17	22.63	Higher-end	21.17	22.11	20.80	18.77	17.15	Middle-class
Fresno, CA	W	22.59	22.80	19.14	18.68	16.79	Middle-class	26.41	22.56	19.11	17.06	14.87	Low-moderate
Sacramento, CA	W	23.94	21.75	18.07	18.11	18.14	Divided	24.23	21.29	20.48	18.57	15.42	Low-moderate
Oakland, CA	W	28.68	22.02	18.27	15.52	15.51	Low-moderate	26.80	21.38	18.13	16.40	17.29	Low-moderate
Mesa, AZ	W	15.47	21.25	21.89	22.86	18.52	Middle-class	15.98	21.92	23.56	21.70	16.84	Middle-class
Honolulu, HI	W	17.42	21.05	19.82	17.78	23.93	Higher-end	21.25	21.19	19.41	17.94	20.22	Balanced
Colorado Springs, CO	W	16.80	22.10	21.48	20.07	19.54	Middle-class	15.48	20.67	22.04	22.12	19.69	Middle-class
Santa Ana, CA	W	15.83	20.34	21.83	22.69	19.30	Middle-class	18.69	24.87	23.30	20.27	12.87	Middle-cass
Anaheim, CA	W	13.67	18.28	20.87	21.70	25.48	Higher-end	17.02	23.13	21.38	20.69	17.78	Middle-class
Aurora, CO	W	8.93	15.00	20.14	27.89	28.04	Higher-end	12.81	21.36	24.36	24.28	17.18	Middle-class
Anchorage, AK	W	12.13	16.46	17.26	19.79	34.37	Higher-end	12.40	17.91	20.72	23.96	25.02	Higher-end
Riverside, CA	W	17.56	19.75	20.00	20.72	21.97	Higher-end	20.08	19.83	19.88	20.36	19.85	Balanced
Bakersfield, CA	W	17.49	18.01	18.07	21.60	24.84	Higher-end	21.32	19.05	19.43	19.79	20.41	Balanced
Stockton, CA	W	23.67	21.59	18.09	19.14	17.51	Low-moderate	26.30	21.31	19.19	18.07	15.12	Low-moderate
Glendale, AZ	W	15.24	19.56	20.31	23.81	21.08	Middle-class	16.99	20.05	21.29	22.39	19.28	Middle-class
Fremont, CA	W	8.72	12.17	17.23	28.51	33.38	Higher-end	8.32	10.32	15.87	26.51	38.98	Higher-end
Scottsdale, AZ	W	11.53	16.41	17.85	21.61	32.60	Higher-end	11.97	15.76	17.47	20.39	34.40	Higher-end
Spokane, WA	W	25.36	22.58	20.29	18.25	13.52	Low-moderate	25.45	23.75	20.48	17.45	12.86	Low-moderate
Glendale, CA	W	18.84	21.43	20.40	17.52	21.81	Balanced	24.23	19.62	19.05	17.39	19.70	Divided
Tacoma, WA	W	24.13	21.64	18.86	19.98	15.39	Low-moderate	22.34	21.27	21.96	19.88	14.56	Low-moderate
West cities (n=31)		*20.57*	*20.96*	*19.55*	*18.59*	*20.33*		*21.60*	*20.95*	*19.61*	*18.69*	*19.15*	
All cities (n = 100)		**24.19**	**21.31**	**19.53**	**17.61**	**17.38**		**24.85**	**21.54**	**19.40**	**17.58**	**16.63**	

Source: Authors' analysis of 1980 and 2000 decennial censuses.

TABLE 7A-2. Largest Changes in Proportion of Households, by Income Category, 100 Largest Cities, 1979–99

Percent

	Largest increases				Largest declines		
City	1979	1999	Change	City	1979	1999	Change
Low-income							
Hialeah, FL	23.1	32.3	9.2	St. Petersburg, FL	28.8	23.5	−5.3
Lubbock, TX	18.2	27.3	9.1	Austin, TX	24.5	19.5	−4.9
Rochester, NY	27.8	35.3	7.5	Tampa, FL	29.3	25.6	−3.7
Houston, TX	15.8	23.1	7.2	Atlanta, GA	33.5	30.2	−3.4
Mobile, AL	22.5	29.1	6.6	Jacksonville, FL	22.3	19.1	−3.2
Lower-middle-income							
Garland, TX	13.5	21.1	7.6	Boston, MA	24.2	20.4	−3.8
Aurora, CO	15.0	21.4	6.4	San Francisco, CA	21.5	18.3	−3.2
Irving, TX	17.7	23.4	5.7	Atlanta, GA	23.2	20.4	−2.8
Anaheim, CA	18.3	23.1	4.9	San Diego, CA	22.3	20.0	−2.3
Cleveland, OH	20.3	25.1	4.7	Austin, TX	23.8	21.5	−2.3
Middle-income							
Aurora, CO	20.1	24.4	4.2	Hialeah, FL	24.6	20.4	−4.2
Anchorage, AK	17.3	20.7	3.5	Yonkers, NY	21.0	18.0	−3.1
Tacoma, WA	18.9	22.0	3.1	Miami, FL	17.8	14.8	−3.0
Garland, TX	20.3	23.0	2.6	Washington, DC	19.7	17.4	−2.3
Arlington, TX	19.3	21.8	2.5	San Francisco, CA	19.9	17.6	−2.3
Upper-middle-income							
Anchorage, AK	19.8	24.0	4.2	Garland, TX	29.4	24.4	−5.0
St. Petersburg, FL	14.3	17.2	2.9	Milwaukee, WI	21.4	17.1	−4.3
Boston, MA	14.2	17.0	2.7	Hialeah, FL	17.6	13.6	−4.0
Austin, TX	16.8	19.2	2.5	Cleveland, OH	17.2	13.3	−3.9
Chesapeake, VA	24.5	26.6	2.1	Houston, TX	20.3	16.4	−3.8
High-income							
Atlanta, GA	13.7	19.8	6.0	Aurora, CO	28.0	17.2	−10.9
Fremont, CA	33.4	39.0	5.6	Garland, TX	29.3	18.9	−10.4
Austin, TX	14.3	19.5	5.1	Anchorage, AK	34.4	25.0	−9.3
Charlotte, NC	20.7	25.6	4.9	Toledo, OH	20.3	12.3	−8.0
San Francisco, CA	18.8	23.5	4.7	Anaheim, CA	25.5	17.8	−7.7

Source: Authors' analysis of 1980 and 2000 decennial censuses.

TABLE 7A-3. Households, by Income Category, Suburbs of 100 Largest Cities, 1979–99[a]

Suburbs of city	Region	Percentage by income category, 1979					Percentage by income category, 1999				
		Low	Lower-middle	Middle	Upper-middle	High	Low	Lower-middle	Middle	Upper-middle	High
Chicago, IL	MW	9.47	12.92	17.25	25.10	35.25	11.24	15.43	18.98	24.87	29.49
Detroit, MI	MW	11.91	13.06	16.98	24.14	33.90	13.19	16.34	18.37	23.59	28.51
Indianapolis, IN	MW	13.29	15.99	19.22	24.58	26.92	12.33	16.51	18.85	24.37	27.94
Columbus, OH	MW	12.54	16.60	19.62	24.98	26.26	12.44	16.20	19.00	23.69	28.67
Milwaukee, WI	MW	8.85	12.73	16.66	26.18	35.57	10.46	15.26	19.18	26.07	29.03
Cleveland, OH	MW	11.73	14.78	18.02	24.61	30.86	14.96	18.59	20.64	22.88	22.94
Kansas City, MO	MW	13.64	16.25	18.38	24.16	27.58	12.63	17.09	20.23	24.06	26.00
Omaha, NE	MW	12.07	16.90	20.70	26.14	24.19	11.19	17.28	20.72	26.79	24.02
Minneapolis, MN	MW	10.08	14.02	19.11	26.83	29.95	9.42	14.78	19.21	27.24	29.35
St. Louis, MO	MW	13.62	15.72	19.14	24.44	27.07	13.82	17.29	19.87	23.34	25.68
Wichita, KS	MW	12.14	14.90	18.79	25.06	29.10	12.34	16.85	21.37	26.01	23.43
Cincinnati, OH	MW	13.72	15.78	18.90	24.77	26.83	13.47	17.19	19.86	23.74	25.75
Toledo, OH	MW	12.54	15.45	18.18	23.89	29.94	13.71	17.79	19.40	22.89	26.21
St. Paul, MN	MW	10.08	14.02	19.11	26.83	29.95	9.42	14.78	19.21	27.24	29.35
Lincoln, NE	MW	10.12	12.84	22.54	26.90	27.60	8.54	12.22	20.11	28.62	30.52
Akron, OH	MW	12.08	15.87	19.37	25.65	27.03	13.87	17.23	20.09	23.71	25.11
Madison, WI	MW	11.29	17.09	20.88	26.13	24.62	9.58	16.64	20.16	28.29	25.32
Fort Wayne, IN	MW	11.31	16.01	20.32	27.03	25.32	11.44	17.44	20.86	26.21	24.06
Des Moines, IA	MW	11.48	15.39	19.35	26.41	27.37	9.90	15.61	19.46	26.04	28.99
Grand Rapids, MI	MW	13.56	16.41	20.17	24.88	24.98	13.38	17.77	21.37	25.25	22.22
Midwest suburbs (n=19)	*MW*	*11.58*	*14.44*	*18.21*	*24.97*	*30.80*	*12.31*	*16.42*	*19.45*	*24.54*	*27.27*
New York, NY	NE	12.78	14.19	17.47	20.95	34.61	13.46	13.55	15.64	19.73	37.62
Philadelphia, PA	NE	13.43	16.66	20.35	23.32	26.24	13.32	16.34	18.73	23.82	27.79
Boston, MA	NE	16.23	17.24	20.45	21.77	24.32	16.39	16.16	18.22	22.23	27.01
Pittsburgh, PA	NE	16.60	17.62	20.07	23.58	22.14	19.77	20.81	19.87	20.33	19.22
Buffalo, NY	NE	13.33	15.96	19.61	25.71	25.40	16.41	18.99	19.94	22.40	22.27
Newark, NJ	NE	13.30	15.34	18.91	22.15	30.30	14.17	14.98	17.09	22.03	31.72
Jersey City, NJ	NE	23.51	19.82	19.36	19.56	17.75	24.45	20.13	19.29	17.98	18.16
Rochester, NY	NE	12.19	16.12	19.57	24.31	27.81	13.85	18.36	20.84	23.90	23.06
Yonkers, NY	NE	12.78	14.19	17.47	20.95	34.61	13.46	13.55	15.64	19.73	37.62
Northeast suburbs (n=8)	*NE*	*14.73*	*16.60*	*19.78*	*22.82*	*26.08*	*15.69*	*17.06*	*18.60*	*22.12*	*26.53*
Houston, TX	S	10.50	11.57	15.25	24.74	37.93	13.05	16.10	18.61	22.84	29.40
Dallas, TX	S	14.94	16.22	18.40	23.27	27.16	13.29	17.14	20.02	23.56	25.98
San Antonio, TX	S	15.03	18.00	20.32	23.25	23.40	14.17	18.29	21.16	23.10	23.28
Jacksonville, FL	S	19.01	21.11	19.69	20.50	19.69	13.88	18.20	20.26	23.08	24.58

City											
Austin, TX	S	21.25	19.57	19.17	20.21	19.80	12.22	15.88	19.59	25.28	27.03
Baltimore, MD	S	10.66	15.10	19.60	24.91	29.73	10.76	15.18	18.65	25.33	30.09
Memphis, TN	S	18.91	17.53	17.04	21.93	24.59	12.93	14.49	18.76	24.84	28.99
Washington, DC	S	9.38	14.07	18.41	22.27	35.88	9.72	14.43	18.66	24.85	32.34
El Paso, TX	S	22.68	31.97	22.25	13.13	9.97	32.38	31.06	19.54	10.79	6.23
Nashville, TN	S	17.91	19.12	20.52	21.96	20.49	14.85	17.85	21.13	23.45	22.71
Charlotte, NC	S	17.39	20.97	22.97	22.49	16.17	15.84	18.25	20.95	23.52	21.45
Fort Worth, TX	S	12.91	15.72	19.55	25.82	26.00	12.22	17.21	20.14	23.56	26.87
Oklahoma City, OK	S	16.63	18.71	20.33	22.19	22.14	18.83	20.71	21.29	20.89	18.29
New Orleans, LA	S	15.22	16.59	18.44	24.46	25.30	19.90	19.90	19.89	20.51	19.81
Virginia Beach, VA	S	19.63	21.61	21.18	20.45	17.13	18.94	21.05	21.51	21.45	17.05
Atlanta, GA	S	14.11	17.38	20.18	22.99	25.34	12.16	17.02	21.08	23.80	25.94
Tulsa, OK	S	18.37	17.32	19.86	23.78	20.67	17.44	19.78	21.37	23.16	18.25
Miami, FL	S	22.34	21.01	20.55	17.41	18.68	23.27	21.15	19.81	17.95	17.82
Arlington, TX	S	12.91	15.72	19.55	25.82	26.00	12.22	17.21	20.14	23.56	26.87
Tampa, FL	S	20.21	26.09	21.93	17.38	14.39	19.56	23.41	21.71	18.99	16.33
Corpus Christi, TX	S	21.21	18.96	18.66	20.06	21.11	26.35	21.98	20.45	17.57	13.66
Raleigh, NC	S	19.96	20.93	20.38	20.53	18.20	16.52	17.76	19.16	21.91	24.65
Lexington-Fayette, KY	S	23.62	22.06	19.53	19.18	15.61	21.28	20.13	20.15	20.74	17.70
Louisville, KY	S	12.96	16.52	20.83	24.61	25.07	14.53	18.34	20.70	22.73	23.69
St. Petersburg, FL	S	20.21	26.09	21.93	17.38	14.39	19.56	23.41	21.71	18.99	16.33
Birmingham, AL	S	17.85	17.93	18.82	21.59	23.81	16.23	17.55	19.52	21.47	25.22
Norfolk, VA	S	19.63	21.61	21.18	20.45	17.13	18.94	21.05	21.51	21.45	17.05
Baton Rouge, LA	S	17.18	15.33	18.02	25.30	24.17	16.88	17.74	19.95	22.73	22.70
Hialeah, FL	S	22.34	21.01	20.55	17.41	18.68	23.27	21.15	19.81	17.95	17.82
Greensboro, NC	S	18.59	20.64	21.65	21.20	17.92	18.51	20.52	21.24	21.67	18.05
Plano, TX	S	14.94	16.22	18.40	23.27	27.16	13.29	17.14	20.02	23.56	25.98
Garland, TX	S	14.94	16.22	18.40	23.27	27.16	13.29	17.14	20.02	23.56	25.98
Montgomery, AL	S	21.52	17.95	18.88	20.37	21.28	18.42	18.83	21.31	22.84	18.61
Shreveport, LA	S	21.44	19.46	20.02	20.55	18.53	23.48	21.04	19.90	19.68	15.91
Augusta-Richmond, GA	S	21.25	20.72	20.37	20.81	16.85	18.88	18.67	19.37	21.52	21.56
Lubbock, TX	S	17.39	21.15	22.08	20.10	19.27	21.43	24.66	21.47	17.77	14.67
Chesapeake, VA	S	19.63	21.61	21.18	20.45	17.13	18.94	21.05	21.51	21.45	17.05
Mobile, AL	S	22.09	19.73	18.81	20.61	18.76	21.26	19.91	21.31	20.63	16.89
Richmond, VA	S	13.29	16.80	20.95	24.81	24.15	12.40	17.83	20.72	24.56	24.49
Irving, TX	S	14.94	16.22	18.40	23.27	27.16	13.29	17.14	20.02	23.56	25.98
South suburbs (n=32)		*15.43*	*17.81*	*19.67*	*22.14*	*24.95*	*14.78*	*17.85*	*20.06*	*22.74*	*24.57*
Los Angeles, CA	W	16.44	18.60	19.79	20.61	24.57	18.86	19.28	19.46	20.21	22.19
Phoenix, AZ	W	17.89	22.12	21.85	19.52	18.62	15.31	19.34	21.42	22.56	21.38

(continued)

TABLE 7A-3. Households, by Income Category, Suburbs of 100 Largest Cities, 1979–99[a] *(continued)*

Suburbs of city	Region	Percentage by income category, 1979					Percentage by income category, 1999				
		Low	Lower-middle	Middle	Upper-middle	High	Low	Lower-middle	Middle	Upper-middle	High
San Diego, CA	W	17.18	21.51	20.84	20.05	20.42	16.21	20.27	20.58	21.09	21.85
San Jose, CA	W	11.15	15.29	19.23	22.27	32.05	11.75	13.41	16.45	21.13	37.26
San Francisco, CA	W	11.02	15.34	17.99	21.83	33.82	13.08	16.00	18.05	21.21	31.66
Seattle, WA	W	11.21	14.33	17.91	24.86	31.59	12.30	16.91	20.24	25.23	25.31
Denver, CO	W	9.45	14.11	17.79	25.34	33.31	9.89	15.24	19.34	25.27	30.26
Portland, OR	W	13.38	16.69	18.92	24.12	26.39	13.35	18.15	21.66	23.82	23.01
Tucson, AZ	W	14.40	18.63	18.48	22.56	25.33	15.14	18.90	20.92	21.72	23.31
Las Vegas, NV	W	15.91	22.26	21.89	20.64	19.31	18.08	22.73	22.74	20.61	15.84
Long Beach, CA	W	16.44	18.60	19.79	20.61	24.57	18.86	19.28	19.46	20.21	22.19
Albuquerque, NM	W	18.91	21.97	20.57	19.24	19.31	19.35	21.27	21.86	19.73	17.78
Fresno, CA	W	17.81	21.45	19.56	19.35	21.84	20.59	21.80	20.39	18.89	18.33
Sacramento, CA	W	14.67	19.04	19.07	22.60	24.63	14.10	17.67	20.14	22.72	25.37
Oakland, CA	W	15.10	15.88	18.44	22.08	28.49	13.79	15.30	18.18	23.00	29.73
Mesa, AZ	W	17.89	22.12	21.85	19.52	18.62	15.31	19.34	21.42	22.56	21.38
Honolulu, HI	W	12.84	19.33	19.87	23.04	24.91	12.63	17.40	20.38	25.75	23.84
Colorado Springs, CO	W	12.14	23.40	21.78	22.79	19.89	10.38	17.82	23.02	25.11	23.67
Santa Ana, CA	W	10.69	14.70	17.57	22.28	34.75	12.70	15.93	18.54	22.70	30.12
Anaheim, CA	W	10.69	14.70	17.57	22.28	34.75	12.70	15.93	18.54	22.70	30.12
Aurora, CO	W	9.45	14.11	17.79	25.34	33.34	9.89	15.24	19.34	25.27	30.26
Anchorage, AK[b]	W										
Riverside, CA	W	19.26	21.61	19.96	20.10	19.07	19.34	19.80	19.90	20.97	19.99
Bakersfield, CA	W	19.62	22.12	19.67	19.76	18.83	25.59	23.25	18.88	17.34	14.93
Stockton, CA	W	18.30	19.62	19.38	21.15	21.56	17.08	18.45	19.87	22.25	22.35
Glendale, AZ	W	17.89	22.12	21.85	19.52	18.62	15.31	19.34	21.42	22.56	21.38
Fremont, CA	W	15.10	15.88	18.44	22.08	28.49	13.79	15.30	18.18	23.00	29.73
Scottsdale, AZ	W	17.89	22.12	21.85	19.52	18.62	15.31	19.34	21.42	22.56	21.38
Spokane, WA	W	15.42	18.85	20.04	23.95	21.74	16.10	20.20	21.40	22.91	19.39
Glendale, CA	W	16.44	18.60	19.79	20.61	24.57	18.86	19.28	19.46	20.21	22.19
Tacoma, WA	W	14.04	19.83	19.11	23.41	23.61	13.25	18.62	21.19	24.93	22.01
West suburbs (n=22)		*14.68*	*17.96*	*19.23*	*21.79*	*26.33*	*15.50*	*18.20*	*19.85*	*22.12*	*24.33*
All suburbs (n = 81)		**14.04**	**16.69**	**19.17**	**22.96**	**27.13**	**14.48**	**17.46**	**19.63**	**22.94**	**25.49**

Source: Authors' analysis of 1980 and 2000 decennial censuses.

a. Suburbs include metropolitan area (as defined in 1999) net of all cities included within the 100 largest. Cities located within the same metro area thus have identical suburban totals.

b. The city of Anchorage is coterminous with the Anchorage metropolitan area.

REFERENCES

Andersson, Fredrik, Harry J. Holzer, and Julia I. Lane. 2003. "Worker Advancement in the Low-Wage Labor Market: The Importance of 'Good Jobs.' " Brookings.

Bernstein, Jared, and Dean Baker. 2003. "The Benefits of Full Employment: When Markets Work for People." Washington: Economic Policy Institute.

Bier, Thomas. 2001. "Moving Up, Filtering Down: Metropolitan Housing Dynamics and Public Policy." Brookings.

Blomquist, Glenn C., Mark C. Berger, and John P. Hoehn. 1998. "New Estimates of Quality of Life in Urban Areas." *American Economic Review* 78 (1): 89–107.

Bowles, Jonathan, and Joel Kotkin. 2003. "Engine Failure." New York: Center for an Urban Future.

Brocht, Chauna. 2001. "EPI Issue Guide: Poverty and Family Budgets." Washington: Economic Policy Institute.

Brookings Metropolitan Policy Program. 2002. "Beyond Merger: A Competitive Vision for the Regional City of Louisville." Brookings.

———. 2003a. "Baltimore in Focus: A Profile from Census 2000." Brookings.

———. 2003b. *Living Cities Databook Series.* Brookings.

———. 2004. "Growing the Middle Class: Connecting All Miami-Dade Residents to Economic Opportunity." Brookings.

Brower, Sidney. 1996. *Good Neighborhoods: A Study of In-Town and Suburban Residential Environments.* Westport, Conn.: Praeger.

Bureau of Labor Statistics. 1997. "Interarea Comparisons of Compensation and Prices." In *Report on the American Workforce.* Washington: Government Printing Office.

Citro, Constance F., and Robert T. Michael, eds. 1995. *Measuring Poverty: A New Approach.* Washington: National Academy Press.

Cloutier, Norman. 1997. "Metropolitan Income Inequality during the 1980s: The Impact of Urban Development, Industrial Mix, and Family Structure." *Journal of Regional Science* 37 (3): 459–78.

Congressional Budget Office. 2003. *Effective Federal Tax Rates, 1997 to 2000.* Washington: Government Printing Office.

Frankel, David M., and Eric D. Gould. 2001. "The Retail Price of Inequality." *Journal of Urban Economics* 49: 219–39.

Frey, William H. 2001. "Melting Pot Suburbs: A Census 2000 Study of Suburban Diversity." Brookings.

Frey, William H., and Alan Berube. 2002. "City Families, Suburban Singles: An Emerging Household Story from Census 2000." Brookings.

Frey, William H., and Elaine L. Fielding. 1995. "Changing Urban Populations: Regional Restructuring, Racial Polarization, and Poverty Concentration." *Cityscape* 1 (2): 1–66.

Gale, William G., and Peter R. Orszag. 2004. "Should the President's Tax Cuts Be Made Permanent?" Brookings.

Glaeser, Edward L., Matthew E. Kahn, and Jordan Rappaport. 2000. "Why Do the Poor Live in Cities?" Working Paper 7636. Cambridge, Mass.: National Bureau of Economic Research.

Hall, Sir Peter. 1998. *Cities and Civilization.* New York: Pantheon.

Jacobs, Jane. 1961. *The Death and Life of Great American Cities.* New York: Random House.

Jargowsky, Paul. 1997. *Poverty and Place.* New York: Russell Sage Foundation.

Jones, Arthur F., Jr., and Daniel H. Weinberg. 2000. "The Changing Shape of the Nation's Income Distribution." Census Bureau Current Population Report P60–204. Washington: U.S. Census Bureau.

Kennedy, Maureen, and Paul Leonard. 2001. "Dealing with Neighborhood Change: A Primer on Gentrification and Policy Choices." Brookings.

Kokoski, Mary, Patrick Cardiff, and Brent Moulton. 1994. "Interarea Price Indices for Consumer Goods and Services: An Hedonic Approach Using CPI Data." BLS Working Paper 256. Washington: Bureau of Labor Statistics.

Ladd, Helen F. 1993. "Fiscal Consequences for U.S. Central Cities of the Changing Urban Form." In *Urban Change in the United States and Western,* ed. A. Summers, P. Cheshire, and L. Seen. Washington: Urban Institute Press.

Lang, Robert E., and Patrick A. Simmons. 2003. " 'Boomburbs': The Emergence of Large, Fast-Growing Suburban Cities." In *Redefining Urban and Suburban America: Evidence from Census 2000,* edited by Bruce Katz and Robert E. Lang. Brookings.

Legislative Analyst Office. 2003. "Teacher Housing Initiatives." San Francisco Board of Supervisors.

Leone, Richard C. 1976. "The Fiscal Decline of Older Cities: Causes and Cures." *National Tax Journal* 29 (3): 257–60.

Madden, Janice F. 2000. *Changes in Income Inequality with U.S. Metropolitan Areas.* Kalamazoo, Mich.: Upjohn Institute.

Martin, Philip, and Elizabeth Midgley. 2003. "Immigration to the United States: Shaping and Reshaping America." *Population Bulletin* 58 (2).

Massey, Douglas S., and Nancy A. Denton. 1993. *American Apartheid: Segregation and the Making of the Underclass.* Harvard University Press.

McMahon, Thomas, Larian Angelo, and John Mollenkopf. 1998. "The Disappearing Urban Middle Class." *Social Policy* 32 (4): 322–35.

Miller, Herman P. 1966. *Income Distribution in the United States.* Department of Commerce. Washington: Government Printing Office.

Mishel, Lawrence, Jared Bernstein, and Heather Boushey. 2003. *The State of Working America 2002–03.* Cornell University Press.

Mondale, Ted, and William Fulton. 2003. "Managing Metropolitan Growth: Reflections on the Twin Cities Experience." Brookings.

Nelson, Arthur C., and others. 2002. "The Link between Growth Management and Housing Affordability: The Academic Evidence." Brookings.

Nelson, Kathryn P. 1988. *Gentrification and Distressed Cities: An Assessment of Trends in Intrametropolitan Migration.* University of Wisconsin Press.

Pack, Janet Rothenberg. 1998. "Poverty and Urban Public Expenditures." *Urban Studies* 35 (11): 1995–2019.

———. 2002. *Growth and Convergence in Metropolitan America.* Brookings.

Research Atlanta. 1997. "A Population Profile of the City of Atlanta: Trends, Causes and Options." Atlanta, Ga.: Research Atlanta.

Rivlin, Alice M., and others. 2003. "Revitalizing Washington's Neighborhoods: A Vision Takes Shape." Brookings.

Ruggles, Patricia. 1990. *Drawing the Line: Alternative Poverty Measures and Their Implications for Public Policy.* Washington: Urban Institute Press.

Rusk, David. 2003. *Cities without Suburbs: A Census 2000 Update.* Baltimore, Md.: Woodrow Wilson Center Press.

Short, Kathleen. 2001a. "Experimental Poverty Measures: 1999." Census Bureau Current Population Report P60-216. Washington: Government Printing Office.

———. 2001b. "Where We Live: Geographic Differences in Poverty Thresholds." Washington: U.S. Census Bureau.

Short, Kathleen, and Thesia Garner. 2002. "A Decade of Experimental Poverty Thresholds: 1990 to 2000." Paper prepared for the annual meeting of the Western Economic Association, Seattle, Wash., July 2.

U.S. Census Bureau. 2003. *Income in the United States, 2002*. Washington.

Varady, David P. 1994. "Middle-Income Housing Programmes in American Cities." *Urban Studies* 31 (8): 1345–66.

Voith, Richard. 1994. "Do Suburbs Need Cities?" Working Paper 93–27/R. Philadelphia: Federal Reserve Bank.

Wilson, William Julius. 1987. *The Truly Disadvantaged: The Inner City, the Underclass, and Public Policy*. University of Chicago Press.

8

Homeownership and Younger Households
Progress among African Americans and Latinos

DOWELL MYERS AND GARY PAINTER

The best housing news from the 1990s is that the United States achieved the largest national gain in the homeownership rate since the 1950s, 2 percentage points, reversing the decline experienced in the 1980s. The increase was so widespread that Simmons termed it a "coast-to-coast expansion" in homeownership.[1]

Several important features of the rebound in homeownership have been documented by previous studies.[2] First, the bulk of the nation's increase in homeownership rates during the 1990s reflects the simple aging of the population into life stages with higher probability of homeownership. The relative decline in number of younger households, whose age group has typically lower homeownership, led to an increase in the nation's overall homeownership rate.

Nonetheless, in contrast to the widespread sharp decline in the homeownership rates of young adults that was recorded in the 1980s, during the 1990s homeownership rates stabilized among young adults in almost all

Adapted from Dowell Myers and Gary Painter, *Homeownership and Younger Households: Progress among African Americans and Latinos* (Census Note 12, October 2003). ©2003 Fannie Mae Foundation, Washington, D.C. Used with permission.

Excellent research assistance was received from Keri Rosenbloom and staff of the University of Southern California's Population Dynamics Research Group, including Sung Ho Ryu, Liang Wei, and Zhou Yu. Julie Park provided skilled supervision and data management. The authors gratefully acknowledge the helpful advice and comments of Patrick Simmons.

1. Simmons (2001a).
2. Simmons (2001a, 2001b); Myers (2001).

the states. The reversal was widespread, with the majority of states experiencing small increases, instead of declines, in homeownership. This finding is especially noteworthy because of the great concerns about the declining homeownership fortunes of the baby boom generation.

A further finding has been that homeownership rates increased for minorities as well as non-Hispanic whites. In fact, among younger adults, the increases for African Americans and Latinos surpassed those for whites, thereby decreasing the gap in homeownership for minorities.[3]

This chapter probes into these changes in greater depth. Trends in homeownership for the baby boom generation are explored in greater detail, examining how minority members of this group have fared. We examine how widespread minority homeownership rate gains were across states and metropolitan areas and identify those metropolitan areas in which minorities have fared best.

METHODOLOGY

Homeownership is one of a handful of variables for which the Census Bureau seeks to obtain information from 100 percent of residents. The resulting data are free of sampling error and are among the first released from Census 2000.

Defining and Measuring Homeownership

Summary File 1 (SF1) of Census 2000 and similar tabulations from the 1980 and 1990 censuses are used to measure overall homeownership trends. Detailed tabulations of homeownership by age, race, and Hispanic origin are drawn from the Summary File 2 (SF2) of the 1980, 1990, and 2000 censuses.

A housing unit is owner-occupied if the owner or co-owner lives in the unit, even if it is mortgaged or not fully paid for. All other occupied housing units are classified as "renter occupied." Traditionally the homeownership rate is defined as the percentage of all occupied housing units that are "owner occupied." The ownership rate is extended to apply to people as well as housing units in the following manner. Every occupied housing unit contains one household, and every household has exactly one householder. The latter is the person in whose name the housing unit is owned or rented. In the cases where multiple parties hold that status, the household designates only one person to hold the status of the reference person (householder) for the household. The characteristics of the householder can then be used to categorize

---

3. Simmons (2001b).

households. In this chapter the homeownership rates of different age groups and race-ethnic groups are compared.

Defining Racial Groups

Analysis of homeownership trends for racial groups is complicated by changes in the definition of racial groups for Census 2000. Unlike previous censuses, in 2000 respondents were asked to check all racial categories that applied to their self-identification. Nationwide, some 2.4 percent of residents identified as multiracial. Thus data are tabulated separately for individuals who identified as African American alone (in other words, not checking any additional racial categories) and for those who identified as African American in combination with one or more other races. The challenge for the current analysis is to decide which of these should be compared to the figures collected in previous censuses.

The solution adopted for this analysis draws upon lessons reported by Myers and James.[4] A useful approximation in 2000 of the racial group that might have been recorded by the techniques used in 1990 is to construct an average of two racial identification alternatives. We have combined the information on household tenure by age from two different tabulations drawn from the SF2 files in 2000, one pertaining to African Americans alone and the other pertaining to the larger group consisting of African Americans alone or in combination with another race. Ownership rates constructed from the two tabulations are simply averaged, under the implicit assumption that roughly half of those African Americans who selected an additional race affiliation in 2000 would have identified as African American in 1990.[5]

In the detailed analysis that follows, the Hispanic portion of African American, white, or other households is removed from tabulations of these racial groups. Hispanic households thus can be of any race, following the convention of the Census Bureau.

Geographic Units for Analysis

Analysis of trends over time requires consistent geographic boundaries that are identifiable in the database. For analysis of 1980–2000 trends we make use of states because these geographic units are most easily identified in the detailed demographic data. However, for 1990–2000 analyses of metropolitan areas, we have recoded the boundary files in the detailed demographic data to

4. Myers and James (2002).
5. See Myers and James (2002).

a consistent definition equivalent to that used in Census 2000. In the New England area this entails detailed matching at the township level, unlike the county units used in most of the United States.

Selecting Age Groups

Homeownership rises rapidly with age. The most critical years for homeownership attainment are ages 25 to 34 and 35 to 44. In the past, the younger group has been considered the prime age for homeownership attainment. Increasing emphasis is now being given to age 35 to 44. In recent years the age at marriage and age of family formation has been delayed substantially, especially in the Northeast and in larger metropolitan areas. This is confounded also with longer periods of education, including increasing professional and postgraduate education. The result is that in some metropolitan areas, the path into homeownership begins at a young age, whereas in others—especially those that are higher-cost and where education levels are also higher—homeownership is delayed. Taking a reading at age 35 to 44 provides a way to measure progress into homeownership of young adults that avoids these variations in lifestyle among people in their twenties.

An additional reason for emphasizing age 35 to 44 is that younger members of the large Baby Boom generation (born between 1946 and 1964) have passed out of the 25-to-34 age group and into the 35-to-44 age group. In 2000 the younger portion of the Baby Boomers occupied age 35 to 44; whereas, in 1990, it was the leading edge of the Baby Boom that was that age. In effect a comparison of the 35-to-44 age group in 1990 and 2000 amounts to a comparison of the homeownership attainments of the earlier and later Baby Boom members when they were at the same stage of life. In turn comparison to the still earlier cohort that occupied age 35 to 44 in 1980 provides an assessment of how the Baby Boomers have fared relative to their predecessors.

In the analysis that follows, we examine trends for both ages 25 to 34 and 35 to 44, but the most detailed analysis is afforded the 35-to-44 age group. As shown in table 8-1, changes in homeownership rates were much more favorable for all groups in the 1990s than in the 1980s. Young adults of all races and Hispanic origin suffered substantial decreases in homeownership rates during the 1980s. Among households in both the 25-to-34 and 35-to-44 age groups, however, there was substantial improvement in homeownership rate trends in the 1990s. Improvement was even greater among blacks and Latinos than it was for non-Hispanic white households or for the age groups as a whole. Asian and Pacific Islander householders age 25 to 34 were the only ones that did not show substantial improvement in homeownership rates between decades.

T A B L E 8 - 1 . Homeownership Rates for Young Adults, by Race and Hispanic Origin, 1980–2000

Percent

Type of household	1980	1990	2000	1980–90 change	1990–2000 change
All households	64.4	64.2	66.2	−0.2	2.0
Non-Hispanic white	68.5	69.1	72.4	0.6	3.4
Black (includes Latino)	44.4	43.4	46.3	−1.0	2.9
Asian/Pacific Islander	52.5	52.2	53.2	−0.3	1.0
Latino	43.4	42.4	45.7	−1.0	3.3
Aged 25–34	51.6	45.3	45.6	−6.3	0.3
Non-Hispanic white	55.7	51.0	53.0	−4.7	1.9
Black (includes Latino)	29.7	23.3	27.3	−6.4	4.0
Asian/Pacific Islander	38.2	34.9	31.8	−3.3	−3.1
Latino	33.9	28.9	32.9	−5.1	4.0
Aged 35–44	71.2	66.2	66.2	−5.0	0.0
Non-Hispanic white	75.6	71.8	73.2	−3.8	1.4
Black (includes Latino)	47.6	43.0	44.6	−4.6	1.5
Asian/Pacific Islander	61.0	58.0	57.8	−3.0	−0.2
Latino	49.6	45.6	48.8	−3.9	3.2

Sources: U.S. Census Bureau, 2000 Census Summary File 1 (SF 1) 100-Percent Data; 1990 Census of Housing: General Housing Characteristics; 1980 Census 5% PUMS data and 1980 Census of Housing Subject Report—Structural Characteristics of the Housing Inventory.

FINDINGS

How common are these patterns of homeownership rebound across the country? This section examines homeownership trends by geography, race and ethnicity, and age during the 1990s.

Homeownership Decline of 1980s Reverses in Most States over 1990s: African American Gains Most Widespread

The number of states with rising homeownership rates in the 1990s greatly exceeded that in the 1980s, reversing the pattern of decline previously seen for homeownership among younger adults. Among all households, all states except Arkansas exhibited increases in homeownership rates during the 1990s. This contrasts with only eighteen states experiencing homeownership increases in the 1980s (see figure 8-1).

Increases were less widespread among young to middle-aged adults but were still substantial in comparison to the previous decade. At age 25 to 34, thirty-two states recorded increased homeownership rates in the 1990s, versus only three states in the 1980s. At age 35 to 44, twenty-one states recorded increased homeownership rates, versus only two states in the 1980s.

Among African American members of the younger generation, even more widespread gains in homeownership rates were achieved. During the

FIGURE 8-1. Number of States with Rising Homeownership Rates, by Age and Race/Ethnicity, 1980–1990 and 1990–2000

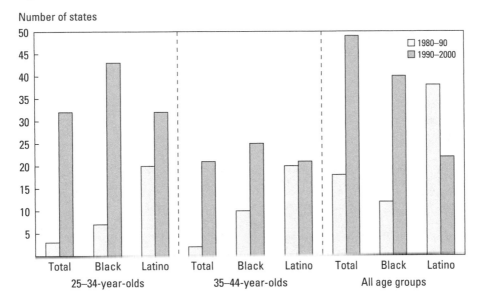

1990s, homeownership rates for black households age 25 to 34 increased in forty-three states, eleven more than for the younger population at large. At age 35 to 44, black homeownership increased in four more states than the average at that age.

Among Latino members of the younger generation, gains in homeownership rates were almost as prevalent as for the younger population at large. During the 1990s homeownership rates for Latino households age 25 to 34 increased in thirty-two states, and at age 35 to 44 in twenty-one states, were almost identical to the number of states where homeownership increased for the younger population at large. Unlike with other young adults, the number of states with Latino homeownership gains was not substantially greater in the 1990s than the 1980s, because Latino gains had been unusually strong in the 1980s.

The greatest rebound in homeownership trends occurred in states where homeownership had declined the most in the previous decade. This is best measured by the correlation between decades of the homeownership rate trends. As shown in table 8-2, there was a substantial, negative correlation (−0.33) for all races and ages combined. This signifies that states with larger declines in homeownership in the 1980s had larger increases in the 1990s.

TABLE 8-2. Correlations of Homeownership Rate Changes for Young Adults between Racial/Ethnic Groups across Decades, 1980–2000

Correlation	All ages	25–34	35–44
Between changes in the 1990s and 1980s			
All races	−0.33	−0.59	−0.46
Black	0.15	0.12	0.05
Latino	0.10	0.01	−0.05
Between changes for groups in the 1980s			
Black and all	0.32	0.24	0.31
Latino and all	0.43	0.31	0.36
Black and Latino	0.16	0.09	0.07
Between changes for groups in the 1990s			
Black and all	0.43	0.28	0.42
Latino and all	0.31	0.35	0.32
Black and Latino	0.36	0.30	0.41

In the case of young adults, the negative correlation is even sharper, −0.59 at age 25 to 34 and −0.46 at age 35 to 44.

A surprising observation is that the same pattern of homeownership reversal does not apply in the case of African Americans and Latinos. The correlation is much weaker and generally positive for all age groups and for young adults (table 8-2). As shown above for African Americans, and especially for Latinos, the number of states with homeownership increases did not expand as greatly as for the total population, largely because the declines in the 1980s were not as widespread. What the correlation analysis adds is that the depth of increases or decreases are not correlated with subsequent trends in the same state. In fact a further set of correlations reported in table 8-2 indicates that, during both the 1980s and 1990s, the trends for African Americans and Latinos were only moderately correlated with the overall homeownership trends in each state. In fact, during the 1980s, the trends in homeownership for African Americans and Latinos were virtually unrelated, whereas in the 1990s the trends for the two minority groups bore a moderate similarity (r = 0.36 for all age groups).

A fuller picture of the correlation between trends of the 1980s and 1990s is provided in figure 8-2. For households age 35 to 44, figure 8-2 shows scatterplots of the homeownership rate changes of the 1990s (vertical axis) against the changes of the 1980s (horizontal axis). Any states that enjoyed increases in both decades would be plotted in the upper right quadrant, whereas those with decreases in both decades would be plotted in the lower left quadrant. Substantial differences are seen among the different racial-ethnic subgroups within the 35-to-44 age category.

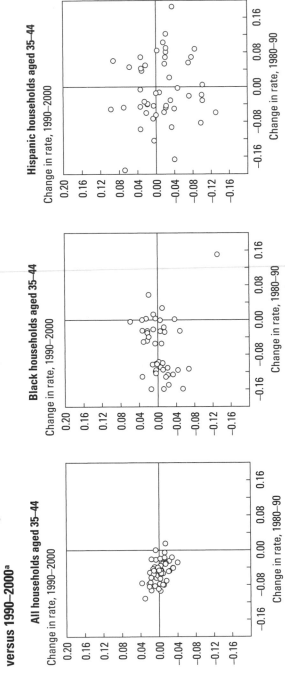

FIGURE 8-2. Changes in State Homeownership Rates for 35- to 44-Year-Olds, by Race/Ethnicity, 1980–90 versus 1990–2000[a]

a. States not shown are Montana, Nevada, North Dakota, South Dakota, Vermont, and Wyoming.

Among all households age 35 to 44, the fifty states cluster in a similar location on the graph. Almost all the states experienced declines in their homeownership rate during the 1980s, varying from a loss of 11 percentage points to an increase of 2 percentage points. During the 1990s, however, the states' rates varied from a 4 percentage point gain to a 4 percentage point decline, a much more compact range. The slight tilt of the data cluster toward the upper left, previously described as a correlation of −0.46 for age 35 to 44, indicates that the states with deeper declines in the 1980s tended to have larger increases in the 1990s.

In the case of African American households age 35 to 44, the data cluster is not as compact, and the correlation between the homeownership trends of the 1980s and 1990s is near zero (0.01). Not all states have substantial African American populations, especially for this narrowly defined age group, and as a result their homeownership trends can vary widely. Data fell outside the plot area for several states, including Vermont, North Dakota, South Dakota, Wyoming, Montana, and Nevada. Only Nevada has any appreciable black population.

Similarly, for Latino households age 35 to 44, population size was small in some states, particularly in 1980. However, the pattern of change for all states but one (Delaware) fell within the plot area. As the scattered pattern of the plot makes clear, states reveal a high degree of variation in their homeownership trends, and the overall correlation is virtually zero (−0.05).

Homeownership Gains Vary across Metropolitan Areas

This section presents analysis of homeownership trends in the 100 largest metropolitan areas.[6] Again we focus on one specific age group, 35 to 44, when homeownership achievement is expected to be attained by the majority of those who are ever going to become homeowners. Comparison of this age group in 1990 and 2000 has the advantage of comparing homeownership attainment for the older half and younger half of the Baby Boom generation.

Homeownership gains for adults age 35 to 44 varied markedly in these 100 metropolitan areas (table 8A-1). During the 1990s, homeownership rates among all households age 35 to 44 increased in fifty-five of the metropolitan areas, with the largest increase observed in Austin, Texas (6.9 percentage points). Albany, New York, experienced the greatest decrease in homeownership rates, 4.8 percentage points.

---

6. We use Metropolitan Statistical Areas (MSAs) and Consolidated Metropolitan Statistical Areas (CMSAs).

Among African American households of the same age, increases occurred in fifty metropolitan areas (table 8A-2). The greatest increase was found in McAllen, Texas (10.9 percentage points), and the greatest decrease in Scranton, Pennsylvania (10.9 percentage points). Few African American households reside in each of these metropolitan areas, making them susceptible to large changes in homeownership rates. In the twenty metropolitan areas with the largest numbers of African American households age 35 to 44, changes in homeownership rates ranged from +6.3 percentage points in Washington, D.C., to −3.3 percentage points in Philadelphia, Pennsylvania.

Among Latino households age 35 to 44, increases occurred in forty-one metropolitan areas (table 8A-3). The largest increase was found in Miami, Florida (9.5 percentage points), whereas the greatest decrease occurred in Lexington, Kentucky (19.2 percentage points), a metropolitan area with fewer than 700 Latino householders age 35 to 44. When the twenty metropolitan areas with the largest numbers of Latino households in this age group are considered, Miami still registers the largest homeownership rate increase, but the largest decline occurs in San Diego, which experienced only a modest drop of 0.6 percentage points.

Minority Homeownership Gains Largest in Areas with Large Minority Populations

We find that increases in homeownership rates during the 1990s for 35- to 44-year-olds were greatest for blacks and Latinos in metropolitan areas where the size of their group was largest. Correlations between homeownership rate changes for 35- to 44-year-olds and the number of households in this age category are 0.23 and 0.29 for blacks and Latinos, respectively. Among metropolitan areas with increasing homeownership rates for 35- to 44-year-old blacks, the median number of black households in this age category was more than 12,000. For metropolitan areas with homeownership rate declines, the median number of young black households was only about 8,000. The contrast for Latinos is even more striking. In metropolitan areas with homeownership rate gains among 35- to 44-year-old Latinos, the median number of young Latino households was more than 11,000. In metropolitan areas with falling Latino homeownership rates, the median number of households was less than 2,000.

The explanation for this size effect is unknown but could reflect several factors. Larger areas might constitute housing markets that present more favorable investment returns for prospective home buyers. Alternatively, the largest metropolitan areas might have been more likely to be selected for home-buyer assistance programs, giving residents greater access to counseling assistance and mortgage programs. Finally, it is also possible that metro-politan areas with the greatest access to homeownership might have attracted a greater number of residents of the given group.

Whatever the reasons for this size effect on trends in homeownership, we note that many of the extreme decreases, and even some of the greatest increases, occurred in metropolitan areas with few households in the desig-nated age-race group. This creates an instability in the measurement of home-ownership rates, and it draws attention to the areas that are smallest and least important. Accordingly, it is potentially misleading to compare the relative increases in homeownership between metropolitan areas of such widely vary-ing sizes. The increases in homeownership rates for African Americans, for example, are obviously more important in New York or Atlanta than are the substantial declines registered in Scranton, Pennsylvania, or Madison, Wisconsin.

To adjust for this size effect, and to better display the homeownership trends, we have plotted the data from the preceding tables of metropolitan areas in a series of maps. The distinctive design of these maps is that each metropolitan area is represented by a circle that is proportional to the size of the targeted population group, for example, number of black household-ers age 35 to 44. The shade of the circle then indicates the amount of change in homeownership rates. Those metropolitan areas with few householders in a given group become only small dots on the map and the larger ones stand out for their size. The maps, of course, also display a third dimension: the location of the metropolitan area.

The pattern of homeownership change for the entire 35-to-44 age group from 1990 to 2000 is displayed in Map 8-1. Increases in the homeownership rate, shown in dark gray, are prevalent across the country, with two notable exceptions. Homeownership in Los Angeles and other California metropol-itan areas declined markedly, as indicated by the black circles. Similarly, throughout the Northeast metropolitan areas experienced declines—or at best minimal changes—in the homeownership rate. The deepest declines were recorded in the smaller metropolitan areas in the region.

In the case of African American households age 35 to 44, substantial gains in homeownership occurred throughout the East Coast and South, with a few notable exceptions (table 8A-2). The deep decline in homeownership among the large Philadelphia black population is unlike that of any other large city. Declines in Jacksonville, Florida, and Houston, Texas, also stand out, as do the deep declines in the small metropolitan areas of Arkansas and Oklahoma. In contrast, substantial gains are observed in Atlanta, Washington, D.C., and New York, metropolitan areas with among the largest black populations.

MAP 8-1. Change in Homeownership Rate, 100 Largest Metropolitan Areas, Households Aged 35 to 44, 1990–2000

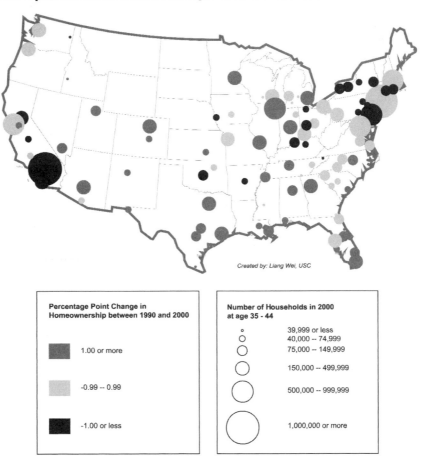

Created by: Liang Wei, USC

Percentage Point Change in Homeownership between 1990 and 2000	
■	1.00 or more
▨	-0.99 -- 0.99
■	-1.00 or less

Number of Households in 2000 at age 35 - 44	
∘	39,999 or less
○	40,000 -- 74,999
○	75,000 -- 149,999
○	150,000 -- 499,999
○	500,000 -- 999,999
○	1,000,000 or more

In the Midwest, gains in homeownership were achieved in Chicago and Indianapolis, but elsewhere in the region only minimal changes or even declines are observed. In the West, minimal changes were recorded in Los Angeles, whereas gains are observed in both northern California and Las Vegas.

Among Latino households age 35 to 44, gains in homeownership are spread throughout the country, including the large metropolitan areas of California, Texas, Florida, the Northeast, and in Chicago (maps 8-2 and 8-3). What stands out, in contrast, is the large number of metropolitan areas with small Latino populations throughout the South and Midwest. Almost all of these areas recorded deep declines in homeownership. In all likelihood, this decline

M A P   8 - 2 .   Change in African American Homeownership Rate, 100 Largest Metropolitan Areas, Households Aged 35 to 44, 1990–2000

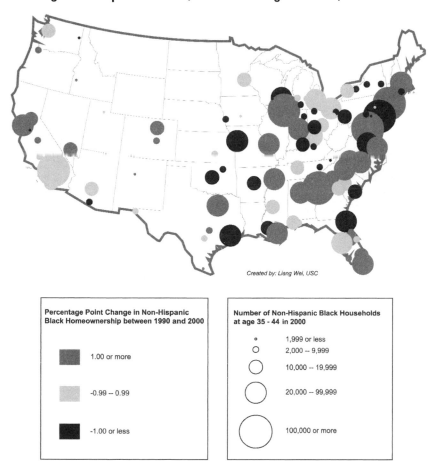

Created by: Liang Wei, USC

Percentage Point Change in Non-Hispanic Black Homeownership between 1990 and 2000	
▨	1.00 or more
▨	-0.99 -- 0.99
■	-1.00 or less

Number of Non-Hispanic Black Households at age 35 - 44 in 2000	
∘	1,999 or less
○	2,000 -- 9,999
○	10,000 -- 19,999
○	20,000 -- 99,999
○	100,000 or more

reflects the rapid growth of the Latino population through migration in the 1990s. Relatively few of these newcomers were likely homeowners, unlike the more settled residents of the large Latino population centers.

CONCLUSION

The decade of the 1990s witnessed the largest secular gain (2 percentage points) in homeownership rates since the 1950s. Overall, young households (aged 25 to 44) experienced lesser gains. Nonetheless these modest gains represented marked improvement over sharply declining homeownership

MAP 8-3. **Change in Hispanic Homeownership Rate, 100 Largest Metropolitan Areas, Households Aged 35 to 44, 1990–2000**

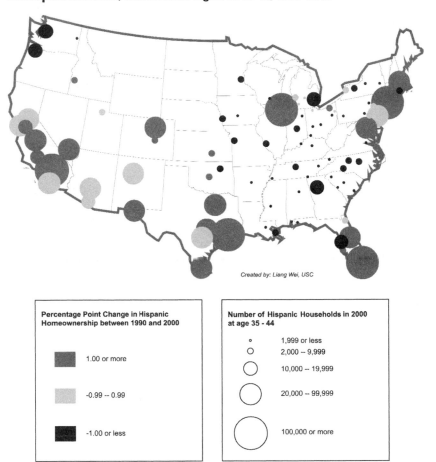

Created by: Liang Wei, USC

Percentage Point Change in Hispanic Homeownership between 1990 and 2000	
■	1.00 or more
▨	-0.99 -- 0.99
■	-1.00 or less

Number of Hispanic Households in 2000 at age 35 - 44	
○	1,999 or less
○	2,000 -- 9,999
○	10,000 -- 19,999
○	20,000 -- 99,999
○	100,000 or more

rates for young households during the 1980s. At the same time, the average gains for African American and Latino households in this age group were much larger, ranging from 1.5 to 4 percentage points. This is in direct contrast to the experience of the 1980s when homeownership rates among black and Latino households fell by 4 to 6.4 percentage points.

The pattern of gains for young households was fairly well distributed across states, with more widespread gains among 25- to 34-year-olds (thirty-two states) than among 35- to 44-year-olds (twenty-one states). The gains among 35- to 44-year-olds are of greatest interest because housing careers are fairly well established by this age and because analysis of this age category in 1990 and 2000 permits comparison of the older and younger halves of the Baby Boom generation. Of this age group, African American and Latino households experienced gains in approximately the same number of states as the overall age group, but their average increase was substantially greater.

The pattern varied more markedly across the 100 largest metropolitan areas in the 1990s. Focusing on adults age 35 to 44, changes in homeownership varied from gains of 6.9 percentage points to losses of 4.7 percentage points. Overall there were gains achieved in 55 of the 100 areas. Gains for African Americans and Latinos occurred in half or slightly fewer of the metropolitan areas, but the positive and negative changes were more extreme for these households.

Finally, homeownership rate gains for minority households tended to occur in those metropolitan areas with the largest populations of those groups. Metropolitan areas with declining African American and Latino homeownership rates tended to have much smaller populations of these groups than areas with rising rates. This suggests that migration and immigration to the smaller metropolitan areas may have played an important role in dampening homeownership rates in those areas, particularly for Latinos.

TABLE 8A-1. **Homeownership Rate Changes for All Households Aged 35–44, 100 Largest Metropolitan Areas, 1990–2000**

2000 rank	Metropolitan area	Total households aged 35–44	Rate change (percent)
1	Austin–San Marcos, TX MSA	117,407	6.86
2	Melbourne–Titusville–Palm Bay, FL MSA	42,809	5.82
3	Colorado Springs, CO MSA	50,440	4.97
4	Las Vegas, NV–AZ MSA	130,395	4.10
5	Fort Myers–Cape Coral, FL MSA	31,533	4.03
6	McAllen–Edinburg–Mission, TX MSA	35,654	3.75
7	Sarasota–Bradenton, FL MSA	41,314	3.55
8	Denver–Boulder–Greeley, CO CMSA	249,735	3.53
9	Daytona Beach, FL MSA	36,465	3.04
10	West Palm Beach–Boca Raton, FL MSA	92,347	2.87
11	Houston–Galveston–Brazoria, TX CMSA	423,595	2.83
12	Raleigh–Durham–Chapel Hill, NC MSA	113,459	2.65
13	El Paso, TX MSA	51,213	2.64
14	Miami–Fort Lauderdale, FL CMSA	333,306	2.49
15	Phoenix–Mesa, AZ MSA	269,679	2.33
16	Memphis, TN–AR–MS MSA	99,874	1.96
17	San Antonio, TX MSA	100,034	1.89
18	Chicago–Gary–Kenosha, IL–IN–WI CMSA	786,762	1.88
19	New Orleans, LA MSA	115,128	1.76
20	Lakeland–Winter Haven, FL MSA	35,688	1.70
21	Atlanta, GA MSA	396,577	1.63
22	Detroit–Ann Arbor–Flint, MI CMSA	482,490	1.61
23	Nashville, TN MSA	115,283	1.56
24	Salt Lake City–Ogden, UT MSA	101,703	1.51
25	Orlando, FL MSA	147,733	1.44
26	Birmingham, AL MSA	79,395	1.41
27	Albuquerque, NM MSA	63,719	1.35
28	Baton Rouge, LA MSA	50,959	1.23
29	Dallas–Fort Worth, TX CMSA	492,658	1.23
30	Wichita, KS MSA	49,368	1.22
31	Charleston–North Charleston, SC MSA	47,809	1.18
32	Mobile, AL MSA	44,455	1.13
33	Boise City, ID MSA	36,974	1.08
34	St. Louis, MO–IL MSA	237,766	1.07
35	Minneapolis–St. Paul, MN–WI MSA	293,803	1.07
36	Stockton–Lodi, CA MSA	43,635	1.04
37	Indianapolis, IN MSA	151,155	1.00
38	Kalamazoo–Battle Creek, MI MSA	37,798	0.94
39	Tampa–St. Petersburg–Clearwater, FL MSA	204,460	0.93
40	Pensacola, FL MSA	34,878	0.89
41	Canton–Massillon, OH MSA	33,872	0.86
42	Charlotte–Gastonia–Rock Hill, NC–SC MSA	139,309	0.83
43	Washington–Baltimore, DC–MD–VA–WV CMSA	714,000	0.74
44	Lansing–East Lansing, MI MSA	38,029	0.70
45	Kansas City, MO–KS MSA	165,222	0.55
46	Des Moines, IA MSA	41,520	0.29
47	Bakersfield, CA MSA	50,984	0.24
48	Jackson, MS MSA	37,877	0.23
49	Cincinnati–Hamilton, OH–KY–IN CMSA	180,321	0.22
50	Greenville–Spartanburg–Anderson, SC MSA	81,595	0.21
51	Columbus, OH MSA	142,619	0.20

(*continued*)

T A B L E 8 A - 1 . Homeownership Rate Changes for All Households Aged 35–44, 100 Largest Metropolitan Areas, 1990–2000 (*continued*)

2000 rank	Metropolitan area	Total households aged 35–44	Rate change (percent)
52	Tucson, AZ MSA	68,714	0.15
53	Columbia, SC MSA	47,912	0.15
54	Augusta–Aiken, GA–SC MSA	41,405	0.10
55	Pittsburgh, PA MSA	198,995	0.09
56	Seattle–Tacoma–Bremerton, WA CMSA	342,458	–0.04
57	Knoxville, TN MSA	59,464	–0.07
58	Grand Rapids–Muskegon–Holland, MI MSA	95,465	–0.08
59	Jacksonville, FL MSA	101,988	–0.20
60	Norfolk–Virginia Beach–Newport News, VA–NC MSA	142,779	–0.25
61	Portland–Salem, OR–WA CMSA	198,595	–0.25
62	San Francisco–Oakland–San Jose, CA CMSA	622,759	–0.32
63	Madison, WI MSA	39,297	–0.33
64	New York–Northern New Jersey–Long Island, NY–NJ–CT–PA CMSA	1,817,110	–0.35
65	Chattanooga, TN–GA MSA	38,687	–0.39
66	Cleveland–Akron, OH CMSA	259,327	–0.53
67	Milwaukee–Racine, WI CMSA	152,569	–0.60
68	Youngstown–Warren, OH MSA	46,915	–0.79
69	Modesto, CA MSA	35,411	–0.79
70	Tulsa, OK MSA	71,028	–0.81
71	Greensboro–Winston-Salem–High Point, NC MSA	110,613	–0.81
72	Richmond–Petersburg, VA MSA	92,099	–0.82
73	Springfield, MA MSA	49,699	–0.83
74	Fort Wayne, IN MSA	44,051	–0.86
75	Boston–Worcester–Lawrence, MA–NH–ME–CT CMSA	532,866	–0.91
76	Omaha, NE–IA MSA	65,143	–1.00
77	Lexington, KY MSA	41,901	–1.00
78	Lancaster, PA MSA	39,619	–1.16
79	Sacramento–Yolo, CA CMSA	158,106	–1.18
80	Spokane, WA MSA	36,171	–1.18
81	Toledo, OH MSA	52,560	–1.18
82	Oklahoma City, OK MSA	94,297	–1.32
83	Philadelphia–Wilmington–Atlantic City, PA–NJ–DE–MD CMSA	535,083	–1.46
84	Dayton–Springfield, OH MSA	81,093	–1.50
85	Louisville, KY–IN MSA	93,081	–1.69
86	Fresno, CA MSA	66,921	–1.72
87	Harrisburg–Lebanon–Carlisle, PA MSA	54,420	–1.78
88	Little Rock–North Little Rock, AR MSA	51,778	–1.80
89	Buffalo–Niagara Falls, NY MSA	101,851	–1.85
90	Scranton–Wilkes-Barre–Hazleton, PA MSA	48,441	–2.00
91	Hartford, CT MSA	107,658	–2.01
92	Los Angeles–Riverside–Orange County, CA CMSA	1,341,877	–2.10
93	Johnson City–Kingsport–Bristol, TN–VA MSA	39,133	–2.25
94	San Diego, CA MSA	239,141	–2.34
95	Honolulu, HI MSA	62,217	–2.55
96	Syracuse, NY MSA	64,734	–2.69
97	Allentown–Bethlehem–Easton, PA MSA	55,117	–3.06
98	Rochester, NY MSA	98,136	–3.47
99	Providence–Fall River–Warwick, RI–MA MSA	103,547	–4.13
100	Albany–Schenectady–Troy, NY MSA	77,577	–4.75

TABLE 8A-2. Homeownership Rate Changes for African American Households Aged 35–44, 100 Largest Metropolitan Areas, 1990–2000

2000 rank	Metropolitan area	Total African American households aged 35–44	Rate change (percent)
1	McAllen–Edinburg–Mission, TX MSA	111	10.87
2	Stockton–Lodi, CA MSA	3,107	9.23
3	West Palm Beach–Boca Raton, FL MSA	13,352	7.45
4	Colorado Springs, CO MSA	3,645	7.21
5	Boise City, ID MSA	235	6.39
6	Washington–Baltimore, DC–MD–VA–WV CMSA	192,106	6.29
7	Atlanta, GA MSA	118,715	6.06
8	Austin–San Marcos, TX MSA	9,397	6.03
9	Lakeland–Winter Haven, FL MSA	5,195	5.46
10	New York–Northern New Jersey–Long Island, NY–NJ–CT–PA CMSA	305,273	4.68
11	Memphis, TN–AR–MS MSA	42,212	4.56
12	Raleigh–Durham–Chapel Hill, NC MSA	25,226	4.26
13	Fort Myers–Cape Coral, FL MSA	2,326	4.13
14	Albuquerque, NM MSA	1,723	4.02
15	Miami–Fort Lauderdale, FL CMSA	65,281	3.73
16	Sarasota–Bradenton, FL MSA	2,770	3.36
17	Las Vegas, NV–AZ MSA	11,749	3.33
10	Orlando, FL MSA	18,803	2.93
19	Springfield, MA MSA	3,261	2.89
20	Boston–Worcester–Lawrence, MA–NH–ME–CT CMSA	26,997	2.77
21	Greenville–Spartanburg–Anderson, SC MSA	14,272	2.55
22	Denver–Boulder–Greeley, CO CMSA	12,496	2.45
23	Hartford, CT MSA	10,073	2.40
24	New Orleans, LA MSA	40,620	2.34
25	Chattanooga, TN–GA MSA	5,568	2.28
26	Indianapolis, IN MSA	20,945	2.22
27	Charlotte–Gastonia–Rock Hill, NC–SC MSA	28,181	2.15
28	Chicago–Gary–Kenosha, IL–IN–WI CMSA	137,858	1.86
29	Daytona Beach, FL MSA	3,227	1.84
30	Birmingham, AL MSA	23,796	1.78
31	Dallas–Fort Worth, TX CMSA	72,405	1.56
32	Sacramento–Yolo, CA CMSA	12,391	1.49
33	Norfolk–Virginia Beach–Newport News, VA–NC MSA	42,800	1.25
34	Honolulu, HI MSA	2,174	1.23
35	San Francisco–Oakland–San Jose, CA CMSA	47,673	1.19
36	Portland–Salem, OR–WA CMSA	5,164	1.18
37	Fresno, CA MSA	3,475	1.10
38	Greensboro–Winston-Salem–High Point, NC MSA	22,314	1.09
39	St. Louis, MO–IL MSA	40,887	1.05
40	Columbus, OH MSA	19,857	0.93
41	Bakersfield, CA MSA	2,876	0.92
42	Allentown–Bethlehem–Easton, PA MSA	1,591	0.86
43	Phoenix–Mesa, AZ MSA	11,270	0.74
44	Nashville, TN MSA	17,611	0.71
45	Detroit–Ann Arbor–Flint, MI CMSA	92,689	0.69
46	Wichita, KS MSA	4,068	0.68
47	Mobile, AL MSA	12,132	0.26
48	Pensacola, FL MSA	5,580	0.05
49	Lansing–East Lansing, MI MSA	3,250	0.04

(*continued*)

TABLE 8A-2. Homeownership Rate Changes for African American Households Aged 35–44, 100 Largest Metropolitan Areas, 1990–2000 (*continued*)

2000 rank	Metropolitan area	Total African American households aged 35–44	Rate change (percent)
50	Cincinnati–Hamilton, OH–KY–IN CMSA	22,234	0.01
51	El Paso, TX MSA	2,022	–0.01
52	San Antonio, TX MSA	9,954	–0.04
53	Melbourne–Titusville–Palm Bay, FL MSA	3,292	–0.07
54	Tampa–St. Petersburg–Clearwater, FL MSA	21,149	–0.15
55	Canton–Massillon, OH MSA	2,274	–0.24
56	Salt Lake City–Ogden, UT MSA	1,336	–0.25
57	San Diego, CA MSA	15,599	–0.35
58	Buffalo–Niagara Falls, NY MSA	12,857	–0.43
59	Los Angeles–Riverside–Orange County, CA CMSA	115,790	–0.46
60	Jackson, MS MSA	16,747	–0.53
61	Grand Rapids–Muskegon–Holland, MI MSA	6,605	–0.62
62	Augusta–Aiken, GA–SC MSA	14,323	–0.64
63	Columbia, SC MSA	15,501	–0.78
64	Cleveland–Akron, OH CMSA	43,281	–0.86
65	Des Moines, IA MSA	1,596	–0.87
66	Minneapolis–St. Paul, MN–WI MSA	15,361	–0.89
67	Seattle–Tacoma–Bremerton, WA CMSA	18,410	–0.90
68	Kansas City, MO–KS MSA	21,069	–1.05
69	Kalamazoo–Battle Creek, MI MSA	3,490	–1.14
70	Jacksonville, FL MSA	21,326	–1.14
71	Providence–Fall River–Warwick, RI–MA MSA	4,088	–1.15
72	Modesto, CA MSA	1,044	–1.30
73	Pittsburgh, PA MSA	16,336	–1.53
74	Charleston–North Charleston, SC MSA	13,717	–1.66
75	Milwaukee–Racine, WI CMSA	21,598	–1.68
76	Houston–Galveston–Brazoria, TX CMSA	68,866	–1.84
77	Dayton–Springfield, OH MSA	11,894	–2.18
78	Richmond–Petersburg, VA MSA	27,414	–2.51
79	Baton Rouge, LA MSA	15,478	–2.57
80	Toledo, OH MSA	6,950	–2.67
81	Knoxville, TN MSA	3,600	–2.68
82	Lexington, KY MSA	4,411	–2.75
83	Omaha, NE–IA MSA	5,504	–2.82
84	Tucson, AZ MSA	2,425	–2.86
85	Fort Wayne, IN MSA	3,429	–3.02
86	Syracuse, NY MSA	4,053	–3.28
87	Philadelphia–Wilmington–Atlantic City, PA–NJ–DE–MD CMSA	102,666	–3.31
88	Youngstown–Warren, OH MSA	4,526	–3.71
89	Johnson City–Kingsport–Bristol, TN–VA MSA	916	–4.12
90	Harrisburg–Lebanon–Carlisle, PA MSA	4,299	–4.13
91	Lancaster, PA MSA	1,072	–4.39
92	Spokane, WA MSA	631	–5.08
93	Albany–Schenectady–Troy, NY MSA	5,031	–5.12
94	Louisville, KY–IN MSA	13,172	–5.25
95	Little Rock–North Little Rock, AR MSA	11,332	–5.43
96	Madison, WI MSA	1,624	–6.04
97	Oklahoma City, OK MSA	10,542	–6.11
98	Rochester, NY MSA	9,632	–7.06
99	Tulsa, OK MSA	6,488	–8.38
100	Scranton–Wilkes-Barre–Hazleton, PA MSA	555	–10.89

TABLE 8A-3. Homeownership Rate Changes for Latino Households
Aged 35–44, 100 Largest Metropolitan Areas, 1990–2000

2000 rank	Metropolitan area	Total Latino households aged 35–44	Rate change (percent)
1	Miami–Fort Lauderdale, FL CMSA	132,338	9.54
2	Chicago–Gary–Kenosha, IL–IN–WI CMSA	102,352	8.93
3	Bakersfield, CA MSA	16,904	7.78
4	Las Vegas, NV–AZ MSA	22,347	6.99
5	Springfield, MA MSA	5,505	6.71
6	Sarasota–Bradenton, FL MSA	2,474	6.42
7	Melbourne–Titusville–Palm Bay, FL MSA	1,831	6.27
8	Houston–Galveston–Brazoria, TX CMSA	101,407	6.24
9	Washington–Baltimore, DC–MD–VA–WV CMSA	37,235	5.36
10	West Palm Beach–Boca Raton, FL MSA	11,349	5.02
11	Lakeland–Winter Haven, FL MSA	2,994	5.01
12	Austin–San Marcos, TX MSA	24,250	4.76
13	Colorado Springs, CO MSA	4,448	4.32
14	Daytona Beach, FL MSA	2,105	4.21
15	McAllen–Edinburg–Mission, TX MSA	31,669	4.19
16	New York–Northern New Jersey–Long Island, NY–NJ–CT–PA CMSA	302,297	4.12
17	Modesto, CA MSA	9,751	3.51
18	Stockton–Lodi, CA MSA	11,320	3.40
19	El Paso, TX MSA	38,329	3.31
20	Fresno, CA MSA	26,666	3.05
21	Dallas–Fort Worth, TX CMSA	78,712	2.73
22	Oklahoma City, OK MSA	4,975	2.60
23	Hartford, CT MSA	8,689	2.58
24	Wichita, KS MSA	2,713	2.53
25	Norfolk–Virginia Beach–Newport News, VA–NC MSA	3,620	2.52
26	Denver–Boulder–Greeley, CO CMSA	33,403	2.36
27	Cleveland–Akron, OH CMSA	5,987	2.28
28	Boston–Worcester–Lawrence, MA–NH–ME–CT CMSA	28,045	2.19
29	Orlando, FL MSA	21,875	2.06
30	Los Angeles–Riverside–Orange County, CA CMSA	449,950	2.02
31	Boise City, ID MSA	2,416	2.00
32	Fort Myers–Cape Coral, FL MSA	2,885	1.15
33	Jacksonville, FL MSA	3,715	0.97
34	Lancaster, PA MSA	2,057	0.60
35	Philadelphia–Wilmington–Atlantic City, PA–NJ–DE–MD CMSA	25,323	0.59
36	Phoenix–Mesa, AZ MSA	52,390	0.50
37	San Antonio, TX MSA	59,921	0.45
38	Milwaukee–Racine, WI CMSA	7,397	0.43
39	Buffalo–Niagara Falls, NY MSA	2,619	0.29
40	Lansing–East Lansing, MI MSA	1,507	0.25
41	San Francisco–Oakland–San Jose, CA CMSA	92,689	0.10
42	Salt Lake City–Ogden, UT MSA	9,086	−0.04
43	Albuquerque, NM MSA	24,306	−0.12
44	Tucson, AZ MSA	17,831	−0.18
45	Grand Rapids–Muskegon–Holland, MI MSA	4,075	−0.20
46	Sacramento–Yolo, CA CMSA	20,148	−0.48
47	Kalamazoo–Battle Creek, MI MSA	969	−0.51
48	San Diego, CA MSA	51,644	−0.56
49	Allentown–Bethlehem–Easton, PA MSA	3,938	−0.81

(*continued*)

T A B L E 8 A - 3 . Homeownership Rate Changes for Latino Households Aged 35–44, 100 Largest Metropolitan Areas, 1990–2000 (*continued*)

2000 rank	Metropolitan area	Total Latino households aged 35–44	Rate change (percent)
50	Toledo, OH MSA	1,889	−0.98
51	Youngstown–Warren, OH MSA	730	−0.99
52	Spokane, WA MSA	724	−1.19
53	Detroit–Ann Arbor–Flint, MI CMSA	10,642	−1.59
54	St. Louis, MO–IL MSA	2,993	−1.82
55	Augusta–Aiken, GA–SC MSA	889	−1.84
56	New Orleans, LA MSA	4,722	−1.95
57	Pensacola, FL MSA	780	−2.06
58	Dayton–Springfield, OH MSA	850	−2.35
59	Tampa–St. Petersburg–Clearwater, FL MSA	19,212	−2.78
60	Chattanooga, TN–GA MSA	464	−2.97
61	Madison, WI MSA	904	−3.41
62	Providence–Fall River–Warwick, RI–MA MSA	7,064	−3.42
63	Honolulu, HI MSA	3,691	−3.55
64	Kansas City, MO–KS MSA	6,373	−3.84
65	Atlanta, GA MSA	16,528	−4.06
66	Minneapolis–St. Paul, MN–WI MSA	6,193	−4.39
67	Columbia, SC MSA	881	−4.40
68	Portland–Salem, OR–WA CMSA	11,708	−4.59
69	Pittsburgh, PA MSA	1,286	−4.65
70	Harrisburg–Lebanon–Carlisle, PA MSA	1,348	−4.68
71	Canton–Massillon, OH MSA	233	−4.96
72	Richmond–Petersburg, VA MSA	1,793	−5.08
73	Seattle–Tacoma–Bremerton, WA CMSA	13,395	−5.15
74	Tulsa, OK MSA	2,540	−5.22
75	Rochester, NY MSA	3,488	−5.29
76	Charleston–North Charleston, SC MSA	843	−5.78
77	Raleigh–Durham–Chapel Hill, NC MSA	4,135	−6.14
78	Birmingham, AL MSA	1,034	−6.81
79	Fort Wayne, IN MSA	1,084	−6.87
80	Des Moines, IA MSA	1,211	−7.20
81	Albany–Schenectady–Troy, NY MSA	1,721	−7.55
82	Knoxville, TN MSA	586	−7.68
83	Cincinnati–Hamilton, OH–KY–IN CMSA	1,667	−7.84
84	Omaha, NE–IA MSA	2,632	−8.03
85	Jackson, MS MSA	276	−8.31
86	Mobile, AL MSA	567	−8.31
87	Syracuse, NY MSA	969	−8.57
88	Memphis, TN–AR–MS MSA	1,684	−8.72
89	Columbus, OH MSA	1,921	−9.25
90	Greenville–Spartanburg–Anderson, SC MSA	1,824	−9.84
91	Nashville, TN MSA	2,550	−10.56
92	Baton Rouge, LA MSA	761	−11.12
93	Scranton–Wilkes-Barre–Hazleton, PA MSA	455	−11.54
94	Charlotte–Gastonia–Rock Hill, NC–SC MSA	4,679	−15.27
95	Indianapolis, IN MSA	2,734	−15.44
96	Little Rock–North Little Rock, AR MSA	847	−17.61
97	Johnson City–Kingsport–Bristol, TN–VA MSA	372	−18.37
98	Greensboro–Winston-Salem–High Point, NC MSA	3,498	−18.79
99	Louisville, KY–IN MSA	1,290	−18.92
100	Lexington, KY MSA	682	−19.17

REFERENCES

Myers, Dowell. 2001. *Advances in Homeownership across the States and Generations: Continued Gains for the Elderly and Stagnation among the Young.* Fannie Mae Foundation Census Note 08, October. Washington: Fannie Mae Foundation.

Myers, Dowell, and Angela James. 2002. *Overlap: A User Guide to Race and Hispanic Origin in Census 2000.* Public Research Report No. 2001–01 (rev.), Race Contours Project. Population Dynamics Research Group, School of Policy, Planning and Development, University of Southern California. Accessed November 3, 2004, at www.usc.edu/schools/sppd/research/census2000/race_census/index.htm.

Simmons, Patrick A. 2001a. "A Coast-to-Coast Expansion: Geographic Patterns of U.S. Homeownership Gains during the 1990s." Census Note 05, June. Washington: Fannie Mae Foundation.

Simmons, Patrick A. 2001b. "Changes in Minority Homeownership during the 1990s." Census Note 07, September. Washington: Fannie Mae Foundation.

9

Rising Affordability Problems among Homeowners

PATRICK A. SIMMONS

During the 1990s the U.S. homeownership rate increased more than at any time since the 1950s. Growth in the number of homeowners was the second largest on record, exceeded only by the gain registered during the 1970s.[1] Minorities shared in this boom, supported by numerous public and private efforts to expand homeownership opportunities for historically under-served population groups.[2]

Recent studies, however, have uncovered a troubling aspect of the 1990s homeownership boom: rapid growth in the number of homeowners facing severe affordability problems. According to a recent study by the Harvard Joint Center for Housing Studies (2003), the total number of homeowners spending more than 50 percent of their income on housing rose by 27 percent between 1997 and 2001. Working families saw an even more pronounced increase. According to Lipman, the number of working families who owned

Adapted from Patrick Simmons, *Rising Affordability Problems among Homeowners: 1990s Homeownership Boom Leaves a Hangover of Owners with Severe Cost Burdens* (Census Note 13, June 2004). ©2004 Fannie Mae Foundation, Washington, D.C.; and Patrick Simmons. *A Tale of Two Cities: Growing Affordability Problems amidst Rising Homeownership for Urban Minorities* (Census Note 14, June 2004). ©2004 Fannie Mae Foundation, Washington, D.C. Used with permission.

The author thanks Amanda Elk for her research assistance. He also thanks Jack Goodman of Hartrey Advisors, Kathryn Pettit of the Urban Institute, and Amy Bogdon and Shelia Maith of the Fannie Mae Foundation for invaluable comments on earlier drafts.

1. Simmons (2001a).
2. Myers and Painter, chapter 8, this volume; Turner and others (2002); Simmons (2001b); Listokin and others (2000).

their homes and paid more than half their incomes for housing rose by 65 percent, or nearly 900,000 households, during 1997–2001.[3]

Rising homeownership affordability problems suggest that millions of homeowners are struggling to sustain homeownership. Loss of the home can impair the creditworthiness and wealth of the affected family and hurt financial institutions and neighborhoods. Even if affordability problems do not lead to home loss, high housing costs can strain the family budget and squeeze expenditures on health care, education, and food.

This chapter uses decennial census data to examine recent trends in severe homeownership affordability problems. Unlike earlier studies that analyze only national data, this chapter examines trends for states and large cities as well. It also describes the characteristics of homeowners with affordability problems and specifically examines changes between 1990 and 2000 in homeownership rates and severe owner cost burdens among blacks and Latinos living in the nation's twenty-five largest cities. The chapter concludes by briefly discussing the policy implications of rapid increases in homeownership affordability problems.

METHODOLOGY

Housing affordability can be defined and measured in a number of ways. This section explains the approach adopted in this chapter.

Measuring Homeownership Affordability

There are two basic types of homeownership affordability indicators. One type quantifies the financial ability of households to purchase homes given typical household income levels and prevailing house prices, interest rates, and mortgage terms. This class of affordability measures includes such well-known indicators as the National Association of Realtors' Housing Affordability Indices and the National Association of Home Builders' Housing Opportunity Index.

The second principal type of housing affordability indicator is the housing cost-to-income ratio. The housing cost-to-income ratio, which is used in this study, compares a household's out-of-pocket housing expenditures with its income.

3. Lipman (2002) defines "working families" as households that meet all of the following criteria: 1) total earnings from wages and salaries exceeding the full-time minimum-wage equivalent; 2) wages and salaries representing more than half of household income; and 3) total household income less than 120 percent of the U.S. Department of Housing and Urban Development (HUD)–adjusted area median family income.

As noted by Goodman, out-of-pocket expenditures are a poor measure of the true economic costs of owner-occupancy.[4] More comprehensive measures of the "user costs" of owned housing would capture not only cash outlays but also noncash costs, such as depreciation, unrealized capital gain, tax benefits, and the opportunity cost of home equity.

Selecting a Standard for Identifying Excessive Housing Cost-to-Income Ratios

Standards used to identify households with excessive housing cost-to-income ratios are somewhat arbitrary and have changed over time. Originally, housing costs consuming more than 25 percent of household income were deemed excessive. This standard derived from the adage "a month's rent should not exceed a week's pay."[5] For federal low-income rental housing assistance programs, this standard of affordability was in place until 1982, at which time it was increased to 30 percent.[6] More recently federal low-income housing policy has focused on helping renters who face severe housing cost burdens, defined as housing costs of at least 50 percent of income.

This chapter adopts the 50 percent standard. Homeowners with housing costs of at least 50 percent of income are labeled "severely cost-burdened" or as having a "severe affordability problem." In addition to identifying homeowners with more serious affordability challenges, adoption of this higher standard removes from the analysis most upper-income owners, for whom higher housing costs are likely to be more manageable.[7] On the other hand, it is important to note that a housing cost-to-income ratio of less than 50 percent can represent a problem for some homeowners with modest incomes.

Cost-to-Income Data

This chapter uses 1990 and 2000 Census Summary File 3 and 4 data to identify homeowners spending at least half their incomes on housing. The data files show selected monthly owner costs as a percent of household income. The

---

4. Goodman (2003).

5. Baer (1976).

6. Mitchell (1985).

7. Census 2000 Summary File 3 tables on housing cost-to-income ratios by household income have a top cost-burden category of 35 percent and thus do not permit analysis of the income distribution of homeowners with severe housing cost burdens. According to tabulations of the 2001 American Housing Survey by the Harvard Joint Center for Housing Studies (2003), however, 84 percent of all homeowners who experience severe housing cost burdens have incomes in the bottom two quintiles of the income distribution (in other words, annual incomes below $32,000).

selected owner-cost component consists of the sum of payments for mortgages, deeds of trust, contracts to purchase, or similar debts on the property; real estate taxes; fire, hazard, and flood insurance on the property; utilities; and fuels. Where applicable, selected monthly owner costs also include monthly condominium fees. In all estimates of severe cost burdens, owners for whom housing cost-to-income was not computed are excluded from the calculations.

Household income is the total pretax income of the householder and all other individuals in the household who are at least fifteen years old. Total income includes wages or salary income; net self-employment income; interest, dividends, or net rental or royalty income or income from estates and trusts; Social Security or railroad retirement income; Supplemental Security Income; public assistance or welfare payments; retirement, survivor, or disability pensions; and all other income.

In decennial census summary data files, housing cost-to-income ratios are tabulated only for "specified" owner-occupied housing units. Specified owner-occupied units include single-family houses on less than ten acres that do not have a business or medical office on the property. Mobile homes, houses with a business or medical office, houses on ten or more acres, and housing units in multi-unit buildings are excluded from this category. Specified units account for only about 80 percent of the nation's owner-occupied units. Although this data constraint should not significantly affect the trends outlined in the chapter, it does mean that the total number of households experiencing severe affordability problems are understated. For a few cities, including Boston, New York, and Chicago, the results may significantly understate the number of severely cost-burdened households and thus should be interpreted with caution. Tables 9A-1 and 9A-2 provide information on specified units' share of the total owner-occupied stock for all states and the large cities included in the analysis.

Summary tape files from the 1990 Census do not include tables showing households with housing cost-to-income ratios of 50 percent or more. The 50 percent cost-to-income category, however, is provided in the printed *Detailed Housing Characteristics* books from the 1990 Census.[8] Because of the challenges associated with converting data from the 1990 Census books to electronic format, the city, rather than the metropolitan area, was selected as the smallest geographic unit of analysis for this chapter, although the latter geographic unit corresponds more closely to an actual housing market.[9]

8. U.S. Bureau of the Census (1993).
9. As used here "city" includes incorporated places, consolidated cities, and Census designated places. It does not refer to the entire metropolitan area of which the cities are part.

Selection of the metropolitan area would have substantially complicated the data conversion process by requiring the aggregation of county-level data for metropolitan areas that were not consistently defined across censuses.

Because at least part of the data used to calculate housing cost-to-income ratios in both 1990 and 2000 were collected on a sample basis, all estimates of severe cost burdens presented here are subject to sampling error.

Race-Ethnicity Data

Census 2000 ushered in significant changes in the collection of data on race.[10] In the most important change, the census questionnaire instructed respondents for the first time to report as many race categories as they felt applied. This chapter presents data only for those persons who reported exclusively in the black, Asian, Pacific Islander, American Indian, Alaska Native, or white racial categories in 2000. All race and Hispanic origin data in this chapter refer to the characteristics of the householder, which in most cases is the person or one of the people in whose name the home is owned, being bought, or rented.

FINDINGS

Census 2000 points to growing affordability problems for homeowners during the 1990s, especially racial and ethnic minorities in cities.

Rise in Severe Affordability Problems Outpaced Homeownership Gains Nationally

The 1990s was one of the best decades for homeownership in American history. The national homeownership rate increased from 64.2 to 66.2 percent, the largest decadal increase since the 1950s.

Unfortunately, some of last decade's strong homeownership growth appears to have come at the expense of rapidly escalating affordability problems. Between 1990 and 2000, the number of homeowners with severe affordability problems rose from 2.8 million to 4.2 million, an increase of 52 percent. During the same period, the total number of homeowners increased by only about 20 percent.

---

10. The decennial census collects information separately on race and Hispanic origin, which for federal statistical purposes are considered to be distinct characteristics of an individual. Thus a person of Hispanic origin may be of any race and a person of a given race may or may not be of Hispanic origin.

Despite rapid growth in the number of severely cost-burdened home-owners during the 1990s, the overall percentage of homeowners experiencing a severe affordability problem remains fairly low. In 2000 7.7 percent of all homeowners experienced severe housing cost burdens, up from 6.1 percent ten years earlier. About 19 percent of renters paid at least half their incomes for housing in 2000.[11]

Census data show that increases in severe homeownership affordability problems were nearly universal during the 1990s: every state and all but two of the nation's fifty largest cities registered a statistically significant increase in the number of homeowners with severe cost burdens. In twenty-seven states and nineteen large cities, severely cost-burdened homeowners grew by at least 50 percent during the 1990s. And in six states (Delaware, Hawaii, Idaho, Nevada, Utah, and Washington), the number of homeowners with severe housing cost burdens more than doubled (table 9A-1). Four of the nation's largest cities (Charlotte, Honolulu, Las Vegas, and Portland, OR) saw a similarly large increase (table 9A-2). In Las Vegas, the number of severely cost-burdened homeowners almost tripled, from just over 3,000 in 1990 to about 9,000 ten years later.

Given the widespread growth in homeownership during the 1990s, it is not surprising that the ranks of severely cost-burdened homeowners also grew.[12] In most states and cities, however, the rate of growth in severe home-ownership affordability problems outstripped the pace of increase in the total number of homeowners. As a result, between 1990 and 2000, the proportion of homeowners experiencing severe affordability problems increased in forty-seven of the fifty states and in forty-three of the nation's fifty largest cities (figure 9-1).

Nationally, less than 8 percent of homeowners experience severe housing affordability problems, but in some states and cities the proportion is sub-stantially higher (tables 9A-1 and 9A-2). In Miami, Los Angeles, and New York, between 15 and 20 percent of homeowners have severe housing cost burdens. Among the states, California and Hawaii have the highest inci-dence of homeownership affordability problems: 11.5 and 10.8 percent, respectively.

---

11. Housing cost-to-income ratios are not strictly comparable for renters and owners. Whereas data on monthly rental and utility payments represent the true economic costs of housing for renters, monthly cash outlays are a poor measure of the economic cost of housing for owners. See Goodman (2003).

12. Simmons (2001a).

FIGURE 9-1. Share of Homeowners with Severe Housing Cost Burdens, States and Top Fifty Cities, 1990 and 2000[a]

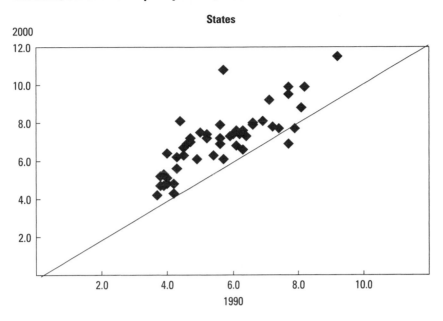

States

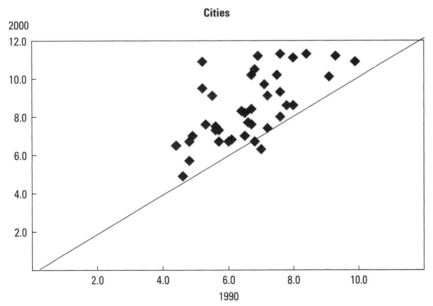

Cities

Source: Author's analysis of U.S. Census Bureau data.

a. Each data point in the graphs represents a single state or city. For a given state or city, the percent of all homeowners experiencing severe housing cost burdens in 1990 is shown on the x-axis and the corresponding statistic for 2000 is shown on the y-axis. Data points lying above the diagonal represent states or cities in which the proportion of owners with severe affordability problems increased during the 1990s.

FIGURE 9-2. Percent Change in Owners and Owners with Severe Cost Burdens, by Race/Ethnicity, Twenty Five Largest Cities, 1990–2000

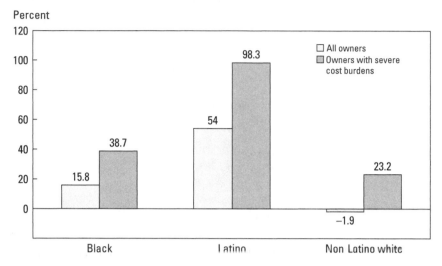

Source: Author's analysis of U.S. Census Bureau data.

Ranks of Minority Homeowners with Severe Cost Burdens Grew Substantially

Urban minorities made impressive homeownership gains during the 1990s. Between 1990 and 2000 the homeownership rates of blacks and Latinos living in the twenty-five largest cities rose by 2.9 and 3.7 percentage points, respectively, exceeding the 2.7 point gain for non-Hispanic whites.[13]

Like homeowners nationwide, however, urban minority homeowners also experienced increased affordability problems. Whereas the number of black homeowners in the nation's twenty-five largest cities expanded by 16 percent last decade, the ranks of black homeowners paying at least half of their incomes for housing grew by 39 percent (figure 9-2). An impressive 54 percent gain in the number of Latino homeowners was overshadowed by a 98 percent jump in Latino homeowners with severe affordability problems. Although the total number of white homeowners fell slightly in major urban centers, the number of severely cost-burdened whites grew by more than 20 percent between 1990 and 2000. Given substantial increases in unemploy-

13. In contrast nationwide homeownership rate gains for blacks (2.9 percentage points) and Latinos (3.3 percentage points) fell just shy of the increase experienced by non-Latino whites (3.4 percentage points).

ment, fuel and utility costs, and home prices since Census 2000, the pace of growth in severe homeowner affordability problems might even have accelerated during the last four years.

Urban minorities in many individual cities experienced growth in severe affordability problems that far outstripped their overall homeownership growth (tables 9A-3 and 9A-4). In Philadelphia, the total number of Latino homeowners increased by 60 percent last decade, but Latino homeowners with severe affordability problems expanded by 167 percent. In total, five cities (Chicago, Los Angeles, New York, Philadelphia, and Phoenix) saw the ranks of severely cost-burdened Latino homeowners grow by 100 percent or more and by at least 2,000 households. Although Memphis saw 40 percent growth in black homeownership, it also registered a 71 percent increase in the number of black owners paying at least half of their incomes for housing. In Washington, D.C., the total number of black homeowners was stable last decade, but black owners with severe affordability problems shot up by more than half. In New York City, Chicago, Memphis, Washington, and Baltimore, the number of severely cost-burdened black owners increased by about 2,000 or more, and the pace of growth was roughly 50 percent or higher during the 1990s.

As of 2000 one in seven (14.1 percent) black homeowners living in the twenty-five largest cities spent at least half of their incomes on housing, and one in eight (12.5 percent) Latino owners faced the same predicament. Both of these proportions were up by more than 2 percentage points from 1990.[14] Overall, the incidence of severe owner cost burdens in 2000 was slightly greater in large cities than in the entire nation and substantially higher for blacks and Latinos than for whites (figure 9-3).

Between 1990 and 2000, most of the nation's largest cities saw an increase in the proportion of owners experiencing severe cost burdens. The proportion of black homeowners experiencing severe affordability problems increased by at least a percentage point in sixteen of the twenty-five largest cities (table 9A-3). Increases of at least a percentage point among Latino owners also occurred in sixteen of the twenty-five cities (table 9A-4).

A couple of major cities managed to buck the trend of rising rates of owner affordability problems. Detroit, which has the second-largest number of black homeowners among the twenty-five largest cities, experienced a slight decline (−0.3 percentage points) between 1990 and 2000 in the proportion of

---

14. Despite the growing incidence of severe affordability problems among homeowners, they are still substantially less likely than renters to experience severe cost burdens. In 2000 24 percent of black renters and 22 percent of Latino renters in the twenty-five largest cities paid at least half of their incomes for housing.

FIGURE 9-3. Share of Homeowners with Severe Cost Burdens, by Race/Ethnicity, United States versus Twenty Five Largest Cities, 2000

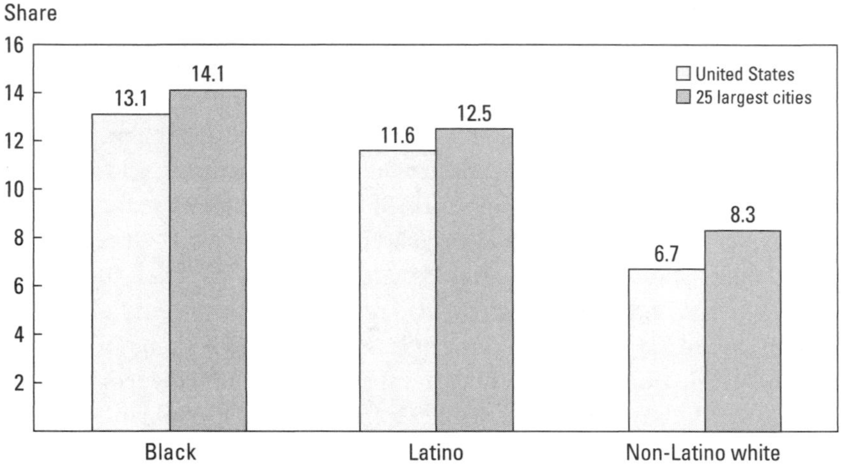

Source: Author's analysis of U.S. Census Bureau data.

black homeowners with severe cost burdens. San Antonio, which led the twenty-five cities in the number of Latino homeowners, experienced a small percentage point decline (0.4) in the proportion of Latino owners experiencing severe cost burdens.

In 2000 Los Angeles led large cities in the likelihood of severe affordability problems for minority homeowners, with one-fifth of both black and Latino owners paying at least half of their incomes for housing. Other cities where substantial proportions of minority owners experienced severe affordability problems include New York City (20 percent of Latinos and 19 percent of blacks), Philadelphia (19 percent of Latinos), and Seattle (17 percent of blacks).

Most Cost-Burdened Homeowners Are Lower-Income; Minorities Make Up Disproportionate Shares

Few tables in the Census 2000 summary files provide information on the attributes of homeowners with housing cost burdens of at least 50 percent. Several tables, however, do cover households with cost burdens of 35 percent or more. Compared with all households, this group tends to have substantially lower incomes and is disproportionately minority. Indeed, among homeowners paying at least 35 percent of their incomes for housing, 27 percent are minorities (compared with 18 percent of all homeowners) and

T A B L E 9 - 1 . Characteristics of Homeowners with Housing Cost Burdens, 2000[a]

Percent of cost-burdened homeowners

Characteristic	Cost-to-income ratio 35 percent or greater	Cost-to-income ratio 50 percent or greater[b]	Specified owner-occupied units[c]
Age of householder			
Under 35	13.9	n.a.	12.5
35 to 64	60.2	n.a.	63.0
65 or older	25.9	n.a.	24.5
Household income			
Under $50,000	84.0	n.a.	44.5
$50,000 to $100,000	14.0	n.a.	37.5
More than $100,000	2.0	n.a.	18.0
Mortgage status			
With mortgage	84.9	83.7	70.0
Without mortgage	15.1	16.3	30.0
Race or Hispanic origin of householder			
White alone, not Hispanic	73.2	71.2	81.7
Minority[d]	26.8	28.8	18.3
Black or African American alone	12.3	13.9	8.2
Asian or Pacific Islander alone	3.7	3.7	2.6
American Indian or Alaska Native alone	0.6	0.7	0.5
Hispanic	8.9	9.1	6.0

Source: Author's analysis of U.S. Census Bureau data.

a. Estimates are based on a sample and may vary from actual values due to sampling variability and other factors.

b. The highest cost-to-income category for tables on age and income in Census 2000 Summary File 3 is 35 percent or more.

c. See text for definition of "specified" owner-occupied units.

d. All persons except white alone, non-Hispanics. Because race and Hispanic origin are two distinct characteristics, individuals may be counted in both the Hispanic and one of the minority racial categories.

84 percent have incomes of less than $50,000 (compared with 45 percent of all homeowners) (table 9-1).

Census data also give us a glimpse of the racial and ethnic characteristics of homeowners with severe cost burdens. As shown in the bottom section of table 9-1, 29 percent of the homeowners spending more than 50 percent of their income on housing are minorities.

CONCLUSION

Rapid and widespread growth of severely cost-burdened homeowners should raise a red flag. Having recently focused much attention on expanding access to owner occupancy, industry leaders and government policymakers might now consider additional emphasis on policies and programs that ensure the sustainability of homeownership. Such efforts could include early detection and remediation of mortgage repayment difficulties and homeowner training programs that address sustainability issues, such as budgeting and home maintenance and repairs.[15] Additional efforts to eliminate predatory lending practices might also help to curtail future growth in severe homeowner affordability problems.

Homeownership sustainability initiatives focusing on low- to moderate-income households and minority homeowners could help preserve the homeownership gains achieved by these groups during the 1990s.[16] In addition, homeownership sustainability initiatives targeted to cities and states that have relatively high proportions of financially distressed homeowners—or that have seen rapid growth in owners with severe cost burdens—could have notable effects. Without such efforts, the long-term benefits of homeownership might slip away from the millions of households barely holding on to the American Dream.

TABLE 9A-1. **Homeowners with Severe Housing Cost Burdens, by State, 1990–2000[a]**

	Number of homeowners with severe housing cost burdens				Percent of all homeowners with severe housing cost burdens		1990–2000 change (percentage points)	Specified units as a percent of all owner-occupied units
			1990–2000 change					
Area	1990	2000	Number	Percent	1990	2000		
United States	2,758,803	4,194,139	1,435,336	52.0	6.1	7.7	1.6	79.1
Alabama	45,688	67,379	21,691	47.5	6.0	7.4	1.4	73.0
Alaska	4,868	7,938	3,070	63.1	6.3	7.6	1.3	76.3
Arizona	49,829	79,124	29,295	58.8	7.4	7.7	0.3	79.8
Arkansas	26,927	33,259	6,332	23.5	6.3	6.6	0.3	71.0
California	436,999	630,382	193,383	44.3	9.2	11.5	2.3	84.4
Colorado	39,811	66,393	26,582	66.8	6.2	7.4	1.2	80.9
Connecticut	44,895	58,963	14,068	31.3	6.9	8.1	1.2	83.7
Delaware	5,569	11,302	5,733	102.9	4.0	6.4	2.4	82.1
Florida	183,924	303,856	119,932	65.2	7.7	9.5	1.8	73.0
Georgia	70,209	119,479	49,270	70.2	6.1	7.6	1.4	78.7
Hawaii	8,419	18,609	10,190	121.0	5.7	10.8	5.0	76.3
Idaho	7,957	16,866	8,909	112.0	4.5	6.7	2.2	75.0
Illinois	98,977	170,610	71,633	72.4	4.7	7.0	2.2	80.0
Indiana	43,426	71,564	28,138	64.8	3.8	5.2	1.4	82.6
Iowa	21,193	28,037	6,844	32.3	3.7	4.2	0.5	80.0
Kansas	21,333	27,930	6,597	30.9	4.2	4.8	0.6	81.0
Kentucky	32,363	48,962	16,599	51.3	4.9	6.1	1.3	71.7
Louisiana	58,287	65,759	7,472	12.8	7.9	7.7	−0.2	76.9

(continued)

15. Wiranski (2003).
16. Myers and Painter (chapter 8, this volume); Simmons (2001b); Belsky and Duda (2002).

TABLE 9A-1. **Homeowners with Severe Housing Cost Burdens, by State, 1990–2000[a]** (*continued*)

Area	Number of homeowners with severe housing cost burdens				Percent of all homeowners with severe housing cost burdens		1990–2000 change (percentage points)	Specified units as a percent of all owner-occupied units
	1990	2000	Number	Percent	1990	2000		
Maine	12,016	17,395	5,379	44.8	5.6	6.9	1.3	68.7
Maryland	46,130	84,531	38,401	83.2	4.7	7.2	2.5	87.9
Massachusetts	72,579	91,735	19,156	26.4	7.2	7.8	0.6	78.8
Michigan	104,042	140,949	36,907	35.5	5.4	6.3	0.9	81.2
Minnesota	35,418	52,722	17,304	48.9	3.9	4.7	0.8	79.1
Mississippi	35,764	45,817	10,053	28.1	8.1	8.8	0.7	70.3
Missouri	43,235	65,553	22,318	51.6	4.3	5.6	1.3	77.1
Montana	6,634	12,256	5,622	84.7	5.0	7.5	2.4	66.8
Nebraska	12,101	17,472	5,371	44.4	3.8	4.7	0.9	82.5
Nevada	13,191	32,983	19,792	150.0	7.1	9.2	2.0	79.5
New Hampshire	15,278	17,130	1,852	12.1	7.7	6.9	−0.8	75.4
New Jersey	121,816	166,699	44,883	36.8	8.2	9.9	1.6	84.6
New Mexico	17,191	27,007	9,816	57.1	6.6	8.0	1.5	71.6
New York	185,148	265,127	79,979	43.2	7.7	9.9	2.2	71.9
North Carolina	63,990	115,924	51,934	81.2	5.2	7.2	2.0	74.4
North Dakota	4,332	5,197	865	20.0	4.2	4.3	0.1	71.3
Ohio	97,934	160,437	62,503	63.8	4.3	6.2	1.9	85.0
Oklahoma	35,241	42,181	6,940	19.7	5.7	6.1	0.4	76.2
Oregon	28,661	51,375	22,714	79.3	5.6	7.9	2.3	76.3
Pennsylvania	134,429	211,391	76,962	57.3	5.2	7.4	2.2	84.8
Rhode Island	11,808	15,937	4,129	35.0	6.6	7.9	1.3	82.5
South Carolina	36,749	56,665	19,916	54.2	5.9	7.3	1.4	70.8
South Dakota	4,550	6,500	1,950	42.9	4.0	4.8	0.8	69.5
Tennessee	52,554	85,646	33,092	63.0	5.6	7.2	1.6	77.2
Texas	181,093	259,168	78,075	43.1	6.1	6.8	0.7	81.6
Utah	13,995	29,379	15,384	109.9	4.6	6.9	2.3	85.2
Vermont	5,689	7,675	1,986	34.9	6.4	7.3	0.9	62.4
Virginia	65,158	94,998	29,840	45.8	5.4	6.3	0.9	82.2
Washington	39,874	93,185	53,311	133.7	4.4	8.1	3.7	78.9
West Virginia	15,797	24,573	8,776	55.6	4.5	6.3	1.8	71.0
Wisconsin	37,207	57,479	20,272	54.5	4.0	5.1	1.1	78.7
Wyoming	3,048	4,992	1,944	63.8	3.9	5.3	1.4	70.5

Source: Author's analysis of U.S. Census Bureau data.

a. A household has a "severe housing cost burden" if it pays at least 50 percent of its income for housing. Data on severely cost-burdened owners are for specified owner-occupied units only. Because specified units are a subset of all owner-occupied units, point-in-time estimates of the number of homeowners experiencing severe affordability problems are understated. Restriction of the data to specified units has an unknown effect on rates of severe owner cost burdens. Underestimates of the magnitude of affordability problems, and potential distortions in trends over time, may be particularly problematic in states where specified units make up a small share of the overall owner stock. Estimates are based on a sample and may vary from actual values due to sampling variability and other factors.

TABLE 9A-2. **Homeowners with Severe Housing Cost Burdens, by City, 1990–2000**[a]

Area	Number of homeowners with severe housing cost burdens		1990–2000 change		Percent of all homeowners with severe housing cost burdens		1990–2000 change (percentage points)	Specified units as a percent of all owner-occupied units
	1990	2000	Number	Percent	1990	2000		
United States	2,758,803	4,194,139	1,435,336	52.0	6.1	7.7	1.6	79.1
Albuquerque	4,927	8,094	3,167	64.3	6.4	8.3	1.9	88.9
Atlanta	6,479	7,906	1,427	22.0	11.5	13.1	1.6	83.3
Austin	4,450	7,316	2,866	64.4	6.5	7.0	0.6	88.0
Baltimore	8,273	12,850	4,577	55.3	6.9	11.2	4.3	89.8
Boston	2,815	3,279	464	16.5	9.9	10.9	1.0	39.5
Charlotte	4,080	8,510	4,430	108.6	5.3	7.6	2.4	90.6
Chicago	18,413	29,545	11,132	60.5	7.6	11.3	3.8	56.8
Cleveland	6,024	9,032	3,008	49.9	8.1	12.2	4.1	81.4
Colorado Springs	3,059	5,103	2,044	66.8	5.7	6.7	1.0	89.0
Columbus	5,176	8,987	3,811	73.6	4.8	6.7	2.0	90.5
Dallas	11,335	15,604	4,269	37.7	7.2	9.1	1.9	88.9
Denver	6,719	9,650	2,931	43.6	7.6	9.3	1.7	83.1
Detroit	18,753	19,540	787	4.2	11.1	12.2	1.2	88.9
El Paso	5,390	8,237	2,847	52.8	6.5	8.2	1.7	91.3
Fort Worth	5,605	7,641	2,036	36.3	6.7	7.6	1.0	93.1
Fresno	3,529	6,748	3,219	91.2	6.8	10.5	3.7	91.7
Honolulu	2,029	4,360	2,331	114.9	5.2	10.9	5.7	61.0
Houston	19,123	24,963	5,840	30.5	7.8	8.6	0.7	89.9
Indianapolis	6,561	11,110	4,549	69.3	4.4	6.5	2.1	92.0
Jacksonville	8,349	11,955	3,606	43.2	6.6	7.7	1.0	87.7
Kansas City	5,096	7,193	2,097	41.1	5.6	7.5	1.8	91.8
Las Vegas	3,146	9,019	5,873	186.7	7.1	9.7	2.6	89.8
Long Beach	4,205	6,455	2,250	53.5	8.1	12.1	4.0	80.5
Los Angeles	49,401	68,057	18,656	37.8	12.4	16.7	4.3	83.9
Memphis	9,323	14,191	4,868	52.2	8.0	11.1	3.0	93.4

(*continued*)

TABLE 9A-2. **Homeowners with Severe Housing Cost Burdens, by City, 1990–2000**[a] (*continued*)

| Area | Number of homeowners with severe housing cost burdens | | | | Percent of all homeowners with severe housing cost burdens | | | Specified units as a percent of all owner-occupied units |
| | 1990 | 2000 | 1990–2000 change | | 1990 | 2000 | 1990–2000 change (percentage points) | |
			Number	Percent				
Mesa	3,448	4,827	1,379	40.0	7.0	6.3	−0.7	79.0
Miami	4,509	6,754	2,245	49.8	14.2	20.2	6.1	72.2
Milwaukee	4,537	5,921	1,384	30.5	5.6	7.3	1.7	78.2
Minneapolis	3,231	4,783	1,552	48.0	4.9	7.0	2.1	82.7
Nashville-Davidson	5,040	7,883	2,843	56.4	5.7	7.3	1.6	88.0
New Orleans	8,550	8,805	255	3.0	12.5	12.1	−0.4	85.0
New York City	36,697	59,028	22,331	60.9	11.0	15.3	4.3	42.9
Oakland	5,823	7,352	1,529	26.3	11.3	14.1	2.7	84.8
Oklahoma City	5,783	7,292	1,509	26.1	6.1	6.8	0.7	89.4
Omaha	3,461	4,862	1,401	40.5	4.8	5.7	0.9	92.7
Philadelphia	27,894	34,788	6,894	24.7	8.4	11.3	2.9	90.2
Phoenix	15,220	21,292	6,072	39.9	8.0	8.6	0.6	88.5
Portland	4,996	10,174	5,178	103.6	5.5	9.1	3.6	90.0
Sacramento	4,525	7,198	2,673	59.1	6.7	10.2	3.5	91.7
San Antonio	10,913	14,330	3,417	31.3	6.8	6.7	−0.1	92.2
San Diego	15,203	20,979	5,776	38.0	9.3	11.2	2.0	84.2
San Francisco	7,676	9,737	2,061	26.8	10.3	12.3	2.1	68.9
San Jose	11,855	14,764	2,909	24.5	9.1	10.1	1.0	85.9
Seattle	5,083	9,697	4,614	90.8	5.2	9.5	4.3	82.1
St. Louis	3,840	4,573	733	19.1	6.7	8.4	1.8	80.0
Tucson	5,130	6,837	1,707	33.3	7.6	8.0	0.5	83.4
Tulsa	4,751	5,598	847	17.8	6.0	6.7	0.7	91.8
Virginia Beach	5,495	6,718	1,223	22.3	7.2	7.4	0.1	90.6
Washington, D.C.	5,477	7,649	2,172	39.7	7.5	10.2	2.7	75.4
Wichita	2,966	3,751	785	26.5	4.6	4.9	0.3	89.3

Source: Author's analysis of U.S. Census Bureau data.

a. See note to table 9A-1.

TABLE 9A-3. All and Severely Cost-Burdened African American Homeowners, Twenty-Five Largest Cities, 1990–2000[a]

Area	All homeowners				Severely cost-burdened owners				Homeownership rate			Percent severely cost-burdened owners			Specified units as a percent of all owner-occupied units
	1990	2000	1990–2000 change Number	Percent	1990	2000	1990–2000 change Number	Percent	1990	2000	1990–2000 change (percentage points)	1990	2000	1990–2000 change (percentage points)	
United States	4,327,265	5,577,734	1,250,469	28.9	401,007	582,745	181,738	45.3	43.4	46.3	2.9	11.6	13.1	1.5	81.5
Austin	7,205	9,038	1,833	25.4	715	917	202	28.3	34.3	36.8	2.5	11.0	11.1	0.1	92.9
Baltimore	55,456	68,104	12,648	22.8	4,513	7,894	3,381	74.9	37.7	44.6	6.9	9.0	12.9	3.9	91.4
Boston	11,565	14,628	3,063	26.5	626	1,012	386	61.7	23.1	28.0	5.0	14.2	16.6	2.4	42.3
Charlotte	16,579	27,517	10,938	66.0	1,327	3,189	1,862	140.3	37.7	42.0	4.3	8.7	12.5	3.8	93.5
Chicago	122,426	134,378	11,952	9.8	9,028	13,415	4,387	48.6	33.8	37.0	3.1	11.7	15.3	3.7	66.3
Columbus	20,169	27,101	6,932	34.4	1,597	2,559	962	60.2	38.5	39.7	1.1	8.6	10.4	1.8	91.9
Dallas	37,922	42,446	4,524	11.9	3,846	4,825	979	25.5	36.9	36.3	-0.6	11.2	12.5	1.3	93.0
Detroit	132,920	144,659	11,739	8.8	14,639	15,978	1,339	9.1	49.0	53.4	4.4	13.1	12.7	-0.3	89.2
El Paso	2,504	3,053	549	21.9	146	266	120	82.2	39.8	46.1	6.3	6.2	9.3	3.1	94.5
Fort Worth	15,639	18,755	3,116	19.9	1,798	2,268	470	26.1	47.1	47.5	0.4	12.5	13.1	0.6	95.5
Houston	64,326	72,046	7,720	12.0	7,609	8,236	627	8.2	39.8	39.1	-0.7	13.1	12.7	-0.5	93.1
Indianapolis[b]	25,653	33,609	7,956	31.0	2,274	3,304	1,030	45.3	42.9	44.3	1.5	9.7	10.6	0.9	94.0
Jacksonville	27,077	36,618	9,541	35.2	3,108	4,336	1,228	39.5	49.2	48.3	-0.9	12.9	12.9	0.0	93.3
Los Angeles	58,770	51,173	-7,597	-12.9	7,583	8,831	1,248	16.5	31.9	30.9	-0.9	15.2	20.5	5.2	86.1
Memphis	50,464	70,517	20,053	39.7	5,615	9,579	3,964	70.6	46.2	50.8	4.6	12.2	14.8	2.6	94.2
Milwaukee	17,999	24,980	6,981	38.8	1,434	2,208	774	54.0	29.7	32.8	3.1	11.4	12.1	0.7	74.3
New York City	144,248	185,818	41,570	28.8	8,697	17,176	8,479	97.5	20.2	24.5	4.4	12.5	18.9	6.4	50.1
Philadelphia	124,554	131,317	6,763	5.4	13,457	16,292	2,835	21.1	56.7	54.7	-2.0	12.1	14.0	1.8	91.8
Phoenix	7,149	9,579	2,430	34.0	888	1,145	257	28.9	41.6	41.0	-0.6	13.4	13.3	-0.1	91.4
San Antonio	10,313	13,224	2,911	28.2	910	1,167	257	28.2	42.1	43.9	1.8	9.7	9.8	0.2	91.9
San Diego	10,875	11,405	530	4.9	1,139	1,542	403	35.4	31.4	33.5	2.1	11.7	15.6	3.9	88.1
San Francisco	8,746	7,196	-1,550	-17.7	903	885	-18	-2.0	28.7	29.6	0.9	13.4	15.8	2.4	79.0
San Jose	4,625	4,407	-218	-4.7	548	539	-9	-1.6	39.4	41.6	2.3	14.0	15.1	1.2	81.6
Seattle	7,229	6,850	-379	-5.2	681	1,019	338	49.6	36.7	36.5	-0.2	10.5	17.5	7.0	86.0
Washington, D.C.	54,332	54,071	-261	-0.5	3,808	5,781	1,973	51.8	35.7	38.8	3.1	8.0	12.4	4.4	88.4
All 25 cities	1,038,745	1,202,489	163,744	15.8	96,889	134,363	37,474	38.7	35.3	38.1	2.9	11.8	14.1	2.3	81.1

Source: Author's analysis of U.S. Census Bureau data.

a. Data are reported for persons indicating black or African American race alone. See also footnote to table 9A-1.

b. Data presented here are for the statistical entity, "Indianapolis city (balance/remainder)," and differ slightly from data for the consolidated city of Indianapolis.

TABLE 9A-4. All and Severely Cost-Burdened Latino Homeowners, Twenty-Five Largest Cities, 1990–2000[a]

Area	All homeowners 1990	2000	1990–2000 change Number	Percent	Severely cost-burdened owners 1990	2000	1990–2000 change Number	Percent	Homeownership rate 1990	2000	1990–2000 change (percentage points)	Percent severely cost-burdened owners 1990	2000	1990–2000 change (percentage points)	Specified units as a percent of all owner-occupied units
United States	2,545,584	4,212,520	1,666,936	65.5	189,718	382,587	192,869	101.7	42.4	45.7	3.3	9.6	11.6	2.0	79.2
Austin	10,820	20,962	10,142	93.7	768	1,649	881	114.7	32.8	36.1	3.3	8.0	9.2	1.2	85.9
Baltimore	1,173	1,288	115	9.8	41	99	58	141.5	44.8	35.5	–9.2	5.3	9.4	4.1	84.9
Boston	2,386	4,073	1,687	70.7	116	186	70	60.3	13.0	15.8	2.8	18.2	13.8	–4.4	33.6
Charlotte	708	2,198	1,490	210.5	42	234	192	457.1	38.9	21.8	–17.1	7.9	12.9	5.0	83.3
Chicago	44,768	75,780	31,012	69.3	1,178	4,541	3,363	285.5	31.7	39.7	8.0	6.8	12.4	5.7	48.8
Columbus	716	1,296	580	81.0	36	89	53	147.2	30.5	24.1	–6.4	7.9	7.5	–0.3	91.4
Dallas	18,219	35,819	17,600	96.6	1,379	2,876	1,497	108.6	33.9	34.2	0.3	8.7	9.1	0.4	89.7
Detroit	3,979	5,504	1,525	38.3	321	378	57	17.8	46.3	45.3	–1.0	11.3	8.8	–2.5	81.3
El Paso	53,041	74,613	21,572	40.7	3,614	6,333	2,719	75.2	55.7	59.7	3.9	7.6	9.5	1.9	90.9
Fort Worth	10,573	20,538	9,965	94.2	621	1,391	770	124.0	47.2	51.6	4.4	6.6	7.4	0.8	92.8
Houston	38,579	69,669	31,090	80.6	3,023	5,484	2,461	81.4	31.8	35.8	4.0	9.0	9.0	0.0	88.6
Indianapolis[b]	1,123	2,287	1,164	103.7	53	144	91	171.7	45.5	27.7	–17.8	6.1	7.3	1.2	86.6
Jacksonville	2,670	4,661	1,991	74.6	183	337	154	84.2	49.2	48.6	–0.6	8.7	8.3	–0.4	87.6
Los Angeles	76,630	112,875	36,245	47.3	9,251	19,461	10,210	110.4	23.5	26.9	3.4	14.5	20.2	5.7	86.2
Memphis	475	1,231	756	159.2	16	72	56	350.0	37.4	25.5	–11.9	4.5	7.8	3.3	75.3
Milwaukee	3,247	6,199	2,952	90.9	126	337	211	167.5	30.9	33.3	2.4	6.5	7.8	1.4	70.0
New York City	66,929	92,230	25,301	37.8	3,180	7,467	4,287	134.8	12.1	14.0	1.9	13.6	20.1	6.5	40.8
Philadelphia	12,035	19,256	7,221	60.0	1,209	3,228	2,019	167.0	46.7	50.8	4.1	12.7	18.9	6.2	91.8
Phoenix	24,529	51,231	26,702	108.9	2,155	5,248	3,093	143.5	47.4	47.7	0.3	10.1	11.9	1.8	87.3
San Antonio	82,072	114,831	32,759	39.9	6,187	8,205	2,018	32.6	54.3	56.4	2.2	8.2	7.8	–0.4	92.7
San Diego	20,240	27,789	7,549	37.3	1,768	3,590	1,822	103.1	34.8	35.3	0.6	10.8	15.7	4.9	83.4
San Francisco	8,723	8,735	12	0.1	619	913	294	47.5	28.2	27.5	–0.7	9.8	13.9	4.2	75.3
San Jose	22,798	27,489	4,691	20.6	2,113	3,222	1,109	52.5	46.1	47.1	0.9	11.0	14.0	3.0	84.5
Seattle	2,008	2,396	388	19.3	156	265	109	69.9	32.1	25.3	–6.8	9.9	13.7	3.8	81.3
Washington, D.C.	2,141	3,422	1,281	59.8	159	224	65	40.9	20.5	24.2	3.7	15.0	10.8	–4.2	61.5
All 25 cities	510,582	786,372	275,790	54.0	38,314	75,973	37,659	98.3	28.6	32.3	3.7	10.0	12.5	2.4	78.6

Source: Author's analysis of U.S. Census Bureau data.

a. Persons of Hispanic/Latino origin may be of any race. See also footnote to table 9A-1.

b. Data presented here are for the statistical entity, "Indianapolis city (balance/remainder)," and differ slightly from data for the consolidated city of Indianapolis.

REFERENCES

Baer, William C. 1976. "The Evolution of Housing Indicators and Housing Standards." *Public Policy* 24 (3): 361–93.

Belsky, Eric S., and Mark Duda. 2002. "Anatomy of the Low-Income Homeownership Boom in the 1990s." In *Low-Income Homeownership: Examining the Unexamined Goal,* edited by Nicolas P. Retsinas and Eric S. Belsky. Brookings.

Goodman, Jack. 2003. "Homeownership and Investment in Real Estate Stocks." *Journal of Real Estate Portfolio Management* 9 (2): 93–105.

Joint Center for Housing Studies of Harvard University. 2003. *State of the Nation's Housing 2003.* Cambridge, Mass.

Lipman, Barbara J. 2002. "America's Working Families and the Housing Landscape 1997–2001." *New Century Housing* 3(2).

Listokin, David, Elvin K. Wyly, Larry Keating, Kristopher M. Rengert, and Barbara Listokin. 2000. "Making New Mortgage Markets: Case Studies of Institutions, Home Buyers, and Communities." Research Report FMFR 180. Washington: Fannie Mae Foundation.

Mitchell, J. Paul. 1985. "Historical Overview of Direct Federal Housing Assistance." In *Federal Housing Policy and Programs,* edited by J. Paul Mitchell. New Brunswick, N.J.: Rutgers University Center for Urban Policy Research.

Myers, Dowell, and Gary Painter. 2003. "Homeownership and Younger Households: Progress among African Americans and Latinos." Census Note 12, October. Washington: Fannie Mae Foundation.

Simmons, Patrick A. 2001a. "A Coast-to-Coast Expansion: Geographic Patterns of U.S. Homeownership Gains during the 1990s." Census Note 05, June. Washington: Fannie Mae Foundation.

Simmons, Patrick A. 2001b. "Changes in Minority Homeownership during the 1990s." Census Note 7. Washington: Fannie Mae Foundation.

Turner, Margery Austin, G. Thomas Kingsley, Kathryn L. S. Pettit, Christopher Snow, and Peter A. Tatian. 2002. *Housing in the Nation's Capital 2002.* Washington: Fannie Mae Foundation.

U.S. Census Bureau. 1993. *1990 Census of Housing. Detailed Housing Characteristics.* 1990 CH-2. Washington.

Wiranski, Mark. 2003. *Sustaining Home Ownership through Education and Counseling.* Washington: Neighborhood Reinvestment Corporation.

The Sheltered Homeless in Metropolitan Neighborhoods

Evidence from the 1990 and 2000 Censuses

BARRETT A. LEE AND CHAD R. FARRELL

Americans expect a lot from their neighborhoods. Many believe that the ideal neighborhood is primarily if not exclusively residential in nature, a safe haven of single-family homes whose owner-occupants keep up their property, get along well together, and want the best for their children. According to this belief, any encroachment of commercial or nonresidential land uses into an area should be resisted, given its potential for undermining the presumed beneficial aspects of neighborhood context. Even quasi-residential facilities such as group homes and halfway houses—no matter how merciful in purpose—are regarded with suspicion by residents. Human service administrators nevertheless try to place their clients in "normal" neighborhoods out of conviction that the desirable features of these settings facilitate treatment, recovery, and rehabilitation, frequently creating tension. In some neighborhoods, preferences for residential purity win out; in others, facilities appear that cater to victims of domestic violence, persons with mental disabilities, HIV/AIDS patients, substance abusers, and similar special-needs groups.

This chapter examines metropolitan neighborhoods with emergency and transitional shelters that house substantial numbers of homeless people.

The authors are grateful to the support staff of the Population Research Institute at Pennsylvania State University for assistance with this project. Special thanks go to Steve Graham of PRI, who played an instrumental role in data extraction and GIS-based analysis. Alan Berube of the Brookings Institution also deserves thanks for his helpful comments on earlier drafts.

These neighborhoods, which we label "critical mass," often have long histories of serving an impoverished clientele, as epitomized by the traditional "skid row" district. Critical-mass neighborhoods of more recent vintage are also evident, some in areas farther away from the city center. One might anticipate the landscape of critical-mass neighborhoods to have shifted since the early 1980s, when a variety of forces converged to increase the size of the U.S. homeless population.[1] To date, however, these neighborhoods remain largely unexplored.

Using census data, this chapter asks four key questions about critical-mass neighborhoods during the 1990–2000 period: (1) In which metropolitan areas are they most and least common? (2) How visible are sheltered homeless persons in critical-mass neighborhoods? (3) How do the intrametropolitan locations of these neighborhoods compare in 2000 and 1990? (4) What are critical-mass neighborhoods like in terms of their demographic, socioeconomic, and housing characteristics?

Answers to the four questions are difficult to predict because multiple factors shape the distribution of shelters at the local level.[2] The conventional pattern—concentration in the central city core—reflects several influences: historical inertia; access to public transportation; cheaper land and lower rental costs; the presence of buildings and zoning suitable for homeless-targeted services; and limited opposition to such services in marginal downtown space. By minimizing the distances among service facilities, this concentrated pattern can be considered an efficient approach to helping homeless people meet their basic needs. Funding formulas for federal homelessness assistance also tend to favor cities, thus guaranteeing at least a portion of the shelters that serve the homeless population will be located there.

Of course, some would rather see shelters and the populations they house located outside the city center. Merchants, developers, and government officials tend to view the spatial concentration of shelters as an impediment to the revitalization of the central business district, not to mention a deterrent to shoppers, tourists, and conventioneers. Consequently, policies ranging from the closure or relocation of shelters to the enforcement of bans on

---

1. The rise of the "new" (post-1980) homelessness—as distinct from the skid row era that preceded it—has been attributed to a housing squeeze (persistent poverty coupled with a decrease in affordable housing units), deteriorating employment opportunities, deinstitutionalization of the mentally ill, a shrinking welfare safety net, the crack cocaine epidemic, and a decline in the attractiveness of marriage, among other forces. Baumohl (1996); Jencks (1994); Lee, Price-Spratlen, and Kanan (2003); Wright, Rubin, and Devine (1998).

2. Brinegar (2003); Hoch (1991); Gaber (1996); Laws (1992).

loitering and panhandling have been implemented, all with an eye toward dispersing the homeless population.[3] Dispersion is popular with some service providers as well. They see "cloistered" shelters in outlying locations as shielding vulnerable homeless groups, especially women and children, from the harmful effects of skid row. Moreover, decentralized shelters address an equity issue, improving access of the suburban poor to services.

Despite these rationales, attempts to open shelters in neighborhoods outside the urban core have typically been greeted with a NIMBY ("not in my backyard") response rather than with open arms. Middle-class residents use a variety of tactics to block shelters, citing the threat posed to property values, safety, public health, and overall quality of life.[4] Similar opposition has increasingly come from low-income areas, whose residents—often racial and ethnic minorities—argue that their neighborhoods are dumping grounds for facilities unwanted elsewhere.

These competing pressures between concentration and dispersion suggest the U.S. metropolis may harbor complex and varied spatial distributions of critical-mass neighborhoods. Few traditional skid rows persist in unaltered form, but neither are we aware of cases in which the sheltered homeless population is spread evenly throughout a central city and its surrounding suburbs. One likelihood is that, given the magnitude of their homelessness problems, the largest metropolitan areas will have the greatest number of critical-mass neighborhoods. We also expect these neighborhoods to be more decentralized in 2000 than 1990, in part because of the growing recognition and use of strategies designed to make shelters more acceptable in the eyes of the public. Smaller facilities in particular may keep the visibility of the sheltered homeless population within limits tolerable to residents across a range of neighborhoods.[5]

The narrow focus of our analysis deserves emphasis. Relying on census data, though integral to our ability to describe the demographic makeup of neighborhoods with sheltered homeless people, precludes examination of the myriad policies and factors that have affected the location and visibility of homelessness in the study areas. These data do not shed light on the size or characteristics of the total homeless population, either nationally or at the

3. National Law Center on Homelessness and Poverty (1996); Simon (1996); Snow and Mulcahy (2001).

4. Dear (1992); National Law Center on Homelessness and Poverty (1997); Takahashi and Dear (1997); Wolch and Dear (1993).

5. Recent evidence suggests that roughly one-half of homeless shelters serve twenty-five persons or fewer per day. Burt, Aron, and Lee (2001); Feins and Fosburg (1999).

metropolitan level.[6] Generalizations about the size and composition of this population are hindered by the fact that many homeless persons spend their days and nights outdoors in hard-to-find spots. Others "double up" with friends and relatives, falling beyond the reach of census enumerators.

In addition to such coverage difficulties, census figures mask the dynamic, transient nature of homelessness. As single-point-in-time estimates, they understate the degree to which frequent entries into, and exits from, the homeless population influence the prevalence of homelessness over longer periods of time.[7] Simply put, our analysis cannot adequately account for individuals who experience only one or two brief episodes of homelessness during their lives.

At best, census data capture the "tip of the iceberg," both temporally and in terms of the types of homeless people covered. Yet by analyzing the changing location of sheltered homeless populations, and the neighborhood circumstances to which they are exposed, we obtain a clearer sense of how economic, policy, and other trends have affected some of society's most vulnerable individuals at the local level.

METHODS

The last two censuses have included special efforts to enumerate homeless people. Shelter count data from these enumerations are particularly useful for describing the 1990–2000 distribution of the most accessible segment of the homeless population across and within metropolitan areas.

Census Data on Homelessness

Data on sheltered homelessness in 2000 come from the Service-Based Enumeration (SBE) conducted during Census 2000. Over a three-day period (March 27–29), people without conventional housing were counted at shelters, soup kitchens, mobile food programs, and predesignated outdoor sites.[8]

---

6. Because census data are not the best way to determine how many are homeless, researchers have tried to tally the homeless population through other means, though the results are still approximations. Using data from a 1996 survey, for example, investigators at the Urban Institute projected that over the course of that year there were at least 2.3 and perhaps as many as 3.5 million people who experienced a spell of homelessness at some time. Burt, Aron, and Lee (2001). Although the composition of the homeless population remains uncertain, evidence suggests that it has become progressively more heterogeneous, with an increase in the number of minorities, families with children, single women, and unaccompanied minors. Baumohl (1996); Lowe and others (2001); Wright, Rubin, and Devine (1998).

7. For period prevalence estimates, see Culhane and others (1994); Link and others (1995); Metraux and others (2001).

8. Smith and Smith (2001).

For comparative purposes, our analysis also draws upon the 1990 S-Night (street and shelter) operation, a similar enumeration fielded by the Census Bureau a decade earlier.[9]

Once the 2000 SBE data were processed, Census Bureau officials proceeded cautiously, changing their minds at least twice about how the components of the SBE should be released. Ultimately only emergency and transitional shelter results were made readily available, and only for census geographic units that met or exceeded a threshold of 100 persons in shelters. Census tabulations aggregated persons counted at soup kitchens, food programs, and outdoor sites in an "other non-institutional group quarters" category (along with persons in certain types of residential care facilities, in domestic violence shelters, and in hospital staff dormitories).[10]

For the nation as a whole, the SBE estimate of the sheltered homeless population provided by Census 2000 equals approximately 170,700. Due to the limitations already noted, the proportion of all homeless people captured in this estimate is impossible to ascertain. The rapid expansion of the shelter supply since the mid-1980s, however, suggests the potential for a significant segment of the homeless population to be in shelters on any particular day.[11] Moreover, postcensus evaluations of the 1990 S-Night data indicate that shelter counts are generally more accurate and complete than counts undertaken at nonshelter sites.[12] In both the S-Night and SBE efforts, Census staff used administrative records and contacts with knowledgeable local informants to develop a master list of emergency and transitional shelters prior to the enumeration date. Afterwards a "mop-up" sought to include any shelters that were missed.

Critical-Mass Neighborhoods in Metropolitan Areas

We rely on census tracts to represent metropolitan neighborhoods.[13] A "critical-mass neighborhood" is defined as a tract with a sheltered homeless population of 100 or more at the time of the census. Members of this population might occupy one large shelter or be spread across several smaller ones.

---

9. Taeuber and Siegel (1991).

10. Smith and Smith (2001); also see U.S. General Accounting Office (2003).

11. Burt, Aron, and Lee (2001).

12. Martin (1992).

13. Census tracts are small geographic areas with between 1,500 and 8,000 residents, and an optimum size of 4,000. The Census Bureau seeks local input in defining tract boundaries, which are designed to remain stable over an extended period. Within metropolitan areas, boundaries frequently follow streets, highways, railroad tracks, rivers, and other visible features of the landscape.

The critical-mass threshold has been set at 100 partly for practical reasons, given the unavailability of 2000 SBE data below that level. The threshold makes sense from a visibility standpoint as well. Homelessness is more likely to be noticed when a nontrivial number of shelter users are spatially concentrated. Shelters themselves are frequently accompanied by facilities and services (for example, soup kitchens, second-hand clothing shops, health clinics) that attract unsheltered homeless clients, and they provide anchors for panhandling, loitering, and related forms of street behavior viewed as problematic by domiciled residents. Thus awareness of homelessness should be heightened in critical-mass neighborhoods.

Because of the heavy urban concentration of homeless people nationally, we limit our attention to critical-mass neighborhoods in metropolitan areas.[14] A total of 331 Metropolitan Statistical Areas (MSAs) and Primary MSAs (PMSAs)—subsets of larger metropolitan areas of 1 million or more people—are recognized in Census 2000. We select a sample of forty-nine MSAs and PMSAs, and most of our results pertain to these areas. Included in this sample are forty-seven of the largest fifty metropolitan areas in 2000—all surpassing the 1 million mark—plus Louisville (ranked sixty-first in population size) and Fresno (ranked sixty-fifth).[15]

Of the approximately 65,450 census tracts defined throughout the United States in 2000, only 358 qualify as critical mass, and the vast majority (353) fall inside metropolitan boundaries. Our sample of forty-nine metropolitan areas accounts for three-fourths (271 out of 358, or 75.7 percent) of all critical-mass tracts.[16] With respect to the 170,700 sheltered homeless people counted during the 2000 SBE, about half (80,300) are located in metropolitan critical-mass tracts, and 39 percent (66,442) in the tracts that make up our forty-nine-metropolitan-area sample. In short most individuals staying in emergency or transitional shelters in metropolitan neighborhoods with significant homeless concentrations at the time of the last census (66,442 out of 80,300, or 83 percent) are represented in the data examined here.

14. According to available estimates over nine-tenths of the homeless live in metropolitan areas, with roughly three-fourths in central cities. Burt, Aron, and Lee (2001); Lee and Price-Spratlen (2004).

15. The three excluded metropolitan areas among the fifty largest are Norfolk-Virginia Beach-Newport News, Pittsburgh, and St. Louis, none of which contained a single critical-mass neighborhood in 2000. We include Louisville and Fresno because they are the only other metropolitan areas among the 100 largest that have at least four critical-mass neighborhoods, and 500 or more sheltered homeless in these neighborhoods.

16. These tracts, however, are not a common feature of the metropolitan scene. Barely 1 percent of all tracts located in the sample metropolitan areas satisfy the critical-mass criterion; among central cities in the sample, the corresponding figure is 2.1 percent.

Comparisons

Our analysis offers comparisons across metropolitan areas, within such areas, and over time. We begin by comparing the distribution of critical-mass neighborhoods and sheltered homelessness across the forty-nine sample metropolitan areas, paying special attention to 1990–2000 changes. We then examine differences in the visibility of homelessness in critical-mass neighborhoods, and in the intrametropolitan location of such neighborhoods. Finally, we compare demographic, housing, and other characteristics of critical-mass neighborhoods to those for adjacent neighborhoods (any tracts with boundaries touching a critical-mass tract), for the surrounding central city, and for the metropolitan area as a whole, using data from Census Summary Files 1 and 3.[17]

FINDINGS

Census data show that sheltered homeless people are found primarily in central city critical-mass neighborhoods of large metropolitan areas, but they make up a small fraction of the total populations in these neighborhoods. Despite considerable locational instability, critical-mass neighborhoods exhibit distinctive demographic, socioeconomic, and housing profiles.

Neighborhoods with Concentrations of Sheltered Homeless Are Metropolitan Phenomena

Critical-mass neighborhoods are, for the most part, a phenomenon associated with large metropolitan areas. Yet metropolitan areas themselves are far from equal in their incidence of such neighborhoods. Our sample of forty-nine large metropolitan areas captures roughly four-fifths of all sheltered homeless individuals residing in metropolitan critical-mass neighborhoods nationwide during Census 2000. Among these large metropolitan areas, New York dominates.[18] Table 10-1 shows that three of every ten critical-mass census tracts in the metropolitan sample are located in New York, as are over one-third of the sheltered homeless people who inhabit those tracts.

17. Census 2000 boundaries are imposed on metropolitan areas, central cities, and tracts in 1990, insuring that any changes observed are not due to a shift in the way that geographic areas are defined.

18. As one of the largest metropolitan areas, New York is likely to have more homeless people. At the same time, the city is also among the few places nationally to have a "right to shelter" decree, prompted by a series of class-action lawsuits in the early 1980s, that guarantees shelter for all homeless individuals who seek it. Gaber (1996). The decree requires that an adequate number of shelters be made available to accommodate those in need. The greater number of critical-mass neighborhoods in New York can be traced in part to this decree.

TABLE 10-1. Top Ten Metropolitan Areas by Sheltered Homeless Population in Critical-Mass Neighborhoods, 2000 and 1990–2000 Change

Metropolitan area	2000		1990–2000 change	
	Sheltered homeless population	*Critical-mass neighborhoods*	*Sheltered homeless population*	*Critical-mass neighborhoods*
New York, NY PMSA	23,111	81	−251	9
Los Angeles-Long Beach, CA PMSA	6,394	16	2,296	−2
Atlanta, GA MSA	2,052	10	460	4
Boston, MA-NH PMSA	2,048	9	−473	−2
Seattle-Bellevue-Everett, WA PMSA	2,026	9	−107	1
Chicago, IL PMSA	1,679	8	−2,101	−10
San Diego, CA MSA	1,660	5	−1,210	0
Washington, DC-MD-VA-WV PMSA	1,442	8	−2,993	−5
Detroit, MI PMSA	1,322	6	383	1
Minneapolis-St. Paul, MN-WI MSA	1,316	5	−169	0
All 49 metro areas	66,442	271	−12,901	−26

Source: U.S. Census Bureau.

After New York, the Los Angeles-Long Beach metropolitan area has the next most—but far fewer—sheltered homeless (6,394 vs. 23,111) and critical-mass neighborhoods (16 vs. 81). The only other metropolitan areas with at least 2,000 sheltered homeless in critical-mass neighborhoods are Atlanta, Boston, and Seattle-Bellevue-Everett. These three areas also have eight or more critical-mass neighborhoods, as do Philadelphia, Chicago, and Washington, D.C. (See table 10A-1 for statistics on all forty-nine metropolitan areas.) By contrast, single critical-mass neighborhoods and modest sheltered homeless populations (less than 300 persons) exist in several of the sample metropolises in 2000.

Overall, between 1990 and 2000, the number of critical-mass neighborhoods declined, as did the number of sheltered homeless in those neighborhoods. In the forty-nine metropolitan areas, critical-mass neighborhoods dropped from 297 to 271, and their combined sheltered homeless population fell off by roughly 16 percent. More metropolitan areas registered declines than increases. Although it is tempting to attribute the downward trend to shrinkage of the national homeless population associated with the economic prosperity of the 1990s, little evidence exists to support that interpretation. More likely reasons include the growing popularity of smaller shelters and nonshelter housing programs, both of which would keep neighborhood shelter populations from reaching the critical-mass threshold.[19]

19. Between 1988 and 1996 an expanding emergency shelter capacity at the national level accompanied the addition of nearly 275,000 permanent and transitional housing units intended for homeless persons. Burt, Aron, and Lee (2001).

Increasing spatial dispersion of shelters—a possibility we consider later—could create a similar outcome.

Amid the overall decline in critical-mass neighborhoods, the picture at the metropolitan level was mixed. The number of critical-mass tracts stayed the same in ten of our forty-nine metropolitan areas and increased in another sixteen. Among the twenty-three areas that saw a decline in these neighborhoods, the drops were greatest in Chicago, San Francisco, Houston, and Washington, D.C. Similarly, San Francisco, Washington, and Chicago also registered the largest declines in the number of sheltered homeless people residing in critical-mass neighborhoods.

By contrast, Los Angeles-Long Beach stands out among the eighteen areas that experienced an increase in sheltered homeless persons living in critical-mass neighborhoods. The large increase it experienced (2,296 persons, or 56 percent) occurred despite a slight drop in the number of critical-mass neighborhoods in the metropolitan area.[20] This combination suggests a trend toward greater spatial concentration of the sheltered homeless, and represents the exception rather than the rule. The more typical pattern, exemplified by Atlanta, Cleveland, and Salt Lake City-Ogden, is that of concomitant gains in critical-mass tracts and in sheltered homeless people within those tracts, although the changes are often modest in absolute terms.

Like Los Angeles, the New York metropolitan area also exhibited a hybrid pattern, but the trends were reversed. New York saw critical-mass neighborhoods increase by about one-eighth, but saw the sheltered homeless population in those neighborhoods fall off slightly. This pattern corresponds to a shift in New York City shelter policy that began in the late 1980s. Faced with mounting resistance from neighborhoods saturated by shelters, municipal officials worked with the boroughs to reduce the size of shelters and distribute them more widely.[21] In contrast to their growing spatial concentration in Los Angeles, then, the sheltered homeless in New York actually "thinned out" spatially during the 1990–2000 period.

20. As was the case in New York, past policy decisions regarding the homeless helped to shape the current shelter landscape in Los Angeles. During the 1970s the Community Redevelopment Agency's "policy of containment" sought to centralize homeless facilities and services in the Central City East area (including the traditional skid row district) proximate to the needy population. As a result the largely single-room occupancy housing stock in the area has stabilized, and delivery of services has expanded, including an increase in the number of shelter beds. Spivak (1998); also see Wolch and Dear (1993).

21. Gaber (1996).

Sheltered Homeless Typically Represent Minority of Neighborhood Populations

The New York and Los Angeles-Long Beach examples imply that critical-mass neighborhoods differ in the visibility of their sheltered homeless. Of course, census data cannot capture many aspects of visibility. For instance, shelter policies—particularly, how long homeless people are allowed to stay in shelters—contribute significantly to the street-level view. Other services offered to homeless clients within the neighborhood may also make their presence more apparent. To measure these factors, we would need information about the number and types of shelters present, details concerning the nonshelter service infrastructure (soup kitchens, drop-in centers), and the ways in which homeless people use public space in the neighborhood. None of these, unfortunately, are available from the SBE data.

Nevertheless, the census figures do permit us to measure three simple dimensions of visibility: the absolute size of a neighborhood's shelter population; the density of the sheltered homeless population within that neighborhood (per square mile); and the percentage of total neighborhood population that the sheltered homeless represent.

Results from our metropolitan area sample indicate that although the sheltered homeless are typically present in noticeable numbers in critical-mass neighborhoods, they account for a relatively small share of neighborhood population. Across all 271 critical-mass neighborhoods in the forty-nine metropolitan areas in 2000, the sheltered homeless average 245 in number, and make up just over 10 percent of the tract population. The small size of the central city census tracts in which shelters are typically located results in a relatively high average density for the sheltered homeless in critical-mass neighborhoods, roughly 1,573 persons per square mile. These overall numbers, however, obscure significant variation from one metropolitan area to the next.

Even within the same metropolitan area, neighborhood shelter populations vary markedly in terms of visibility. Table 10-2 presents the high and low values on each dimension of visibility for the metropolitan areas in our sample with at least eight critical-mass neighborhoods. The gap between highest and lowest is especially notable in Los Angeles-Long Beach and New York. Both have neighborhoods with sheltered homeless populations of 1,000 or more and densities above 10,000 sheltered homeless per square mile. Such neighborhoods presumably contain multiple shelters, including some of substantial size. At the same time, each contains at least one critical-mass neighborhood where the sheltered homeless account for only a small fraction of the population.

TABLE 10-2. Visibility Measures for Sheltered Homeless Population in Critical-Mass Neighborhoods, Selected Metropolitan Areas, 2000

	Neighborhood-sheltered homeless		
Metropolitan area	Population	Population per square mile	Population share
New York, NY PMSA			
Average	285	3,750	11.3
High	1,264	18,057	97.3
Low	102	11	0.6
Los Angeles-Long Beach, CA PMSA			
Average	400	1,285	9.3
High	2,529	10,538	50.6
Low	102	78	1.5
Atlanta, GA MSA			
Average	205	250	4.7
High	506	888	16.1
Low	101	27	1.7
Boston, MA-NH PMSA			
Average	228	758	12.6
High	386	1,627	58.9
Low	109	94	1.4
Seattle-Bellevue-Everett, WA PMSA			
Average	225	552	8.1
High	391	1,006	17.2
Low	107	22	1.9
Chicago, IL PMSA			
Average	210	1,282	14.4
High	411	2,308	38.2
Low	107	210	2.5
Washington, DC-MD-VA-WV PMSA			
Average	180	884	6.5
High	470	2,338	25.3
Low	111	43	1.7
Philadelphia, PA-NJ PMSA			
Average	132	748	7.0
High	184	1,121	15.2
Low	103	568	1.4
All 49 metro areas (average)	245	1,573	10.0

Source: U.S. Census Bureau.

In 2000, there were only three critical-mass neighborhoods—two in New York and one in Los Angeles-Long Beach—in which sheltered homeless people make up a majority of the total neighborhood population. In fact, the same Los Angeles neighborhood registers the highest values on all three visibility dimensions. These neighborhoods are outliers. Critical-mass tracts are more commonly marked by a noticeable but much more moderate homeless presence. As other research confirms, few contemporary neighborhoods approach the high-profile characteristics of traditional skid rows.[22]

22. Lee (1980); Lee and Price-Spratlen (2004); Wolch and Dear (1993).

Critical-Mass Neighborhoods Are Mostly in Central Cities, but Locations Shifted in 1990s

Evidence that the number of critical-mass neighborhoods, and the sheltered homeless population living within them, declined during the 1990s suggests that shelters may have downsized or dispersed within metropolitan areas. Even so, 86 percent of the critical-mass neighborhoods in our metropolitan area sample in 2000 are located inside central cities. Did the homeless population disperse within central cities in the 1990s, or do sheltered homeless people still live largely in critical-mass neighborhoods?

Critical-mass neighborhoods encompass a large share of their cities' sheltered homeless population.[23] Nearly three-fourths (73 percent) of all central city shelter inhabitants, including persons in census tracts not reaching the 100-sheltered-homeless threshold, reside in critical-mass neighborhoods. Cities such as San Diego (99 percent), Sacramento (93 percent), Denver (88 percent), Orlando (86 percent), and New York (85 percent) have even higher proportions of their total sheltered homeless population in critical-mass neighborhoods. By contrast, some cities, such as Baltimore (26 percent), Oakland (27 percent), and New Orleans (33 percent), exhibit much more dispersed sheltered populations, suggesting that a greater number of smaller shelters are scattered across more census tracts.[24]

Mapping the location of critical-mass neighborhoods in 2000 highlights the variety of ways in which shelters are spatially configured. Although no two metropolitan areas are identical, we detect certain tendencies. The first

23. To demonstrate this point, we focus on the thirty-five metropolitan areas in the sample for which the number of sheltered homeless is reported for each component central city. Recall that data in 2000 are suppressed for any geographic unit—cities as well as census tracts—with sheltered homeless populations under 100. The eleven metropolitan areas affected by such suppression and thus excluded here are Austin-San Marcos, Charlotte-Gastonia-Rock Hill, Cleveland-Lorain-Elyria, Greensboro-Winston Salem-High Point, Milwaukee-Waukesha, Orange County, Providence-Fall River-Warwick, Raleigh-Durham-Chapel Hill, Riverside-San Bernardino, Salt Lake City-Ogden, and Seattle-Bellevue-Everett. In addition, Las Vegas has been excluded because of a data inconsistency problem, and Bergen-Passaic and Nassau-Suffolk are omitted due to their suburban character, which precludes calculations involving central cities as units.

24. Although we adhere to Census Bureau precedent in defining central cities, some researchers have focused on primary cities instead, limiting their attention to the first city listed in the official (Office of Management and Budget [OMB]) metropolitan area name plus any other city in the name with at least 100,000 residents. Application of the primary city rule—which excludes smaller central cities that fail to reach the critical-mass threshold (for example, dropping San Marcos from Austin and Bellevue and Everett from Seattle; see note 22)—boosts the number of cases from thirty-five to forty-four for this part of the analysis. It does not, however, change the results. Under the new rule, the average proportion of primary city sheltered homeless located in critical-mass neighborhoods equals 62.8 percent (versus 63 percent of central city homeless).

tendency, the traditional "skid row" configuration, is exemplified by Seattle, where critical-mass neighborhoods are geographically contiguous and near the downtown. Phoenix-Mesa, San Diego, and San Francisco share a similar pattern, though each exhibits a few additional outlying pockets of sheltered homelessness.[25] As in Seattle, critical-mass tracts in Chicago are found mainly within the central city. In Chicago, however, they can also be found to the north, west, and south of the downtown Loop.[26] This "checkerboard" pattern is also common to the Cleveland-Lorain-Elyria, Detroit, and Houston metropolitan areas. Finally, Atlanta offers a sharp contrast to the Seattle and Chicago cases. Despite some clustering in the core, the majority of Atlanta's critical-mass neighborhoods occupy outlying positions in the suburban ring. Fort Lauderdale, another Sunbelt metropolitan area, shows a similar pattern of suburbanizing critical-mass tracts.

Of course, many metropolitan areas have too few critical-mass neighborhoods to justify a search for patterns. Others constitute mixed cases, combining elements of two or more of the ideal types—clustering and checkerboard tendencies appear in Philadelphia, and Boston exhibits both of those tendencies plus a degree of suburbanization. The actual distribution of critical-mass neighborhoods in 2000 is too messy to distill into a few spatial generalizations applicable to most metropolitan areas.

One generalization that does hold pertains to locational change: critical-mass neighborhoods have become somewhat more decentralized since 1990. We document this change by measuring the distance of each critical-mass neighborhood from the central business district (CBD) of its respective central city.[27] In 1990 critical-mass neighborhoods were located an average of 4.3 miles from the CBD; by 2000 the average distance had risen to 5.4 miles. Figure 10-1 shows a sizeable increase in the percentage of neighborhoods located three miles or farther from the CBD.[28]

25. Further analysis of the spatial distribution of shelters in Phoenix-Mesa can be found in Brinegar (2003). The geography of homelessness in San Francisco is examined in Lee and Price-Spratlen (2004).

26. The emergence of the checkerboard pattern is documented by Hoch (1991).

27. We have defined CBDs on a tract basis, using information from the 1982 Census of Retail Trade. (The CBD tract identification program was discontinued after 1982.) Distance is measured between the geographic centroid of the critical-mass tract and the centroid of the tract or tracts that make up the CBD. In the case of multiple central cities with multiple CBDs, we use the distance to the nearest CBD.

28. To account for the possibility that the disproportionate number of critical-mass tracts in New York may be driving these changes, we replicated the distance analysis for non-New York tracts. The basic patterns reported for the full sample hold when New York tracts are deleted: the average distance of critical-mass neighborhoods from the CBD rose from 3.5 to five miles between 1990 and 2000, and the percentage of such neighborhoods three miles or farther from the CBD increased significantly as well. Additional tests show the results for the rest of our analysis to be similarly robust; that is, they are not unduly influenced by New York's sample dominance.

FIGURE 10-1. Location of Critical-Mass Neighborhoods by Proximity to CBD, 1990–2000

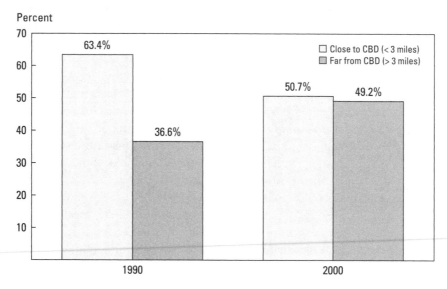

Source: U.S. Census Bureau.

Given the preponderance of critical-mass neighborhoods inside central city boundaries at both time points, decentralization appears to have occurred intracity rather than on a metro-wide basis. The 1990–2000 changes, however, involve more than increasing distance from the CBD; the landscape of sheltered homelessness is in a general state of flux. The majority of critical-mass neighborhoods in our sample achieved that status in one of the census years, but not both. Our sample of forty-nine metropolitan areas contains 456 unique tracts that had a critical-mass population in either 1990 or 2000 (table 10-3). Out of this total, 185 (or 41 percent) satisfied the critical-mass criterion in 1990 only; another 159 (35 percent) in 2000 only. Stable critical-mass tracts, which meet or exceed the 100+ sheltered homeless threshold in both years, are by far the smallest category (112 tracts, or 25 percent).[29] In short, only one-

29. The sheltered homeless populations in stable critical-mass neighborhoods average more than 300 members at both time points, compared to a 1990 average of 203 in the 1990-only neighborhoods and a 2000 average of 186 in the 2000-only neighborhoods. Mean homeless density exceeds 2,000 persons per square mile in the stable neighborhoods, nearly double the level in the other two types of neighborhoods. Finally, sheltered homeless persons constitute an average of 14–17 percent of all residents in stable critical-mass neighborhoods, but 7–10 percent in the 1990-only and 2000-only neighborhoods.

T A B L E   1 0 - 3 .   Stability of Critical-Mass Neighborhoods, Top Ten Metropolitan Areas, 1990–2000

Metropolitan area	Critical-mass neighborhoods			Percent stable[a]
	1990	*2000*	*1990 and 2000*	
New York, NY PMSA	40	49	32	26.4
Los Angeles-Long Beach, CA PMSA	13	11	5	17.2
Atlanta, GA MSA	3	7	3	23.1
Boston, MA-NH PMSA	6	4	5	33.3
Seattle-Bellevue-Everett, WA PMSA	5	6	3	21.4
Chicago, IL PMSA	13	3	5	23.8
San Diego, CA MSA	3	3	2	25.0
Washington, DC-MD-VA-WV PMSA	9	4	4	23.5
Detroit, MI PMSA	3	4	2	22.2
Minneapolis-St. Paul, MN-WI MSA	1	1	4	66.7
All 49 metro areas	185	159	112	24.6

Source: U.S. Census Bureau.

a. Percentage of neighborhoods identified as critical mass in either 1990 or 2000 meeting criteria at both times.

fourth of neighborhoods identified as critical mass in 1990 or 2000 held that designation at both points in time.

With few exceptions, stable critical-mass tracts make up a minority of the critical-mass neighborhoods in our sample (see last column of table 10-3). Indeed, many of the metropolitan areas exhibit minimal stability (under 30 percent), underscoring the spatially unsettled nature of sheltered homeless populations at the local level.

The New York and Los Angeles-Long Beach metropolitan areas (see maps 10-1 and 10-2) illustrate this point. In both areas, a majority of neighborhoods qualify as critical mass in either 1990 or 2000, but not in both years. In New York City's midtown and downtown neighborhoods, new critical-mass neighborhoods emerged in the 1990s, though not in nearly the same number as existed there at the beginning of the decade. In Los Angeles, some new critical-mass neighborhoods formed adjacent to neighborhoods that previously held significant sheltered populations, close to the CBD, whereas others appeared farther out.

The instability of critical-mass neighborhoods in these cities may reflect minor, temporary fluctuations in some tracts, with sheltered homeless populations barely exceeding the 100-person threshold in one census year, and dipping just below it the next (or vice versa). The nature of local shelter systems, however, is volatile: new shelters open rather frequently whereas others close, relocate, or downsize in response to shifting needs, resources, and policy. As these changes accumulate over the course of a decade, they may significantly modify the spatial distribution of sheltered homelessness.

MAP 10-1. Critical-Mass Neighborhoods in New York Metropolitan Area, 1990–2000

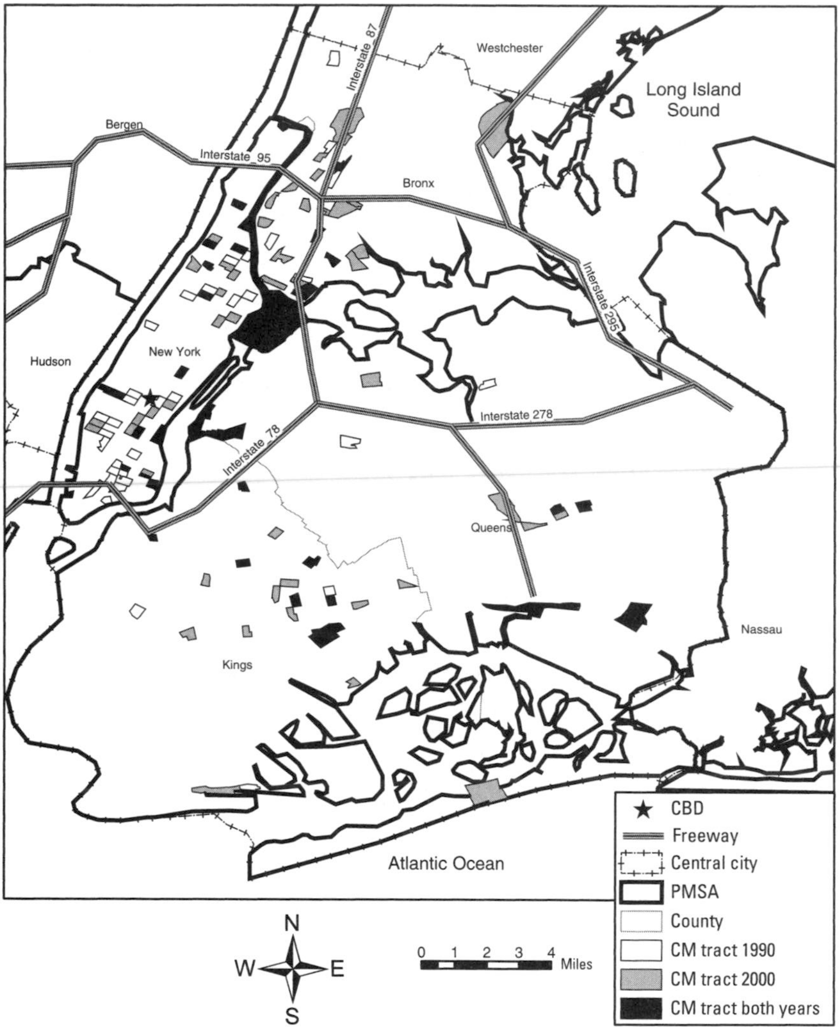

Source: U.S. Census Bureau.

MAP 10-2. Critical-Mass Neighborhoods in Los Angeles-Long Beach Metropolitan Area, 1990–2000

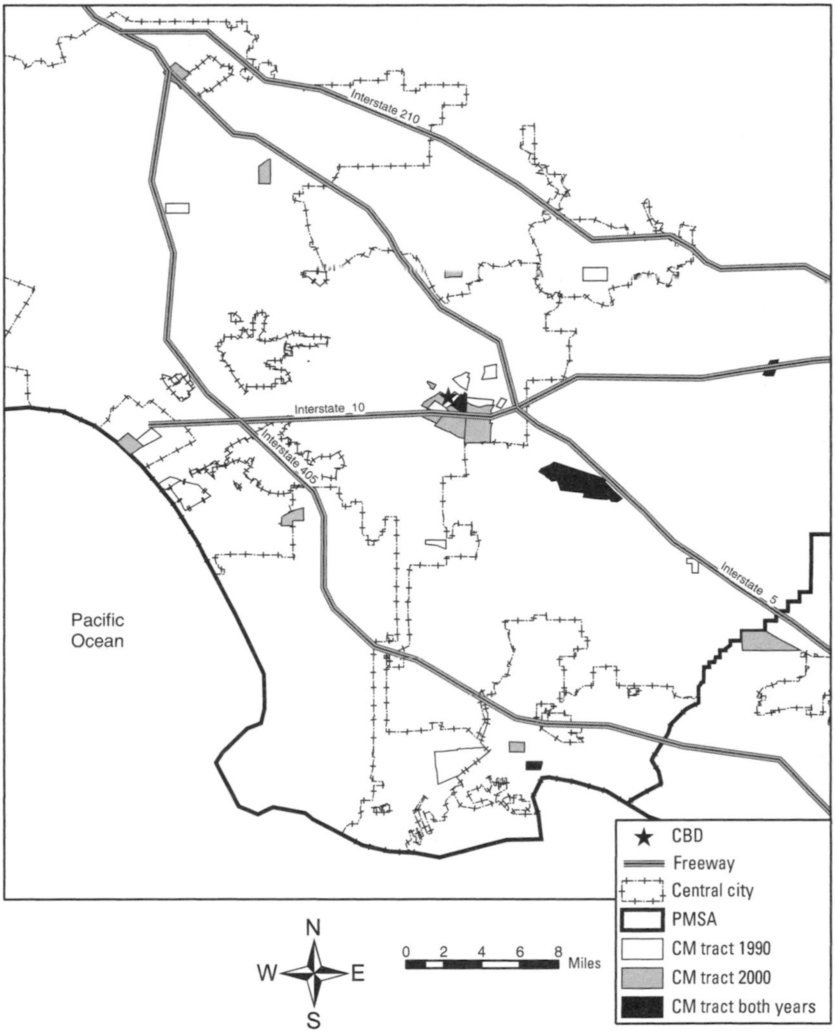

Interstate 210
Interstate 10
Interstate 405
Interstate 5
Pacific Ocean
CBD
Freeway
Central city
PMSA
CM tract 1990
CM tract 2000
CM tract both years
N
W
E
S
0 2 4 6 8 Miles

Source: U.S. Census Bureau.

TABLE 10-4. **Characteristics of Metropolitan Critical-Mass Neighborhoods and Comparison Geographies, 2000**

Percent, unless otherwise noted

Characteristic	Critical-mass neighborhoods	Adjacent neighborhoods	Central cities	Metropolitan areas
Sex ratio (men per 100 women)	127.1	114.5	96.1	96.4
Non-white or Hispanic	71.8	66.1	52.1	36.2
Married-couple households	26.9	32.5	38.2	50.6
High school graduates[a]	63.5	67.7	76.8	81.7
Unemployed[b]	21.2	11.5	7.5	5.0
Below poverty	34.0	25.1	17.6	11.0
Households without vehicle	45.8	36.4	17.4	10.1
Disabled[c]	28.9	24.7	21.4	18.4
In multiunit structures	51.4	37.6	24.0	17.3
Renter-occupied units	75.2	65.2	50.7	36.6
Vacant units	10.5	8.6	7.6	6.3
Crowded units[d]	16.6	15.5	9.4	7.0

Source: U.S. Census Bureau.

a. Of persons 25 years old or older.

b. Of civilian labor force 16 years old or older.

c. Physical, mental, or emotional disability that limits functional activities.

d. 1.01+ persons per room.

Critical-Mass Neighborhoods Exhibit High Degrees of Economic and Social Disadvantage

As the sheltered homeless account for only 10 percent of the population in critical-mass neighborhoods, on average, they can exert only so much direct influence on the overall characteristics of those neighborhoods. Yet these neighborhoods appear to exhibit qualities one might generally associate with homeless populations themselves, indicating that extant community characteristics continue to play a large role in the siting of shelters. In table 10-4 we compare the 271 critical-mass tracts in our metropolitan area sample to adjacent census tracts, to the central city as a whole, and to the entire metropolitan area along three dimensions: demographic composition, economic and social disadvantage, and housing.

The top panel of the table indicates that critical-mass neighborhoods tend to be heavily male and heavily minority in composition relative to the other three comparison units. The first feature is consistent with traditional skid row districts, the second with the profile of the new (post-1980) homelessness. Also notable is the dearth of married-couple households in these communities— one-person, single-parent, and nonfamily households are more common in critical-mass neighborhoods than elsewhere. Finally, fewer adults in critical-mass tracts hold a high school diploma.

The demographic character of these neighborhoods implies that they suffer from multiple forms of disadvantage. The second panel of table 10-4 shows that average unemployment and poverty rates in 2000 are two to four times greater in critical-mass neighborhoods than in the surrounding central city or metropolitan area, respectively. These rates also far exceed those in adjacent neighborhoods. Residents of critical-mass neighborhoods are more physically isolated than their counterparts, as nearly half lack access to a car, compared to one-tenth of all metropolitan dwellers. Moreover, approximately three in ten people in critical-mass neighborhoods have a physical, mental, or emotional disability that restricts their routine functioning. When the characteristics of residents are considered as a whole, it becomes apparent that sheltered homelessness remains concentrated in the types of areas least able to defend themselves from land uses deemed undesirable by the general public.

The average critical-mass neighborhood also possesses a distinctive housing profile. One-half of the housing units in critical-mass neighborhoods are located in buildings with ten or more units—suggesting zoning conducive to shelters—and those units are often small (29 percent consist of one or two rooms). Rental units predominate, composing three-fourths of the housing stock. The vacancy rate in critical-mass neighborhoods is somewhat higher than elsewhere, but much higher rates of overcrowding prevail. Twice the proportion of critical-mass units satisfies the standard definition of crowding (1.01 or more persons per room) compared to all metropolitan housing units. In line with the generally compressed nature of the built environment, mean population density in critical-mass neighborhoods (25,821 persons per square mile) dwarfs the metropolitan average (1,055). These average characteristics reflect not just the influence of large metropolitan areas like New York and Los Angeles, but persist across most of the metropolitan areas in our sample.[30]

The profile of suburban critical-mass neighborhoods is somewhat less distinctive. Only a handful of suburban critical-mass neighborhoods exist in our metropolitan area sample (38 out of 271), and although they exhibit higher levels of disadvantage than their metropolitan areas overall, they do differ systematically from critical-mass tracts in central cities. They tend to contain

30. We repeated the comparisons for the twenty-five metropolitan areas in our sample with at least three critical-mass neighborhoods and sheltered homeless populations of 700 or more in the year 2000. The critical-mass tracts exhibit a higher sex ratio (on average) than does their respective metropolitan area in twenty-four of the twenty-five cases, a lower proportion of married-couple households in twenty-four, and a higher minority percentage and lower percentage of high school graduates in all twenty-five. Similar consistency is apparent on the measures of disadvantage and housing conditions described in table 10-4.

TABLE 10-5. Changes in Mean Characteristics of Types of Metropolitan Critical-Mass Neighborhoods, 1990–2000

Percent

	Critical-mass neighborhoods		
Characteristic	1990 only n = 185	2000 only n = 159	1990 and 2000 n = 112
Minority			
1990	57.0	62.6	70.4
2000	60.5	70.9	73.1
Married-couple households			
1990	29.7	32.4	24.5
2000	26.6	29.9	22.6
Poor			
1990	30.6	29.7	42.2
2000	28.0	31.3	37.8
In multiunit structures			
1990	49.6	48.6	53.9
2000	50.0	48.6	55.4

Source: U.S. Census Bureau.

smaller proportions of minority residents, and more married couples and high school graduates. They also fare better than their central city counterparts on indicators of unemployment, poverty, and the quality of the housing stock.

Stable critical-mass neighborhoods, which met the threshold level for sheltered homelessness in both 1990 and 2000, reveal even more disadvantage than critical-mass neighborhoods generally. In table 10-5 selected characteristics of the stable tracts are compared to those of tracts qualifying as critical mass in just one of the census years. The stable neighborhoods have a higher average percentage of minority residents, relatively fewer married couples, more poor people, and a larger share of housing units in multi-unit structures in both census years than the 1990-only and 2000-only neighborhoods. Moreover, with the exception of the poverty rate, these characteristics moved farther away from metropolitan norms over the course of the decade.

CONCLUSION

At the national level, few neighborhoods have truly substantial sheltered homeless populations. Of the more than 65,000 census tracts in Census 2000, fewer than 400 meet the critical-mass threshold. The majority of these are located in large metropolitan areas, with New York claiming a disproportionate share. Moreover, the overwhelming proportion of these metropolitan, critical-mass neighborhoods falls inside central city limits, and contains a majority of all homeless shelter inhabitants metro-wide. Comparing 1990 and 2000 census data shows that the number of critical-mass neighborhoods declined in many metropolitan areas. Although the reasons for this decline are uncertain, it probably does not owe to any shrinkage in the overall size of the homeless population.

The decline is, however, consistent with a gradual dispersion of the sheltered homeless population. Our analysis reveals a variety of spatial configurations across metropolitan settings, ranging from the relatively concentrated pattern evident in Seattle to the more suburbanized shelter population of Atlanta. Nevertheless, two findings stand out regarding the geography of metropolitan homelessness. First, critical-mass neighborhoods are more decentralized in 2000 than they were a decade earlier. Second, little overlap exists between the neighborhoods qualifying as critical mass at both points in time. Shelter downsizing, closure, and relocation, as well as the opening of smaller facilities for specialized groups, appear to have spread sheltered homelessness to different locations throughout the metropolis.

This shift away from traditional skid rows means that more neighborhoods now have experience with shelters. How are they affected? With respect to visibility, the impact may not be large. Our results indicate that homeless people staying in emergency and transitional shelters constitute only about one-tenth of the total population in the average critical-mass neighborhood. Of course, many shelters are not big enough to push the host neighborhood beyond the 100-person critical-mass threshold. Such shelters may have physical designs more compatible with their surroundings, and house clienteles such as women and children, as opposed to single men. Shelter operating procedures (including daily schedule and amount of supervision provided), effects on congestion (traffic, parking, noise), and the types of human service-oriented facilities already present in a neighborhood are among the other factors that could influence shelter visibility and hence how domiciled residents respond.[31] Unfortunately, census sources offer no details on the number of shelters let alone their characteristics.

As neighborhood residents encounter the sheltered homeless, their reactions are not necessarily negative. Indeed, exposure to homelessness, including the presence of homeless people in one's neighborhood, can make an individual's attitudes toward homelessness more favorable or sympathetic, at least in the abstract.[32] Those attitudes can change quickly, however, when residents

---

31. Dear (1992); Takahashi and Dear (1997); National Law Center on Homelessness and Poverty (1997).

32. Henig (1994); Lee, Farrell, and Link (2004).

perceive their own place-based interests, such as property values and safety, to be at stake. NIMBY-ism is often prompted by concerns over the stigma associated with homeless shelters and occupants; residents do not want that stigma to "rub off" on them.[33] As our research implies, certain neighborhoods are less able than others to mount campaigns against the placement of shelters. Disadvantaged areas of the central city tend to be particularly vulnerable to shelter overload.

This final finding highlights the equity issues and policy choices facing local governments. Localities have invoked "fair share" principles with increasing frequency to balance the burden of human service facilities across neighborhoods.[34] Encouraging shelter may also increase the accessibility of shelters and essential services to poor people living in outlying parts of the metropolis. As permanent housing programs replace emergency and transitional shelters as the primary strategy for addressing chronic homelessness, efforts to achieve greater dispersal may ease. A trend in this direction is already apparent.[35]

Other contemporary factors suggest that we keep a close eye on the trends explored in this chapter. For example, will local social service reforms and urban redevelopment efforts alter the number or location of critical-mass neighborhoods? What implications might current economic woes, an affordable housing squeeze, and federal policies pertaining to homelessness and housing vouchers have for the geography of urban homelessness? Future researchers should give greater attention to these questions as they affect the geographic and demographic setting for sheltered homelessness in the nation's large metropolitan areas.

33. Takahashi (1997).
34. Gaber (1996); Takahashi and Dear (1997).
35. Burt, Aron, and Lee (2001).

TABLE 10A-1. Sheltered Homeless Population in Critical-Mass Neighborhoods by Metropolitan Area, 2000 and 1990–2000 Change

Metropolitan area	2000 Sheltered homeless population	2000 Critical-mass neighborhoods	1990–2000 change Sheltered homeless population	1990–2000 change Critical-mass neighborhoods
New York, NY PMSA	23,111	81	−251	9
Los Angeles-Long Beach, CA PMSA	6,394	16	2,296	−2
Atlanta, GA MSA	2,052	10	460	4
Boston, MA-NH PMSA	2,048	9	−473	−2
Seattle-Bellevue-Everett, WA PMSA	2,026	9	−107	1
Chicago, IL PMSA	1,679	8	−2,101	−10
San Diego, CA MSA	1,660	5	−1,210	0
Washington, DC-MD-VA-WV PMSA	1,442	8	−2,993	−5
Detroit, MI PMSA	1,322	6	383	1
Minneapolis-St. Paul, MN-WI MSA	1,316	5	−169	0
Philadelphia, PA-NJ PMSA	1,315	10	−1,369	−3
Las Vegas, NV-AZ MSA	1,293	3	741	1
Denver, CO PMSA	1,217	3	−47	−1
San Francisco, CA PMSA	1,125	5	−3,416	−9
Dallas, TX PMSA	1,037	3	−42	−1
Portland-Vancouver, OR-WA PMSA	983	3	−355	−1
Cleveland-Lorain-Elyria, OH PMSA	957	6	729	5
Miami, FL PMSA	951	4	195	2
Phoenix-Mesa, AZ MSA	926	5	−862	0
Salt Lake City-Ogden, UT MSA	896	5	475	3
Houston, TX PMSA	763	4	−597	−5
Raleigh-Durham-Chapel Hill, NC MSA	746	4	423	2
Louisville, KY-IN MSA	734	4	126	0
Orange Co., CA PMSA	725	4	187	0
Fort Lauderdale, FL PMSA	702	5	372	3
Fresno, CA MSA	683	4	119	1
San Jose, CA PMSA	577	4	−432	−1
Cincinnati, OH-KY-IN PMSA	531	2	−346	−1
Newark, NJ PMSA	500	4	−1,506	−3
Orlando, FL MSA	500	2	−35	−1
Sacramento, CA PMSA	486	1	−341	−2
Charlotte-Gastonia-Rock Hill, NC-SC MSA	450	2	−28	0
Columbus, OH MSA	404	2	60	0
Oakland, CA PMSA	403	2	−721	−3
San Antonio, TX MSA	380	2	−213	−1
Fort Worth-Arlington, TX PMSA	379	1	−419	−2
Nashville, TN MSA	377	1	−206	−1
Kansas City, MO-KS MSA	366	2	214	1
Greensboro-Winston-Salem-High Point, NC MSA	325	1	−37	−1
Bergen-Passaic, NJ PMSA	296	2	−105	0
Riverside-San Bernardino, CA PMSA	294	2	−334	0
Nassau-Suffolk, NY PMSA	292	1	292	1
Austin-San Marcos, TX MSA	289	1	−52	0
Baltimore, MD PMSA	285	2	−433	−2
Tampa-St. Petersburg-Clearwater, FL MSA	281	1	−726	−4
Indianapolis, IN MSA	279	2	95	1
Milwaukee-Waukesha, WI PMSA	230	2	119	1
New Orleans, LA MSA	212	1	−464	−3
Providence-Fall River-Warwick, RI-MA MSA	203	2	203	2
Total	66,442	271	−12,901	−26

Source: U.S. Census Bureau.

REFERENCES

Baumohl, Jim, ed. 1996. *Homelessness in America.* Phoenix, Ariz.: Oryx Press.

Brinegar, Sarah J. 2003. "The Social Construction of Homeless Shelters in the Phoenix Area." *Urban Geography* 24: 61–74.

Burt, Martha R., Laudan Y. Aron, and Edgar Lee. 2001. *Helping America's Homeless: Emergency Shelter or Affordable Housing?* Washington: Urban Institute Press.

Culhane, Dennis P., and others. 1994. "Public Shelter Admission Rates in Philadelphia and New York City: The Implications of Turnover for Sheltered Population Counts." *Housing Policy Debate* 7: 327–65.

Dear, Michael. 1992. "Understanding and Overcoming the NIMBY Syndrome." *Journal of the American Planning Association* 58: 288–300.

Feins, Judith D., and Linda B. Fosburg. 1999. "Emergency Shelter and Services: Opening a Front Door to the Continuum of Care." In *Practical Lessons: The 1998 National Symposium on Homelessness Research,* edited by Linda B. Fosburg and Deborah L. Dennis. Washington: Government Printing Office.

Gaber, Sharon L. 1996. "From NIMBY to Fair Share: The Development of New York City's Municipal Shelter Siting Policies, 1980–1990." *Urban Geography* 17: 294–316.

Henig, Jeffrey R. 1994. "To Know Them Is to . . . ? Proximity to Shelters and Support for the Homeless." *Social Science Quarterly* 75: 741–54.

Hoch, Charles. 1991. "The Spatial Organization of the Urban Homeless: A Case Study of Chicago." *Urban Geography* 12: 137–54.

Jencks, Christopher. 1994. *The Homeless.* Harvard University Press.

Laws, Glenda. 1992. "Emergency Shelter Networks in an Urban Area: Serving the Homeless in Metropolitan Toronto." *Urban Geography* 13: 99–126.

Lee, Barrett A. 1980. "The Disappearance of Skid Row: Some Ecological Evidence." *Urban Affairs Quarterly* 16: 81–107.

Lee, Barrett A., Chad R. Farrell, and Bruce G. Link. 2004. "Revisiting the Contact Hypothesis: The Case of Public Exposure to Homelessness." *American Sociological Review* 68: 40–63.

Lee, Barrett A., and Townsand Price-Spratlen. 2004. "The Geography of Homelessness in American Communities: Concentration or Dispersion?" *City & Community* 3: 3–27.

Lee, Barrett A., Townsand Price-Spratlen, and James W. Kanan. 2003. "Determinants of Homelessness in Metropolitan Areas." *Journal of Urban Affairs* 25: 335–55.

Link, Bruce G., and others. 1995. "Lifetime and Five-Year Prevalence of Homelessness in the United States: New Evidence on an Old Debate." *American Journal of Orthopsychiatry* 65: 347–54.

Lowe, Eugene, Art Slater, James Welfley, and Doreen Hardie. 2001. "A Status Report on Hunger and Homelessness in America's Cities." Washington: U.S. Conference of Mayors.

Martin, Elizabeth. 1992. "Assessment of S-Night Street Enumeration in the 1990 Census." *Evaluation Review* 16: 418–38.

Metraux, Stephen, and others. 2001. "Assessing Homeless Population Size through the Use of Emergency and Transitional Shelter Services in 1998: Results from the Analysis of Administrative Data from Nine U.S. Jurisdictions." *Public Health Reports* 116: 344–52.

National Law Center on Homelessness and Poverty. 1996. *Mean Sweeps: A Report on Anti-Homeless Laws, Litigation, and Alternatives in 50 United States Cities.* Washington.

———. 1997. *Access Delayed, Access Denied: Local Opposition to Housing and Services for Homeless People across the United States.* Washington.

Simon, Harry. 1996. "Municipal Regulation of the Homeless in Public Spaces." In *Homelessness in America,* edited by Jim Baumohl. Phoenix, Ariz.: Oryx Press.

Smith, Annetta C., and Denise I. Smith. 2001. "Emergency and Transitional Shelter Population: 2000." U.S. Census Bureau, Census 2000 Special Reports, Series CENSR/01–2. Washington: Government Printing Office.

Snow, David A., and Michael Mulcahy. 2001. "Space, Politics, and the Survival Strategies of the Homeless." *American Behavioral Scientist* 45: 149–69.

Spivak, Donald R. 1998. "CRA's Role in the History and Development of Skid Row Los Angeles." Accessed June 2004 at www.weingart.org/institute/research/colloquia/pdf/HistoryofSkidRow.pdf.

Taeuber, Cynthia M., and Paul M. Siegel. 1991. "Counting the Nation's Homeless Population in the 1990 Census." In *Enumerating Homeless People: Methods and Data Needs,* edited by Cynthia M. Taeuber. Washington: Government Printing Office.

Takahashi, Lois M. 1997. "The Socio-Spatial Stigmatization of Homelessness and HIV/AIDS: Toward an Explanation of the NIMBY Syndrome." *Social Science and Medicine* 45: 903–14.

Takahashi, Lois M., and Michael J. Dear. 1997. "The Changing Dynamics of Community Opposition to Human Service Facilities." *Journal of the American Planning Association* 63: 79–93.

U.S. General Accounting Office. 2003. "Decennial Census: Methods for Collecting and Reporting Data on the Homeless and Others without Conventional Housing Need Refinement." Report to Congressional Requesters, GAO-03-227. Washington.

Wolch, Jennifer R., and Michael J. Dear. 1993. *Malign Neglect: Homelessness in an American City.* San Francisco: Jossey-Bass.

Wright, James D., Beth A. Rubin, and Joel A. Devine. 1998. *Beside the Golden Door: Policy, Politics, and the Homeless.* New York: Aldine de Gruyter.

11

Patterns and Trends in Overcrowded Housing
Results from Census 2000

PATRICK A. SIMMONS

O vercrowded tenements in the immigrant neighborhoods of large U.S. cities helped galvanize the housing reform movement of the early twentieth century. As immigration subsided, families shrank, and home building boomed during the postwar period, however, residential overcrowding declined dramatically. Sharp drops in household densities were accompanied by waning interest in overcrowding as a research topic and housing policy issue.

The decline in overcrowding came to an abrupt end during the 1980s, when both the number and proportion of overcrowded households increased for the first time in four decades. Recently released data from Census 2000 indicate that overcrowding expanded by an even greater amount during the 1990s. While the number of overcrowded households increased by 900,000 during the 1980s, the nation added 1.5 million overcrowded households during the past decade. By 2000 overcrowding affected 6.1 million households, the largest number since 1960. The rate of overcrowding reached 5.8 percent, the highest level in nearly three decades.

New census data reveal that overcrowding is most prevalent in the western and southwestern United States and in immigration gateways across the

Adapted from Patrick Simmons, *Patterns and Trends in Overcrowded Housing: Early Results from Census 2000* (Census Note 09, August 2002). ©2002 Fannie Mae Foundation, Washington, D.C. Used with permission.

The author thanks Amy Bogdon of the Fannie Mae Foundation for valuable comments on an earlier version of this chapter. He also thanks Kris Rengert, Carol Bell, and Kathy Litzenberg of the Fannie Mae Foundation for editorial and graphics assistance.

nation. These data also indicate that a growing number of small suburbs and rural towns outside of these areas experience high rates of overcrowding.

This chapter describes these trends and patterns in detail. It analyzes the number of overcrowded households and the overcrowding rate at multiple levels of geography, ranging from the nation to small towns. It also considers whether the recent upswing in overcrowding warrants renewed attention from researchers and policymakers.

METHODOLOGY

This brief section outlines how housing researchers typically define and measure overcrowding.

Definition of Overcrowding

At the outset of the housing reform movement in the late 1800s, the number of families per housing unit was commonly used to measure household density in the United States.[1] Since the 1920s, however, the number of occupants per room has been the principal measure of household density.[2]

In order to measure overcrowding, the objective indicator of occupants per room must be paired with a normative standard that identifies unacceptably high household densities.[3] As noted by Myers, Baer, and Choi, the standard used to denote overcrowding changed twice between 1940 and 1960.[4] The overcrowding cutoff dropped first from 2.0 to 1.5 persons per room, and then to 1.0 person per room, the standard still in use today. Changes in the overcrowding standard coincided with substantial improvements in U.S. housing conditions. During the two decades following 1940 the United States experienced a 40 percent decline in the proportion of overcrowded households

---

1. Baer (1976).

2. The decennial census counts only whole rooms used for living purposes. Living rooms, dining rooms, kitchens, bedrooms, finished recreation rooms, enclosed porches suitable for year-round use, and lodger's rooms are included in the Census Bureau definition. Excluded from the definition are bathrooms, strip or Pullman kitchens, open porches, balconies, halls or foyers, half rooms, utility rooms, unfinished attics or basements, or other unfinished space used for storage.

3. Baer (1976, p. 362) provides useful definitions of the concepts of "standard" and "indicator." The former is "an established criterion or recognized level of excellence [measured by an indicator] used as a determinant of achievement," whereas the latter is "a measure [usually a time series] that permits comparison in the item measured at different points in time so as to detect fluctuation in rates of change and long-term trends."

4. Myers, Baer, and Choi (1996).

(measured using the 1.0 person per room standard), a 60 percent drop in the share of housing units with incomplete plumbing facilities, and a 40 percent increase in the homeownership rate.[5]

Aside from changing standards, measurement of overcrowding is complicated further by the use of two different cutoffs to capture gradations of overcrowding. A standard of more than 1.0 person per room typically denotes overcrowding, whereas a higher cutoff of 1.50 occupants per room generally signifies severe overcrowding. This chapter uses both standards to measure national and regional trends, but for simplicity only analyzes overcrowding for smaller geographic areas.

To get a better sense of the living conditions implied by these two standards, it is helpful to consider them in relationship to the typical American home, which contains five rooms.[6] For the typical house to be overcrowded, it would need to have at least six occupants.[7] The typical home would need to have at least eight occupants for it to be classified as severely overcrowded.

Overcrowding standards reflect somewhat arbitrary judgments about acceptable household densities.[8] A scientific basis for establishing overcrowding standards has never existed, and determining an appropriate cutoff has become even more difficult as the nation has grown more diverse. Today the housing expectations of older native-born persons—many of whom have become accustomed to ever-increasing housing size and quality during their housing careers—are juxtaposed against those of young immigrants who originate from countries with lower housing standards and who have different outlooks on what constitutes "normal" living arrangements. These different expectations clash with increasing frequency in the diversifying neighborhoods of cities, suburbs, and small towns.[9] The result is discord between long-standing residents and newcomers over neighborhood parking, home upkeep, and noise. Clashing expectations have also caused conflict between long-term residents and city officials over housing code enforcement.

---

5. Simmons (2000).

6. According to the 2000 census, the median number of rooms for all housing units is 5.3. The modal number of rooms is 5.

7. Note that this house would not be overcrowded if it contained five occupants because the overcrowding standard requires more than 1.0 person per room.

8. Myers, Baer, and Choi (1996).

9. Haya El Nassar, "U.S. Neighborhoods Grow More Crowded," *USA Today,* July 2, 2002, p. A1; Jo Becker, "Suburban Crowding Arouses Tensions," *Washington Post,* May 3, 2002, p. A1; Miguel Bustillo, "A Sign of the Times: Once-Quaint Oxnard Community Strives to Weather Transition," *Los Angeles Times,* August 8, 1994, p. B1.

Data

Summary tabulations of the decennial census of population and housing are the source of all data analyzed in this chapter. Data on occupants per room for 2000 are from the U.S. Bureau of the Census's *Demographic Profile: 2000, Table DP-4: Profile of Selected Housing Characteristics,* released in May and June of 2002. Summary File 1 of the 1990 census is the source of data for 1990.[10]

Because data prior to 2000 were obtained from the census short-form questions, which were asked of all households, they are not subject to sampling error. The 2000 data on number of rooms were collected on the census long-form questionnaire, which was sent to one in six households, and thus are subject to sampling variability. Instances in which sampling variability might affect the results are discussed in notes to the tables and text.

The number of overcrowded (severely overcrowded) households is the number of occupied housing units that have more than 1.0 (1.5) persons per room.[11] The rate of overcrowding is the proportion of all households that exceed a given standard of occupants per room.

Overcrowding was analyzed for the nation, states, counties, and small places.[12] For the purposes of this analysis, small places are defined as those with between 1,000 and 10,000 households. The minimum household threshold is used because numerous places have few households and thus could distort the analysis. For example, largely rural states, such as North Dakota and South Dakota, have many places with fewer than 100 households and some places with even fewer than 10.

The analyses for counties and small places focus on areas with at least twice the national overcrowding rate in 2000. This cutoff corresponds to an overcrowding rate of 11.5 percent, which is roughly equal to the 1960 national overcrowding rate.

10. U.S. Bureau of the Census (n.d.). Data prior to 1990 are obtained from Simmons (2001).

11. A household is conceptually equivalent to an occupied housing unit and, in a true census, the count of households equals the count of occupied housing units. Because the estimates of occupied housing units in this chapter are based on weighted sample data from Census 2000, however, they do not necessarily equal household counts obtained from the 100 percent data. For the smallest geographic areas examined here, any difference between the estimate of occupied housing units and the count of households is generally less than a few percent.

12. This chapter uses the U.S. Bureau of the Census definition of "place," which includes local concentrations of population with legally prescribed limits, powers, or functions and those designated by the Bureau solely for statistical purposes. To qualify as a place, the concentration of population must have a name, be locally recognized, and not be part of any other place (U.S. Bureau of the Census [1994]). In decennial census reports, places include incorporated places, consolidated cities, and census designated places (CDPs).

Two measurement issues might affect assessment of overcrowding trends using the decennial census. The first relates to census coverage. According to the U.S. Bureau of the Census's Executive Steering Committee for Accuracy and Coverage Evaluation Policy, the net population undercount likely declined between the 1990 and 2000 censuses.[13] The extent to which the change in coverage between censuses affected measurement of overcrowding trends is unknown.

The potential effect of the second measurement issue, which relates to a change in the definition of a household, is easier to gauge. In the 1980 and 1990 censuses, living arrangements consisting of nine or more persons not related to the person in charge were classified as noninstitutional group quarters and were thus removed from the household universe, from which overcrowding estimates are calculated. In the 2000 census this classification rule was dropped, leading to the possibility of an increase in the number of large, and potentially overcrowded, households. The potential impact of this change on overcrowding estimates is minuscule, however. The 2000 census counted fewer than 30,000 nonfamily households with seven or more persons.[14] Such households accounted for less than 0.1 percent of all households.

FINDINGS

Analysis of Census 2000 reveals a trend towards greater overcrowding nationwide, with conditions concentrated in a relatively small but diverse and growing set of places across the United States.

Overcrowding Increased for the Second Consecutive Decade

Prior to the 1980s the number of overcrowded households in the United States decreased for four consecutive decades, with the decline accelerating in each successive decade (figure 11-1). Between 1940 and 1980 the number of overcrowded households fell by nearly 50 percent, and the number of severely overcrowded households declined by 63 percent. In comparison, the total number of households in the United States increased by 131 percent during this period. By 1980 fewer than 4 million of the nation's 80 million households were overcrowded, and only 1.1 million were severely overcrowded (table 11-1).

13. U.S. Census Bureau (2001).
14. In Census 2000 Summary File 1 tabulations, the largest household-size category is seven or more persons. Nonfamily households, as opposed to all households, are used in this calculation because the classification rule for identifying noninstitutional group quarters is based on counts of persons not related to the person in charge.

FIGURE 11-1. Change in the Number of Overcrowded Households, by Decade, United States, 1940 to 2000

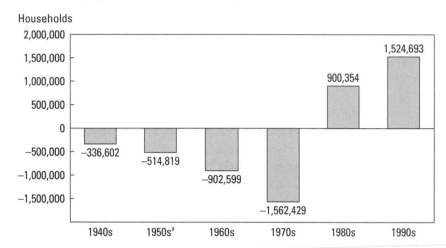

Source: Author's analysis of census data; Simmons (2001).

a. The decline in overcrowding during the 1950s is understated for two reasons. First, Alaska and Hawaii are included in the 1960 national total, but not the 1950 total. Second, the 1950 count of overcrowded households included only those households reporting persons per room, thus excluding some overcrowded households who did not report. Overcrowded households have more than 1.0 person per room.

TABLE 11-1. Overcrowding in the United States, 1940–2000

	Overcrowding[a]				*Severe overcrowding*[b]			
Year	*Number (millions)*	*Change from preceding decade (millions)*	*Percent*	*Change from preceding decade (percentage points)*	*Number (millions)*	*Change from preceding decade (millions)*	*Percent*	*Change from preceding decade (percentage points)*
1940[c]	7.0		20.2		3.1		9.0	
1950[c]	6.6	−0.3	15.7	−4.5	2.6	−0.5	6.2	−2.8
1960	6.1	−0.5	11.5	−4.2	1.9	−0.7	3.6	−2.6
1970	5.2	−0.9	8.2	−3.3	1.4	−0.5	2.2	−1.4
1980	3.6	−1.6	4.5	−3.7	1.1	−0.3	1.4	−0.8
1990	4.5	0.9	4.9	0.4	1.9	0.8	2.1	0.7
2000	6.1	1.5	5.8	0.8	2.9	1.0	2.7	0.6

Source: Author's analysis of data from U.S. Census Bureau; Simmons (2001).

a. Households with more than 1.0 person per room.

b. Households with more than 1.5 persons per room.

c. Data for 1940 and 1950 are based on households reporting persons per room. All other years are based on total households.

During the 1980s the trend in overcrowding reversed abruptly, as the number of overcrowded households increased by 900,000. Severely overcrowded households, which increased by 777,000, accounted for most of the total growth in overcrowding.

During the 1990s, overcrowding expanded even more rapidly. The number of overcrowded households grew by 1.5 million and the number of severely overcrowded households rose by 963,000.[15] By decade's end, 6.1 million households were overcrowded and 2.9 million were severely overcrowded.

Despite the recent growth in overcrowding, the likelihood of living in an overcrowded home remains small. Nationwide, only 5.8 percent of all households were overcrowded in 2000, up from 4.9 percent in 1990. The rate of severe overcrowding was only 2.7 percent in 2000, up from 2.1 percent a decade earlier. Although proportionately few households are affected by overcrowding, the current overcrowding rate is greater than at any time since 1970, and the rate of severe overcrowding is at the highest level since 1960.

Overcrowding Most Prevalent in the West and Southwest

The national statistics described in the preceding section mask considerable geographic variation in overcrowding. Overcrowding rates are substantially higher in the western and southwestern United States than in the remainder of the nation. The Pacific Division (Alaska, Washington, Oregon, California, Hawaii) leads the nation in overcrowding by a substantial margin (12.8 percent). The second most overcrowded census division is the West South Central (Texas, Oklahoma, Arkansas, Louisiana) (7.6 percent).

The West and Southwest are home to the six states with the highest overcrowding rates in the nation (table 11-2). In California and Hawaii more than 15 percent of all households are overcrowded, a rate roughly 6 percentage points higher than in any other state. During the 1990s California surpassed Hawaii and became the state with the highest rate of severe overcrowding (9.1 percent). California's current rates of overcrowding and severe overcrowding are at the highest levels ever recorded in that state.

At the other end of the overcrowding spectrum, twenty-one states had overcrowding rates in 2000 of less than 3 percent and nineteen states had

15. It is interesting to note that increased overcrowding during the 1990s coincided with declining household sizes and increasing housing unit sizes. Between 1990 and 2000 average household size declined from 2.63 to 2.59 persons and the median number of rooms per housing unit increased from 5.2 to 5.3.

TABLE 11-2. **Most Overcrowded States in 2000**[a]

Highest overcrowding rates (percent)		Highest rates of severe overcrowding (percent)		Largest numbers of overcrowded households		Largest numbers of severely overcrowded households	
Hawaii	15.5	California	9.1	California	1,749,998	California	1,048,338
California	15.2	Hawaii	7.8	Texas	698,082	Texas	335,787
Texas	9.4	Texas	4.5	New York	550,559	New York	267,046
Arizona[b]	8.6	Nevada[c]	4.3	Florida	410,840	Florida	195,096
Nevada[b]	8.6	Arizona[c]	4.2	Illinois	223,434	Illinois	94,481
Alaska[b]	8.6						

Source: Author's analysis of data from U.S. Census Bureau.

a. Overcrowded households have more than 1.0 person per room. Severely overcrowded households have more than 1.5 persons per room.

b. Overcrowding rates for Arizona, Nevada, and Alaska are not significantly different at the 90-percent confidence level.

c. Rates of severe overcrowding for Nevada and Arizona are not significantly different at the 90-percent confidence level.

severe overcrowding rates of less than 1 percent.[16] States with the lowest rates tend to be located in the Northeast, Midwest, and in relatively slow growth areas of the Southeast.

Because of its high rate of overcrowding and its large size, California far surpasses any other state in numbers of overcrowded households. The Golden State is home to 1.7 million overcrowded and 1 million severely overcrowded households, more than twice as many as in any other state. The number of severely overcrowded households in California today is almost equal to the number of such households in the entire nation in 1980. Since 1970 the number of severely overcrowded households in the United States has roughly doubled, but the number in California has grown almost sixfold.

Just two states, California and Texas, were home to two-fifths of the nation's overcrowded households and nearly half of all severely overcrowded households in 2000. These states accounted for less than one-fifth of the nation's total households. California alone accounted for over one-quarter of the nation's overcrowded households and one-third of its severely overcrowded households, but only one in nine total households.

Overcrowding Affects Several Different Types of Counties

Map 11-1, which shows overcrowding rates at the county level, provides a more detailed picture of regional variations in overcrowding. The map

16. For all twenty-one states the estimated overcrowding rate was significantly less than 3.0 at the 90 percent confidence level. In three of the nineteen states with estimated rates of severe overcrowding of less than 1.0, the estimate was not significantly different from 1.0 at the 90 percent confidence level.

MAP 11-1. **Overcrowding in the United States, by County, 2000**

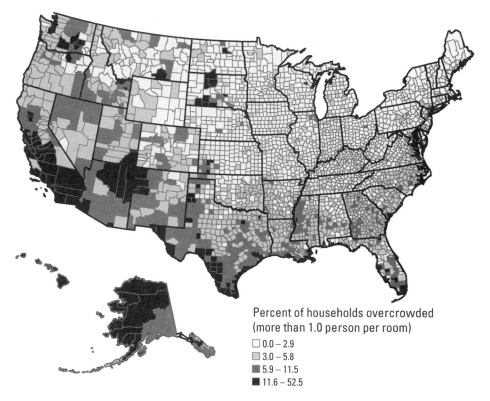

Percent of households overcrowded
(more than 1.0 person per room)
☐ 0.0 – 2.9
▨ 3.0 – 5.8
▨ 5.9 – 11.5
■ 11.6 – 52.5

Source: Author's analysis of census data.

reveals that the majority of U.S. counties have low overcrowding rates. In 2000 85 percent of all counties had overcrowding rates that fell below the national rate (5.8 percent), and 55 percent had rates that were less than half that of the nation.

In only 104 of the nation's 3,141 counties was the rate of overcrowding at least twice the national rate (table 11A-1).[17] Roughly half of these counties are located in just two states, Texas and California. The remainder of this section identifies several different types of counties with high overcrowding rates.

Large Multiethnic Urban Counties. Many of the nation's overcrowded households are in large, ethnically diverse urban counties. Of the nation's fifty most populous counties, fourteen have overcrowding rates at least twice

17. In 26 of the 104 counties with estimated overcrowding rates of at least twice the national rate, the estimate was not significantly different from twice the national rate at the 90 percent confidence level.

as high as the nation's. Half of these counties are located in California, but also include Kings, Queens, and Bronx counties in New York; Harris and Dallas counties in Texas; Miami-Dade County, Florida; and Honolulu County, Hawaii. Together, these fourteen counties contain 2.1 million overcrowded households, or one-third of the national total. Southern California alone contains five such counties (Los Angeles, Orange, San Diego, San Bernardino, and Riverside) that together account for 1.1 million overcrowded households, or nearly 20 percent of the national total.

Urban counties with the highest rates of overcrowding tend to be ethnically diverse and have substantial foreign-born populations. In thirteen of the fourteen large urban counties with high overcrowding rates, at least two of the major racial/ethnic minority groups (Latinos, Asian or Pacific Islanders, and blacks) are overrepresented relative to their share of the U.S. population. The foreign-born population makes up between 19 and 51 percent of the total population in these fourteen counties, compared with 11 percent nationally.

American Indian and Alaskan Native Counties in the West and Upper Midwest. Although large urban counties contain a substantial share of the nation's overcrowded households, the highest rates of overcrowding are found in rural western and midwestern counties with concentrations of American Indians and Alaskan Natives.[18] In 29 of the 104 counties with at least twice the national overcrowding rate, American Indians or Alaskan Natives compose at least 20 percent of the population. In the four counties with the highest rates of overcrowding in the nation (Wade Hampton Census Area, Alaska; Shannon County, South Dakota; Northwest Arctic Borough, Alaska; and Bethel Census Area, Alaska), American Indians or Alaskan Natives account for more than 80 percent of the population.

As these examples illustrate, most of the overcrowded counties with large American Indian or Alaskan Native populations are found in Alaska, the Upper Midwest (particularly South Dakota), and the Four Corners area of the Southwest. In addition to experiencing high rates of overcrowding, these areas tend to have substantially higher proportions of physically inadequate housing units than the nation as a whole. For example, in the four counties with the highest overcrowding rates, between 13 and 52 percent of housing

18. It should be noted that many of these counties are small and in some cases contain only a few thousand, or even a few hundred, households. In some neighborhoods of comparable size in urban areas, it is possible that overcrowding rates approach those found in these sparsely populated American Indian and Alaskan Native areas. At the time this chapter was written Census 2000 data on occupants per room were not available at the neighborhood level.

units lack complete plumbing facilities. In comparison, less than 1 percent of units nationally lack complete plumbing.

Predominantly Latino Counties in the Rio Grande Valley of Texas. One of the largest agglomerations of counties with high overcrowding rates is found along the Rio Grande River in Texas. Of the 104 counties with at least twice the national overcrowding rate, 18 are found along the Rio Grande from El Paso County at the western edge of Texas to Cameron County at the southernmost tip of the state. These counties tend to have large Latino populations (between 45 and 98 percent) and above-average concentrations of immigrants (thirteen of the eighteen counties have a higher proportion of foreign-born residents than the nation as a whole). They have somewhat above-average proportions of physically inadequate housing units (between 1 and 5 percent lack complete plumbing facilities), although this problem is much less frequent than in the American Indian and Alaskan Native counties described above.

Agricultural Counties on the West Coast and in Texas and Florida. Agricultural areas in the West and South are home to the final type of county with high overcrowding rates. This category includes farming areas such as Glenn and Colusa counties in California; Grant and Adams counties in Washington; and Hardee and Hendry counties in Florida. It also includes counties with large livestock industries such as Deaf Smith, Parmer, and Castro in Texas.

Census 2000 employment data show the importance of the agriculture industry in these counties. According to these data, the agriculture industry accounted for between 14 and 26 percent of total civilian employment in the counties noted above, compared with only 2 percent nationally.[19] The heavy reliance of the agriculture industry on Latino labor is also reflected in the census data, which shows that the Latino population in these counties ranges from 30 to nearly 60 percent of the total population. The majority of the Latino population in these areas is Mexican in origin.

Small-Town Overcrowding Spreads during the 1990s

Although the county provides a convenient unit of analysis for examining regional patterns of overcrowding, substantial variations in overcrowding can occur within a county. For example, a suburban immigrant enclave

---

19. The industry category used in these calculations includes agriculture, forestry, fishing and hunting, and mining.

TABLE 11-3. **Number of Small Places with High Overcrowding Rates, by State, 1990 and 2000**[a]

State	1990	2000	State	1990	2000
Alabama	0	1	Montana	0	0
Alaska	4	4	Nebraska	0	2
Arizona	17	19	Nevada	0	1
Arkansas	0	1	New Hampshire	0	0
California	123	175	New Jersey	0	8
Colorado	0	6	New Mexico	6	9
Connecticut	0	0	New York	8	12
Delaware	0	1	North Carolina	0	1
Florida	43	71	North Dakota	0	0
Georgia	1	12	Ohio	0	0
Hawaii	31	35	Oklahoma	0	0
Idaho	1	2	Oregon	2	7
Illinois	5	14	Pennsylvania	0	0
Indiana	0	0	Rhode Island	0	0
Iowa	0	1	South Carolina	0	1
Kansas	0	4	South Dakota	0	0
Kentucky	0	0	Tennessee	0	0
Louisiana	1	3	Texas	59	83
Maine	0	0	Utah	0	0
Maryland	4	7	Vermont	0	0
Massachusetts	0	0	Virginia	2	3
Michigan	0	0	Washington	7	13
Minnesota	0	0	West Virginia	0	0
Mississippi	5	2	Wisconsin	0	0
Missouri	1	0	Wyoming	0	0
			Total	320	498

Source: Author's analysis of data from U.S. Census Bureau.

a. Small places are those with between 1,000 and 10,000 households. Only places with estimated overcrowding (more than 1.0 person per room) rates of at least twice the 2000 national rate, or 11.5 percent, are counted. Sampling variability is not considered.

might have a substantially higher rate of overcrowding than its host county, a fact that can be hidden when the county is the unit of analysis. To get a better sense of variations in overcrowding at a finer geographic scale, this section examines overcrowding in small places, defined as those with between 1,000 and 10,000 households.

In 2000 some 498 of 7,470 small places had an overcrowding rate of at least twice the national average (table 11-3). The number of highly overcrowded small towns has increased 56 percent since 1990, when there were 320 such places. During the same period, the total number of small places grew by only 7 percent.

In 1990 just four states—California, Texas, Florida, and Hawaii—accounted for 80 percent of all small towns with high overcrowding rates. These states still accounted for the large majority of such places in 2000, but their share of the national total had fallen to 73 percent. This decline coincided with an increase in small-town overcrowding in states with few or no such places in 1990. For example, New Jersey, Colorado, and Kansas had no highly over-crowded small towns in 1990, but by 2000 they were home to eight, six, and four such places, respectively. In 1990 Georgia had only one highly over-crowded small town, but by 2000 it had twelve.

Although it is beyond the scope of this chapter to systematically explore the nature and causes of overcrowding in small-town America, preliminary analysis suggests that at least two types of small places experienced significant increases in overcrowding during the 1990s. These two types of small towns are described below.

Small Suburbs in Large Metropolitan Areas. Like their larger urban counterparts, small suburbs with high overcrowding rates tend to be ethnically diverse and home to many immigrants. They also tend to have experienced rapid population growth during the past decade.

Norcross, Georgia—a town of 8,400 located less than twenty miles north-east of Atlanta—provides an example of the substantial increase in over-crowding that can accompany rapid population growth and diversification. In 1990 the overcrowding rate in Norcross was 4.7 percent, roughly in line with the national rate. By 2000, however, the overcrowding rate had increased to 15.8 percent, nearly three times that of the nation. During this period the number of overcrowded households in Norcross quadrupled, from 107 to 427.

Growth in overcrowding corresponded with rapid expansion of Norcross's population, and in particular its Latino immigrants. Between 1990 and 2000 the town's population increased by 41 percent. In 1990 Latinos accounted for only 5 percent of the town's population, but by 2000 this proportion had mushroomed to 41 percent. The foreign-born population exhibited a similar jump from 10 to 42 percent of the town's population.

In some of these small suburbs both the rate of overcrowding and the level of diversity can rival corresponding statistics for the nation's most diverse big cities. Chamblee, Georgia, a suburb of 10,000 persons located less than ten miles north of Atlanta, is a case in point. Chamblee had an overcrowding rate in 2000 of 35 percent, a figure far higher than that of Atlanta (7 percent) and also substantially higher than rates found in the nation's most crowded big cities. For example, the overcrowding rate in Miami and Los Angeles, the nation's two most overcrowded large cities, is roughly 26 percent.

Like Miami and Los Angeles, Chamblee's population is diverse. Latinos make up 56 percent of Chamblee's population, Asians account for 14 percent, and immigrants compose 64 percent. All of these proportions exceed the corresponding figures for Los Angeles.

Small Towns with Recent Influxes of Latino Immigrants. Even some small towns far removed from large cities experienced rapidly rising overcrowding during the 1990s. For many of these places, the catalyst appears to be a rapid influx of Latino immigrants attracted by employment opportunities in meat processing plants or textile mills. Two small towns—one in Nebraska and one in North Carolina—provide examples of the substantial transformations that occurred in such places during the 1990s.

For Lexington, a town located about 220 miles west of Omaha in south-central Nebraska, rapid change followed the 1990 opening of a large beef processing plant.[20] In that year, Lexington had a population of 6,600, of which 94 percent was non-Hispanic white, 5 percent was Latino, and only 1 percent was foreign-born. By 2000, the town's population had increased to 10,000, and the Latino and foreign-born shares had grown to 51 and 34 percent, respectively. Overcrowding rose dramatically along with the population influx, from 2 percent in 1990 to 16 percent in 2000. Lexington had 47 overcrowded households at the beginning of the 1990s, whereas by the end of the decade it was home to 481.

In Siler City, located about thirty miles southeast of Greensboro, North Carolina, the impetus for change was employment in the town's chicken processing plants and textile mills.[21] As was the case in Lexington, these job opportunities attracted numerous Latino immigrants. Between 1990 and 2000 the town's population grew by 45 percent, from 4,800 to 7,000. During the same period the Latino share of the population increased from just 4 percent to almost 40 percent, and the foreign-born share grew from 3 percent to 35 percent. A sharp increase in household density accompanied these changes, as Siler City's overcrowding rate jumped from 3 to 16 percent between 1990 and 2000. During the same period, the number of overcrowded households in the town grew from 53 to 370.

CONCLUSION

Recently released data from Census 2000 indicate that residential overcrowding increased during the 1990s and is now more widespread than it has been in decades. These data also show that high overcrowding rates are found in a greater number and variety of locations today than a decade ago.

---

20. Alva James-Johnson, "Room to Grow, Little to Live In," *Omaha World Herald,* March 19, 1995, p. A1.

21. Andres Viglucci, "Small Town Gives Immigrants a Hesitant 'Bienvenido'; Newcomers Fuel Economy, Debate," *New Orleans Times-Picayune,* January 16, 2000, p. A26.

Despite these trends, overcrowding remains geographically limited in scope and affects a small proportion of the total U.S. population. The limited extent of overcrowding is illustrated by a comparison with housing affordability problems. Although roughly 6 percent of all households are overcrowded, almost 30 percent have housing costs that exceed 30 percent of income, a standard often used to denote a housing affordability problem. Moreover, although less than 3 percent of households are severely overcrowded, 12 percent have housing costs that consume at least 50 percent of household income.[22]

A comparison of overcrowding and affordability begs the question of the relationship between the two problems. In some instances, increases in overcrowding are the effect of insufficient affordable housing options for lower income households, which are forced to double up to save on housing costs. In a study using summary files from the decennial census, however, Myers, Baer, and Choi found no evidence of a strong link between rental overcrowding and housing market conditions such as low rental vacancy rates or high rental cost burdens.[23]

This finding might reflect the limitations of housing market indicators available from the census summary files, but it might also indicate the greater tolerance of some ethnic groups for higher household densities. For example, the Myers, Baer, and Choi study showed that Hispanics and Asians maintain relatively high household densities even after achieving middle- or upper-income status. The possibility that different ethnic groups might have varying tolerances for overcrowding is particularly important given the rapid increase in the U.S. foreign-born population in recent decades. Although many native-born persons might find eight people living in a five-room house to be objectionable, immigrants originating from close-contact societies with higher average residential densities might not perceive such a living arrangement as problematic. The likelihood that different ethnic groups have different conceptions of unacceptable household densities creates challenges for both researchers and policymakers, who have never had a rigorous scientific basis for establishing standards of overcrowding for use in research or policy formulation.

Despite the limited extent of overcrowding and the likelihood that it does not always reflect a problem for the affected household, it warrants greater attention from researchers and policymakers for several reasons. First, the

---

22. Analysis of 1999 American Housing Survey data in Joint Center for Housing Studies of Harvard University (2002).

23. Myers, Baer, and Choi (1996).

rise in overcrowding undoubtedly indicates a lack of affordable housing options for many lower-income households. Providing decent and affordable housing has been a long-standing challenge for some of the overcrowded areas profiled here, such as large urban counties and areas with concentrations of Native Americans. The continued rise in overcrowding suggests that these challenges may be intensifying. Insufficient affordable housing is also likely to be an acute problem in overcrowded small towns, some of which have not experienced population growth and have not produced significant new housing in decades.

Second, overcrowding can pose a threat to health or safety. Some overcrowded households have members living in basements or attics without adequate egress or are exposed to an increased fire risk because of overburdened home electrical systems. Indeed, fire fatalities involving overcrowded housing have motivated some public officials to tighten housing occupancy codes or step up enforcement.[24]

Finally, even if overcrowded households do not always suffer ill effects, their neighbors sometimes associate overcrowding with negative externalities such as increased traffic and noise, falling property values, and rising taxes. In addition, local public officials are becoming increasingly concerned about the impact of overcrowding on public infrastructure such as schools, roads, and water and sewer systems.[25] Despite these concerns, local officials have often been unable or unwilling to tighten occupancy codes and step up enforcement. Change has been inhibited by insufficient inspection staff and fears that tougher codes and enforcement might increase homelessness or discriminate against families or minorities.[26]

For these reasons, overcrowding is likely to be a significant and vexing public policy issue in those areas experiencing rapidly rising household densities. Researchers might inform better policy responses through further study of the geographic and demographic variations in overcrowding rates. For example, other data from Census 2000 will permit examination of overcrowding among renters and recent immigrants, groups that tend to have

24. Marc Lifsher, "Santa Ana Councilmen Press Lawmakers for Lower Occupancy Limits," *Orange County Register,* March 24, 1994, p. B5.

25. Daryl Kelley, Daniel Yi, and Hector Becerra, "Crowding Now Way of Life in California," *Los Angeles Times,* June 10, 2002, p. 1, metro; Andrea Jones, "Occupancy Limits Growing as Issue," *Atlanta Journal and Constitution,* July 22, 2001, p. 1JJ; Gebe Martinez, "Putting the Squeeze on Crowding," *Los Angeles Times,* January 2, 1992, p. A1.

26. Marc Lifsher, "Santa Ana Councilmen Press Lawmakers for Lower Occupancy Limits," *Orange County Register,* March 24, 1994, p. B5; Jo Becker, "Suburban Crowding Arouses Tensions," *Washington Post,* May 3, 2002, p. A1.

substantially higher overcrowding rates than the general population. Future research might also examine the differing perceptions of household density across ethnic groups and the household- and community-level consequences of overcrowding. Such research would help policymakers and local public officials understand the circumstances under which overcrowding represents a problem and the possible ramifications of inaction.

The revival of overcrowding demonstrates the complexities of studying housing conditions and the difficulties of maintaining the nation's high housing standards in a time of rapid demographic and social change. Successfully meeting these challenges has important implications not only for households that experience overcrowding directly, but also for those that believe their quality of life is indirectly compromised by this growing problem.

T A B L E 1 1 A - 1 .   Counties with High Overcrowding Rates in 2000[a]

2000 Rank[b]	County or county equivalent	Overcrowding rate (percent)
1	Wade Hampton Census Area, AK	52.5
2	Shannon County, SD	39.1
3	Northwest Arctic Borough, AK	37.4
4	Bethel Census Area, AK	37.1
5	Apache County, AZ	30.5
6	Nome Census Area, AK	29.9
7	McKinley County, NM	27.4
8	Zavala County, TX	26.5
9	Webb County, TX	26.4
10	Starr County, TX	26.1
11	North Slope Borough, AK	25.3
12	Yukon-Koyukuk Census Area, AK	24.5
13	Maverick County, TX	24.1
14	Hidalgo County, TX	24.1
15	San Juan County, UT	24.0
16	Los Angeles County, CA	23.0
17	Todd County, SD	22.8
18	Imperial County, CA	22.2
19	Cameron County, TX	21.8
20	Willacy County, TX	21.0
21	Dillingham Census Area, AK	20.8
22	Monterey County, CA	20.6
23	Zapata County, TX	20.5
24	Merced County, CA	20.1
25	Miami-Dade County, FL	20.0
26	Bronx County, NY	19.7
27	Tulare County, CA	19.3
28	Franklin County, WA	18.5
29	Navajo County, AZ	18.3
30	Lake and Peninsula Borough, AK	18.2
31	Madison County, ID	17.9
32	Colusa County, CA	17.9
33	Buffalo County, SD	17.7
34	Fresno County, CA	17.1
35	Sioux County, ND	16.7
36	Maui County, HI	16.5
37	Queens County, NY	16.4
38	Honolulu County, HI	16.1
39	Ziebach County, SD	16.1
40	Orange County, CA	15.8
41	Hendry County, FL	15.7
42	Kings County, CA	15.6
43	Dimmit County, TX	15.6
44	Kings County, NY	15.6
45	Santa Cruz County, AZ	15.4
46	Hardee County, FL	15.3
47	Madera County, CA	15.3
48	Kern County, CA	15.0
49	Frio County, TX	14.9
50	Jackson County, SD	14.8
51	San Benito County, CA	14.8
52	Clark County, ID*	14.7
53	Yuma County, AZ	14.7
54	San Bernardino County, CA	14.7
55	Adams County, WA	14.4

(*continued*)

2000 Rank[b]	County or county equivalent	Overcrowding rate (percent)
56	Santa Clara County, CA	14.3
57	Val Verde County, TX	14.3
58	Castro County, TX	14.3
59	Yakima County, WA	14.2
60	Big Horn County, MT	14.2
61	El Paso County, TX	14.2
62	Corson County, SD	14.0
63	San Joaquin County, CA	14.0
64	Stanislaus County, CA	13.9
65	San Juan County, NM	13.6
66	Seward County, KS	13.5
67	Dewey County, SD*	13.3
68	Finney County, KS	13.1
69	Uvalde County, TX	13.1
70	Harris County, TX	13.0
71	Dallas County, TX	13.0
72	Santa Barbara County, CA	12.9
73	Hawaii County, HI	12.8
74	Brooks County, TX*	12.8
75	Glenn County, CA*	12.8
76	La Salle County, TX*	12.7
77	Riverside County, CA	12.7
78	Aleutians West Census Area, AK*	12.5
79	Grant County, WA	12.5
80	San Francisco County, CA	12.4
81	Ventura County, CA	12.4
82	Deaf Smith County, TX*	12.4
83	Kauai County, HI*	12.4
84	Kodiak Island Borough, AK*	12.3
85	Titus County, TX*	12.3
86	San Mateo County, CA	12.3
87	Alameda County, CA	12.2
88	Morrow County, OR*	12.2
89	Parmer County, TX*	12.2
90	Thurston County, NE*	12.1
91	Reagan County, TX*	12.1
92	Coconino County, AZ*	12.1
93	Moore County, TX*	12.0
94	Presidio County, TX*	12.0
95	Menominee County, WI*	12.0
96	Gaines County, TX*	11.9
97	Bennett County, SD*	11.8
98	San Diego County, CA	11.8
99	Hudspeth County, TX*	11.8
100	Edwards County, TX*	11.7
101	Cibola County, NM*	11.7
102	Sharkey County, MS*	11.7
103	Benson County, ND*	11.6
104	Southeast Fairbanks Census Area, AK*	11.5

Source: Author's analysis of data from U.S. Census Bureau (2002).

a. Table shows counties with estimated overcrowding (more than 1.0 person per room) rate of at least twice the 2000 national rate, or a rate of at least 11.5 percent. For counties with an * next to the name, the overcrowding rate estimate was not significantly different from 11.5 percent.

b. Ranks are based solely on estimated overcrowding rates and do not consider sampling variability. Ranks based on a complete enumeration could vary from those shown here.

REFERENCES

Baer, William C. 1976. "The Evolution of Housing Indicators and Housing Standards." *Public Policy* 24 (3): 361–93.

Joint Center for Housing Studies of Harvard University. 2002. *State of the Nation's Housing.* Cambridge, Mass.

Myers, Dowell, William C. Baer, and Seong-Youn Choi. 1996. "The Changing Problem of Overcrowded Housing." *Journal of the American Planning Association* 62 (1): 66–84.

Simmons, Patrick A. 2000. "Shelter Indicator." In *Calvert-Henderson Quality of Life Indicators,* edited by Hazel Henderson, Jon Lickerman, and Patrice Flynn. Bethesda, Md.: Calvert Group.

Simmons, Patrick A. 2001. *Housing Statistics of the United States.* 4th ed. Lanham, Md.: Bernan Press.

U.S. Census Bureau. 1994. *Geographic Areas Reference Manual.* Washington.

U.S. Census Bureau. 2001. *Report of the Executive Steering Committee for Accuracy and Coverage Evaluation Policy on Adjustment for Non-Redistricting Uses.* Washington.

Contributors

Alan Berube
Brookings Institution

Chad R. Farrell
Pennsylvania State University

William H. Frey
Brookings Institution

Paul A. Jargowsky
University of Texas at Dallas

Bruce Katz
Brookings Institution

Robert E. Lang
Virginia Tech

Barrett A. Lee
Pennsylvania State University

Shannon McConville
University of California, Los Angeles

Dowell Myers
University of Southern California

Paul Ong
University of California, Los Angeles

Gary Painter
University of Southern California

Patrick A. Simmons
Fannie Mae Foundation

Audrey Singer
Brookings Institution

Thacher Tiffany
Brookings Institution

Index